Redemption Songs

1000 Hymns & Choruses

Collins

Index to Subjects

Collins, a division of
HarperCollins Publishers
1 London Bridge Street
London SE1 9GF

Harper Collins Publishers
Macken House, 39/40 Mayor Street Upper,
Dublin 1, D01 C9W8

Printed and Bound in the UK using 100% Renewable Electricity at CPI Group (UK) Ltd

17

978 0 00 721238 5 Words (Cased)
978 0 00 721237 8 Words (Limp)

Owners of copyright are gratefully
thanked for the permission given to use
the hymns which are owned by them.
Detailed acknowledgements will be
found in the Music Edition.

Printed and bound by
CPI Group (UK) Ltd,
Croydon, CR0 4YY

REDEMPTION SONGS

PRAISE AND OPENING

ALL hail the power of Jesus's name!
  Let angels prostrate fall ;
Bring forth the royal diadem,
  And crown Him Lord of all.

Crown Him, ye martyrs of your God,
  Who from His altar call ;
Extol the stem of Jesse's rod,
  And crown Him Lord of all.

Ye chosen seed of Israel's race,
  A remnant weak and small,
Hail Him who saves you by His grace,
  And crown Him Lord of all.

Ye Gentile sinners, ne'er forget
  The wormwood and the gall ;
Go, spread your trophies at His feet,
  And crown Him Lord of all.

Let every kindred, every tribe,
  On this terrestrial ball,
To Him all majesty ascribe,
  And crown Him Lord of all.

O that with yonder sacred throng
  We at His feet may fall,
Join in the everlasting song,
  And crown Him Lord of all !

BREAK Thou the bread of life,
  Dear Lord, to me,
As Thou didst break the loaves
  Beside the sea.
Beyond the sacred page
  I seek Thee, Lord ;
My spirit pants for Thee,
  O Living Word !

Break Thou the bread of life,
  O Lord, to me,
That hid within my heart
  Thy Word may be :
Mould Thou each inward thought,
  From self set free,
And let my steps be all
  Controlled by Thee.

Open Thy Word of Truth,
  That I may see
Thy message written clear
  And plain for me ;

Then in sweet fellowship
  Walking with Thee,
Thine image on my life
  Engraved will be.

4 Bless Thou the truth, dear Lord,
  To me, to me,
As Thou didst bless the bread
  By Galilee :
Then shall all bondage cease,
  All fetters fall ;
And I shall find my peace,
  My All in All !

3 WE come before Thy throne to-day,
  Thy promised presence claim ;
O come and enter now our hearts,
  And set our souls aflame.

Lord, send Thy blessing, Lord, send Thy
  blessing,
Lord, send Thy blessing on our waiting souls.

2 We know that Thou art present here,
  Thy grace to us reveal ;
We fain would know Thy blessed will,
  Thy holy presence feel.

3 O send to us Thy quickening power,
  All guilt and dross remove ;
O let our waiting hearts be filled,
  Dear Saviour, with Thy love.

4 Accept the homage that we bring,
  O Lord, we humbly pray ;
Bestow Thy richest blessings now,
  And meet with us to-day.

4 THE name of Jesus is so sweet,
  I love its music to repeat ;
It makes my joys full and complete,
  The precious name of Jesus.

  " Jesus," oh, how sweet the name !
  " Jesus," every day the same ;
  " Jesus," let all saints proclaim
    Its worthy praise for ever.

2 I love the name of Him Whose heart
Knows all my griefs and bears a part;
Who bids all anxious fears depart—
  I love the name of Jesus.

3 That name I fondly love to hear,
  It never fails my heart to cheer,
  Its music dries the falling tear ;
    Exalt the name of Jesus !

4 No word of man can ever tell
  How sweet the name I love so well ;
  Oh, let its praises ever swell !
    Oh, praise the name of Jesus !

5 WHEN upon life's billows you are
    tempest tossed,
  When you are discouraged, thinking
    all is lost,
  Count your many blessings, name
    them one by one,
  And it will surprise you what the
    Lord hath done.

Count your blessings, name them one by one,
Count your blessings, see what God hath done ;
Count your blessings, name them one by one,
And it will surprise you what the Lord hath
    done.

2 Are you ever burdened with a load
    of care ?
  Does the cross seem heavy you are
    called to bear ?
  Count your many blessings, every
    doubt will fly,
  And you will be singing as the days
    go by.

3 When you look at others with their
    lands and gold,
  Think that Christ has promised you
    His wealth untold,
  Count your many blessings, money
    cannot buy
  Your reward in heaven, nor your
    home on high.

4 So amid the conflict, whether great
    or small,
  Do not be discouraged, God is over
    all,
  Count your many blessings, angels
    will attend,
  Help and comfort give you to your
    journey's end.

6 GOD is here, and that to bless us
    With the Spirit's quickening
      power :
  See, the cloud already bending,
    Waits to drop the grateful shower.

Let it come, O Lord, we pray Thee,
  Let the shower of blessing fall ;
We are waiting, we are waiting,
  Oh, revive the hearts of all.

2 God is here ! we feel His presence
    In this consecrated place ;
  But we need the soul refreshing
    Of His free, unbounded grace.

3 God is here ! oh, then, believing,
    Bring to Him our one desire,
  That His love may now be kindled
    Till its flame each heart inspire.

4 Saviour, grant the prayer we offer,
    While in simple faith we bow,
  From the windows of Thy mercy
    Pour us out a blessing now.

7 TO God be the glory, great things
    He hath done,
  So loved He the world that He gave
    us His Son,
  Who yielded His life an atonement
    for sin,
  And opened the Life Gate that all
    may go in.

Praise the Lord, praise the Lord,
  Let the earth hear His voice !
Praise the Lord, praise the Lord,
  Let the people rejoice !
O come to the Father, through Jesus the Son,
And give Him the glory, great things He hath
    done.

2 O perfect redemption, the purchase
    of blood,
  To every believer the promise of God ;
  The vilest offender who truly believes
  That moment from Jesus a pardon
    receives.

3 Great things He hath taught us,
    great things He hath done,
  And great our rejoicing through
    Jesus the Son ;
  But purer, and higher, and greater
    will be
  Our wonder, our transport when
    Jesus we see.

8 WHO is on the Lord's side ?
    Who will serve the King ?
  Who will be His helpers,
    Other lives to bring ?
  Who will leave the world's side ?
    Who will face the foe ?
  Who is on the Lord's side ?
    Who for Him will go ?
  By Thy call of mercy,
    By Thy grace divine,
  We are on the Lord's side,
    Saviour, we are Thine !

2 Not for weight of glory,
   Nor for crown and palm,
   Enter we the army,
     Raise the warrior psalm ;
But for love that claimeth
   Lives for whom He died :
He whom Jesus nameth
   Must be on His side !
By Thy love constraining,
   By Thy grace divine,
We are on the Lord's side,
   Saviour, we are Thine !

3 Jesus, Thou hast bought us,
   Not with gold or gem,
But with Thine own life-blood
   For Thy diadem ;
With Thy blessing filling
   All who come to Thee,
Thou hast made us willing,
Thou hast made us free.
By Thy grand redemption,
   By Thy grace divine,
We are on the Lord's side,
   Saviour, we are Thine !

4 Fierce may be the conflict,
   Strong may be the foe ;
But the King's own army
   None can overthrow :
Round His standard ranging,
   Victory is secure,
For His truth unchanging
   Makes the triumph sure.
Joyfully enlisting,
   By Thy grace divine,
We are on the Lord's side,
   Saviour, we are Thine !

I MUST have the Saviour with me,
   For I dare not walk alone,
I must feel His presence near me,
   And His arm around me thrown.

   Then my soul....shall fear no ill,....
   Let Him lead....me where He will,....
   I will go without a murmur,
   And His footsteps follow still.

I must have the Saviour with me,
   For my faith, at best, is weak ;
He can whisper words of comfort,
   That no other voice can speak.

I must have the Saviour with me,
   In the onward march of life,
Through the tempest and the sun-
     shine,
   Through the battle and the strife.

4 I must have the Saviour with me,
   And His eye the way must guide,
   Till I reach the vale of Jordan,
   Till I cross the rolling tide.

10 HERE in Thy name we are
     gathered,
   Come and revive us, O Lord ;
  " There shall be showers of blessing,"
   Thou hast declared in Thy Word.

   Oh, graciously hear us,
     Graciously hear us, we pray :
   Pour from Thy windows upon us
   Showers of blessing to-day.

2 Oh ! that the showers of blessing
   Now on our souls may descend,
While at the footstool of mercy
   Pleading Thy promise we bend !

3 " There shall be showers of blessing,"
   Promise that never can fail ;
Thou wilt regard our petition ;
   Surely our faith will prevail.

4 Showers of blessing, we need them,
   Showers of blessing from Thee ;
Showers of blessing, oh, grant them !
   Thine all the glory shall be.

11 MY song shall be of Jesus,
     His mercy crowns my days,
He fills my cup with blessings,
   And tunes my heart to praise ;
My song shall be of Jesus,
   The precious Lamb of God,
Who gave Himself my ransom,
   And bought me with His blood.

2 My song shall be of Jesus,
   When sitting at His feet,
I call to mind His goodness,
   In meditation sweet :
My song shall be of Jesus,
   Whatever ill betide ;
I'll sing the grace that saves me,
   And keeps me at His side.

3 My song shall be of Jesus,
   While pressing on my way,
To reach the blissful region
   Of pure and perfect day ;
And when my soul shall enter
   The gate of Eden fair,
A song of praise to Jesus
   I'll sing for ever there.

12 PRAISE Him! praise Him! Jesus
  our blessed Redeemer,
Sing, O earth, His wonderful love
  proclaim.
Hail Him! hail Him! highest
  archangels in glory,
Strength and honour give to His
  holy name.
Like a shepherd Jesus will guard
  His children,   [day long.
In His arms He carries them all
O ye saints that dwell on the moun-
  tain of Zion,
Praise Him! praise Him! ever
  in joyful song.

2 Praise Him! praise Him! Jesus, our
  blessed Redeemer,
For our sins He suffered and bled
  and died;
He, our rock, our hope of eternal
  salvation.
Hail Him! hail Him! Jesus the
  crucified.   [sorrow,
Loving Saviour, meekly enduring
Crowned with thorns that cruelly
  pierced His brow;
Once for us rejected, despised, and
  forsaken,   [now.
Prince of Glory, ever triumphant

3 Praise Him! praise Him! Jesus our
  blessed Redeemer,
Heavenly portals, loud with
  hosannahs ring.   [ever,
Jesus, Saviour, reigneth for ever and
Crown Him, crown Him, Prophet
  and Priest and King!
Death is vanquished! tell it with
  joy ye faithful,   [grave?
Where is now thy victory, boasting
Jesus lives! no longer thy portals
  are cheerless,
Jesus lives, the mighty and strong
  to save.

13 STANDING on the promises of
  Christ our King,   [ring:
Through eternal ages let His praises
Glory in the highest, I will shout
  and sing,
  Standing on the promises of God.

  Stand...ing, stand...ing,
Standing on the promises of God my Saviour,
  Stand...ing, stand...ing,
I'm standing on the promises of God.

2 Standing on the promises that
  cannot fail,
When the howling storms of doub
  and fear assail,   [prevail
By the living Word of God I sha'
  Standing on the promises of God.

3 Standing on the promises I now ca
  see   [blood for me
Perfect, present cleansing in th
Standing in the liberty where Chris
  makes free,
  Standing on the promises of God.

4 Standing on the promises of Chris
  the Lord,
Bound to Him eternally by love'
  strong cord,   [sword
Overcoming daily with the Spirit'
  Standing on the promises of God.

14 THE wondrous work the Lord ha
  done
Let every voice proclaim!
And for the work of grace begun,
The wondrous battle fought and won
Give glory to His name!

  We pleaded for the Spirit,
    He came in mighty power!
  We pleaded for the droppings,
    And, lo, He sent the shower!

2 Unto the Lord doth praise belong,
  O tell it everywhere!
Let every ransomed soul prolong
The loud hosannah of the song—
The Lord doth answer prayer!

3 We'll sing the power of Jesus' name
  And His atoning blood;
To-day and evermore the same,
The vilest sinner to reclaim,
  And bring him back to God.

4 Let every heart and every tongue
  As one united host   [done—
Praise God for what His arm hat
Praise God the Father, God the Son
  And God the Holy Ghost!

15 COME, O my soul, my every powe
  awaking,
  Look unto Him whose goodnes
    crowns thy days;
While into song angelic choirs ar
  breaking,
  O let thy voice in thankful tribut
    raise!

ell how alone the path of death He trod ;
ell how He lives, thine Advocate with God ;
ift up thy voice, while heaven's triumphant
    throng
well at His feet the everlasting song.

Think, O my soul, how patiently He
    sought thee,   [steep,
  Far, far away upon the mountain
Then in His arms how tenderly He
    brought thee,   [ing sheep.
  Home to His fold a weary, wander-

Sing, O my soul, and let thy pure
    devotion
  Rise to His throne, thy Saviour,
    Friend, and Guide ;
Sing of His love, that, like a mighty
    ocean   [beside.
  Flows unto thee, and all the world

Soon, O my soul, thine earthly house
    forsaking,
  Soon shalt thou rise the better
    land to see ;   [awaking,
Then will thy harp, a nobler strain
  Praise Him who died to purchase
    life for thee.

6 O LOVE, that wilt not let me go,
  I rest my weary soul in Thee ;
I give Thee back the life I owe,
That in Thine ocean depths, its flow
  May richer, fuller be.

O Light, that followest all my way,
  I yield my flickering torch to Thee ;
My heart restores its borrowed ray,
That in Thy sunshine's blaze, its day
  May brighter, fairer be.

O Joy, that seekest me through pain,
  I cannot close my heart to Thee ;
I trace the rainbow through the rain,
And feel the promise is not vain,
  That morn shall tearless be.

O Cross, that liftest up my head,
  I dare not ask to fly from Thee ;
I lay in dust life's glory dead,   [red,
And from the ground, there blossoms
  Life that shall endless be.

7 I WILL sing of my Redeemer,
  And His wondrous love to me ;
On the cruel Cross He suffered,
  From the curse to set me free.

  Sing, oh sing...of my Redeemer,...
    With His blood...He purchased me,...
  On the Cross...He sealed my pardon,...
    Paid the debt...and made me free....

2 I will tell the wondrous story,
    How my lost estate to save,
  In His boundless love and mercy,
    He the ransom freely gave.

3 I will praise my dear Redeemer,
    His triumphant power I'll tell,
  How the victory He giveth,
    Over sin, and death, and hell.

4 I will sing of my Redeemer,
    And His heavenly love to me ;
  He from death to life hath brought me,
    Son of God, with Him to be.

18 THE God of Abraham praise
    Who reigns enthroned above,
  Ancient of everlasting days,
    And God of love !
  Jehovah ! great I AM !
    By earth and heaven confest.
  I bow, and bless the sacred Name,
    For ever blest.

2 The God of Abraham praise,
    At whose supreme command
  From earth I rise, and seek the joys
    At His right hand.
  I all on earth forsake,
    Its wisdom, fame, and power ;
  And Him my only portion make,
    My shield and tower.

3 He by Himself hath sworn ;
    I on His oath depend ;
  I shall, on eagles' wings upborne,
    To heaven ascend.
  I shall behold His face,
    I shall His power adore,
  And sing the wonders of His grace
    For evermore.

4 There dwells the Lord our King,
    The Lord our righteousness,
  Triumphant o'er the world and sin :
    The Prince of Peace.
  On Zion's sacred height
    His kingdom still maintains,
  And glorious with His saints in light,
    For ever reigns.

5 The whole triumphant host
    Give thanks to God on high ;
  "Hail, Father, Son, and Holy Ghost !"
    They ever cry.
  Hail, Abraham's God and mine !
    I join the heavenly lays ;
  All might and majesty are Thine,
    And endless praise.

19 MY Shepherd is the Lamb,
The living Lord, who died ;
With all things good I ever am
By Him supplied.
He richly feeds my soul
With blessings from above,
And leads me where the rivers roll
Of endless love.

2 My soul He doth restore
Whene'er I go astray ;
He makes my cup of joy run o'er
From day to day.
His love, so full, so free,
Anoints my head with oil ;
Mercy and goodness follow me,
Fruit of His toil.

3 When faith and hope shall cease,
And love abides alone,
Then shall I see Him face to face,
And know as known.
Still shall I lift my voice,
His praise my song shall be ;
And I will in His love rejoice
Who died for me.

20 WITH harps and with vials there
stand a great throng
In the presence of Jesus and sing
this new song.

Unto Him who hath loved us and washed us
from sin,
Unto Him be the glory for ever ! Amen !

2 All these once were sinners, defiled
in His sight,
Now arrayed in pure garments in
praise they unite.

3 He maketh the rebel a priest and
a king,
He hath bought us and taught us
this new song to sing.

4 How helpless and hopeless we
sinners had been,
If He never had loved us till cleansed
from our sin ?

5 Aloud in His praises our voices
shall ring,
So that others, believing, this new
song shall sing.

21 HARK, hark, my soul ! angelic
songs are swelling
O'er earth's green fields and
ocean's wave-beat shore ;

How sweet the truth those blesse
strains are telling
Of that new life when sin sha
be no more !

Angels of Jesus, angels of light,
Singing to welcome the pilgrims of the nigh

2 Onward we go, for still we hear the
singing, [bids you come :
" Come, weary souls, for Jest
And through the dark, its echoo
sweetly ringing, [hom
The music of the gospel leads

3 Far, far away, like bells at evenin
pealing,
The voice of Jesus sounds o'
land and sea,
And laden souls, by thousand
meekly stealing,
Kind Shepherd, turn their wear
steps to Thee.

4 Angels, sing on, your faithful watch
keeping ;
Sing us sweet fragments of th
songs above,
Till morning's joy shall end th
night of weeping,
And life's long shadows break i
cloudless love.

22 FOR all the Lord has done for m
I never will cease to praise Him
And for His grace so rich and free,
I never will cease to praise Him

I never will cease to praise Him,
My Saviour ! My Saviour !
I never will cease to praise Him,
He's done so much for me.

2 He gives me strength for every day
I never will cease to praise Him
He leads and guides me all the way
I never will cease to praise Him.

3 Although the world His love negled
I never will cease to praise Him
I could not such a friend reject,
I never will cease to praise Him.

4 He saves me every day and hour,
I never will cease to praise Him
Just now I feel His cleansing powe
I never will cease to praise Him.

5 While on my journey here below,
I never will cease to praise Him ;
And when to that bright world I g
I never will cease to praise Him.

23 O GOD of Bethel, by whose hand
    Thy people still are fed,
Who through this weary pilgrimage
    Hast all our fathers led ;

2 Our vows, our prayers we now present
    Before Thy throne of grace :
God of our fathers, be the God
    Of their succeeding race.

3 Through each perplexing path of life
    Our wandering footsteps guide ;
Give us each day our daily bread,
    And raiment fit provide.

4 O spread Thy covering wings around,
    Till all our wanderings cease,
And at our Father's loved abode,
    Our souls arrive in peace.

5 Such blessings from Thy gracious
      hand
    Our humble prayers implore ;
And Thou shalt be our chosen God,
    And portion evermore.

24 AWAKE, my soul, and with the
      sun
Thy daily stage of duty run ;
Shake off dull sloth, and joyful rise,
To pay the morning sacrifice.

2 Wake, and lift up thyself, my heart,
And with the angels bear thy part,
Who all night long unwearied sing
High praise to the eternal King.

3 Lord, I my vows to Thee renew ;
Disperse my sins as morning dew ;
Guard my first springs of thought
    and will,
And with Thyself my spirit fill.

4 Direct, control, suggest, this day,
All I design, or do, or say,   [might,
That all my powers, with all their
In Thy sole glory may unite.

25 HOLY, holy, holy, Lord God
     Almighty !
  Early in the morning our song
    shall rise to Thee ;
Holy, holy, holy, merciful and
    mighty,   [Trinity !
  God in Three Persons, blessed

2 Holy, holy, holy ! all the saints
    adore Thee,
  Casting down their golden crowns
    around the glassy sea ;

Cherubim and seraphim falling down
    before Thee,
  Which wert, and art, and evermore
    shalt be.

3 Holy, holy, holy ! though the dark-
    ness hide Thee,
  Though the eye of sinful man Thy
    glory may not see ;
Only Thou art holy ! there is none
    beside Thee.
  Perfect in power, in love, and
    purity.

4 Holy, holy, holy, Lord God Almighty !
  All Thy works shall praise Thy
    name, in earth, and sky, and sea ;
Holy, holy, holy, merciful and
    mighty,
  God in Three Persons, blessed
    Trinity !

26 ALL people that on earth do
    dwell,   [voice ;
  Sing to the Lord with cheerful
Him serve with mirth, His praise
    forth tell !
  Come ye before Him and rejoice.

2 Know that the Lord is God indeed ;
  Without our aid He did us make :
We are His flock, He doth us feed,
  And for His sheep, He doth
    us take.

3 Oh, enter then His gates with praise,
  Approach with joy His courts
    unto ;
Praise, laud, and bless His Name
    always,
  For it is seemly so to do.

4 For why ? the Lord our God is good,
  His mercy is for ever sure ;
His truth at all times firmly stood,
  And shall from age to age endure.

27 JESUS has loved me—wonderful
    Saviour !
  Jesus has loved me, I cannot tell
    why ;   [less,
Came He to rescue sinners all worth-
  My heart He conquered, for Him
    I would die.

    Glory to Jesus—wonderful Saviour !
    Glory to Jesus, the One I adore ;
    Glory to Jesus—wonderful Saviour !
    Glory to Jesus, and praise evermore.

2 Jesus has saved me—wonderful
    Saviour!   [how;
  Jesus has saved me, I cannot tell
  All that I know is He was my ransom,
  Dying on Calvary with thorns
    on His brow.

3 Jesus will lead me—wonderful
    Saviour!
  Jesus will lead me, I cannot tell
    where;   [sorrow,
  But I will follow through joy or
  Sunshine or tempest, sweet peace
    or despair.

4 Jesus will crown me—wonderful
    Saviour!   [when;
  Jesus will crown me, I cannot tell
  White throne of splendour hail I
    with gladness,
  Crowned with the plaudits of
    angels and men.

28 CLEANSED in our Saviour's
    precious blood,
  Filled with the fulness of our God,
  Walking by faith the path He trod,
    Hallelujah! hallelujah!

2 Leaning our heads on Jesus' breast,
  Knowing the joy of that sweet rest,
  Finding in Him, the chief, the best,
    Hallelujah! hallelujah!

3 Kept by His power from day to day,
  Held by His hand, we cannot stray,
  Glory to glory all the way,
    Hallelujah! hallelujah!

4 Living in us His own pure life,
  Giving us rest from inward strife,
  From strength to strength, from
    death to life,
    Hallelujah! hallelujah!

5· Oh, what a Saviour we have found,
  Well may we make the world resound,
  With one continual, joyous sound,
    Hallelujah! hallelujah!

29 NOW in a song of grateful praise,
  To Thee, O Lord, my voice I'll
    raise;
  With all Thy saints I'll join to tell,
  My Jesus has done all things well.

  And above the rest this note shall swell,
  This note shall swell, this note shall swell,
  And above the rest this note shall swell,
  My Jesus has done all things well.

2 How sov'reign, wonderful and free,
  Has been Thy love to sinful me!
  Thou sav'dst me from the jaws of
    hell;
  My Jesus has done all things well.

3 Since e'er my soul has known His
    love,
  What mercies He has made me
    prove!
  Mercies which do all praise excel!
  My Jesus has done all things well.

4 And when to that bright world I rise,
  And join the anthems of the skies,
  Above the rest this note shall swell,
  My Jesus has done all things well.

30 COME, sing, my soul, and praise
    the Lord,
  Who hath redeemed thee by His
    blood;
  Delivered thee from chains that
    bound,
  And brought thee to redemption
    ground.

  Redemption ground, the ground of peace!
  Redemption ground, O wondrous grace!
  Here let our praise to God abound,
  Who saves us on redemption ground!

2 Once from my God I wandered far,
  And with His holy will made war;
  But now my songs to God abound,
  I'm standing on redemption ground.

3 Oh, joyous hour when God to me
  A vision gave of Calvary:
  My bonds were loosed, my soul
    unbound;
  I sang upon redemption ground.

4 No works of merit now I plead,
  But Jesus take for all my need;
  No righteousness in me is found,
  Except upon redemption ground.

5 Come, weary soul, and here find rest,
  Accept redemption, and be blest:
  The Christ who died by God is
    crowned
  To pardon on redemption ground.

31 WORTHY, worthy, is the Lamb,
  Worthy, worthy, is the Lamb,
  Worthy, worthy, is the Lamb,
    That was slain.

  Praise Him, hallelujah! Praise Him, hallelujah!
  Praise Him, hallelujah! Praise the Lamb!

We the crown of life shall wear,
We the palm of victory bear,
All our Father's blessings share,
    In the Lamb.

And when landed safe above,
In the kingdom of His love,
We shall all the fulness prove
    Of the Lamb.

Now revive Thy work, O Lord,
By Thy Spirit and Thy Word ;
Now revive Thy work, O Lord,
    Through the Lamb.

Strike the stoutest sinner through,
Start the cry, " What must I do ? "
Make him weep till born anew,
    Through the Lamb.

2 PRAISE, my soul, the King of
    heaven ;
    To His feet thy tribute bring ;
Ransomed, healed, restored, forgiven,
    Who like thee His praise shall sing ?
        Praise Him ! praise Him !
    Praise the everlasting King !

Praise Him for His grace and favour
    To our fathers in distress ;
Praise Him, still the same as ever,
    Slow to chide, and swift to bless :
        Praise Him ! praise Him !
    Glorious in His faithfulness !

Father-like He tends and spares us ;
    Well our feeble frame He knows ;
In His hands He gently bears us,
    Rescues us from all our foes :
        Praise Him ! praise Him !
    Widely as His mercy flows.

Angels, help us to adore Him,
    Ye behold Him face to face !
Sun and moon, bow down before Him,
    Dwellers all in time and space.
        Praise Him ! praise Him !
    Praise with us the God of grace !

3 LOOK, ye saints, the sight is
    glorious ;
    See the " Man of Sorrows " now
From the fight return victorious :
    Every knee to Him shall bow !
        Crown Him ! crown Him !
    Crowns become the Victor's brow.

Crown the Saviour ! Angels, crown
    Him !
Rich the trophies Jesus brings :

In the seat of power enthrone Him,
    While the vault of Heaven rings !
        Crown Him ! crown Him !
    Crown the Saviour King of kings !

3 Sinners in derision crowned Him,
    Mocking thus the Saviour's claim :
Saints and angels crowd around Him,
    Own His title, praise His name.
        Crown Him ! crown Him !
    Spread abroad the Victor's fame.

4 Hark ! those bursts of acclamation !
    Hark ! those loud triumphant
    chords !
Jesus takes the highest station,
    Oh, what joy the sight affords !
        Crown Him ! crown Him !
    King of kings and Lord of lords !

34 WHO is He in yonder stall,
    At whose feet the shepherds fall ?
    'Tis the Lord, O wondrous story,
    'Tis the Lord, the King of Glory !
    At His feet we humbly fall—
    Crown Him, crown Him Lord of all !

2 Who is He in deep distress,
    Fasting in the wilderness ?

3 Who is He the people bless
    For His word of gentleness ?

4 Who is He to Whom they bring
    All the sick and sorrowing ?

5 Who is He Who stands and weeps
    At the grave where Lazarus sleeps ?

6 Who is He the gathering throng
    Greet with loud triumphant song ?

7 Lo, at midnight, who is He
    Prays in dark Gethsemane ?

8 Who is He on yonder tree
    Dies in grief and agony ?

9 Who is He Who from the grave
    Comes to succour, help, and save ?

10 Who is He Who from His throne
    Rules through all the world alone ?

35 WE are never, never weary of the
    grand old song ;
    Glory to God, hallelujah !
We can sing it loud as ever with our
    faith more strong :
    Glory to God, hallelujah !
O, the children of the Lord have a right to
    shout and sing,
For the way is growing bright, and our souls
    are on the wing,   [King !
We are going by-and-bye to the palace of a
    Glory to God, hallelujah !

2 We are lost amid the rapture of
    redeeming love ;
  Glory to God, hallelujah !
We are rising on its pinions to the
    hills above ;
  Glory to God, hallelujah !

3 We are going to a palace that is built
    of gold ;
  Glory to God, hallelujah !
Where the King in all His splendour
    we shall soon behold ;
  Glory to God, hallelujah !

4 There we'll shout redeeming mercy
    in a glad new song ;
  Glory to God, hallelujah !
There we'll sing the praise of Jesus
    with the blood-washed throng;
  Glory to God, hallelujah !

36 WE praise Thee, O God, for the
    Son of Thy love.
For Jesus, who died and is now gone
    above.

    Hallelujah ! Thine the glory !
    Hallelujah ! Amen !
    Hallelujah ! Thine the glory !
    Revive us again.

2 We praise Thee, O God, for Thy
    Spirit of light,
Who has shown us our Saviour, and
    scattered our night.

3 All glory and praise to the Lamb that
    was slain,
Who has borne all our sins, and has
    cleansed every stain.

4 All glory and praise to the God of all
    grace,
Who has bought us, and sought us,
    and guided our way.

5 Revive us again ; fill each heart with
    Thy love ;
May each soul be rekindled with fire
    from above.

37 MY God, I have found
    The thrice blessed ground,
Where life and where joy and true
    comfort abound.

    Hallelujah ! Thine the glory !
    Hallelujah ! Amen !
    Hallelujah ! Thine the glory !
    Revive us again.

2 'Tis found in the blood
    Of Him who once stood
My refuge and safe y, my sure
    with God.

3 He bore on the tree
    The sentence for me,
And now both the Surety and sinn
    are free.

4 And though here below
    'Mid sorrow and woe,
My place is in heaven with Jesu
    I know.

5 And this I shall find,
    For such is His mind.
He'll not be in glory and leave n
    behind.

38 REJOICE and be glad ! t
    Redeemer has come !
Go look on His cradle, His Cros
    and His tomb.

Sound His praises, tell the story of Him wl
    was slain !
Sound His praises, tell with gladness, He live
    again !

2 Rejoice and be glad ! it is sunshir
    at last !
The clouds have departed, t
    shadows are past.

3 Rejoice and be glad ! for the bloc
    hath been shed ;
Redemption is finished, the pri
    hath been paid.

4 Rejoice and be glad ! now the pardo
    is free !
The Just for the unjust had died
    the tree.

5 Rejoice and be glad ! for the Lam
    that was slain
O'er death is triumphant, and live
    again.

6 Rejoice and be glad ! for our Kir
    is on high ;
He pleadeth for us on His thro
    in the sky.

7 Rejoice and be glad for He come
    again ;
He cometh in glory, the Lamb th
    was slain.

Sound His praises, tell the story of Him wl
    was slain !
Sound His praises, tell with gladness, He come
    again !

39 WE plough the fields and scatter
 The good seed o'er the land,
But it is fed and watered
 By God's Almighty Hand ;
He sends the snow in winter,
 The warmth to swell the grain,
The breezes and the sunshine,
 And soft refreshing rain.
  All good gifts around us
   Are sent from Heaven above,
  Then thank the Lord, O thank the Lord,
   For all His love.

2 He only is the Maker
 Of all things near and far ;
He paints the wayside flower,
 He lights the evening star ;
The winds and waves obey Him,
 By Him the birds are fed ;
Much more to us His children
 He gives our daily bread.

3 We thank Thee, then, O Father,
 For all things bright and good,
The seed-time and the harvest,
 Our life, our health, our food.
Accept the gifts we offer
 For all Thy love imparts,
And, what Thou most desirest,
 Our humble, thankful hearts.

40 O COME all ye faithful,
 Joyfully triumphant,
To Bethlehem hasten now with glad
 accord ;
  Lo ! in a manger
  Lies the King of Angels !
  O come, let us adore Him,
  O come, let us adore Him,
  O come, let us adore Him,
   Christ the Lord !

2 Raise, raise, choirs of angels,
 Songs of loudest triumph :
Through heaven's high arches be
 your praises poured :
  Now to our God be
  Glory in the highest !

3 Amen ! Lord, we bless Thee,
 Born for our salvation,
O Jesus ! for ever be Thy name adored;
 Word of the Father,
 Now in flesh appearing.

41 HOW firm a foundation, ye saints
 of the Lord,
Is laid for your faith in His excellent
 Word !

What more can He say than to you
 He hath said,
You who unto Jesus for refuge have
 fled.

2 Fear not, I am with thee, O be not
 dismayed !
I, I am thy God, and will still give
 thee aid ;
I'll strengthen thee, help thee, and
 cause thee to stand,
Upheld by My righteous, omnipotent
 hand.

3 When through the deep waters I call
 thee to go,
The rivers of grief shall not thee
 overflow ;
For I will be with thee in trouble to
 bless, [distress.
And sanctify to thee thy deepest

4 The soul that on Jesus hath leaned
 for repose,
I will not, I will not desert to its foes;
That soul, though all hell should
 endeavour to shake,
I'll never, no never, no never forsake!

42 HARK ! the herald angels sing,
 " Glory to the new-born King,
Peace on earth and mercy mild,
God and sinners reconciled."
Joyful, all ye nations rise,
Join the triumph of the skies ;
With the angelic host proclaim,
" Christ is born in Bethlehem."
  Hark ! the herald angels sing,
  " Glory to the new-born King."

2 Christ, by highest heaven adored,
Christ, the everlasting Lord,
Late in time behold Him come,
Offspring of a Virgin's womb.
Veiled in flesh the God-head see !
Hail, the Incarnate Deity !
Pleased as Man with man to dwell,
Jesus our Emmanuel.

3 Hail, the heaven-born Prince of
 Peace !
Hail, the Sun of righteousness !
Light and life to all He brings,
Risen with healing in His wings.
Mild He lays His glory by,
Born that man no more may die,
Born to raise the sons of earth,
Born to give them second birth.

43 TEN thousand times ten thousand,
In sparkling raiment bright,
The armies of the ransomed saints
Throng up the steeps of light.
'Tis finished, all is finished,
Their fight with death and sin ;
Fling open wide the golden gates,
And let the victors in.

2 What rush of Alleluias
Fill all the earth and sky !
What ringing of a thousand harps
Bespeak the triumph nigh !
O day, for which creation
And all its tribes were made !
O joy, for all its former woes
A thousandfold repaid !

3 Oh, then what raptured greetings
On Canaan's happy shore,
What knitting severed friendships up,
Where partings are no more !
Then eyes with joy shall sparkle
That brimmed with tears of late ;
Orphans no longer fatherless,
Nor widows desolate.

44 HE hath spoken, " Be still," the
Rebuker of seas :
The command was for me, and my
heart is at ease ;
He hath hushed into silence the
waves and the winds,
By applying His blood, and removing
my sins.

He's the Prince of peacemakers, all glory to God,
To redeem me, and cleanse me, He shed His
own blood ;
My adoption is sealed, I'm a child of the King,
And for ever and ever of Jesus I'll sing.

2 He hath quickened my soul by a
life from above,
It was done by the Spirit, its essence
is love ;
He hath pardoned and washed me
as white as the snow,
And my heart with His love does
this moment o'erflow.

3 He's a wonderful Jesus, this Saviour
of mine,
He's the great Son of God, a Redeemer Divine ;
He's my Strength, and my Wisdom,
my Life and my Lord,
And enthroned in my heart to be
loved and adored.

4 I will love Him, and serve Him from
now till I die,
For His love fills my heart, and His
beauty my eye ;
He's the fairest and dearest of all
to my soul,
And our lives shall be one, while
eternities roll.

45 REST of the weary, Joy of the sad,
Hope of the dreary, Light of the
glad ;
Home of the stranger, Strength to
the end ;
Refuge from danger, Saviour and
Friend.

2 Pillow where, lying, love rests its
head ;
Peace of the dying, Life of the dead
Path of the lowly, Prize at the end
Breath of the holy, Saviour and
Friend.

3 When my feet stumble, I to Thee cry,
Crown of the humble, Cross of the high
When my steps wander, over me bend
Truer and fonder, Saviour and
Friend.

4 Ever confessing Thee, I will raise
Unto Thee blessing, glory and praise
All my endeavour, world without
end,
Thine to be ever, Saviour and Friend

46 SING on, ye joyful pilgrims,
Nor think the moments long ;
My faith is heavenward rising
With every tuneful song ;
Lo ! on the mount of blessing,
The glorious mount, I stand,
And, looking over Jordan,
I see the promised land.

Sing on ; oh ! blissful music !
With every note you raise
My heart is filled with rapture,
My soul is lost in praise.

2 Sing on, ye joyful pilgrims,
While here on earth we stay,
Let songs of home and Jesus
Beguile each fleeting day ;
Sing on the grand old story
Of His redeeming love,
The everlasting chorus
That fills the realms above.

Sing on, ye joyful pilgrims,
  The time will not be long
Till in our Father's kingdom
  We swell a nobler song,
Where those we love are waiting
  To greet us on the shore,
We'll meet beyond the river,
  Where surges roll no more.

7 O GOD, our help in ages past,
    Our hope for years to come,
  Our shelter from the stormy blast,
    And our eternal home !

Under the shadow of Thy throne
  Thy saints have dwelt secure ;
Sufficient is Thine arm alone,
  And our defence is sure.

Before the hills in order stood,
  Or earth received her frame,
From everlasting Thou art God,
  To endless years the same.

A thousand ages in Thy sight
  Are like an evening gone,   [night
Short as the watch that ends the
  Before the rising sun.

Time, like an ever rolling stream,
  Bears all its sons away ;
They fly forgotten, as a dream
  Dies at the opening day.

O God, our help in ages past,
  Our hope for years to come,
Be Thou our guard while troubles last,
  And our eternal home.

8 ETERNAL Father, strong to save,
    Whose arm hath bound the rest-
      less wave,
  Who bidd'st the mighty ocean deep
  Its own appointed limits keep ;
  O hear us when we cry to Thee
  For those in peril on the sea.

O Christ, whose voice the waters
    heard,   [word,
And hushed their raging at Thy
Who walkedst on the foaming deep,
And calm amid the storm didst sleep ;
O hear us when we cry to Thee
For those in peril on the sea.

O Holy Spirit, Who did'st brood
Upon the waters dark and rude,
And bid their angry tumult cease,
And give, for wild confusion, peace ;
O hear us when we cry to Thee
For those in peril on the sea.

4 O Trinity of love and power,
  Our brethren shield in danger's hour ;
  From rock and tempest, fire and foe,
  Protect them, wheresoe'er they go ;
  Thus evermore shall rise to Thee
  Glad hymns of praise from land and
    sea.

49 O LORD of heaven and earth and
      sea,
  To Thee all praise and glory be ;
  How shall we show our love to Thee.
    Who givest all ?

2 Thou didst not spare Thine only Son,
  But gav'st Him for a world undone ;
  And freely with the Blessed One
    Thou givest all.

3 We lose what on ourselves we spend,
  We have as treasure without end
  Whatever Lord, to Thee, we lend,
    Who givest all.

4 To Thee, from whom we all derive
  Our life, our gifts, our power to give !
  O may we ever with Thee live,
    Who givest all !

50 THE Church's one foundation
      Is Jesus Christ her Lord ;
  She is His new creation
    By water and the word.
  From heav'n He came and sought her
    To be His holy bride ;
  With His own blood He bought her
    And for her life He died.

2 Elect from every nation,
    Yet one o'er all the earth,
  Her charter of salvation
    One Lord, one faith, one birth.
  One holy name she blesses,
    Partakes one holy food,
  And to one hope she presses,
    With every grace endued.

3 Though with a scornful wonder
    Men see her sore oppressed,
  By schisms rent asunder,
    By heresies distressed,
  Yet saints their watch are keeping,
    Their cry goes up, " How long ? "
  And soon the night of weeping
    Shall be the morn of song.

4 'Mid toil and tribulation,
    And tumult of her war,
  She waits the consummation
    Of peace for evermore ;

Till with the vision glorious
Her longing eyes are blest,
And the great Church victorious
Shall be the Church at rest.

5 Yet she on earth hath union
With God the Three in One,
And mystic sweet communion
With those whose rest is won.
O happy ones and holy !
Lord, give us grace that we
Like them, the meek and lowly,
On high may dwell with Thee.

51 O JESUS, I have promised
To serve Thee to the end ;
Be Thou for ever near me,
My Master and my Friend !
I shall not fear the battle
If Thou art by my side,
Nor wander from the pathway
If Thou wilt be my Guide.

2 O let me feel Thee near me ;
The world is ever near,
I see the sights that dazzle,
The tempting sounds I hear ;
My foes are ever near me,
Around me and within ;
But, Jesus, draw Thou nearer,
And shield my soul from sin.

3 O let me hear Thee speaking
In accents clear and still,
Above the storms of passion,
The murmurs of self-will.
O speak to reassure me,
To hasten or control ;
O speak, and make me listen,
Thou Guardian of my soul !

4 O Jesus, Thou hast promised
To all who follow Thee,
That where Thou art in glory
There shall Thy servant be ;
And, Jesus, I have promised,
To serve Thee to the end :
O give me grace to follow,
My Master and my Friend !

52 STAND up, stand up for Jesus !
Ye soldiers of the cross ;
Lift high His royal banner,
It must not suffer loss.
From vict'ry unto vict'ry
His army shall He lead,
Till every foe is vanquished,
And Christ is Lord indeed.

Stand up, stand up for Jesus !
Ye soldiers of the cross ;
Lift high His royal banner,
It must not suffer loss.

2 Stand up ! stand up for Jesus !
The trumpet call obey ;
Forth to the mighty conflict,
In this His glorious day !
" Ye that are men, now serve Him,
Against unnumbered foes ;
Let courage rise with danger,
And strength to strength oppose.

3 Stand up ! stand up for Jesus !
Stand in His strength alone ;
The arm of flesh will fail you—
Ye dare not trust your own ;
Put on the gospel armour,
And, watching unto prayer,
Where duty calls, or danger,
Be never wanting there.

4 Stand up ! stand up for Jesus !
The strife will not be long ;
This day, the noise of battle,
The next the victor's song.
To him that overcometh,
A crown of life shall be ;
He with the King of glory
Shall reign eternally.

53 THINE arm, O Lord, in days of
old,
Was strong to heal and save ;
It triumphed o'er disease and death
O'er darkness and the grave.
To Thee they went, the blind, the
dumb,
The palsied and the lame,
The leper with his tainted life,
The sick with fevered frame.

2 And lo ! Thy touch brought life an
health,   [sight
Gave speech, and strength, an
And youth renewed and frenz
calmed
Owned Thee the Lord of light ;
And now, O Lord, be near to bless
Almighty as of yore,
In crowded street, by restless couch
As by Gennesareth's shore.

3 Be Thou our great Deliverer still,
Thou Lord of life and death ;
Restore and quicken, soothe an
bless,
With Thine Almighty breath.

To hands that work, and eyes that
　　see,
　Give wisdom's heavenly lore,
That whole and sick and weak and
　　strong
　May praise Thee evermore.

54 ROLLING downward through the
　　midnight,　　　[song ;
　Comes a glorious burst of heavenly
'Tis a chorus full of sweetness—
　And the singers are an angel throng.

　" Glory ! glory in the highest !
　　On the earth good-will and peace to men ! "
　Down the ages send the echo ;
　　Let the glad earth shout again !

Wond'ring shepherds see the glory,
　Hear the word the shining ones
　　declare ;
At the manger fall in worship,
　While the music fills the quiv'ring
　　air.

Christ the Saviour, God's Anointed,
　Comes to earth our fearful debt
　　to pay ;
Man of sorrows, and rejected,
　Lamb of God, that takes our sin
　　away.

55 OH, bliss of the purified ! bliss of
　　the free !
I plunge in the crimson tide opened
　for me ;　　　　　[I stand,
O'er sin and uncleanness exulting
And point to the print of the nails
　in His hand.

　Oh, sing of His mighty love !
　Sing of His mighty love !
　Sing of His mighty love,
　　Mighty to save !

Oh, bliss of the purified ! Jesus is
　mine !　　　　　[I pine ;
No longer in dread condemnation
In conscious salvation I'll sing of
　His grace,　　　　[face.
Who lifted upon me the light of His

Oh, bliss of the purified ! bliss of the
　pure !
No wound hath the soul that His
　blood cannot cure ;
No sorrow bowed head but may
　sweetly find rest ;
No tears—but may dry them on
　Jesus's breast.

4 Oh, Jesus the crucified ! Thee will
　　I sing.!
My blessed Redeemer, my God, and
　my King !
My soul, filled with rapture, shall
　shout o'er the grave,
And triumph in death in the
　" Mighty to save."

56 SING, O sing, the dear old story
　　Of our Saviour's matchless love ;
Sing of Jesus and His glory
　With the ransomed host above.

　Sing, O sing the love of Jesus—
　　Sound His praises far and near ;
　Sing the wondrous story over,
　　Till the whole wide world shall hear.

2 Sing of love to you so precious,
　Tell, in song, how Jesus died ;
Let sweet music draw the millions
　To the dear Redeemer's side.

3 Ye redeemed ones, sing the story !
　Sing it o'er and o'er again,
Until every tribe and nation
　Join to sing the glad refrain.

57 O FOR a thousand tongues to sing
　　My great Redeemer's praise,
The glories of my God and King,
　The triumphs of His grace !

2 My gracious Master and my God,
　Assist me to proclaim,
And spread through all the earth
　abroad
　The honour of Thy name.

3 Jesus ! the name that charms our
　　fears,
　That bids our sorrows cease ;
'Tis music in the sinner's ears,
　'Tis life and health and peace.

4 He breaks the power of cancelled sin,
　He sets the prisoner free ;
His blood can make the foulest clean,
　His blood avails for me.

58 O FOR a faith that will not shrink
　　Though pressed by many a foe,
That will not tremble on the brink
　Of poverty or woe ;

2 That will not murmur nor complain
　Beneath the chastening rod,
But, in the hour of grief or pain,
　Can lean upon its God.

3 A faith that shines more bright and
    clear
  When tempests rage without,
That when in danger knows no fear,
  In darkness feels no doubt.

4 A faith that keeps the narrow way
  Till life's last spark is fled,
And with a pure and heavenly ray
  Lights up a dying bed.

5 Lord, give me such a faith as this,
  And then, whate'er may come,
I taste even now the hallowed bliss
  Of an eternal home.

59 COME let us to the Lord our God
  With contrite hearts return :
Our God is gracious, nor will leave
  The desolate to mourn.

2 His voice commands the tempest
    forth,
  And stills the stormy wave ;
And though His arm be strong to
    smite,
  'Tis also strong to save.

3 Long hath the night of sorrow
    reigned,
  The dawn shall bring us light ;
God shall appear, and we shall rise
  With gladness in His sight.

4 Our hearts, if God we seek to know,
  Shall know Him and rejoice ;
His coming like the morn shall be,
  Like morning songs His voice.

5 As dew upon the tender herb,
  Diffusing fragrance round ;
As showers that usher in the spring,
  And cheer the thirsty ground,

6 So shall His presence bless our souls
  And shed a joyful light ;
That hallowed morn shall chase away
  The sorrows of the night.

60 HARK, the glad sound, the
  Saviour comes,
The Saviour promised long :
Let every heart prepare a throne,
  And every voice a song.

2 He comes, the prisoners to release,
  In Satan's bondage held :
The gates of brass before Him burst,
  The iron fetters yield.

3 He comes from thickest films of vice
  To clear the mental ray,
And on the eyeballs of the blind,
  To pour celestial day.

4 He comes, the broken heart to bind
  The bleeding soul to cure,
And with the treasures of His grace
  To enrich the humble poor.

5 Our glad hosannas, Prince of Peace,
  Thy welcome shall proclaim ;
And heaven's eternal arches ring
  With Thy beloved name.

61 O THOU, my soul, bless God the
  Lord,
  And all that in me is
Be stirred up, His holy name
  To magnify and bless.

2 Bless, O my soul, the Lord thy God
  And not forgetful be
Of all His gracious benefits
  He hath bestowed on thee.

3 All thine iniquities who doth
  Most graciously forgive ;
Who thy diseases all and pains
  Doth heal, and thee relieve.

4 Who doth redeem thy life, that thou
  To death may'st not go down :
Who thee with loving kindness doth
  And tender mercies crown.

62 I TO the hills will lift mine eyes,
  From whence doth come mine
    aid ;
My safety cometh from thee Lord,
  Who heaven and earth hath made

2 Thy foot He'll not let slide, nor will
  He slumber that thee keeps :
Behold, He that keeps Israel,
  He slumbers not, nor sleeps.

3 The Lord thee keeps, the Lord thy
    shade
  On thy right hand doth stay :
The moon by night thee shall not
    smite,
  Nor yet the sun by day.

4 The Lord shall keep thy soul : He
    shall
  Preserve thee from all ill ;
Henceforth thy going out and in
  God keep for ever will.

63 TO Him that loved the souls of
men,
And washed us in His blood,
To royal honours raised our head,
And made us priests to God ;
To Him let every tongue be praise,
And every heart be love !
All grateful honours paid on earth,
And nobler songs above !

Behold, on flying clouds He comes !
His saints shall bless the day ;
While they that pierced Him sadly
mourn
In anguish and dismay.

I am the First, and I the Last,
Time centres all in Me ;
Th' Almighty God, who was, and is,
And evermore shall be.

64 WHAT though no flow'rs the fig-
tree clothe,
Though vines their fruit deny,
The labour of the olive fail,
And fields no meat supply ?

Though from the fold, with sad sur-
My flock cut off I see ;   [prise,
Though famine pine in empty stalls,
Where herds were wont to be ;

Yet in the Lord will I be glad,
And glory in His love ;
In Him I'll joy, who will the God
Of my salvation prove.

He to my tardy feet shall lend
The swiftness of the roe ;
Till, rais'd on high, I safely dwell
Beyond the reach of woe.

God is the treasure of my soul,
The source of lasting joy ;
A joy which want shall not impair,
Nor death itself destroy.

65 REVIVE Thy work, O Lord !
Thy mighty arm make bare ;
Speak with the voice that wakes
the dead,
And make Thy people hear !
Revive Thy work, O Lord,
While here to Thee we bow ;
Descend, O gracious Lord, descend
Oh, come and bless us now !
Revive Thy work, O Lord !
Disturb this sleep of death ;
Quicken the smould'ring embers now
By Thine Almighty breath.

3 Revive Thy work, O Lord !
Create soul-thirst for Thee ;
And hung'ring for the Bread of life,
Oh, may our spirits be !

4 Revive Thy work, O Lord !
Exalt Thy precious name :
And by the Holy Ghost, our love
For Thee and Thine inflame.

66 I WILL sing the wondrous story
Of the Christ who died for me ;
How He left His home in glory,
For the Cross on Calvary.
Yes, I'll sing the wondrous story
Of the Christ who died for me ;
Sing it with the saints in glory,
Gathered by the crystal sea.

2 I was lost ; but Jesus found me—
Found the sheep that went astray ;
Threw His loving arms around me,
Drew me back into His way.

3 I was bruised ; but Jesus healed me—
Faint was I from many a fall ;
Sight was gone and fears possessed
me ;
But He freed me from them all.

4 Days of darkness still come o'er me ;
Sorrow's paths I often tread ;
But the Saviour still is with me,
By His hand I'm safely led.

5 He will keep me till the river
Rolls its waters at my feet ;
Then He'll bear me safely over,
Where the loved ones I shall meet.

67 LOVE divine, all love excelling,
Joy of heaven, to earth come
down !
Fix in us Thy humble dwelling,
All Thy faithful mercies crown.
Jesus, Thou art all compassion,
Pure, unbounded love Thou art ;
Visit us with Thy salvation,
Enter every trembling heart.

2 Breathe, oh, breathe Thy loving
Spirit
Into every troubled breast !
Let us all in Thee inherit,
Let us find the promised rest ;
Take away the love of sinning,
Alpha and Omega be ;
End of faith, as its beginning,
Set our hearts at liberty.

3 Come, almighty to deliver,
    Let us all Thy grace receive !
Suddenly return, and never,
    Never more Thy temples leave,
Thee we would be always blessing,
    Serve Thee as Thy hosts above,
Pray, and praise Thee without ceas-
    Glory in Thy perfect love.   [ing,

4 Finish then Thy new creation,
    Pure and spotless may we be ;
Let us see our whole salvation
    Perfectly secured by Thee !
Changed from glory into glory,
    Till in Heaven we take our place ;
Till we cast our crowns before Thee,
    Lost in wonder, love, and praise.

68 THE Head that once was crowned
        with thorns
    Is crowned with glory now :
A royal diadem adorns
    The mighty Victor's brow.

2 The highest place that heaven affords
    Is His by sovereign right :
The King of kings and Lord of lords,
    He reigns in perfect light.

3 The joy of all who dwell above,
    The joy of all below
To whom He manifests His love,
    And grants His name to know.

4 To them the Cross, with all its shame,
    With all its grace, is given :
Their name, an everlasting name,
    Their joy, the joy of heaven.

69   ARISE, my soul, arise,
        Shake off thy guilty fears !
    The bleeding sacrifice
        In my behalf appears ;
Before the throne my Surety stands,
His name is written on His hands.

2 He ever lives above
    For me to intercede ;
His all-redeeming love,
    His precious blood will plead ;
His blood atoned for all our race,
And sprinkles now the throne of
    grace.

3 Five bleeding wounds He bears,
    Received on Calvary ;
They pour effectual prayers,
    They strongly plead for me ;
" Forgive him, oh, forgive," they cry,
" Nor let that ransomed sinner die."

4 My God is reconciled,
    His pard'ning voice I hear ;
He owns me for His child,
    I can no longer fear ;
With confidence I now draw nigh,
And " Father, Abba Father ! " cry.

70 THERE is no name so sweet o
        earth,
    No name so sweet in heaven,
The name, before His wondrou
        birth,
    To Christ the Saviour given.

        We love to sing of Christ our King,
        And hail Him blessed Jesus !
        For there's no word ear ever heard
        So dear, so sweet as " Jesus."

2 And when He hung upon the tree
    They wrote this name above Hir
That all might see the reason we
    For evermore must love Him.

3 So now, upon His Father's throne—
    Almighty to release us
From sin and pain—He ever reign
    The Prince and Saviour, Jesus.

4 O Jesus ! by that matchless Name
    Thy grace shall fail us never ;
To-day as yesterday the same,
    Thou art the same for ever !

71 IN the field with their flock
        abiding,
    They lay on the dewy ground ;
And glimmering under the starligh
    The sheep lay white around,
When the light of the Lord sprea
        o'er them,
    And lo ! from the heaven above
An angel leaned from the glory
    And sang his song of love—

        He sang, that first sweet Christmas,
        The song that shall never cease,
        " Glory to God in the highest,
        On earth good-will and peace."

2 " To you in the City of David,
    A Saviour is born to-day ! "
And suddenly a host of the heaven
        ones
    Flashed forth to join the lay.
O never hath sweeter message
    Thrilled home to the souls of me
And the heavens themselves ha
        never heard
    A gladder choir, till then.

For they sang that Christmas carol,
   That never on earth shall cease,
" Glory to God in the highest,
   On earth good-will and peace."

And the shepherds came to the manger,
   And gazed on the Holy Child ;
And calmly o'er that rude cradle
   The Virgin Mother smiled ;
And the sky, in the starlight silence,
   Seem'd full of the angel lay ;
" To you in the City of David
   A Saviour is born to-day ; "

O they sang—and I ween that never
   The carol on earth shall cease,
" Glory to God in the highest,
   On earth good-will and peace."

72 WE sing the praise of Him who died,
   Of Him who died upon the Cross,
The sinner's hope—though men deride,
   For Him we count the world but loss.

2 Inscribed upon the Cross we see,
   In shining letters, " God is Love!"
The Lamb who died upon the tree
   Has brought us mercy from above.

3 The Cross, it takes our guilt away,
   It holds the fainting spirit up ;
It cheers with hope the gloomy day,
   And sweetens every bitter cup.

4 It makes the coward spirit brave,
   And nerves the feeble arm for fight ;
It takes its terror from the grave,
   And gilds the bed of death with light.

73 O WORSHIP the King all glorious above,
O gratefully sing His power and His love,
Our Shield and Defender, the Ancient of Days,
Pavilioned in splendour, and girded with praise.

2 O tell of His might, O sing of His grace,
Whose robe is the light, whose canopy space.

His chariots of wrath deep thunder-clouds form,
And dark is His path on the wings of the storm.

3 This earth with its store of wonders untold,
Almighty, Thy power hath founded of old,
Hath 'stablished it fast by a changeless decree,
And round it hath cast, like a mantle, the sea.

4 Thy bountiful care what tongue can recite ?
It breathes in the air ; it shines in the light ;
It streams from the hills ; it descends to the plain,
And sweetly distils in the dew and the rain.

74 YE servants of God,
   Your Master proclaim,
   And publish abroad
     His Wonderful Name ;
   The Name all victorious
     Of Jesus extol ;
   His kingdom is glorious,
     And rules over all.

2 God ruleth on high,
   Almighty to save ;
   And still He is nigh,
     His presence we have !
   The great congregation
     His triumph shall sing,
   Ascribing salvation
     To Jesus our King.

3 " Salvation to God
   Who sits on the throne "
   Let all cry aloud,
     And honour the Son.
   The praises of Jesus
     All angels proclaim,
   Fall down on their faces,
     And worship the Lamb.

4 Then let us adore
   And give Him His right,
   All glory and power,
     All wisdom and might ;
   All honour and blessing,
     With angels above ;
   And thanks never-ceasing,
     And infinite love.

75 I AM a stranger here within a
    foreign land,
  My home is far away upon a golden
    strand;
  Ambassador to be of realms beyond
    the sea,
  I'm here on business for my King.

  This is the message that I bring,
  A message angels fain would sing:
  "Oh, be ye reconciled,"
  Thus saith my Lord and King,
  "Oh, be ye reconciled to God!"

2 This is the King's command, that
    all men everywhere
  Repent and turn away from sin's
    seductive snare;
  That all who will obey, with Him
    shall reign for aye,
  And that's my business for my King.

3 My home is brighter far than
    Sharon's rosy plain,
  Eternal life and joy throughout its
    vast domain;
  My Sovereign bids me tell how
    mortals there may dwell,
  And that's my business for my King.

76 THAT grand word, "Whosoever,"
    is ringing through my soul,
  Whosoever will may come;
  In rivers of salvation the living
    waters roll,
  Whosoever will may come.

  Oh, that "Who...soev...er!"
  Whosoever will may come;
  The Saviour's invitation is freely sounding
  Whosoever will may come.   [still,

2 Whenever this sweet message in
    God's own Word I see,
  Whosoever will may come;
  I know 'tis meant for sinners, I
    know 'tis meant for me,
  Whosoever will may come.

3 I heard the loving message, and now
    to others say,
  Whosoever will may come;
  Seek now the precious Saviour, and
    He'll be yours to-day,
  Whosoever will may come.

4 To God be all the glory! His only
    Son He gave,
  Whosoever will may come;

And those who come believing, He'll
    to the utmost save,
  Whosoever will may come.

77 UNDER the burden of guilt and
    care,
  Many a spirit is grieving,
  Who in the joy of the Lord might
    share,
  Life everlasting receiving.

  Life! life! eternal life!
  Jesus alone is the Giver!
  Life! life! abundant life!
  Glory to Jesus for ever!

2 Burdened one, why will you longer
    bear
  Sorrows from which He releases?
  Open your heart and rejoicing share
  Life "more abundant" in Jesus.

3 Leaving the mountain, the streamlet
    grows,
  Flooding the vale with a river;
  So, from the hill of the Cross there
    flows
  Life "more abundant" for ever.

4 Oh for the floods on the thirsty land!
  Oh for a mighty revival!
  Oh for a sanctified, fearless band,
  Ready to hail its arrival.

78 WOULD you be free from your
    burden of sin?
  There's power in the blood, power
    in the blood.
  Would you o'er evil a victory win?
  There's wonderful power in the
    blood.

  There is power,..power,..wonder-working
    power,
  In the blood..of the Lamb,..
  There is power,..power,...wonder-working
    power,
  In the precious blood of the Lamb.

2 Would you be free from your passion
    and pride?
  There's power in the blood, power
    in the blood.
  Come for a cleansing to Calvary's
    tide,
  There's wonderful power in the
    blood.

Would you be whiter, much whiter
    than snow ?
There's power in the blood, power
    in the blood.   [flow,
Sin stains are lost in its life-giving
    There's wonderful power in the
    blood.

Would you do service for Jesus your
    King ?
There's power in the blood, power
    in the blood.
Would you live daily His praises to
    sing ?
There's wonderful power in the
    blood.

79 YOU may have the joy-bells
    ringing in your heart,
And a peace that from you never
    will depart ;
    Walk the straight and narrow
    way,
    Live for Jesus every day,
He will keep the joy-bells ringing
    in your heart.
    Joy..bells....ringing in your heart,
    Joy..bells....ringing in your heart ;
    Take the Saviour here below,
    With you everywhere you go ;
    He will keep the joy-bells
    Ringing in your heart.

Love of Jesus in its fulness you may
    know,
And this love to those around you
    sweetly show;
    Words of kindness always say,
    Deeds of mercy do each day,
Then He'll keep the joy-bells ringing
    in your heart.

You will meet with trials as you
    journey home,
Grace sufficient He will give to over-
    come ;
    Though unseen by mortal eye,
    He is with you, ever nigh,
And He'll keep the joy-bells ringing
    in your heart.

Let your life speak well of Jesus
    every day,
Own His right to every service you
    can pay ;
    Sinners you can help to win,
    If your life is pure and clean,
And you keep the joy-bells ringing in
    your heart.

80 THEY tell me the story of Jesus
    is old,
    And they ask that we preach
    something new;
They say that the Babe and the Man
    of the cross   [do.
For the wise of this world will not
    It can never grow old, it can never grow old,
    Though a million times over the story is told;
    While sin lives unvanquished, and death rules
    the world,
    The story of Jesus can never grow old.

2 Yet the story is old, as the sunlight
    is old,
    Though it's new every morn all
    the same;
    As it floods all the world with its
    gladness and light,
    Kindling far away stars by its
    flame.

3 For what can we tell to the weary of
    heart,   [sin?
    If we preach not salvation from
    And how can we comfort the souls
    that depart,
    If we tell not how Christ rose again?

4 So, with sorrow we turn from the
    wise of this world
    To the wanderers far from the fold;
    With hearts for the message they'll
    join in our song,
    That the story can never grow old.

81 WAS it for me, for me alone,
    The Saviour left His glorious
    throne,
    The dazzling splendours of the sky?
    Was it for me He came to die ?
    It was for me,...yes, all for me,....
    O love of God,.....so great, so free,....
    O wondrous love,.....I'll shout and sing,....
    He died for me,.....my Lord and King !

2 Was it for me sweet angel strains
    Came floating o'er Judea's plains,
    That starlight night so long ago ?
    Was it for me God planned it so ?

3 Was it for me the Saviour said,
    " Pillow thy weary, aching head,
    Trustingly on thy Saviour's breast?"
    Was it for me ? Can I thus rest ?

4 Was it for me He wept and prayed,
    My load of sin before Him laid,
    That night within Gethsemane ?
    Was it for me, that agony ?

5 Was it for me He bowed His head
Upon the Cross, and freely shed
His precious blood—that crimson
tide ?
Was it for me the Saviour died ?

82 THERE'S a hill lone and grey, in
a land far away,
In a country beyond the blue sea,
Where beneath that fair sky went ·a
Man forth to die   [me.
For the world and for you and for

Oh, it bows down the heart,
And the tear-drops will start
When in memory that grey hill I see,
For 'twas there on its side
Jesus suffered and died,
To redeem a poor sinner like me.

2 Behold ! faint on the road, 'neath a
world's heavy load,
Comes a thorn-crowned Man on
the way,
With a cross He is bowed, but still on
through the crowd   [grey.
He's ascending that hill lone and

3 Hark ! I hear the dull blow of the
hammer swung low ;
They are nailing my Lord to the
tree,
And the cross they upraise while the
multitude gaze
On the blest Lamb of dark
Calvary.

4 How they mock Him in death, to
His last labouring breath,
While His friends sadly weep o'er
the way !
But though lonely and faint, still no
word of complaint
Fell from Him on the hill lone and
grey.

5 Then the darkness came down and
the rocks rent around,   [air ;
And a cry pierced the grief-laden
'Twas the voice of our King who
received death's dark sting,
All to save us from endless despair.

6 Let the sun hide its face, let the earth
reel apace,
Over men who their Saviour have
slain ;
But behold from the sod, comes the
blest Lamb of God,
Who was slain and is risen again.

83 COME, sinner, behold what Jesu
hath done,
Behold how He suffered for thee
They crucified Him, God's innocen
Son,
Forsaken, He died on the tree !

They crucified Him, they crucified Him,
They nailed Him to the tree ;
And so there He died, a King crucified
To save a poor sinner like me.

2 From heaven He came, He love
you—He died ;
Such love as His never was known
Behold, on the Cross your Kin
crucified,   [throne
To make you an heir to Hi

3 No pitying eye, a saving arm, none
He saw us and pitied us then ;
Alone, in the fight, the victory H
won ;
O praise Him, ye children of men

4 They crucified Him, and yet H
forgave,   [cried
" My Father, forgive them," H
What must He have borne, th
sinner to save,
When under the burden He died

5 So what will you do with Jesus you
King ?   [last
Say, how will you meet Him a
What plea in the day of wrath wi
you bring,
When offers of mercy are past ?

84 THE atoning blood is flowing—
Let all the tidings hear ;
The gospel word is showing
How sinners may draw near.
The atoning blood's relieving
The prisoners from their chains,
And sinners in believing
Lose all their guilty stains.

It is the blood,.....the precious blood,.....
It is the blood,.....the precious blood,.....
It is the blood that maketh an atonement fo
the soul.

2 The atoning blood is saving
Sinners of deepest dye,
And multitudes are having
Free titles to the sky.
The atoning blood is healing
The souls that sin had slain ;
Rejoicing saints are feeling
The promised " latter rain."

3 The atoning blood is bringing
Poor lost ones to the fold,
And heavenly hosts are singing
O'er multitudes untold.
The atoning blood is speaking
To every precious soul
Who is salvation seeking,
" Believe, and be made whole."

4 The atoning blood is staying
The great avenging rod,
While men are still delaying
To yield themselves to God.
The atoning blood is sealing
The world's eternal doom ;
But, to thy soul appealing,
Says, " Lost one, to Me come."

35   THERE is no love like the love
of Jesus—
Never to fade or fall,
Till into the fold of the peace of God
He has gathered us all.

Jesus' love, precious love,
Boundless and pure and free ;
Oh, turn to that love weary wandering soul,
Jesus pleadeth with thee !

2 There is no eye like the eye of Jesus,
Piercing so far away ;   [light
Ne'er out of the sight of its tender
Can the wanderer stray.

3 There is no voice like the voice of
Jesus—
Tender and sweet its chime,
Like musical ring of a flowing spring
In the bright summer time.

4 There is no heart like the heart of
Jesus,
Filled with a tender love ;
No throb nor throe that our hearts
can know,
But He feels it above.

36   A HAND all bruised and bleeding
is knocking at the door,
Is knocking at the door of your
heart ;
It is the hand of Jesus, who long has
knocked before,   [depart.
Though oft you have told Him to

Oh, don't you hear Him knocking, knocking
at the door ?
He's knocking at the door to come in ;
He wants an invitation to cross your threshold
o'er,
Then Jesus will save you from all sin.

2 How often when in sickness, your
body racked with pain,
This knocking resounded in your
ears !
How often in the night-time the
knock would come again,
So loud it would fill your soul with
fears !

3 While standing by the casket of
some departed friend,
With sorrow your heart was sick
and sore ;
What caused that train of thinking
of how your life would end ?
That hand was then knocking at
the door.

4 Why will you keep Him knocking ?
why don't you let Him in ?
He'll fill your pathway with
delight ;
That hand so torn and bleeding will
wash away your sin,
Oh, welcome the Saviour in
to-night.

87   COME away to Jesus ; He is
willing to forgive,
His love will shine around you every
moment that you live ;
You'll find Him good and true, the
pilgrim journey through,
He'll do better for you than this
world can do.

He'll do better for you than this world can do,
He's a mighty Saviour, He is good and true ;
He'll save you by His grace, until you see His
face,
He'll do better for you than this world can do.

2 Come away to Jesus ; let illusive
trifles go,
For everlasting blessing He is able to
bestow ;
He'll answer when you pray, He'll
take your sins away,
Lead you up and onward to His
perfect day.

3 Come away to Jesus ; from your
earthly idols part,
And take His great salvation, for it
satisfies the heart ;
He'll open to your view His treasures
ever new,
He'll do better for you than this
world can do.

88 OH, the best friend to have is
Jesus,
When the cares of life upon you roll ;
He will heal the wounded heart,
He will strength and grace impart;
Oh, the best friend to have is Jesus.

The best friend to have is Je..sus,
The best friend to have is Je..sus.
He will help you when you fall,
He will hear you when you call ;
Oh, the best friend you have is Jesus.

2 What a friend I have found in Jesus !
Peace and comfort to my soul He
brings ;
Leaning on His mighty arm,
I will fear no ill or harm ;
Oh, the best friend to have is Jesus.

3 Though I pass through the night of
sorrow,
And the chilly waves of Jordan roll,
Never need I shrink or fear,
For my Saviour is so near ;
Oh, the best friend to have is Jesus.

4 When at last to our home we gather
With the loved ones who have gone
before,
We will sing upon the shore,
Praising Him for evermore ;
Oh, the best friend to have is Jesus.

89 " MAN of Sorrows," what a name
For the Son of God who came
Ruined sinners to reclaim !
Hallelujah ! what a Saviour !

2 Bearing shame and scoffing rude,
In my place condemned He stood ;
Sealed my pardon with His blood :
Hallelujah ! what a Saviour !

3 Guilty, vile, and helpless we,
Spotless Lamb of God was He,
" Full atonement," can it be ?
Hallelujah ! what a Saviour !

4 Lifted up was He to die,
" It is finished," was His cry,
Now in heaven exalted high ;
Hallelujah ! what a Saviour !

5 When He comes, our glorious King,
All His ransomed home to bring,
Then anew this song we'll sing :
Hallelujah ! what a Saviour !

90 WHEN I think of Him who hath
loved me so, [woe,
Who left His home for this vale of
Was cradled in a manger low—
Oh, it's a precious old story !

Oh, the dear old story, the precious story,
That fills my heart with grace and glory,
The sweetest song in heaven I'll sing,
'Twill be...the old, old story !

2 How He healed the sick and restored
the blind, [pined,
And cheered the heart that in sorrow
The tender Saviour, loving, kind,
Oh, it's a precious old story !

3 As wearied He sat at Samaria's well,
The story of love did sweetly tell,
His gracious words of mercy fell,
Oh, it's a precious old story !

4 My griefs He carried, my sorrows
bore, [He wore,
His brow was scarred by the thorns
But now He reigns for evermore,
Oh, it's a precious old story !

91 IS there any one can help us, one
who understands our hearts,
When the thorns of life have
pierced them till they bleed ;
One who sympathises with us, who
in wondrous love imparts
Just the very, very blessing that
we need ?

Yes, there's One,...only One,...
The blessed, blessed Jesus, He's the One !
When afflictions press the soul,
When waves of trouble roll,
And you need a friend to help you,
He's the One.

2 Is there anyone can help us, who can
give a sinner peace,
When his heart is burdened down
with pain and woe ;
Who can speak the word of pardon
that affords a sweet release,
And whose blood can wash and
make us white as snow ?

3 Is there anyone can help us, when
the end is drawing near,
Who will go through death's dark
waters by our side ;
Who will light the way before us, and
dispel all doubts and fear,
And will bear our spirits safely o'er
the tide ?

92 BY Samaria's wayside well,
    Once a blessed message fell
On a woman's thirsty soul,
    Long ago ;
And to eyes that long were sealed
Was the glorious light revealed,
Through a fountain that was opened
    Long ago.

There's a fountain that was opened
    Long ago, long ago,
For the healing of the nation is its flow ;
Along the line of ages the prophets and the sages
Taught the singing of its waters,
    Long ago....

2 And a little captive maid
By a leper undismayed,
Told to him a simple story
    Long ago ;
That the stream where he might lave
Had alone the power to save,
Through his trust in that old fountain,
    Long ago.

3 And a woman in a crowd,
Without word or cry aloud,
Just stooped down and touched His
    garment
    Long ago ;
As her urgent need appealed,
So her sinful soul was healed
In that fountain that was opened
    Long ago.

4 As the eunuch tried to read
Philip taught him of his need,
And baptized him in the stream
    Long ago ;
As the outward seal and sign
Of an inward work divine,
That was wrought through that old
    fountain
    Long ago.

93 " WHOSOEVER heareth ! "
    shout, shout the sound !
Send the blessed tidings all the world
    around !   [man is found :
Spread the joyful news wherever
    " Whosoever will may come."

Whosoever will ! " " whosoever will ! "
Send the proclamation over vale and hill ;
'Tis the loving Father calls the wanderer home ;
    Whosoever will may come."

Whosoever cometh need not delay ;
Now the door is open, enter while
    you may ;   [Way ;
Jesus is the true and only Living
    " Whosoever will may come."

3 " Whosoever will ! " the promise is
    secure ;
" Whosoever will," for ever shall
    endure ;   [more ;
" Whosoever will "—'tis life for ever-
    " Whosoever will may come."

94 " THOUGH your sins be as
    scarlet,
They shall be as white as snow ;
Though they be red....like crimson,
    They shall be as wool ;
Though your sins be as scarlet,
    They shall be as white as snow."

2 Hear the voice that entreats you,
    Oh, return ye unto God !
He is of great....compassion,
    And of wondrous love ;
Hear the voice that entreats you,
    Oh, return ye unto God !

3 He'll forgive your transgressions,
    And remember them no more ;
" Look unto Me,.....ye people,"
    Saith the Lord your God ;
He'll forgive your transgressions,
    And remember them no more.

95 SOFTLY and tenderly Jesus is
    calling—
    Calling for you and for me.
See on the portals He's waiting and
    watching—
    Watching for you and for me.

Come home,...come home,...
Ye who are weary, come home....
Earnestly, tenderly Jesus is calling—
Calling, " O sinner, come home ! "

2 Why should we tarry when Jesus is
    pleading,—
    Pleading for you and for me ?
Why should we linger and heed not
    His mercies,—
    Mercies for you and for me ?

3 Time is now fleeting, the moments
    are passing,—
    Passing from you and from me.
Shadows are gathering, death-beds
    are coming,—
    Coming for you and for me.

4 Oh, for the wonderful love He has
    promised,—
    Promised for you and for me.
Though we have sinned He has
    mercy and pardon,—
    Pardon for you and for me.

96 COME, sinners, to the Living One,
He's just the same Jesus
As when He raised the widow's son,
The very same Jesus.

> The very same Jesus,
> The wonder-working Jesus ;
> Oh ! praise His name, He's just the same,
> The very same Jesus.

2 Come, feast upon the Living Bread,
He's just the same Jesus
As when the multitudes He fed,
The very same Jesus.

3 Come, tell Him all your griefs and fears,
He's just the same Jesus
As when He shed those loving tears,
The very same Jesus.

4 Still follow Him for clearer light,
He's just the same Jesus   [sight,
As when He gave the blind their
The very same Jesus.

5 Then calm 'midst waves of trouble
He's just the same Jesus   [be,
As when He hushed the raging sea,
The very same Jesus.

6 Some day our raptured eyes shall see
He's just the same Jesus,
Oh, blessed day for you and me !
The very same Jesus.

97 WONDROUS love of Jesus !
spread the news around—
Pardon freely offered, what a joyful sound !
Jesus, loving Saviour, died to set me   [free ;
Oh ! that blessed "Whosoever,"
that means me.

> Pardon freely offered all who will believe ;
> Whosoever cometh Jesus will receive ;
> Jesus, loving Saviour, died to set us free :
> Hallelujah ! " Whosoever," that means me.

2 "Whosoever" means me better than my name,   [same ?
Any one, every one, is not that the
Believing is salvation, present, full,
and free ;   [means me.
"Whosoever" is the message, that

3 Whosoever cometh may the promise claim,   [every stain.
Precious blood of Jesus cleanseth
The Son of God has loved me,
wonder, can it be ?
"Whosoever," saith the Saviour,
that means me.

4 Do not trust your feelings, trust His
Word alone,
Prayer can never save you, tear
cannot atone.
Finished ! cried the Saviour ; noth
ing now to do,
Come, believe this "Whosoever," that
means you.

98 I'VE a message from the Lord,
hallelujah !
The message unto you I'll give,
'Tis recorded in His Word, halle
lujah !   [live.
It is only that you " look and
" Look and live,"...my brother, live,...

> Look to Jesus now and live ;
> 'Tis recorded in His Word, Hallelujah
> It is only that you " look and live."

2 I've a message full of love, hallelujah
A message, O my friend, for you
'Tis a message from above, halle
lujah !
Jesus said it, and I know 'tis true

3 Life is offered unto you, hallelujah
Eternal life your soul shall have,
If you'll only look to Him, halle
lujah !
Look to Jesus, who alone can save

99 WHAT can wash away my stain
Nothing but the blood of Jesus
What can make me whole again ?
Nothing but the blood of Jesus.

> Oh, precious is the flow
> That makes me white as snow ;
> No other fount I know,
> Nothing but the blood of Jesus.

2 For my cleansing this I see—
Nothing but the blood of Jesus ;
For my pardon this my plea,—
Nothing but the blood of Jesus.

3 Nothing can for sin atone,
Nothing but the blood of Jesus ;
Nought of good that I have done,
Nothing but the blood of Jesus.

4 This is all my hope and peace—
Nothing but the blood of Jesus ;
He is all my righteousness—
Nothing but the blood of Jesus.

5 Now by this I overcome ;
Nothing but the blood of Jesus !
Now by this I'll reach my home :
Nothing but the blood of Jesus.

100   OUT in the desert, seeking,
     seeking,
   Sinner, 'tis Jesus seeking for thee ;
Tenderly calling, calling, calling,
   "Hither, thou lost one, oh, come
     unto Me."

   Jesus is seeking, Jesus is calling,
     Why dost thou linger, why tarry away ?
     Run to Him quickly, say to Him gladly,
     Lord, I am coming, coming to-day.

2 Still He is waiting, waiting, waiting,
   Oh, what compassion beams in
     His eye,
   Hear Him repeating, gently, gently,
   "Come to the Saviour, oh, why
     wilt thou die ? "

3 Lovingly pleading, pleading, plead-
     ing,
   Mercy, though slighted, bears with
     thee yet ;
   Thou canst be happy, happy, happy,
   Come, ere thy life star for ever
     shall set.

4 Spirits in glory, watching, watching,
   Long to behold thee safe in the
     fold ;
   Angels are waiting, waiting, waiting,
   When shall thy story with rapture
     be told ?

101   WE'RE bound for the land of
     the pure and the holy,
   The home of the happy, the
     kingdom of love ;
Ye wanderers from God in the broad
     road of folly,   [above ?
   Oh ! say, will you go to the Eden

     Will you go ?
   Oh ! say, will you go to the Eden above ?

2 In that blessed land neither sighing
     nor anguish
   Can breathe in the fields where the
     glorified rove ;
   Ye heart-burdened ones, who in
     misery languish,   [above ?
   Oh ! say, will you go to the Eden

3 March on, happy pilgrims, the land
     is before you,
   And soon its ten thousand delights
     we shall prove ;
   Yes, soon we shall march o'er the
     hills of bright glory,
   And drink the pure joys of the
     Eden above ?

102   THERE'S a stranger at the door,
     Let....Him in....
He has been there oft before,
     Let....Him in....
Let Him in, ere He is gone,
Let Him in, the Holy One,
Jesus Christ, the Father's Son,
     Let....Him in....

2 Open now to Him your heart,
     Let....Him in ;....
If you wait He will depart,
     Let....Him in ;....
Let Him in, He is your Friend,
He your soul will sure defend,
He will keep you to the end,
     Let....Him in....

3 Hear you now His loving voice ?
     Let....Him in ;....
Now, oh now, make Him your choice,
     Let....Him in ;....
He is standing at the door,
Joy to you He will restore,
And His name you will adore,
     Let....Him in....

4 Now admit the heavenly Guest,
     Let....Him in ;....
He will make for you a feast,
     Let....Him in ;....
He will speak your sins forgiven,
And when earth ties all are riven,
He will take you home to heaven,
     Let....Him in.....

103   CHRIST has for sin atonement
     made,
   What a wonderful Saviour !
We are redeemed ! the price is paid ;
   What a wonderful Saviour !

   What a wonderful Saviour is Jesus, my Jesus !
   What a wonderful Saviour is Jesus, my Lord !

2 I praise Him for the cleansing blood,
   What a wonderful Saviour !
That reconciled my soul to God,
   What a wonderful Saviour !

3 He dwells within me day by day,
   What a wonderful Saviour !
And keeps me faithful all the way,
   What a wonderful Saviour !

4 He gives me overcoming power,
   What a wonderful Saviour !
And triumph in each conflict hour,
   What a wonderful Saviour !

5 To Him I've given all my heart,
   What a wonderful Saviour!
The world shall never share a part,
   What a wonderful Saviour!

104 BLESSED be the fountain of
            blood,
   To a world of sinners revealed;
Blessed be the dear Son of God;
   Only by His stripes are we healed.
Though I've wandered far from His
            fold,   [woe,
   Bringing to my heart pain and
Wash me in the blood of the Lamb,
   And I shall be whiter than snow.

   Whit - - er than the snow....
   Whit - - er than the snow,....
   Wash me in the blood of the Lamb,....
   And I shall be whiter than snow.....

2 Thorny was the crown that He wore,
   And the cross His body o'ercame;
Grievous were the sorrows He bore,
   But He suffered thus not in vain.
May I to that Fountain be led,
   Made to cleanse my sins here
            below;
Wash me in the blood that He shed,
   And I shall be whiter than snow.

3 Father, I have wandered from Thee,
   Often has my heart gone astray;
Crimson do my sins seem to me:
   Water cannot wash them away.
Jesus, to that Fountain of Thine,
   Leaning on Thy promise I go,
Cleanse me by Thy washing divine,
   And I shall be whiter than snow.

105 COME to Jesus, come to Jesus,
            Come to Jesus just now;
Just now come to Jesus,
            Come to Jesus just now.

   2 He will save you.
   3 He is able.
   4 Only trust Him.
   5 Call upon Him.
   6 He will hear you.
   7 Look to Jesus.
   8 He'll forgive you.
   9 Don't reject Him.
  10 Hallelujah. Amen.

106 BEHOLD Me standing at the
            door,
And hear Me pleading evermore,

With gentle voice, oh, heart of sin,
May I come in? may I come in?

   Behold Me standing at the door,
   And hear Me pleading evermore;
   Say, weary heart, opprest with sin,
   May I come in? may I come in?

2 I bore the cruel thorns for thee,
I waited long and patiently,
Say, weary heart, opprest with sin,
May I come in? may I come in?

3 I would not plead with thee in vain;
Remember all My grief and pain!
I died to ransom thee from sin,
May I come in? may I come in?

4 I bring thee joy from heaven above,
I bring thee pardon, peace, and love;
Say, weary heart, opprest with sin,
May I come in? may I come in?

107 THERE is a story sweet to hear,
            I love to tell it too;
It fills my heart with hope and cheer,
   'Tis old, yet ever new.

      'Tis old,....yet ever new,
      'Tis old,....yet ever new,
      I know,....I feel 'tis true,
      'Tis old, yet ever new.

2 It tells me God the Son came down
   From glory's throne to die,
That I might live and wear a crown,
   And reign with Him on high.

3 It says He bore the Cross for me,
   And suffered in my place,
That I from sin might ransomed be,
   And praise Him for His grace.

4 Oh wondrous love, so great, so vast,
   So boundless and so free!
Lord, at Thy feet myself I cast:
   My all I give to Thee!

108 ONE there is above all others,
            Oh, how He loves!
His is love beyond a brother's,
            Oh, how He loves!
Earthly friends may fail or leave us,
One day soothe, the next day grieve
            us,
But this Friend will ne'er deceive us,
            Oh, how He loves!

2 'Tis eternal life to know Him,
            Oh, how He loves!   [Him,
Think, oh think, how much we owe
            Oh, how He loves!

With His precious blood He bought
  us,
In the wilderness He sought us,
To His fold He safely brought us,
   Oh, how He loves!

We have found a Friend in Jesus,
   Oh, how He loves!
'Tis His great delight to bless us,
   Oh, how He loves!
How our hearts delight to hear Him,
Bid us dwell in safety near Him!
Why should we distrust or fear Him?
   Oh, how He loves!

Through His name we are forgiven,
   Oh, how He loves!
Backward shall our foes be driven,
   Oh, how He loves!
Best of blessings He'll provide us,
Nought but good shall e'er betide us,
Safe to glory He will guide us,
   Oh, how He loves!

109   HARK! 'tis the Shepherd's
      voice I hear,
Out in the desert dark and drear,
Calling the lambs who've gone astray,
Far from the Shepherd's fold away.

> Bring them in, bring them in,
> Bring them in from the fields of sin;
> Bring them in bring them in,
> Bring the wandering ones to Jesus.

Who'll go and help this Shepherd
   kind,
Help Him the wandering lambs to
   find?
Who'll bring the lost ones to the fold,
Where they'll be sheltered from the
   cold?

Out in the desert hear their cry;
Out on the mountain wild and high;
Hark! 'tis the Master speaks to
   thee,   [be."
"Go, find My lambs, where'er they

110   THERE'S not a Friend like the
      lowly Jesus,
   No, not one! no, not one!
None else can heal all our soul's
  diseases,
   No, not one! no, not one!

> Jesus knows all about our struggles.
> He will guide till the day is done.
> There's not a friend like the lowly Jesus,
> No, not one! no, not one!

2 No friend like Him is so high and
   holy,
   No, not one! no, not one!
And yet no friend is so meek and
   lowly,
   No, not one! no, not one!

3 There's not an hour that He is not
   near us,
   No, not one! no, not one!
No night so dark but His love can
   cheer us,
   No, not one! no, not one!

4 Did ever saint find this Friend for-
   sake him?
   No, not one! no, not one!
Or sinner find that He would not
   take him?
   No, not one! no, not one!

5 Was e'er a gift like the Saviour given?
   No, not one! no, not one!
Will He refuse us a home in heaven?
   No, not one! no, not one!

111   WHENE'ER we meet you
      always say,
   What's the news?
Pray what's the order of the day?
   What's the news?
Oh! I have got good news to tell,
My Saviour hath done all things well,
And triumphed over death and hell,
   That's the news.

2 The Lamb was slain on Calvary,
   That's the news.
To set a world of sinners free,
   That's the news.
For us He bowed His sacred head,
For us His precious blood was shed:
And now He's risen from the dead,
   That's the news.

3 The Lord has pardoned all my sin,
   That's the news.
I feel the witness now within,
   That's the news.
And since He took my guilt away,
And taught me how to watch and
   pray,
I'm happy now, from day to day,
   That's the news.

4 And Jesus Christ can save you too,
   That's the news.
Your sinful heart He can renew,
   That's the news.

This moment, if for sin you grieve,
This moment, if you do believe,
A ready pardon you'll receive,
   That's the news.

5 And then if anyone should say,
   What's the news?
Oh, tell them you've begun to pray,
   That's the news.
That you have joined the conquering
   band,   [mand
And now with joy at God's com-
You're marching to the better land,
   That's the news.

112 WE'RE marching on to heaven
   above,
   Will you go?
To sing the Saviour's dying love—
   Will you go?   [shore,
Millions have reached that blissful
Their trials and their labours o'er,
And yet there's room for millions
   more—
   Will you go?

2 The way to heaven is strait, but plain,
   Will you come?
Repent, believe, be born again,
   Will you come?
Christ offers pardon free to all,
Who will accept His loving call,
And at His feet repentant fall—
   Will you come?

3 How blessed 'tis to serve Him here!
   Praise the Lord!
Redeemed from every doubt and fear
   Praise the Lord!
Though tribulation cross our way,
Affliction or adversity,
Yet Jesus saves us every day,
   Praise the Lord!

4 And when our day of fighting's o'er,
   Home at last!
We'll praise Him on the other shore,
   Home at last!
We'll join again in songs of praise
With those who see the Master's face,
And ever sing redeeming grace—
   Home at last!

113 COME, for the feast is spread;
   Hark to the call!
Come to the Living Bread,
   Broken for all;

Come to His " house of wine,"
Low on His breast recline,
All that He hath make thine;
   Come, sinner, come.

2 Come, where the fountain flows—
   River of life—
Healing for all thy woes,
   Doubting and strife:
Millions have been supplied,
No one was e'er denied;
Come to the crimson tide,
   Come, sinner, come.

3 Come to the Throne of Grace,
   Boldly draw near;
He who would win the race
   Must tarry here;
Whate'er thy want may be,
Here is the grace for thee,
Jesus thy only plea;
   Come, Christian, come.

4 Jesus, we come to Thee,
   Oh, take us in!
Set Thou our spirits free;
   Cleanse us from sin;
Then, in yon land of light,
All clothed in robes of white,
Resting not day nor night,
   Thee will we sing.

114 GOD loved the world of sinner
   lost
   And ruined by the fall,
Salvation full at highest cost,
   He offers free to all.

   Oh, 'twas love, 'twas wondrous love,
     The love of God to me;
   It brought my Saviour from above,
     To die on Calvary.

2 Eternal praises, Lord, to Thee,
   Thou blessed Son of God;
For Thy deep love in cleansing me,
   In Thy most precious blood!

3 Even now by faith, I know I'm
   Thine,
   'Tis in Thy faithful Word;
Oh, height, oh, depth of love divine
   In Thee, the risen Lord!

4 Oh, help me, Lord, to spread Th
   fame,
   And tell of all Thy grace,
To all the world Thy love proclaim
   Until I see Thy face.

115 JESUS, my Saviour, to Beth-
        lehem came,
Born in a manger to sorrow and
   shame ;
Oh, it was wonderful—blest be His
   name !
     Seeking for me, for me !

     Seeking for me ! for me !..
     Seeking for me ! for me !..
   Oh, it was wonderful—blest be His Name !
     Seeking for me, for me !

2 Jesus, my Saviour, on Calvary's tree,
Paid the great debt, and my soul He
   set free ;   [be ?
Oh, it was wonderful—how could it
     Dying for me, for me !

     Dying for me ! for me !..
     Dying for me ! for me !..
   Oh, it was wonderful—how could it be?
     Dying for me, for me !

3 Jesus, my Saviour, the same as of
   old,   [fold,
When I was wand'ring afar from the
Gently and long He did plead with
   my soul,
     Calling for me, for me !

     Calling for me ! for me !..
     Calling for me ! for me !..
   Gently and long did He plead with my soul,
     Calling for me, for me !

4 Jesus, my Saviour, shall come from
   on high—
Sweet is the promise as weary years
   fly ;   [sky,
Oh, I shall see Him descending the
     Coming for me, for me !

     Coming for me ! for me !
     Coming for me ! for me !..
   Oh, I shall see Him descending the sky,
     Coming for me, for me !

116 OH, sing of Jesus, " Lamb of
       God,"
Who died on Calvary !
And for a ransom shed His blood
For you, and even me !

   I'm redeem'd,..I'm redeem'd,..
     Through the blood of the Lamb that
       was slain,..
   I'm redeem'd,..I'm redeem'd,..
     Hallelujah to God and the Lamb !

2 Oh, wondrous power of love divine !
So rich, so full, so free !
It reaches out to all mankind,
   Embraces even me !

3 All glory now to Christ the Lord,
   And evermore shall be !
He hath redeemed a world of sin,
   And ransomed even me !

117 ONE there is who loves thee,
       Waiting still for thee ;
Canst thou yet reject Him ?
   None so kind as He !
Do not grieve Him longer,
   Come, and trust Him now !
He has waited all thy days ;
   Why waitest thou ?

     One there is who loves thee,
       Oh, receive Him now !
     He has waited all the day ;
       Why waitest thou ?

2 Graciously He woos thee,
   Do not slight His call ;
Though thy sins are many,
   He'll forgive them all.
Turn to Him, repenting,
   He will cleanse thee now ;
He is waiting at thy heart :
   Why waitest thou ?

3 Jesus still is waiting ;
   Sinner, why delay ?
To His arms of mercy
   Rise and haste away !
Only come believing,
   He will save thee now ;
He is waiting at the door,
   Why waitest thou ?

118 A RULER once came to Jesus
       by night,   [light ;
To ask Him the way of salvation and
The Master made answer in words
   true and plain,
   " Ye must be born again."...

     " Ye must be born again !
     " Ye must be born again !
     " I verily, verily say unto you—
     " Ye must be born again ! "

2 Ye children of men, attend to the
   word   [Lord.
So solemnly uttered by Jesus, the
And let not this message to you be
   in vain,
   " Ye must be born again."...

3 O ye who would enter the glorious rest,
And sing with the ransomed the song
   of the blest ;   [obtain,
The life everlasting if ye would
   " Ye must be born again."...

4 A dear one in heaven thy heart
    yearns to see,
At the beautiful gates may be
    watching for thee ;
Then list to the note of this solemn
    refrain,
" Ye must be born again.".....

119 WILL you come, will you come,
    with your poor broken heart,
Burdened and sin oppressed ?
Lay it down at the feet of the
    Saviour and Lord,
    Jesus will give you rest.

> O happy rest, sweet happy rest,
>   Jesus will give you rest...   [faith ?
> Oh ! why won't you come in simple trusting
>   Jesus will give you rest.

2 Will you come, will you come ? there
    is mercy for you,
Balm for your aching breast :
Only come as you are and believe
    on His name,
    Jesus will give you rest.

3 Will you come, will you come ? you
    have nothing to pay ;
Jesus who loves you best,
By His death on the cross purchased
    life for your soul ;
    Jesus will give you rest.

4 Will you come, will you come ? how
    He pleads with you now !
Fly to His loving breast ;
And whatever your sin or your
    sorrow may be,
    Jesus will give you rest.

120 'TIS the grandest theme
    through the ages rung ;
'Tis the grandest theme for a mortal
    tongue ;
'Tis the grandest theme that the
    world e'er sung :
    " Our God is able to deliver thee."

> He is a..ble to deliver thee,
> He is a..ble to deliver thee ;
> Tho' by sin opprest, go to Him for rest ;
>   Our God is able to deliver thee.

2 'Tis the grandest theme in the earth
    or main ;   [strain ;
'Tis the grandest theme for a mortal
'Tis the grandest theme, tell the
    world again :
    " Our God is able to deliver thee."

3 'Tis the grandest theme, let th
    tidings roll   [soul
To the guilty heart, to the sinfu
Look to God in faith, He will mak
    thee whole :
    " Our God is able to deliver thee."

121 THERE is a green hill far away
    Without a city wall,
Where the dear Lord was crucified
    Who died to save us all.

> Oh, dearly, dearly has he loved !
>   And we must love Him too ;
> And trust in His redeeming love,
>   And try His works to do.

2 We may not know, we cannot tell
    What pains He had to bear ;
But we believe it was for us
    He hung and suffered there.

3 He died that we might be forgiven
    He died to do us good,
That we might go at last to heaven
    Saved by His precious blood.

4 There was no other good enough
    To pay the price of sin ;
He only could unlock the gate
    Of heaven, and let us in.

122 HAVE you any room for Jesus
    He who bore your load of sin
As He knocks and asks admission,
    Sinner, will you let Him in ?

> Room for Jesus, King of glory,
>   Hasten now, His word obey !
> Swing the heart's door widely open,
>   Bid Him enter while you may.

2 Room for pleasure, room for busines
    But for Christ the crucified,
Not a place that He can enter,
    In your heart for which He died

3 Have you any time for Jesus,
    As in grace He calls again ?
Oh, to-day is time accepted,
    To-morrow you may call in vain

4 Room and time now give to Jesus,
    Soon will pass God's day of grace
Soon thy heart left cold and silent,
    And thy Saviour's pleading cease

123 COME to the Saviour, make n
    delay ;
Here in His Word He has shown u
    the way ;

Here in our midst He's standing
    to-day,
    Tenderly saying, " Come ! "

Joyful, joyful will the meeting be,
When from sin our hearts are pure and free,
And we shall gather, Saviour, with Thee,
    In our eternal home.

" Suffer the children ! " oh, hear His
    voice !   [rejoice ;
Let every heart leap forth and
And let us freely make Him our
    choice,
    Do not delay, but come.

Think once again, He's with us
    to-day ;   [obey ;
Heed now His blest command, and
Hear now His accents tenderly say,
    " Will you, My children, come ? "

24 SINNER, how thy heart is
    troubled !
    God is coming very near ;
Do not hide thy deep emotion,
    Do not check that falling tear.

Oh, be saved, His grace is free !
Oh, be saved, He died for thee !

Jesus now is bending o'er thee,
    Jesus lowly, meek, and mild ;
To the Friend who died to save thee,
    Wilt thou not be reconciled ?

Art thou waiting till the morrow ?
    Thou may'st never see its light !
Come at once ! accept His mercy :
    He is waiting—come to-night !

With a lowly contrite spirit,
    Kneeling at the Saviour's feet,
Thou canst feel, this very moment,
    Pardon—precious, pure and sweet.

Let the angels bear the tidings
    Upward to the courts of heaven !
Let them sing, with holy rapture,
    O'er another soul forgiven !

25 GOD is calling the prodigal,
    come without delay,
Hear, oh, hear Him calling, calling
    now for thee,
Though you've wandered so far from
    His presence, come to-day,
Hear His loving voice calling still...

Call..ing now for thee,..
    Oh ! wea..ry prodigal, come...
Call..ing now for thee,..
    Oh ! wea..ry prodigal, come..

2 Patient, loving, and tenderly still the
    Father pleads,
    Hear, oh, hear Him calling, calling
    now for thee,
Oh ! return while the Spirit in mercy
    intercedes,
    Hear His loving voice calling still...

3 Come, there's bread in the house of
    thy Father, and to spare,
    Hear, oh, hear Him calling, calling
    now for thee,
Lo ! the table is spread and the feast
    is waiting there,
    Hear His loving voice calling still...

126 THE love that Jesus had for me,
    To suffer on the cruel tree,
That I a ransomed soul might be,
    Is more than tongue can tell !

His love is more than tongue can tell !..
His love is more than tongue can tell !..
The love that Jesus had for me
Is more than tongue can tell !

2 The bitter sorrow that He bore,
    And oh, that crown of thorns He
    wore,
That I might live for evermore,
    Is more than tongue can tell.

3 The peace I have in Him, my Lord,
    Who pleads before the throne of God,
The merit of His precious blood,
    Is more than tongue can tell !

4 The joy that comes when He is near,
    The rest He gives, so free from fear,
The hope in Him, so bright and clear,
    Is more than tongue can tell !

127 O SWEET is the story of Jesus,
    The wonderful Saviour of men,
Who suffered and died for the sinner—
    I'll tell it again and again !

Oh, won..derful, wonderful sto..ry,
    The dea..rest that ever was told...
I'll repeat it in glo..ry, the wonderful sto..ry,
    Where I..shall His beauty behold...

2 He came from the brightest of glory ;
    His blood as a ransom He gave,
To purchase eternal redemption,
    And oh, He is mighty to save !

3 His mercy flows on like a river,
    His love is unmeasured and free ;
His grace is for ever sufficient,
    It reaches and purifies me.

128 THERE'S a song my heart is singing;
In my soul its tones are ringing,
Peace and rest and joy 'tis bringing :
Jesus Christ has power to save !

..Sing it over and over again to me..
In its wonderful sweet simplicity ;
Tell it o'er...the ocean wave,
Jesus Christ..has power to save !

2 Oh, that song my soul is thrilling !
Jesus saves the soul that's willing,
Precious truth my heart 'tis filling :
Jesus Christ has power to save !

3 Sinner come ! if thou'lt receive Him,
Look to Jesus and believe Him ;
All your life and service give Him :
Jesus Christ has power to save !

129 COME, sing the gospel's joyful sound,
Salvation full and free ;
Proclaim to all the world around,
The year of jubilee !

Salvation, salvation, the grace of God
doth bring :
Salvation, salvation thro' Christ our Lord
and King.

2 Ye mourning souls aloud rejoice ;
Ye blind, your Saviour see !
Ye prisoners sing with thankful voice,
The Lord hath made you free ;

3 With rapture swell the song again,
Of Jesus' dying love ;
'Tis peace on earth, good will to men,
And praise to God above.

130 WE can tell it as we journey toward the mansion built above,
The grand old story of salvation ;
We sing it out with gladness, in the melodies of love,
The grand old story of salvation.

Ring it out. .ring it out,..
Ring to every tribe and nation,...
Ring it out,.. ring it out,..
The grand old story of salvation.

2 His hand can lift the fallen and His blood can make them white,
The grand old story of salvation ;
His love can pierce the darkness with a never-fading light,
The grand old story of salvation.

3 We'll sing it in the battle, and i
notes shall victory be,
The grand old story of salvatio
We'll sing it in our trials, till tl
passing shadows flee,
The grand old story of salvation

4 The angels look with wonder, y
their harps can never tell
The grand old story of salvatior
His ransomed, clothed with beaut
shall the praise of Jesus swell
The grand old story of salvation

131 COME, ye sinners, poor ar needy,
Weak and wounded, sick and sor
Jesus ready stands to save you,
Full of pity, love, and power.
Now, ye needy, come and welcome
God's free bounty glorify,
True belief and true repentance,
Every grace that brings you nig

2 Let not conscience make you ling
Nor of fitness fondly dream,
All the fitness He requireth
Is to feel your need of Him.
Come, ye weary, heavy laden,
Bruised and mangled by the fal
If you tarry till you're better,
You will never come at all.

132 TELL me the old, old story
Of unseen things above,
Of Jesus and His glory,
Of Jesus and His love.
Tell me the story simply,
As to a little child ;
For I am weak and weary,
And helpless and defiled.

Tell me the old, old story,
Tell me the old, old story,
Tell me the old, old story
Of Jesus and His love.

2 Tell me the story slowly,
That I may take it in—
That wonderful redemption,
God's remedy for sin.
Tell me the story often,
For I forget so soon !
The " early dew " of morning
Has passed away at noon.

3 Tell me the story softly,
With earnest tones, and grave;
Remember ! I'm the sinner
Whom Jesus came to save.

Tell me the story always,
  If you would really be
In any time of trouble
  A comforter to me.

Tell me the same old story,
  When you have cause to fear
That this world's empty glory
  Is costing me too dear.
Yes, and when that world's glory
  Is dawning on my soul,
Tell me the old, old story,
  " Christ Jesus makes thee whole."

133 JESUS is tenderly calling thee
    home—
  Calling to-day ! calling to-day !
Why from the sunshine of love wilt
    thou roam—
  Farther and farther away ?

  Call..ing to-day,..call..ing to-day,..
  Jesus is calling, is tenderly calling to-day !

Jesus is calling the weary to rest—
  Calling to-day ! calling to-day !
Bring Him thy burden and thou
    shalt be blest—
  He will not turn thee away.

Jesus is waiting, oh, come to Him
    now—
  Waiting to-day ! waiting to-day !
Come with thy sins—at His feet
    lowly bow—
  Come and no longer delay.

Jesus is pleading, oh, list to His
    voice—   [day !
  Hear Him to-day ! hear Him to-
They who believe on His name shall
    rejoice— ·
  Quickly arise, come away.

134 'TWAS Jesus, my Saviour, who
    died on the tree,   [me,
To open a fountain for sinners like
His blood is the fountain that pardon
    bestows,   [flows.
And cleanses the foulest wherever it
For the conquering Saviour shall break every
    chain,
And give us the victory again and again.

And when I was willing with all
    things to part,   [my heart,
He gave me my bounty, His love in
So now I am joined with the con-
    quering band,   [command.
Who are marching to glory at Jesus'

3 Though round me the storms of
    adversity roll,
  And the waves of destruction encom-
    pass my soul.
  In vain this frail vessel the tempest
    shall toss.   [the Cross.
  My hopes rest secure on the blood of

4 And when with the ransomed of
    Jesus. my Head,
  From fountain to fountain I then
    shall be led,
  I'll fall at His feet and His mercy
    adore,   [evermore.
  And sing of the blood of the Cross

5 Come, sinners, to Jesus ! no longer
    delay !
  A full free salvation He offers to-day,
  Arouse your dark spirits, awake
    from your dream,
  And Christ will support you in
    coming to Him.

135 REPEAT the story o'er and o'er,
    Of grace so full and free ;
  I love to hear it more and more,
    Since grace has rescued me.

      The half....was never told,....
      The half....was never told ;....
      Of grace divine, so wonderful,
      The half was never told.

2 Of peace I only knew the name,
    Nor found my soul its rest,
  Until the sweet-voiced angel came,
    To soothe my weary breast.

      The half....was never told,....
      The half....was never told ;....
      Of peace divine, so wonderful,
      The half was never told.

3 My highest place is—lying low
    At my Redeemer's feet ;
  No real joy in life I know
    But in His service sweet.

      The half....was never told,....
      The half....was never told ;....
      Of joy divine, so wonderful,
      The half was never told.

4 And oh, what rapture will it be
    With all the host above,
  To sing through all eternity
    The wonders of His love.

      The half....was never told,....
      The half....was never told ;....
      Of love divine, so wonderful,
      The half was never told.

136 WHILE Jesus whispers to you,
  Come, sinner, come !
While we are praying for you,
  Come, sinner, come !
Now is the time to own Him,
  Come, sinner, come !
Now is the time to know Him,
  Come, sinner, come !

2 Are you too heavy laden ?
  Come, sinner, come !
Jesus will bear your burden,
  Come, sinner, come !
Jesus will not deceive you,
  Come, sinner, come !
Jesus will now receive you,
  Come, sinner, come !

3 Oh, hear His tender pleading,
  Come, sinner, come !
Oh, now receive the blessing !
  Come, sinner, come !
While Jesus whispers to you,
  Come, sinner, come !
While we are praying for you,
  Come, sinner, come !

137 THERE is a fountain filled
    with blood,
  Drawn from Immanuel's veins ;
And sinners plunged beneath that
    flood
  Lose all their guilty stains !

  I do believe, I will believe,
  * That Jesus died for me !*
  That on the Cross He shed His blood,
  * From sin to set me free.*

2 The dying thief rejoiced to see
  That fountain in His day ;
And there may I, though vile as he,
  Wash all my sins away.

3 Dear dying Lamb ! Thy precious
    blood
  Shall never lose its power,
Till all the ransomed church of God
  Be saved to sin no more.

4 E'er since by faith I saw the stream
  Thy flowing wounds supply,
Redeeming love has been my theme,
  And shall be till I die.

  The following chorus may be substituted :—
  Hallelujah, to the Lamb,
  * Who died on Mount Calvary ;*
  Hallelujah ! Hallelujah !
  * Hallelujah ! Amen.*

138 OH, how dark the night tha
    wrapt my spirit round !
Oh, how deep the woe my Saviou
    found
When He walked across the water
    of my soul,
Bade my night disperse and mad
    me whole !

  All the way to Calvary He went for m
  He went for me, He went for me,
  All the way to Calvary He went for m
  He died to set me free.

2 Trembling a sinner bowed befor
    His face,
Naught I knew of pardon—God'
    free grace,
Heard a voice so melting, " Ceas
    thy wild regret,
Jesus bought thy pardon, paid th
    debt."

3 Oh, 'twas wondrous love the Saviou
    showed for me,
When He left His throne for Calvary
When He trod the wine-press, tro
    it all alone,
Praise His name for ever, make i
    known.

139 PRAISE be to Jesus, His merc
    is free ;
  Mercy is free, mercy is free ;
Sinner, that mercy is flowing fo
    thee,
  Mercy is boundless and free.
If thou art willing on Him to believ
  Mercy is free, mercy is free,
Life everlasting thy soul may receiv
  Mercy is boundless and free.

  Jesus, the Saviour, is looking for thee,
  Looking for thee, looking for thee ;
  Lovingly, tenderly calling for thee,
  Calling and looking for thee.

2 Why on the mountains of sin wil
    thou roam ?
  Mercy is free, mercy is free ;
Gently the Spirit is calling " Com
    home,"
  Mercy is boundless and free.
Thou art in darkness, oh, come t
    the light,
  Mercy is free, mercy is free.
Jesus is waiting, He'll save the
    to-night,
  Mercy is boundless and free.

Think of His goodness, and patience
    and love ;
Mercy is free, mercy is free ;
Pleading thy cause with His Father
    above,
    Mercy is boundless and free.
Come and repenting, oh, give Him
    thy heart,
Mercy is free, mercy is free.
Grieve Him no longer, but come as
    thou art,
    Mercy is boundless and free.

Yes, there is pardon for all who
    believe ;
Mercy is free, mercy is free ;
Come and this moment a blessing
    receive,
    Mercy is boundless and free.
Jesus is waiting, oh, hear Him
    proclaim
Mercy is free, mercy is free !
Cling to His mercy, believe on His
    name,
    Mercy is boundless and free.

40 SHE only touched the hem of
    His garment
As to His side she stole,
Amid the crowd that gathered
    around Him,
    And straightway she was whole.

Oh, touch the hem of His garment,
    And thou, too, shalt be free !
His saving power this very hour
    Shall give new life to thee.

She came in fear and trembling
    before Him,
She knew her Lord had come ;
She felt that from Him virtue had
    healed her,
    The mighty deed was done.

He turned with, " Daughter, be of
    good comfort,
Thy faith hath made thee whole;"
And peace that passeth all under-
    standing
    With gladness filled her soul.

41 IN tenderness He sought me,
    Weary and sick with sin,
And on His shoulders brought me
    Back to His fold again ;
While angels in His presence sang
Until the courts of heaven rang.

Oh, the love that sought me !
Oh, the blood that bought me !
Oh, the grace that brought me to the fold.
Wondrous grace that brought me to the fold !

2 He washed the bleeding.sin-wounds,
    And poured in oil and wine ;
He whispered to assure me,
    " I've found thee, thou art Mine;"
I never heard a sweeter voice,
It made my aching heart rejoice.

3 He pointed to the nail-prints ;
    For me His blood was shed,
A mocking crown so thorny,
    Was placed upon His head :
I wonder what He saw in me
To suffer such deep agony.

4 I'm sitting in His presence,
    The sunshine of His face,
While with adoring wonder
    His blessings I retrace.
It seems as if eternal days
Are far too short to sound His praise.

5 So while the hours are passing,
    All now is perfect rest ;
I'm waiting for the morning,
    The brightest and the best,
When He will call us to His side,
To be with Him, His spotless bride.

142 I STAND all amazed at the
    love Jesus offers me,
Confused at the grace that so fully
    He proffers me ;
I tremble to know that for me He
    was crucified,
That for me a sinner, He suffered,
    He bled, and died.

Oh! it is wonderful that He should care for me,
    Enough to die for me.
Oh ! it is wonderful, wonderful to me !

2 I marvel that He would descend
    from His throne divine,
To rescue a soul so rebellious and
    proud as mine ;
That He should extend His great
    love unto such as I,   [justify.
Sufficient to own, to redeem and to

3 I think of His hands pierced and
    bleeding to pay the debt !
Such mercy, such love and devotion
    can I forget ?   [mercy seat,
No, no, I will praise and adore at the
Until at the glorified throne I kneel
    at His feet.

143 ON the golden streets of heaven
all men hope to walk some day,
Yet so many are not willing to accept
the living way ;
But while others build on good works
or opinions if they may,
Hallelujah ! hallelujah ! I'm depending on the blood.

In the soul-cleansing blood of the Saviour,
I've been washed in the crimson flood ;
Tho' the world may say there is hope some other
I'm depending on the blood.   [way.

2 Some will tell us that God's mercy is
their only hope and plea,
That a soul He could not punish
throughout all eternity ;
But I read that my dear Saviour
died for sinners just like me,
Hallelujah ! hallelujah ! I'm depending on the blood.

3 As we look back through the ages
where the kings and prophets trod,
We may see their altars reeking with
the sacrifice and blood,
But those types were only pointing
to the Paschal Lamb of God,
Hallelujah ! hallelujah ! I'm depending on the blood.

4 'Tis the burden of that chorus over
on the streets of light,
That the blood from Calvary's
mountain hath washed all their
garments white ;
So I'll shout along life's pathway till
I reach that land so bright :
" Hallelujah ! hallelujah ! I'm depending on the blood."

144 OH, now I see the cleansing wave,
The fountain deep and wide !
Jesus, my Lord, mighty to save,
Points to His wounded side.

The cleansing stream I see. I see !
I plunge, and oh, it cleanseth me !
Oh, praise the Lord ! it cleanseth me ;
It cleanseth me, yes, cleanseth me.

2 I see the new creation rise ;
I hear the speaking blood !
It speaks polluted nature dies !
Sinks 'neath the cleansing flood.

3 I rise to walk in heaven's own light,
Above the world and sin, [white,
With heart made pure and garment
And Christ enthroned within.

4 Amazing grace ! 'tis heaven below
To feel the blood applied ;
And Jesus, only Jesus know,
My Jesus crucified.

145 GOD calling yet ! shall I ne
hear ?   [dear
Earth's pleasures shall I still ho
Shall life's sweet passing years all fl
And still my soul in slumber lie

Call...ing yet ! oh, hear Him !
Call...ing yet ! oh, hear Him !
God is calling yet! oh, hear Him! calling, callin
Call...ing yet ! oh, hear Him !
Call...ing yet ! oh, hear Him !
God is calling yet ! oh, hear Him calling yet !

2 God calling yet ! shall I not rise ?
Can I His loving voice despise,
And basely His kind care repay
He calls me still : can I delay ?

3 God calling yet ! and shall He knoc
And I my heart the closer lock ?
He still is waiting to receive ;
And shall I dare His Spirit grieve

4 God calling yet ! and shall I give
No heed but still in bondage live
I wait ; but He does not forsake ;
He calls me still : my heart, awake

5 God calling yet ! I cannot stay ;
My heart I yield without delay :
Vain world, farewell ! from thee
part ;   [hear
The voice of God has reached n

146 WHY do you wait, dear brothe
Oh, why do you tarry so long
Your Saviour is waiting to give ye
A place in His sanctified throng

Why not ? why not ?
Why not come to Him now ?

2 What do you hope, dear brother,
To gain by a further delay ?
There's no one to save you b
Jesus,
There's no other way but His wa

3 Do you not feel, dear brother,
His spirit now striving within ?
Oh, why not accept His salvation
And throw off your burden of sin

4 Why do you wait, dear brother ?
The harvest is passing away,
Your Saviour is longing to bless yo
There's danger and death in dela

47 SOWING the seed by the day-
     light fair,   [glare,
Sowing the seed by the noon-day
Sowing the seed by the fading light,
Sowing the seed in the solemn night;
     Oh, what shall the harvest be ?

own..in the dark..ness or sown..in the light..
own..in our weak..ness or sown..in our might,...
     Gather'd in time or eternity,
     Sure, ah, sure will the harvest be...

Sowing the seed by the wayside high,
Sowing the seed on the rocks to die,
Sowing the seed where the thorns will
     spoil,
Sowing the seed in the fertile soil;
     Oh, what shall the harvest be ?

Sowing the seed of a lingering pain,
Sowing the seed of a maddened brain,
Sowing the seed of a tarnished name,
Sowing the seed of eternal shame;
     Oh, what shall the harvest be ?

Sowing the seed with an aching
     heart,   [start,
Sowing the seed while the teardrops
Sowing in hope till the reapers come
Gladly to gather the harvest home :
     Oh, what shall the harvest be ?

48 TO-DAY the Saviour calls;
     Ye wanderers come;
O ye benighted souls,
     Why longer roam ?

To-day the Saviour calls;
     O hear Him now;
Before your day is gone,
     To Jesus bow.

To-day the Saviour calls :
     For refuge fly;
The storm of vengeance falls;
     Ruin is nigh.

The Spirit calls to-day :
     Yield to His power;
O grieve Him not away;
     'Tis mercy's hour.

49 TO-DAY Thy mercy calls me,
     To wash away my sin;
However great my trespass,
     Whate'er I may have been.
However long from mercy
     I may have turned away,
Thy blood, O Christ, can cleanse me,
     And make me white to-day.

2 To-day Thy gate is open,
     And all who enter in
Shall find a Father's welcome,
     And pardon for their sin;
The past shall be forgotten.
     A present joy be given,
A future grace be promised—
     A glorious crown in heaven.

3 To-day the Father calls me;
     The Holy Spirit waits;
The blessed angels gather
     Around the heavenly gates.
No question will be asked me,
     How often I have come :
Although I oft have wandered,
     It is my Father's home.

4 O all-embracing mercy,
     Thou ever-open door !
What shall I do without thee,
     When heart and eyes run o'er ?
When all things seem against me,
     To drive me to despair,
I know one gate is open,
     One ear will hear my prayer.

150 COME, contrite one, and seek
     His grace,
     Jesus is passing by;
See in His reconciled face
     The sunshine of the sky.

     Pass...ing by,...pass...ing by...
     Hasten to meet Him on the way,
     Jesus is passing by to-day,
     Pass...ing by,...pass...ing by....

2 Come, hungry one, and tell your
     Jesus is passing by;   [need,
The Bread of Life your soul will feed,
     And fully satisfy.

3 Come, weary one, and find sweet rest,
     Jesus is passing by;
Come where the longing heart is
     blessed,
     And on His bosom lie.

4 Come, burdened one, bring all your
     care,
     Jesus is passing by;
The love that listens to your prayer
     Will " no good thing " deny.

151 THE Gospel bells are ringing,
     Over land, from sea to sea :
Blessed news of free salvation
     Do they offer you and me.

" For God so loved the world
   That His only Son He gave,
Whosoe'er believeth in Him
   Everlasting life shall have."

Gospel bells,...how they ring ;...
Over land from sea to sea ;
Gospel bells, ..freely bring...
   Blessed news to you and me.

2 The Gospel bells invite us
   To a feast prepared for all ;
Do not slight the invitation,
   Nor reject the gracious call.
" I am the Bread of life ;
   Eat of Me, thou hungry soul,
Though your sins be red as crimson
   They shall be as white as wool."

3 The Gospel bells give warning
   As they sound from day to day,
Of the fate which doth await them
   Who for ever will delay.
" Escape thou for thy life ;
   Tarry not in all the plain,
Nor behind thee look, oh, never,
   Lest thou be consumed in pain."

4 The Gospel bells are joyful,
   As they echo far and wide,
Bearing notes of perfect pardon,
   Through a Saviour crucified.
" Good tidings of great joy
   To all people do I bring,
Unto you is born a Saviour,
   Which is Christ the Lord and
     King."

152 ART thou weary, art thou
     languid,
   Art thou sore distressed ?
" Come to Me," saith One, " and
     coming,
   Be at rest."

2 Hath He diadem as monarch,
   That His brow adorns ?
Yes, a crown of very surety,
   But of thorns.

3 If I ask Him to receive me,
   Will He say me nay ?
Not till earth, and not till heaven,
   Pass away.

4 Finding, following, keeping, strug-
   ls He sure to bless ?   [gling,
Angels, martyrs, saints, and pro-
   Answer, " Yes ! "   [phets

153 ON Calvary's brow my Saviour
     died,
"Twas there my Lord was crucified,
'Twas on the Cross He bled for me
And purchased there my pardon free

O Calvary ! dark Calvary !
Where Jesus shed His blood for me,...
   O Calvary ! blest Calvary !
'Twas there my Saviour died for me.

2 'Mid rending rocks and darkening
     skies,
My Saviour bows His head and dies
The opening veil reveals the way
To heaven's joys and endless day.

3 O Jesus, Lord, how can it be,
That Thou shouldst give Thy life for
     me,
To bear the Cross and agony
In that dread hour on Calvary !

154 THERE'S a royal highway
     leading
   To the King's sublime abode ;
And I seek a home in glory,
   Walking in that royal road.

Oh, the bless...ed royal road,...
Oh, the bless...ed royal road,...
Will you go...with me to glo...ry,
   Walking in...that royal road ?

2 O'er the highway Jesus travelled,
   Up the hill of Calvary trod,
That He might a path make open
   Leading to the throne of God.

3 As I journey o'er the highway
   To the country of my King,
Oft by faith I hear the echo
   From the land where angels sing

4 Oft a glad, entrancing vision
   To my spirit is bestowed ;
'Tis the city, bright, eternal,
   Whither leads the royal road.

155 TENDERLY the Shepherd,
     O'er the mountains cold,
Goes to bring His lost one
    Back to the fold.

Seeking to save, seeking to save,
Lost one, 'tis Jesus, seeking to save.

2 Patiently the owner
   Seeks with earnest care,
In the dust and darkness
   Her treasure rare.

3 Lovingly the Father
    Sends the news around :
"He once dead now liveth—
    Once lost is found."

56 LORD Jesus, I long to be
    perfectly whole,
I want Thee for ever to live in my
    soul ;   [every foe—
Break down every idol, cast out
Now wash me, and I shall be whiter
    than snow.

Whiter than snow ; yes, whiter than snow ;
Now wash me, and I shall be whiter than
snow.

Lord Jesus, let nothing unholy
    remain,
Apply Thine own blood and extract
    every stain ;   [forgo—
To get this blest cleansing I all things
Now wash me, and I shall be whiter
    than snow.

Lord Jesus, look down from Thy
    throne in the skies,
And help me to make a complete
    sacrifice ;   [know—
I give up myself and whatever I
Now wash me, and I shall be whiter
    than snow.

Lord Jesus, for this I most humbly
    entreat,   [feet ;
I wait, blessed Lord, at Thy crucified
By faith, for my cleansing I see Thy
    blood flow—
Now wash me, and I shall be whiter
    than snow.

Lord Jesus, Thou seest I patiently
    wait ;   [heart create ;
Come now, and within me a new
To those who have sought Thee Thou
    never saidst, " No "—
Now wash me, and I shall be whiter
    than snow.

57 THE whole world was lost in
    the darkness of sin,
The Light of the world is Jesus ;
Like sunshine at noon-day His glory
    shone in,
    The Light of the world is Jesus.

Come to the Light, 'tis shining for thee ;
Sweetly the Light has dawn'd upon me.
Once I was blind, but now I can see :
    The Light of the world is Jesus.

2 No darkness have we who in Jesus
    abide,
    The Light of the world is Jesus ;
We walk in the light when we follow
    our guide,
    The Light of the world is Jesus.

3 Ye dwellers in darkness, with sin-
    blinded eyes,
    The Light of the world is Jesus ;
Go, wash at His bidding, and light
    will arise,
    The Light of the world is Jesus.

4 No need of the sunlight in heaven,
    we're told,
    The Light of the world is Jesus ;
The Lamb is the Light in the City
    of Gold,
    The Light of the world is Jesus.

158 IF you could see Christ stand-
    ing here to-night—
    His thorn-crowned head and
    pierced hands could view ;
Could see those eyes that beam with
    heaven's own light,
    And hear Him say, " Beloved,
    'twas for you : "

Would you believe,...and Jesus receive,...
If He were stand...ing here ?...

2 If you could see that face so calm
    and sweet,
    Those lips that spake words only
    pure and true ;
Could see the nail prints in His
    tender feet,
    And hear Him say, " Beloved,
    'twas for you : '

3 He whispers to your heart, turn not
    away,
    For He's beside you in your
    narrow pew ;
If you will listen, you will hear Him
    say,
    In loving tones, " Beloved, 'twas
    for you : "

Will you believe,...and Jesus receive,..
For He is stand...ing here?..

159 I WAS drifting away on life's
    pitiless sea,
And the angry waves threatened
    my ruin to be,

When away at my side, there I
dimly descried
A stately old vessel, and loudly I
cried—
"Ship, a-hoy!
Ship, a-hoy!"
And loudly I cried,
"Ship, a-hoy!"

2 'Twas the "old ship of Zion," thus
sailing along,
All aboard her seemed joyous, I
heard their sweet song;
And the Captain's kind ear, ever
ready to hear,
Caught my wail of distress, as I
cried out in fear—
"Ship, a-hoy!
Ship, a-hoy!"
As I cried out in fear,
"Ship, a-hoy."

3 The good Captain commanded a
boat to be low'red,
And with tender compassion, He
took me on board;
And I'm happy to-day, all my sins
washed away
In the blood of my Saviour; and
now I can say—
"Bless the Lord!
Bless the Lord!"
From my soul I can say,
"Bless the Lord!"

4 O soul, sinking down 'neath sin's
merciless wave,
The strong arm of our Captain is
mighty to save;
Then trust Him to-day, no longer
delay;
Board the old ship of Zion, and
shout on your way—
"Jesus saves!
Jesus saves!"
Shout and sing on your way,
"Jesus saves!"

160 JESUS the water of life will give
Freely, freely, freely;
Jesus the water of life will give
Freely to those who love Him.
Come to that fountain, oh, drink and
live!
Freely, freely, freely;   [live!
Come to that fountain, oh, drink and
Flowing for those that love Him!

The Spirit and the Bride say, Come,
Freely, freely, freely:
And he that is thirsty let him come,
And drink of the water of life.

The fountain of life is flowing,
Flowing, freely flowing;
The fountain of life is flowing,
Is flowing for you and for me.

2 Jesus has promised a home in heaven
(*Repeat*
Treasures unfading will there be
given,   (*Repeat*

3 Jesus has promised a robe of white
(*Repeat*
Kingdoms of glory and crowns of
light,   (*Repeat*

4 Jesus has promised eternal day,
(*Repeat*
Pleasures that never shall pass away
(*Repeat*

161 O CHRIST, what burden
bowed Thy head!
Our load was laid on Thee;
Thou stoodest in the sinner's stead,
Didst bear all ill for me.
A Victim led, Thy blood was shed,
Now there's no load for me.

2 Death and the curse were in our cup,
O Christ, 'twas full for Thee!
But Thou hast drained the last dark
drop,
'Tis empty now for me.
That bitter cup, love drank it up,
Now blessing's draught for me.

3 The tempest's awful voice was
heard,
O Christ, it broke on Thee!
Thy open bosom was my ward,
It braved the storm for me:
Thy form was scarred, Thy visage
marred,
Now cloudless peace for me.

4 For me, Lord Jesus, Thou hast died,
And I have died in Thee:
Thou'rt risen—my bands are all
untied;
And now Thou liv'st in me;
When purified, made white and
Thy glory then for me!   [tried

162 THE gospel of Thy grace
    My stubborn heart has won,
For God so loved the world,
    He gave His only Son,
That " Whosoever will believe,
Shall everlasting life receive."

The serpent " lifted up,"
    Could life and healing give ;
So Jesus on the Cross
    Bids me to look and live ;
For " Whosoever will believe,
Shall everlasting life receive ! "

" The soul that sinneth dies : "
    My awful doom I heard ;
I was for ever lost,
    But for Thy gracious word
That " Whosoever will believe,
Shall everlasting life receive ! "

" Not to condemn the world "
    The " Man of Sorrows " came ;
But that the world might have
    Salvation through His name ;
For " Whosoever will believe,
Shall everlasting life receive ! "

" Lord, help my unbelief ! "
    Give me the peace of faith,
To rest with child-like trust
    On what Thy gospel saith,
That " Whosoever will believe,
Shall everlasting life receive ! "

163 AT even, ere the sun was set,
    The sick, O Lord, around
    Thee lay ;
O in what divers pains they met !
O with what joy they went away !

Once more 'tis eventide and we,
    Oppressed with various ills, draw
    near ;
What if Thy form we cannot see,
We know and feel that Thou art here.

O Saviour Christ, our woes dispel :
    For some are sick, and some are sad,
And some have never loved Thee
    well,   [had.
    And some have lost the love they

And some are pressed with worldly
    care,   [doubt,
    And some are tried with sinful
And some such grievous passions
    tear,   [out.
    That only Thou canst cast them

5 And some have found the world is
    vain,
    Yet from the world they break not
    free ;
And some have friends who give
    them pain ;
    Yet have not sought a friend in
    Thee.

6 O Saviour Christ ! Thou too art Man;
    Thou hast been troubled, tempted,
    tried ;   [scan,
Thy kind but searching glance can
    The very wounds that shame
    would hide !

7 Thy touch has still its ancient power,
    No word from Thee can fruitless
    fall ;
Hear in this solemn evening hour,
And in Thy mercy heal us all.

164 ROCK of Ages, cleft for me,
    Let me hide myself in Thee !
Let the water and the blood,
From Thy riven side which flow'd,
Be of sin the double cure ;
Cleanse me from its guilt and pow'r.

2 Not the labour of my hands
Can fulfil Thy law's demands ;
Could my zeal no respite know,
Could my tears for ever flow,
All for sin could not atone ;
Thou must save, and Thou alone.

3 Nothing in my hand I bring,
Simply to Thy Cross I cling ;
Naked, come to Thee for dress ;
Helpless, look to Thee for grace ;
Foul, I to the fountain fly ;
Wash me, Saviour, or I die.

4 While I draw this fleeting breath,
When my eyelids close in death ;
When I soar to worlds unknown,
See Thee on Thy judgment throne,
Rock of Ages, cleft for me,
Let me hide myself in Thee.

165 OH, this uttermost salvation !
    'Tis a fountain full and free,
Pure, exhaustless, ever flowing,
    Wondrous grace ! it reaches me !

    It reaches me ! it reaches me !
    Wondrous grace ! it reaches me !
    Pure, exhaustless, ever flowing :
    Wondrous grace ! it reaches me !

2 How amazing God's compassion,
   That so vile a worm should prove
This stupendous bliss of heaven,
   This unmeasured wealth of love!

3 Jesus, Saviour, I adore Thee!
   Now Thy love I will proclaim!
I will tell the blessed story,
   I will magnify Thy name!

166   OH! we are going to wear a
      crown,
Oh, we are going to wear a crown,
Oh, we are going to wear a crown,
   To wear a starry crown.

Away over Jordan, with our blessed Jesus,
Away over Jordan, to wear a starry crown.

2 You must be saved to wear a crown.

3 You must be cleansed, to wear that
   crown.

4 You must live upright, to wear that
   crown.

5 You must fight the fight, to wear
   that crown.

6 You must bear the cross, to win
   that crown.

167   WE know there's a bright and
      a glorious home,
   Away in the heavens high,
Where all the redeem'd shall with
     Jesus dwell,
   Will you be there, and I ?

Will you be there and I ? (Repeat.)
Where all the redeemed shall with Jesus
   Will you be there, and I ?   [dwell.

2 In robes of white, o'er streets of gold,
   Beneath a cloudless sky,
They'll walk in the light of their
     Father's love.
   Will you be there, and I ?

Will you be there and I ? (Repeat.)
They'll walk in the light of their Father's
   Will you be there and I ?   [love.

3 If we find the loving Saviour now,
   And follow Him faithfully,
When He gathers His children in
     that bright home,
   Then you'll be there, and I !

Yes, you'll be there and I (Repeat)
When He gathers His children in that bright
  home,
   Yes, you'll be there, and I.

4 If we are sheltered by the Cross,
   And through the blood brough[t]
     nigh ;
Our utmost gain we'll count but los[s]
   Since you'll be there, and I.

Since you'll be there and I (Repent),
Our utmost gain we'll count but loss,
   Since you'll be there and I.

168   HARK! there comes a whispe[r]
     Stealing on thine ear ;
'Tis the Saviour calling,
   Soft, soft and clear.

" Give thy heart to Me,.....
   Once I died for thee....."
Hark ! hark ! thy Saviour calls ;
   Come, sinner, come !

2 With that voice so gentle,
   Dost thou hear Him say ?
Tell Me all thy sorrows ;
   Come, come away ! "

3 Wouldst thou find a Refuge
   For thy soul opprest ?
Jesus kindly answers,
   " I am thy rest."

4 At the Cross of Jesus,
   Let thy burden fall ;
While He gently whispers,
   " I'll bear it all."

169   THERE is life for a look at th[e]
     Crucified One,
   There is life at this moment f[or]
     thee ;
Then look, sinner, look unto Hi[m]
     and be sav'd,   [tre
Unto Him who was nail'd to th[e]

Look ! look ! look and live !
There is life for a look at the crucified One,
There is life at this moment for thee.

2 It is not thy tears of repentance n[or]
     pray'rs,   [soul
But the blood that atones for th[y]
On Him then believe, and a pardo[n]
     receive,
   For His blood now can make the[e]
     quite whole.

3 We are healed by His stripes[,]
     wouldst thou add to the word[?]
And He is our righteousness made[,]
The best robe of heaven He bi[ds]
     thee to wear,   [arrayed
Oh, couldst thou be bett[er]

Then doubt not thy welcome, since
  God has declared   [done :
There remaincth no more to be
That once in the end of the world
  He appeared,   [begun.
And completed the work He'd
But take, with rejoicing, from
  Jesus at once,
The life everlasting He gives ;
And know with assurance thou never
  canst die,   [lives.
Since Jesus thy righteousness

70 SEEKING the lost, yes, kindly
    entreating   [astray ;
Wanderers on the mountains
" Come unto Me." His message
  repeating,   [day.
Words of the Master speaking to-

Going afar....upon the mountain,....
Bringing the wand'rer back again....
Into the fold....of my Redeemer,....
Jesus the Lamb for sinners slain....

Seeking the lost, and pointing to Jesus,
Souls that are weak, and hearts
  that are sore ;   [salvation,
Leading them forth in ways of
Showing the path to life evermore.

Thus I would go on missions of
  mercy,   [day ;
Following Christ from day unto
Cheering the faint, and raising the
  fallen ;
Pointing the lost to Jesus the way.

71 HAVE you been to Jesus for
    the cleansing pow'r ?
Are you washed in the blood of the
  Lamb ?   [this hour ?
Are you fully trusting in His grace
Are you washed in the blood of
  the Lamb ?

Are you wash'd...in the blood,...
In the soul-cleansing blood of the Lamb ?...
Are your garments spotless ? are they white
  as snow ?
Are you wash'd in the blood of the Lamb ?

Are you walking daily by the
  Saviour's side ?
Are you washed in the blood of
  the Lamb ?   [Crucified ?
Do you rest each moment in the
Are you washed in the blood of
  the Lamb ?

3 When the Bridegroom cometh will
  your robes be white—
Pure and white in the blood of the
  Lamb ?
Will your soul be ready for the
  mansions bright,
And be washed in the blood of the
  Lamb ?

4 Lay aside the garments that are
  stain'd by sin,   [Lamb :
And be washed in the blood of the
There's a fountain flowing for the
  soul unclean,   [Lamb.
Oh. be washed in the blood of the

172 THERE'S a wonderful story
    I've heard long ago.
'Tis called " The sweet story of
  old,"
I hear it so often, wherever I go.
That same old story is told ;
And I've thought it was strange that
  so often they'd tell
That story, as if it were new ;
But I've found out the reason they
  loved it so well,
That old, old story is true.

That old, old story is true,....
That old, old story is true.....
But I've found out the reason they lov'd
  it so well,
That old, old story is true.....

2 They told of a Saviour so lovely and
  pure,
That came to the earth to dwell ;
To seek for His lost ones, and make
  them secure
From death and the power of hell.
That He was despised, and with
  thorns He was crowned, [view;
On the cross was extended to
But oh, what sweet peace in my
  heart since I've found
That old, old story is true !

That old, old story is true,....
That old, old story is true.....
But oh, what sweet peace in my heart
  since I've found
That old, old story is true.....

3 He arose and ascended to heaven,
  we're told,
Triumphant o'er death and hell ;
He's preparing a place in that city
  of gold,.   [dwell;
Where lov'd ones for ever may

Where our kindred we'll meet, and
   we'll never more part,
And oh, while I tell it to you,
It is peace to my soul, it is joy to
   my heart,
   That old, old story is true.

    That old, old story is true,.....
    That old, old story is true.....
    It is peace to my soul, it is joy to my heart,
    That old, old story is true.....

4 Oh, that wonderful story, I love to
   repeat,
Of peace and good-will to men ;
There's no story to me that is half
   so sweet,
   As I hear it again and again.
He invites you to come—He will
   freely receive,   [you :
   And this message He sendeth to
" There's a mansion in glory for all
   who believe,"
   That old, old story is true.

    That old, old story is true,.....
    That old, old story is true.....
    " There's a mansion in glory for all who
    believe,"
    That old, old story is true....

173   O WHAT a Saviour that He
   died for me !
From condemnation He hath made
   me free ;   [saith He,
" He that believeth on the Son,"
   "*Hath* everlasting life."

    Verily, verily, I say unto you,
    Verily, verily, message ever new ·
    " He that believeth on the Son," 'tis true !
    " Hath everlasting life."

2 All my iniquities on Him were laid,
All my indebtedness by Him was
   paid ;   [hath said,
All who believe on Him, the Lord,
   " *Have* everlasting life."

3 Tho' poor and needy, I can trust my
   Lord ;   [Word ;
Tho' weak and sinful, I believe His
O glad message ! ev'ry child of God,
   " *Hath* everlasting life."

4 Tho' all unworthy, yet I will not
   doubt,   [cast out ;
For him that cometh He will not
" He that believeth," Oh, the good
   news shout,
   " HATH everlasting life."

174 I HEARD the voice of Jesus say
   " Come unto Me and rest;
Lay down, thou weary one, lay
   down
   Thy head upon My breast."

2 I came to Jesus as I was—
   Weary, and worn, and sad ;
I found in Him a resting place,
   And He has made me glad.

3 I heard the voice of Jesus say,
   " Behold, I freely give
The living water—thirsty one,
   Stoop down, and drink, and live.

4 I came to Jesus and I drank
   Of that life-giving stream ;
My thirst was quench'd, my soul
   revived,
   And now I live in Him.

5 I heard the voice of Jesus say,
   " I am this dark world's Light ;
Look unto Me, thy morn shall rise
   And all thy day be bright."

6 I looked to Jesus, and I found
   In Him my Star, my Sun ;
And in that Light of Life I'll walk
   Till travelling days are done.

175 O WORD, of words the sweetest
   O word, in which there lie
All promise, all fulfilment,
   And end of mystery !
Lamenting, or rejoicing,
   With doubt or terror nigh,
I hear the " Come ! " of Jesus,
   And to His Cross I fly.

    " Come ! oh, come to Me !....
    Come ! oh, come to Me ! "....
    " Weary, heavy-laden,
    Come ! oh, come to Me ! "

2 O soul ! why shouldst thou wander
   From such a loving Friend ?
Cling closer, closer to Him,
   Stay with Him to the end ;
Alas ! I am so helpless,
   So very full of sin,
For I am ever wand'ring,
   And coming back again.

3 Oh, each time draw me nearer,
   That soon the " Come " may be
Nought but a gentle whisper,
   To one close, close to Thee ;

Then, over sea and mountain,
    Far from or near my home,
I'll take Thy hand and follow,
    At that sweet whisper, "Come!"

76 OH, turn ye, oh, turn ye, for
        why will ye die,
When God in great mercy is drawing
    so nigh?
Now Jesus invites you, the Spirit
    says, "Come,"
And angels are waiting to welcome
    you home.

How vain the delusion, that while
    you delay,
Your hearts may grow better by
    staying away!
Come wretched, come thirsty, come
    just as you be,
While streams of salvation are
    flowing so free.

In riches, in pleasures, what can you
    obtain,
To sooth your affliction, or banish
    your pain,
To bear up your spirits when
    summon'd to die,
Or take you to Christ in the clouds
    of the sky?

77 SING them over again to me,
        Wonderful words of life!
Let me more of their beauty see,
    Wonderful words of life!
Words of life and beauty,
Teach me faith and duty!
    Beautiful words! wonderful words!
      Wonderful words of life!

Christ, the blessed One gives to all,
    Wonderful words of life!
Sinner list to the loving call,
    Wonderful words of life!
All so freely given,
Wooing us to heaven!

Sweetly echo the gospel call,
    Wonderful words of life!
Offer pardon and peace to all.
    Wonderful words of life!
Jesus, only Saviour,
Sanctify for ever!

78 SOUND the gospel of grace
        abroad,
    There's life in the risen Lord!

Spread the news of the gift of God,
    There's life in the risen Lord.
    God above desires it!
    Sinful man requires it!
    Tell it around, let it abound,
    There's life in the risen Lord!

2 All by nature are doomed to die,
    So saith the Holy Word;
Welcome, therefore, the joyful cry,
    There's life in the risen Lord!
    Welcome news of gladness—
    Antidote of sadness.

3 Saints, apostles, and prophets, all
    Published with one accord,
This deliverance from the fall—
    This life in the risen Lord!
    Glory be to Jesus,
    Who from bondage freed us.

4 Pardon, power, and perfect peace
    The words of this life afford;
Never, then, let the tidings cease,
    Of life in the risen Lord.
    Open wide the portal,
    Unto every mortal.

179 HAVE thy affections been
        nailed to the Cross?
    Is thy heart right with God?
Dost thou count all things for Jesus
    but loss?
    Is thy heart right with God?
    Is thy heart right with God,
      Washed in the crimson flood,
    Cleansed and made holy, humble and lowly,
      Right in the sight of God?....

2 Hast thou dominion o'er self and
    o'er sin?
    Is thy heart right with God?
Over all evil without and within?
    Is thy heart right with God?

3 Is there no more condemnation for
    sin?
    Is thy heart right with God?
Does Jesus rule in the temple
    within?
    Is thy heart right with God?

4 Are all thy powers under Jesus'
    control?
    Is thy heart right with God?
Does He each moment abide in thy
    soul?
    Is thy heart right with God?

5 Art thou now walking in heaven's
     pure light ?
   Is thy heart right with God ?
   Is thy soul wearing the garment of
     white ?
   Is thy heart right with God ?

180 WILL your anchor hold in the
     storms of life,
   When the clouds unfold their wings
     of strife ?
   When the strong tide lifts, and the
     cables strain,   [remain ?
   Will your anchor shift, or firm

   We have an anchor that keeps the soul
   Steadfast and sure while the billows roll,
   Fasten'd to the Rock which cannot move,
   Grounded firm and deep in the Saviour's love.

2 It is safely moor'd, 'twill the storm
     withstand,
   For 'tis well secured by the Saviour's
     hand ;
   And the cables, pass'd from His
     heart to mine,   [divine.
   Can defy the blast, thro' strength

3 It will firmly hold in the straits of
     fear,
   When the breakers have told the
     reef is near ;
   Tho' the tempest rave, and the wild
     winds blow,   [o'erflow.
   Not an angry wave shall our barque

4 It will surely hold in the floods of
     death,   [breath ;
   When the waters cold chill our latest
   On the rising tide it can never fail,
   While our hopes abide within the
     veil !

5 When our eyes behold, thro' the
     gathering night,
   The city of gold, our harbour bright,
   We shall anchor fast by the heav'nly
     shore,   [more.
   With the storms all past for ever-

181 THERE were ninety and nine
     that safely lay
   In the shelter of the fold,
   But one was out on the hills away,
   Far off from the gates of gold ;
   Away on the mountains wild and
     bare,   [care.
   Away from the tender Shepherd's

2 " Lord, Thou hast here Thy nine
     and nine,
   Are they not enough for Thee ?
   But the Shepherd made answer
     " This of Mine
   Has wandered away from Me ;
   And, although the road be roug
     and steep,
   I go to the desert to find My sheep

3 But none of the ransomed ev
     knew
   How deep were the waters cross'd
   Nor how dark was the night that t
     Lord pass'd through,   [los
   Ere He found His sheep that wa
   Out in the desert He heard its cry-
   Sick, and helpless, and ready to di

4 " Lord, whence are those bloo
     drops all the way,   [track ?
   That mark out the mountain
   " They were shed for one who ha
     gone astray   [back
   Ere the Shepherd could bring hi
   " Lord, whence are Thy hands
     rent and torn ? "
   " They are pierced to-night b
     many a thorn."

5 But all through the mountair
     thunder-riven,
   And up from the rocky steep,
   There arose a cry to the gate
     heaven :   [sheep !
   " Rejoice ! I have found M
   And the angels echoed around t
     throne,   [His own !
   " Rejoice ! for the Lord brings bac

182 WHEN tossed on Galilee
     rough wave,   [oppresse
   And fear their anxious hear
   The Master's voice spoke firm an
     clear,   [res
   And calm'd the angry waves

   It was His voice that still'd the wave,
   His healing touch new vision gave ;
   His might has triumph'd o'er the grave,
   Our Christ alone has power to save.

2 When he who sight had nev
     known,   [voic
   Came to the Lord with pleadir
   That word and touch made darkne
     flee,
   And bade the sorrowful rejoice.

When crucified on Calvary,
  And in the tomb was laid away,
He rose triumphant o'er the grave,
  And lives and reigns with bound-
    less sway.

When trials thick my path surround,
  When hope departs and gloom
    descends,
A gentle voice speaks from above,
  And ev'ry dark foreboding ends.

33 IN the soul's bright home
      beyond the sky,   [die,
In a land where the ransomed never
There will be a royal banquet by and
      by—   [the Lamb.
  'Tis the great marriage supper of

  Are you going to be there,
  Are you going to be there,
At the great marriage supper of the Lamb ?
  With your wedding garments on,
  Will you meet the lov'd ones gone ?
At the great marriage supper of the Lamb ?

Oh, the bride shall shine in bright
      array,   [away ;
With her tears all for ever wiped
There will be a great rejoicing on
      that day—   [the Lamb.
  At the great marriage supper of

From all sin for evermore released,
  They will come from the west and
    from the east,
For all nations will be gathered at
      the feast,   [the Lamb.
  Of the great marriage supper of

We shall praise Him by the crystal
      tide,   [glorified,
When the Lamb that was slain is
And the ransomed Church of God
  shall be the bride,
    At the great marriage supper of
      the Lamb.

34 A GLORIOUS invitation
      Now calls you to the feast;
Each soul is now invited,
  The greatest and the least.
Come, all ye heavy burdened,
  With sorrow or with care—
To-day you are invited,
  Your burden Christ will bear.

e Spirit says come, the Bride says come ;
t him that heareth say, come, let him that
    thirsteth come,   [of life freely.
d whosoever will, let him take of the water

2 That blessed invitation
    Oh, hear to-day and heed !
  The Spirit now is calling,
    Why longer dwell in need ?
  Thy soul to-day is fainting
    For Christ, the living bread ;
  Accept the invitation,
    Come while the feast is spread.

3 Repeat the invitation !
    Pass on the blessed news ;
  Let none forsake His mercy,
    Or pardon now refuse.
  'Tis Jesus that is calling—
    All things are ready, come—
  The Spirit will direct you,
    The Bride will welcome home.

185 WHEN none was found to
        ransom me,
    He was found worthy.
  To set a world of sinners free,
    He was found worthy.
      Oh, the bleeding Lamb !
      He was found worthy.

2 To take the book and loose the seal,
    To bruise the head that bruised His
      heel.

3 To bridge the gulf 'twix man and
      God,
    And save the rebels by His blood.

4 To open wide the gates of heaven,
    To Him all majesty be given !

5 To reign o'er all the ransomed race,
    I've tasted of His saving grace.

6 His blood has washed me white as
      snow,
    And all His fulness I shall know.

186 FREE from the law, oh, happy
        condition,   [mission ;
  Jesus hath bled, and *there* is re-
  Curs'd by the law and bruised by
      the fall,
  Grace hath redeemed us once for all.
      Once for all, oh, sinner, receive it,
      Once for all, oh, brother believe it ;
      Cling to the Cross, the burden will fall,
      Christ hath redeemed us once for all.

2 Now are we free—there's no con-
      demnation,
  Jesus provides a perfect salvation ;
  "Come unto *Me*," oh, hear His
      sweet call !
  Come, and He saves us once for all.

3 " Children of God," oh, glorious
    calling !
Surely His grace will keep us from
    falling ;
Passing from death to life at His call,
Blessed salvation once for all.

187 O MY brother, do you know
    the Saviour,
    Who is wondrous kind and true ?
" He's the Rock of your salvation ! "
    There's Honey in the Rock for you.

Oh, there's Honey in the Rock, my brother,...
There's Honey in the Rock for you ;...
Leave your sins for the blood to cover,
There's Honey in the Rock for you....

2 Have you " tasted that the Lord is
    gracious " ? [new ?
Do you walk in the way that's
Have you drunk from the living
    Fountain ? [you.
There's Honey in the Rock for

3 Do you pray unto God the Father,
    "What wilt Thou have me to do?"
Never fear, He will surely answer ;
There's Honey in the Rock for you.

4 Then go out thro' the streets and
    bye-ways, [few ;
Preach the Word to the many or
Say to ev'ry fallen brother,
    There's Honey in the Rock for you.

188 HEAR the Saviour at the door,
    Let Him in,...let Him in,...
        let Him in.
He has often knocked before,
    Let Him in,...let Him in,... let
        Him in.

'Tis the Saviour standing at the door,....
He's been watching, waiting there before ;....
Open wide the heart of sin,
Let the blessed Saviour in ;
Let Him in,...let Him in.

2 He's your best and truest Friend,
One who always will defend.

3 Do not let Him knock in vain,
He may never come again.

4 Hear His gentle, loving voice,
Bid Him welcome, and rejoice.

189 JESUS is waiting, oh sinner ! for
    thee, [Me ; "
Calling so tenderly, " Come unto

Waiting His mercy and peace
    impart, [thy hea
Come then, oh wanderer, give H

Come to Him now, He's waiting for thee
Turn not away from His mercy so free,
Jesus is waiting, waiting for thee,
Calling so tenderly, " Come unto Me."

2 Come from the path that see
    pleasant and wide.
Narrow the way if thou walk
    His side—
Narrow, yet brighten'd with ble
    ings untold, [go
Leading thee home to the city

3 Come to the Saviour whose grace
    so free, [for the
Come to Him now while He call
Enter the fold by the only true do
Come, quickly come, lest He c
    thee no more.

190 WHEN the sinner turns from s
    How they sing up yonder
Come to Christ sweet peace to w
    How they sing up yonder !
Asks for cleansing in the blood,
Sinks beneath the healing flood,
Rises, cleansed and owned of Go
    How they sing up yonder !

2 When the wanderer seeks his hor
    How they sing up yonder !
Just a servant to become,
    How they sing up yonder !
Leave the byways cold and bare
Seeks again a Father's care,
All His wealth of love to share,
    How they sing up yonder !

3 Brother, would you join the song
    In the home up yonder ?
Sing while ages roll along,
    In the home up yonder ?
Then forsake the paths so cold,
Fly to Jesus and His fold,
That your name may be enrolled,
    In the home up yonder !

191 OH, why thus stand w
    reluctant feet, [swe
Just on the verge of this rest
While God invites and your st
    will greet ?
    Come away to Jesus now.
    Come away....to Jesus,....
    Come away to Jesus now.

The Spirit strives, and yet there you
    stand,
In sight of bliss and the glory land ;
Retreat is death in the sinking sand,
    Come away to Jesus now.

Your loved ones gone to the other
    shore,   [o'er ;
With unseen hands seem to beckon
Their voices hush'd, yet they still
    implore,
    Come away to Jesus now.

92   DOWN at the Cross where my
        Saviour died,
Down where for cleansing from sin
    I cried,   [applied ;
There to my heart was the blood
    Glory to His name !

    Glory to His name !
    Glory to His name !
There to my heart was the blood applied ;
    Glory to His name !

I am so wondrously sav'd from sin,
Jesus so sweetly abides within,
There at the Cross where He took
    me in :
    Glory to His name !

Oh, precious fountain, that saves
    from sin !
I am so glad I have enter'd in ;
There Jesus saves me and keeps me
    clean :
    Glory to His name !

Come to this fountain, so rich and
    sweet,
Cast thy poor soul at the Saviour's
    feet ;   [complete.
Plunge in to-day, and be made
    Glory to His name !

93   THIS is the day the Lord hath
        made,
He calls the hours His own ;
Let heaven rejoice, let earth be glad,
    And praise surround the throne.

To-day He rose and left the dead,
    And Satan's empire fell :
To-day the saints His triumph spread,
    And all His wonders tell.

Hosanna to the anointed King,
    To David's holy Son !
Help us, O Lord ! descend and bring
    Salvation from Thy throne.

4 Blest be the Lord, who comes to
     men,
  With messages of grace ;
Who comes in God His Father's
    name,
  To save our sinful race.

5 Hosanna ! in the highest strains,
  The Church on earth can raise ;
The highest heavens in which He
    reigns
  Shall give Him nobler praise.

194   IS there a heart that is waiting,
        Longing for pardon to-day ?
Hear the glad message proclaiming,
    Jesus is passing this way.

    Jesus is passing this way,....
    This way,....to-day ;.... ◁
    Jesus is passing this way,....
    Is passing this way to-day.

2 Is there a heart that has wandered ?
  Come with thy burden to-day ;
Mercy is tenderly pleading,
    Jesus is passing this way.

3 Is there a heart that is broken ?
  Weary and sighing for rest ?
Come to the arms of thy Saviour,
  Pillow thy head on His breast.

4 Come to thy only Redeemer,
  Come to His infinite love ;
Come to the gate that is leading
  Homeward to mansions above.

195   DEAR to the heart of the
        Shepherd,
  Dear are the sheep of His fold ;
Dear is the love that He gives them,
  Dearer than silver or gold.
Dear to the heart of the Shepherd,
  Dear are His " other " lost sheep ;
Over the mountains He follows,
  Over the waters so deep.

    Out in the desert they wander,
    Hungry and helpless and cold ;
    Off to the rescue He hastens,
    Bringing them back to the fold.

2 Dear to the heart of the Shepherd,
  Dear are the lambs of His fold ;
Some from the pastures are straying,
  Hungry, and helpless, and cold.
See, the good Shepherd is seeking,
  Seeking the lambs that are lost ;
Bringing them in with rejoicing,
  Saved at such infinite cost.

3 Dear to the heart of the Shepherd,
  Dear are the " ninety and nine,"
Dear are the sheep that have
    wandered
  Out in the desert to pine.
Hark ! He is earnestly calling,
  Tenderly pleading to-day ;
" Will you not seek for My lost ones,
  Far from My shelter astray ? "

196 COME, ev'ry soul by sin
    oppress'd,
  There's mercy with the Lord,
And He will surely give you rest,
  By trusting in His word.

  Only trust Him ! Only trust Him !
    Only trust Him now !
  He will save you ! He will save you !
    He will save you now !

2 For Jesus shed His precious blood,
  Rich blessings to bestow ;
Plunge now into the crimson flood,
  That washes white as snow.

3 Yes, Jesus is the Truth, the Way,
  That leads you into rest ;
Believe in Him without delay,
  And you are fully blest.

4 Come, then, and join this holy band,
  And on to glory go ;
To dwell in that celestial land,
  Where joys immortal flow.

197 O TELL me o'er and o'er again
    the tale I love so well,
  Of how the King of Glory left
    His throne,
And came a humble man among our
    sinful race to dwell,
  That He might save and claim us
    for His own.

Oh, tell the sweet old story once again,...
  Of how the Saviour loved the sons of men,...
He loved them, oh, so well, He came on earth
    to dwell,
  Oh, tell the sweet old story once again.

2 I am both weak and sinful, but one
    thing I surely know,
  That Jesus fills my heart with
    grace and love ;
That He will guide me safely thro'
    my journey here below,
  And then will take me to Himself
    above.

3 O tell again the story of His mercy
    and His grace,
  The story that is told of Him
    alone ;
Of how He died in torment, in the
    helpless sinner's place,
  And conquered, and is now upon
    His throne.

198 I HEAR the Saviour say,
    " Thy strength indeed is
      small ;
Come to Me—I'll be thy stay,
  Find in Me thine all in all."

    Jesus paid it all,
      All to Him I owe—
    Sin had left a crimson stain,
      He washed it white as snow.

2 For nothing good have I
  Whereby Thy grace to claim ;
Jesus died my soul to save,
  And blessed be His name.

3 When from my dying bed
  My ransomed soul shall rise,
" Jesus died my soul to save,"
  Shall rend the vaulted skies.

4 And when before the throne,
  I stand, in Him complete :
" Jesus died my soul to save,"
  My lips shall still repeat.

199 TELL it ! let the people hear
    it,
  " Jesus saves from sin ! "
Let the breezes bear the message,
  " Jesus makes men clean ;
That He shed His blood to save us !
  Tell it far and wide,
" In no other is redemption
  Save the Crucified ! "

    Tell it far and wide,
    Tell it far and wide,
    " In no other is redemption,
      Save the Crucified ! "

2 Tell it to the lone and weary,
  To the blithe and gay ;
To the aged with their burdens,
  To the child at play.
" There is full and free salvation ! "
  Here the blessed word,
" There is mercy and true healing
  In the Saviour's blood ! "

Free the mercy, full of pardon,
  Jesus died to give !
Sweet the welcome that the sinner
  Surely will receive.
Weary, weak, and heavy laden,
  Come to Him to-day ;
Let the cleansing blood of Jesus
  Wash your sins away.

200 WE have heard a joyful sound,
  Jesus saves ! Jesus saves !
Spread the gladness all around,
  Jesus saves ! Jesus saves !
Bear the news to ev'ry land,
  Climb the steeps and cross the
    waves,
Onward ! 'tis our Lord's command,
  Jesus saves ! Jesus saves !

Waft it on the rolling tide,
  Jesus saves ! Jesus saves !
Tell to sinners far and wide,
  Jesus saves ! Jesus saves !
Sing, ye islands of the sea,
  Echo back, ye ocean caves,
Earth shall keep her Jubilee,
  Jesus saves ! Jesus saves !

Sing above the battle's strife,
  Jesus saves ! Jesus saves !
By His death and endless life,
  Jesus saves ! Jesus saves !
Sing it softly thro' the gloom,
  When the heart for mercy craves ;
Sing in triumph o'er the tomb,
  Jesus saves ! Jesus saves !

Give the wind a mighty voice,
  Jesus saves ! Jesus saves !
Let the nations now rejoice,
  Jesus saves ! Jesus saves !
Shout salvation full and free,
  Highest hills and deepest caves,
This our song of victory,
  Jesus saves ! Jesus saves !

201 WHOEVER receiveth the
  Crucified One,
Whoever believeth on God's only
  Son,
A free and a perfect salvation shall
  have,
For He is abundantly able to save.
  y brother, the Mas..ter is calling for thee ;...
  is grace and His mer..cy are wondrously free;..
  is blood as a ran..som for sinners He gave,...
  nd He is abun..dantly able to save.

2 Whoever receiveth the message of
  God,
  And trusts in the pow'r of the soul-
    cleansing blood,
  A full and eternal redemption shall
    have,   [save.
  For He is both able and willing to

3 Whoever repents and forsakes ev'ry
  sin,   [come in,
  And opens his heart for the Lord to
  A present and perfect salvation shall
    have,   [save,
  For Jesus is ready this moment to

202 FAIREST of all the earth
  beside,
  Chiefest of all unto Thy bride,
  Fulness divine in Thee I see,
  Wonderful Man of Calvary !

      That Man of Calvary
      Has won my heart from me,
      And died to set me free,
      Blest Man of Calvary !

2 Granting the sinner life and peace,
  Granting the captive sweet release ;
  Shedding His blood to make us free,
  Merciful Man of Calvary !

3 Giving the gifts obtained for men,
  Pouring out love beyond our ken,
  Giving us spotless purity,
  Bountiful Man of Calvary !

4 Comfort of all my earthly way,
  Jesus, I'll meet Thee some sweet
    day ;
  Centre of glory, Thee I'll see,
  Wonderful Man of Calvary !

203 SHOUT the tidings of salvation
  To the aged and the young,
  Till the precious invitation
  Waken ev'ry heart and tongue.

  Send the sound the earth around,
    From the rising to the setting of the sun,
  Till each gath'ring crowd shall proclaim aloud,
    " The glorious work is done."

2 Shout the tidings of salvation
  North and south and east and west,
  Till each gath'ring congregation
  With the gospel sound is blest.

3 Shout the tidings of salvation
  Mingling with the ocean's roar,
  Till the ships of ev'ry nation
  Bear the news from shore to shore.

4 Shout the tidings of salvation
  O'er the islands of the sea,
Till, in humble adoration,
  All to Christ shall bow the knee.

204 AS when the Hebrew prophet rais'd
  The brazen serpent high,
The wounded look'd and straight were cur'd,
  The people ceased to die :

2 So from the Saviour on the Cross
  A healing virtue flows ;
Who looks to Him with lively faith
  Is saved from endless woes.

3 For God gave up His Son to death,
  So generous was His love,
That all the faithful might enjoy
  Eternal life above.

4 Not to condemn the sons of men
  The Son of God appeared !
No weapons in His hand are seen,
  Nor voice of terror heard.

5 He came to raise our fallen state,
  And our lost hopes restore ;
Faith leads us to the mercy-seat,
  And bids us fear no more.

6 But vengeance just for ever lies
  Upon the rebel race,
Who God's eternal Son despise,
  And scorn His offered grace.

205 FATHER of peace and God of love !
  We own Thy power to save,
That power by which our Shepherd rose
  Victorious o'er the grave.

2 Him from the dead Thou brought'st again,
  When by His sacred blood,
Confirmed and sealed for evermore,
  Th' eternal covenant stood.

3 Oh, may Thy Spirit seal our souls,
  And mould them to Thy will,
That our weak hearts no more may stray,
  But keep Thy precepts still.

4 That to perfection's sacred height
  We nearer still may rise ;
And all we think, and all we do,
  Be pleasing in Thine eyes.

206 BEHOLD th' amazing gift of love
  The Father hath bestow'd
On us, the sinful sons of men,
  To call us sons of God !

2 Conceal'd as yet this honour lies
  By this dark world unknown,
A world that knew not when He came,
  Ev'n God's eternal Son.

3 High is the rank we now possess,
  But higher we shall rise ;
Though what we shall hereafter be
  Is hid from mortal eyes.

4 Our souls, we know, when He appears,
  Shall bear His image bright ;
For all His glory, full disclos'd,
  Shall open to our sight.

5 A hope so great, and so divine,
  May trials well endure ;
And purge the soul from sense and sin,
  As Christ Himself is pure.

207 HO ! ev'ry one that is thirsty in spirit,
  Ho ! ev'ry one that is weary and sad :
Come to the fountain, there's fulness in Jesus,
  All that you're longing for, come and be glad.

" I will pour water on him that is thirsty,
I will pour floods upon the dry ground ;
Open your heart for the gift I am bringing
  While ye are seeking Me, I will be found

2 Child of the world, are you tired of your bondage ?
  Weary of earth-joys, so false, untrue ?
Thirsting for God and His fulness of blessing ?
  List to the promise, a message for you.

3 Child of the kingdom, be filled with the Spirit !
  Nothing but fulness thy longing can meet ;
'Tis the induement for life and for service ;
  Thine is the promise, so certain, so sweet.

208 IN evil long I took delight,
    Unawed by shame or fear,
Till a new object met my sight,
    And stopp'd my wild career.

> Oh, the Lamb ! the bleeding Lamb !
>   The Lamb upon Calvary !
> The Lamb that was slain,
> That liveth again
>   To intercede for me !

I saw One hanging on a tree
    In agonies and blood,
Who fixed His languid eyes on me,
    As near His Cross I stood.

My conscience felt and owned my
    guilt,
    And plunged me in despair ;
I saw my sins His blood had spilt,
    And help'd to nail Him there.

A second look He gave, which said,
    " I freely all forgive ;
This blood is for thy ransom paid ;
    I die that thou may'st live."

Thus while His death my sin displays
    In all its blackest hue
(Such is the mystery of grace),
    It seals my pardon, too.

209 HAVE you found the Saviour
    precious,
More than all on earth beside,
He who gave His life to save you,
    Who for your transgressions died ?

> Have you found...the Saviour precious ?
> Can you slight...such love as this ?
> Surely there...can be no greater !
>   Would you give...your life for His ?

Have you found the Saviour
    precious,   [grave,
Who for you passed thro' the
Broke the bonds of death asunder,
    Have you " prov'd His power to
    save " ?

Have you found the Saviour
    precious ?
Do you know the peace and rest
That doth fill each soul that trusts
    Him,
Who in His deep love is blest ?

Have you found the Saviour
    precious ?
Seek Him then without delay,
Taste the sweetness of His pardon,
He will take your sins away.

210 WHEN sorrows and trouble
    like sea billows roll,
Tell me the story of Jesus ;
When evil assails me and doubts
    fill my soul,
Tell me the story of Jesus.

> Tell....it to me,.....
> Tell....it to me,.....
> Tell me the story of Jesus :
>   Tell....it to me.....

2 When weary from labour I rest by
    the way,
    It strengthens my purpose and
    brightens the day.

3 In times of affliction, when suff'ring
    from pain,
    It softens my pillow, revives me
    again.

4 When life here is over, and time i
    no more,
    Oh, tell it again on the beautifu
    shore.

211 JESUS died for you and me ;
    Is it not good news ?
Now there's pardon full and free ;
    Is it not good news ?
On the Cross our sins He bore,
That on heav'n's eternal shore
We might live for evermore ;
    Is it not good news ?

> Is it not good news ?
> Is it not good news ?
> On the Cross our sins He bore ;
>   Oh, is it not good news ? ·

2 " It is finished," Jesus said ;
    Is it not good news ?
Sin and death are captive led ;
    Is it not good news ?
In the grave our Lord was laid,
And the last great tribute paid,
Free the sacrifice He made ;
    Is it not good news ?

> Is it not good news ?
> Is it not good news ?
> Free the sacrifice He made ;
>   Oh, is it not good news ?

3 From the grave the Saviour rose ;
    Is it not good news ?
Gain'd the vict'ry o'er His foes ;
    Is it not good news ?

Christ the law did satisfy,
Christ ascended up on high,
We shall meet Him by and bye ;
Is it not good news ?

> Is it not good news ?
> Is it not good news ?
> We shall meet Him by and bye ;
> Oh, is it not good news ?

4 Now He pleads for us on high ;
Is it not good news ?
Pleads that we may never die;
Is it not good news ?
Soon He'll come to claim His own,
All who trust in Him alone,
We shall gather round His throne ;
Is it not good news ?

> Is it not good news ?
> Is it not good news ?
> We shall gather round His throne ;
> Oh, is it not good news ?

212 HARK ! the gospel news is
sounding,
Christ has suffered on the tree ;
Streams of mercy are abounding,
Grace for all is rich and free.
Now poor sinner,
Come to Him who died for thee.

2 Oh ! escape to yonder mountain,
Refuge find in Him to-day ;
Christ invites you to the fountain,
Come and wash your sins away.
Do not tarry,
Come to Jesus while you may.

3 Grace is flowing like a river,
Millions there have been supplied ;
Still it flows as fresh as ever
From the Saviour's wounded side.
None need perish,
All may live, for Christ hath died.

4 Christ alone shall be our portion,
Soon we hope to meet above ;
Then we'll bathe in the full ocean
Of the great Redeemer's love ;
All His fulness
We shall then for ever prove.

213 COME unto Jesus, all ye that
labour,
All that are weary, sad, and
oppressed ;
Still He is calling, oh, friend and
neighbour, [you rest."
" Come unto Me, and I will give

Down thro' the ages, sweetly 'tis ringing,
This word of Jesus, come and be blest ;
Sweeter than carols angels are singing,
" Come unto Me, and I will give you rest.

2 Bring Him the burden, heavil
pressing, [breast
Tell Him the sorrow hid in you
Sin and transgression freely con
fessing, [you rest
Come unto Him and He will giv

3 Lose not a moment, haste to you
Saviour,
Ere the bright day-beams fade i
the west ; [favou
Asking His mercy, seeking Hi
Come unto Him and He will giv
you rest.

4 Come unto Jesus, Saviour an
Brother, [best
Surely you need Him, purest an
Truer than father, fonder tha
mother, [you res
Come unto Him and He will giv

214 " GIVE Me thy heart," say
the Father above,
No gift so precious to Him as ou
love ; [ar
Softly He whispers wherever tho
" Gratefully trust Me, and give M
thy heart."

> " Give Me thy heart, give Me thy heart,"
> Hear the soft whisper, wherever thou art ;
> From this dark world He would draw you apar
> Speaking so tenderly, " Give Me thy heart."

2 " Give Me thy heart," says th
Saviour of men,
Calling in mercy again and again ;
" Turn now from sin, and from ev
depart,
Have I not died for thee ? give M
thy heart."

3 " Give Me thy heart," says th
Spirit divine, [resign
" All that thou hast to My keepin
Grace more abounding is Mine t
impart, [heart.
Make full surrender, and give Me th

215 THERE'S no one like m
Saviour,
No friend can be like Him ;
My never-failing sunshine
When earthly lights grow dim ;

When summer flow'rs are blooming,
   The brightness of my joy,
Oh, may His happy service
   My heart and life employ !

No one, no one like my precious Saviour,
  No one, no one such a friend can be ;
No one, no one like my precious Saviour,
  Glory ! glory ! Jesus cares for me.

There's no one like my Saviour ;
   In seasons of distress,
He draws me closer to Him,
   To comfort and to bless ;
He gives me, in temptation,
   The strength of His right arm ;
His angels camp around me,
   To keep me from all harm.

There's no one like my Saviour,
   He pardons all my sin ;
And gives His Holy Spirit,
   A springing well within ;
He leads me out to service,
   With gentle touch and mild ;
Oh, wonder of all wonders,
   That I should be His child !

There's no one like my Saviour,
   Come now, and find it true,
He gave His life a ransom,
   His blood was shed for you ;
Then, when we reach the city
   Of everlasting light,
We'll sing with saints and angels,
   All honour, pow'r, and might.

16 I HEAR the words of love,
   I gaze upon the blood,
I see the mighty sacrifice,
   And I have peace with God.

'Tis everlasting peace !
   Sure as Jehovah's name ;
'Tis stable as His steadfast throne,
   For evermore the same.

The clouds may go and come,
   And storms may sweep my sky—
This blood-sealed friendship changes
   not,
   The Cross is ever nigh.

My love is oft-times low,
   My joy still ebbs and flows ;
But peace with Him remains the
   same—
   No change Jehovah knows.

5 I change, He changes not,
   The Christ can never die ;
His love, not mine, the resting place,
   His truth, not mine, the tie.

217 NOT all the blood of beasts
     On Jewish altars slain
Could give the guilty conscience
    peace
   Or wash away the stain.

2 But Christ, the heavenly Lamb,
   Takes all our sins away ;
A sacrifice of nobler name
   And richer blood than they.

3 My faith would lay her hand
   On that dear head of Thine,
While like a penitent I stand
   And there confess my sin.

4 My soul looks back to see
   The burdens Thou didst bear,
When hanging on the cursed tree,
   And knows her guilt was there.

5 Believing, we rejoice
   To see the curse remove ;
We bless the Lamb with cheerful
   voice
   And sing His bleeding love !

218 HEAR the promise of the Lord,
   As recorded in His Word,
  " Unto you is everlasting life ! "
Heavy laden and distress'd,
Come, and I will give you rest ;
  " Unto you is everlasting life ! "

" Everlasting life," the promise reads,
While at God's right hand the Saviour pleads ;
Will you come to-day, making Christ your stay?
For with Him is everlasting life.

2 Weary pilgrim on the road
   To the judgment seat of God,
  " Unto you is everlasting life ! "
If on Jesus you believe,
And His blessed Word receive,
  " Unto you is everlasting life ! "

3 Cast on Jesus all your care,
   And your burden He will bear,
  " Unto you is everlasting life ! "
In the strait and narrow way,
He will lead you day by day !
  " Unto you is everlasting life ! "

219   THERE's nothing like the old,
      old story,
   Grace is free, grace is free !
Which saints and martyrs tell in
      glory,
   Grace is free, grace is free !
It brought them thro' the flood and
      flame,
By it they fought and overcame,
And now they cry thro' His dear
      name,
   Grace is free, grace is free !

   There's nothing like the old, old story,
      Grace is free, Grace is free !
   Which saints and martyrs tell in glory,
      Grace is free, Grace is free !

2 There's only hope in trusting Jesus,
      Grace is free, grace is free !
   From sin that doomed He died to
      free us.
      Grace is free, grace is free !
   Who would not tell the story sweet
   Of love so wondrous, so complete,
   And fall in rapture at His feet !
      Grace is free, grace is free !

3 From age to age the theme is telling,
      Grace is free, grace is free !
   From shore to shore the strains are
      swelling.
      Grace is free, grace is free !
   And when that time shall cease to be,
   And faith is crowned with victory,
   'Twill sound thro' all eternity,
      Grace is free, grace is free !

220   WOULD I know Him if He
      stood here
   By my side, by my side ?
Do the cruel, cruel nail-prints
   Yet abide, yet abide ?
Would He show to me His beauty,
   So divine, so divine,
That in rapture I would feel Him
   To be mine, to be mine ?

2 When to Satan thou dost answer,
   " Flee from me, flee from me ! "
When between thee and the Master
   Naught shall be, naught shall be ;
On thine eyes shall flash a vision,
   Wondrous fair, wondrous fair—
Lo ! a pierced and thorn-crowned
      Saviour,
   Standeth there, standeth there.

3 Could I hear Him if He called me,
   Waiting here, waiting here ?
Would His words of magic sweetne
   Pierce my ear, pierce my ear ?
Could the world with all its lurin
   Drown that tone, drown that ton
And He pass me by and leave me
   All alone, all alone ?

4 When thou criest in thine anguish
   " Saviour, hear ; Saviour, hear
It will reach Him thro' the clamou
   Never fear, never fear !
Tho' sometimes thine ears a
      deafened
   By the din, by the din,
He is list'ning for the summons,
   " Lord, come in ; Lord, come in

221   I HAD wander'd far away
      In the land of mighty foes,
And my soul had felt the bitterne
      of sin ;
   I was marching with the hosts
   That the truth of God oppose,
And among the sav'd I was n
      counted in.

   Counted in.... Counted in,....
Whosoever will believe is counted in ;....
What a jubilee of joy in the heavens then
      heard,
When a soul among the saved is counted ir

2   But I found it written down,
      Whosoever will believe
   In the Son of God is sav'd fro
      ev'ry sin ;
   And I bless His holy name
      That the promise I receive—   [i
   In that " whosoever " I am count

3   When the pardon full and free,
      That is promised in His Word,
   Is received by faith, and Jesus enters i
      What a jubilee of joy
   In the heavens then is heard,
   And a soul among the sav'd
      counted in.

4   Oh, my sinner friend, beware !
      A revealing day is near,
   That will show the secrets of t
      heart within ;
   Have it cleansed by grace divin
   And when Jesus shall appear,
   He will then among His jewels cou
      you in.

222 THEY nail'd my Lord upon the tree,
And left Him, dying, there ;
Thro' love He suffered there for me,
'Twas love beyond compare.

Crucified ! Crucified !
And nailed upon the tree !
With pierced hands and feet and side !
For you !...For me !....

Upon His head a crown of thorns,
Upon His heart my shame ;
For me He prayed, for me He died,
And, dying, spoke my name.

"Forgive him, O forgive!" He cried,
Then bow'd His sacred head ;
"O Lamb of God ! my sacrifice ! "
For me Thy blood was shed.

His voice I hear, His love I know ;
I worship at His feet ;
And kneeling there, at Calvary's Cross,
Redemption is complete.

223 O MOURNER in Zion, how blessed art thou,
For Jesus is waiting to comfort thee now ; [God ;
Fear not to rely on the Word of thy
Step out on the promise—get under the blood.

O ye that are hungry and thirsty, rejoice !
For ye shall be filled ; do you hear that sweet voice [God ?
Inviting you now to the banquet of
Step out on the promise—get under the blood.

Who sighs for a heart from iniquity free ?
O, poor troubled soul ; there's a promise for thee.
There's rest, weary one, in the bosom of God ;
Step out on the promise—get under the blood.

Step out on this promise, and Christ thou shalt win.
" The blood of His Son cleanseth us from all sin ; " [God !
It cleanseth me now, hallelujah to
I rest on His promise—I'm under the blood.

224 SOULS of men ! why will yo scatter
Like a crowd of frightened sheep ?
Foolish hearts, why will ye wander
From a love so true and deep ?

2 Was there ever kindest shepherd
Half so gentle, half so sweet,
As the Saviour, who would have us
Come and gather round His feet ?

3 There's a wideness in God's mercy,
Like the wideness of the sea ;
There's a kindness in His justice,
Which is more than liberty.

4 For the love of God is broader
Than the measures of man's mind ;
And the heart of the Eternal
Is most wonderfully kind.

5 There is plentiful redemption
In the blood that has been shed ;
There is joy for all the members
In the sorrows of the Head.

6 Pining souls ! come nearer Jesus,
And oh, come not doubting thus,
But with faith that trusts more bravely
His great tenderness for us.

7 If our love were but more simple,
We should take Him at His Word ;
And our lives would be all sunshine
In the sweetness of our Lord.

225 A FRIEND I have called Jesus,
Whose love is strong and true,
And never fails howe'er 'tis tried,
No matter what I do.
I've sinn'd against this love of His,
But when I knelt to pray,
Confessing all my guilt to Him,
The sin clouds rolled away.

It's just like Jesus to roll the clouds away,
It's just like Jesus to keep me day by day,
It's just like Jesus all along the way,
It's just like His great love.

2 Sometimes the clouds of trouble
Bedim the sky above ;
I cannot see my Saviour's face,
I doubt His wondrous love.
But He, from heaven's mercy-seat,
Beholding my despair,
In pity bursts the clouds between,
And shows me He is there.

3 When sorrow's clouds o'ertake me,
  And break upon my head,
When life seems worse than useless,
  And I were better dead ;
I take my grief to Jesus then,
  Nor do I go in vain,
For heav'nly hope He gives that cheers,
  Like sunshine after rain.

4 O, I could sing for ever
  Of Jesus' love divine,
Of all His care and tenderness,
  For this poor life of mine.
His love is in and over all,
  And winds and waves obey
When Jesus whispers ," Peace, be
  still ! "
  And rolls the clouds away.

226 COME to the Saviour, come to
    the Saviour,
  Thou sin-stricken offspring of man ;
    He left His throne above,
    To reveal His wondrous love,
  And to open a fountain for sin.

  I do believe it ! I do believe it !
  I'm saved thro' the blood of the Lamb
  My happy soul is free,
  For the Lord has pardoned me,
  Hallelujah to His blessed name !

2 Pardon is offer'd, pardon is offer'd,
  A pardon, full, present, and free ;
    The mighty debt was paid,
    When on Calvary Jesus died,
  To atone for a rebel like me.

3 Plunge in the fountain, plunge in the
    fountain,   [soul ;
  The fountain which cleanses the

'Tis cleansing far and near,
  And its streams are flowing here
Oh, believe it, and thou art made
  whole.

227 LISTEN to the blessed in
    vitation,
  Sweeter than the notes of angel song
  Chiming softly with a heav'nly
    cadence,
  Calling to the passing throng.

  Him that cometh unto Me,....
  Him that cometh unto Me,....
  Him that cometh unto Me,....
  I will in no wise cast out.

2 Weary toiler, sad and heavy laden,
  Joyfully the great salvation see ;
  Close beside thee stands the Burden
    Bearer,
  Strong to bear thy load and thee

3 Come, ye thirsty, to the living
    waters,
  Hungry, come, and on His bounty
    feed ;   [Him
  Not thy fitness is the plea to bring
  But thy pressing utmost need.

4 Whoso cometh, blind, or maimed, or
    sinful,
  Cometh for his healing to the Lord
  Claims the cleansing of the blood so
    precious,
  Proves anew this gracious word.

5 Coming humbly daily to this Saviour
  Breathing all the heart to Him in
    pray'r ;   [mansions
  Coming some day to the heav'nly
  He will give thee welcome there

WARNING AND ENTREATY

228 OH, why not say Yes to the
    Saviour to-night ?
  He's tenderly pleading with thee
  To come to Him now with thy sin-
    burden'd heart,
  For pardon so full and so free....

  Why not say Yes to-night ?....
  Why not ? Why not ?
  While He so gently, so tenderly pleads,
  Oh, accept Him to-night !....

2 For with you the Spirit will not
    always plead—
  O do not reject Him to-night !

To-morrow may bring you the
  darkness of death,
Unbroken by heavenly light....

3 Take Christ as your Saviour, then
    all shall be well,
  The morrow let bring what it may
His love shall protect you, His Spirit
    shall guide,
  And safely keep you in His way..

229 DRIFTING away from the
    Saviour,
  Drifting to lands unknown,

Drifting away by night and by day,
Drifting, yes, drifting alone.
Drifting away from the Saviour,
Drifting away from His love ;
While the Saviour is tenderly calling,
You are drifting away from God.

Drifting away from the Saviour,
He who would bear your load ;
Drifting away by night and by day,
Drifting, yes, drifting from God.

Drifting away from the Saviour,
Fearlessly on you go ;
Drifting away by night and by day,
Drifting to regions of woe.

Drifting away from the Saviour,
Even the angels weep ;
Still you drift on with mirth and
with song,
Out on the fathomless deep.

30 O SINNER, the Saviour is
calling for thee,   [vain ;
Long, long has He called thee in
He called thee when joy lent its
'crown to thy days,
He called thee in sorrow and pain.
h, turn, while the Saviour in mercy is waiting,
And steer for the harbour light ;
or how do you know but your soul may be
drifting
Over the dead-line to-night ?

O sinner, thine ears have been deaf
to His voice,
Thine eyes to His glory been dim ;
The calls of thy Saviour have so
wearied thee,   [Him ?
Oh, what if they should weary

O sinner, the Spirit is striving with
thee ;   [more,
What if He should strive never
But leave thee alone in thy darkness
to dwell,
In sight of the heavenly shore ?

O sinner, God's patience may weary
some day,
And leave thy sad soul in the
blast ;   [away,
By wilful resistance you've drifted
Over the dead-line at last.

31 LIFE at best is very brief,
Like the falling of a leaf,
Like the binding of a sheaf,
Be in time.

Fleeting days are telling fast
That the die will soon be cast,
And the fatal line be passed,
Be in time.
Be in time,.....Be in time,.....
While the voice of Jesus calls you,
Be in time.....
If in sin you longer wait
You may find no open gate,
And your cry be just too late.
Be in time.

2 Fairest flowers soon decay,
Youth and beauty pass away,
Oh, you have not long to stay,
Be in time.
While God's Spirit bids you come,
Sinner, do no longer roam,
Lest you seal your hopeless doom,
Be in time.

3 Time is gliding swiftly by,
Death and judgment draweth nigh,
To the arms of Jesus fly,
Be in time.
Oh, I pray you, count the cost,
Ere the fatal line be crossed,
And your soul in hell be lost,
Be in time.

4 Sinner, heed the warning voice,
Make the Lord your final choice,
Then all heaven will rejoice,
Be in time.
Come from darkness into light,
Come, let Jesus make you right,
Come, and start for heaven to-night,
Be in time.

232 ON the happy golden shore,
Where the faithful part no
more,
When the storms of life are o'er,
Meet me there ;
When the night dissolves away,
Into pure and perfect day,
I am going home to stay.
Meet me there.
Meet me there,.....meet me there,.....
Where the tree of life is blooming,
Meet me there.....
When the storms of life are o'er,
On the happy golden shore,
Where the faithful part no more,
Meet me there.

2 Here our fondest hopes are vain,
Dearest links are rent in twain,
But in heaven no throb of pain—
Meet me there ;

By the river sparkling bright,
In the city of delight,
Where our faith is lost in sight,
  Meet me there.

3 Where the harps of angels ring,
And the blest for ever sing,
In the palace of the King,
  Meet me there;
Where in sweet communion blend,
Heart with heart, and friend with
    friend,
In a world that ne'er shall end,
  Meet me there.

233 YOU are drifting far from
        shore, leaning on an idle oar,
You are drifting, slowly drifting,
    drifting down;
You are drifting with the tide, to
    the ocean wild and wide,
You are drifting, slowly drifting,
    drifting down.

You are drift..ing..down,..drift..ing..down
  To the dark and awful sea;
You are drift..ing..down,
  From a Father's loving care,
  To the blackness of despair;
You are drifting, slowly drifting, drifting down.

2 Lights upon the homeland shore give
      you warning o'er and o'er,
  You are drifting, slowly drifting,
      drifting down.
  Soon beyond the harbour bar will
      your boat be carried far.
  You are drifting, slowly drifting,
      drifting down.

3 Voices from the homeland shore
      fainter grow as they implore;
  You are drifting, slowly drifting,
      drifting down.
  O my brother, do not wait! heed
      them ere it be too late,
  Ere for ever you have drifted,
      drifted down.

234 STILL out of Christ, when so
        oft He has call'd you,
Why will you longer refuse to
    believe ?
What can you hope from the world
    or its pleasure ?
How can you trust them when
    both will deceive ?

Come, come to Jesus, weary, heavy-hearted,
  Come, come to Jesus while you may;
Now He is waiting, waiting to receive you,
  Hark! He is calling you to-day.

2 Still out of Christ, and the moment
      so precious,
  Night is approaching, oh, what
      will you do ?
  Still out of Christ, yet there's room
      at the fountain,
  Free are its waters, and flowing
      for you.

3 Still out of Christ, yet for you there
      is mercy,
  If you are willing to turn from
      your sin;
  Yonder He stands at the door of
      salvation,
  Waiting to pardon and welcome
      you in.

4 Still out of Christ, and the love He
      has promised;
  How you are longing that love
      to receive!
  Haste where the star of your faith
      is directing,
  Haste, and this moment repent
      and believe.

235 NO beautiful chamber,
        No soft cradle bed,
No place but a manger,
  Nowhere for His head;
No praises of gladness,
  No thought of their sin,
No glory, but sadness,
  No room in the inn.

No room, no room for Jesus!
  Oh, give Him welcome free,
Lest you should hear at heaven's gate,
  There is no room for thee!

2 No sweet consecration,
    No seeking His part,
No humiliation,
  No place in the heart;
No thought of the Saviour,
  No sorrow for sin,
No prayer for His favour,
  No room in the inn.

3 No one to receive Him,
    No welcome while here,
No balm to relieve Him,
  No staff but a spear;
No seeking His treasure,
  No weeping for sin,
No doing His pleasure,
  No room in the inn.

36 OVER the river faces I see,
Fair as the morning, looking
for me ;
Free from their sorrow, grief, and
despair, [there.
Waiting **and watching** patiently

Looking this way, yes, looking this way ;
Loved ones are waiting, looking this way ;
Fair as the morning, bright as the day,
Dear ones in glory looking this way.

Father and mother safe in the vale,
Watch for the boatman, wait for
the sail,
Bearing the loved ones over the tide,
Into the harbour, near to their side.

Brother and sister, gone to that clime,
Wait for the others, coming some-
time ;
Safe with the angels, whiter than
snow, [below.
Watching for dear ones waiting

Sweet little darling, light of the
home,
Looking for someone, beckoning
come ; [dew,
Bright as a sunbeam, pure as the
Anxiously looking, mother, for you.

Jesus the Saviour, bright morning
star,
Looking for lost ones straying afar ;
Hear the glad message, why will you
roam ? [home."
Jesus is calling, " Sinner, come

37 OH, come, sinner come, 'tis
mercy's call ;
Here at Jesu's feet !
Oh, come, and repenting, lay thy all
Down at Jesu's feet !

Oh, lay it down, lay it down,
Lay thy weary burden down ;
Oh, lay it down, lay it down,
Down at Jesu's feet.

Oh come, and believing, seek thy rest
Here, at Jesu's feet !
Thy heart, with its heavy weight
opprest,
Lay at Jesu's feet.

Oh come where thy faith can make
thee whole,
Here at Jesu's feet ! [soul
Oh come, and thy weary, troubled
Lay at Jesu's feet !

c

4 Oh come ! bless the Lord, there's
room for thee,
Here at Jesu's feet !
Thy burden of sin, whate'er it be,
Lay at Jesu's feet !

238 BEHOLD a Stranger at the
door,
He gently knocks, has knock'd
before ;
Has waited long—is waiting still :
You treat no other friend so ill !

Oh, let the dear Saviour come in,....
He'll cleanse the heart from sin !....
Oh, keep Him no more out at the door,
But let the dear Saviour come in !....

2 Oh, lovely attitude, He stands
With melting heart and open hands :
Oh, matchless kindness ! and He
shows
That matchless kindness to His foes.

3 But will He prove a Friend indeed ?
He will—the very Friend you need :
The Friend of sinners ? Yes, 'tis
He,
With garments dyed on Calvary !

4 Rise, touch'd with gratitude divine,
Turn out His enemy and thine,
That soul-destroying monster, sin,
And let the Heav'nly Stranger in.

5 Admit Him ere His anger burn ;
His feet departed, ne'er return ;
Admit Him ! or the hour's at hand
You'll at His door rejected stand.

239 ONCE I heard a sound at my
heart's dark door,
And was roused from the slumber
of sin ;
It was Jesus knock'd, He had
knock'd before ;
Now I said, " Blessed Master,
come in ! "

Then open ! open ! open ! let the Master in....
For the heart will be bright with a heav'nly
light,
When you let the Master in.

2 Then He spread a feast of redeeming
love, [guest ;
And He made me His own happy
In my joy I thought that the saints
above [blest.
Could be hardly more favour'd or

3 In the holy war with the foes of
 truth,
   He's my shield; He my table
     prepares.   [youth,
 He restores my soul, He renews my
 And gives triumph in answer to
   pray'rs.

4 He will feast me still with His
     presence dear,
   And the love He so freely hath
     giv'n;   [Him here,
 While His promise tells, as I serve
 Of the banquet of glory in heav'n.

240 OUT of Christ, without a
       Saviour,
   Oh! can it, can it be?
 Like a ship without a rudder,
   On a wild and stormy sea!

   Oh, to be without a Saviour,
     With no hope nor refuge nigh!
   Can it be, O blessed Saviour,
     One without Thee dares to die?

2 Out of Christ, without a Saviour,
   Lonely and dark the way;
 With no light, no hope in Jesus,
   Making bright the cheerless day.

3 Out of Christ, without a Saviour,
   No help nor refuge nigh;
 How can you, my friend and brother,
   Dare to live, or dare to die?

4 Out of Christ, without a Saviour,
   Dark will the voyage be;
 Clouds will gather, storms surround
     you,
   Oh, to Christ for refuge flee!

5 Out of Christ, without a Saviour,
   Give to Him now your heart,
 Ere the door of mercy closes,
   And you hear His word, "Depart."

241 THERE'S a great day coming,
       a great day coming,
   There's a great day coming by
     and by,
 When the saints and the sinners
     shall be parted right and left.
 Are you ready for that day to
     come?

   Are you ready, are you ready,
     Are you ready for the judgment day?
   Are you ready, are you ready
     For the judgment day?

2 There's a bright day coming,
     bright day coming,
   There's a bright day coming
     and by,
 But its brightness shall only come
     them that love the Lord,
 Are you ready for that day to come

3 There's a sad day coming, a sad d
     coming,   [b
   There's a sad day coming by a
 When the sinner shall hear his door
   "Depart, I know you not."
 Are you ready for that day
     come?

242 SINNERS, whither will y
       wander?
   Whither will you stray?
 Oh, remember, life is slender,
   'Tis but a short day.

   Death is coming, coming, coming,
     And the judgment day;
   Hasten sinner, hasten sinner,
     Seek the narrow way.

2 Satan has resolv'd to have you
   For his lawful prey;
 Jesus Christ has died to save you;
   Haste, oh, haste away!

3 Listen to the invitation,
   Whilst He's crying, "Come!"
 If you miss the great salvation,
   Hell will be your doom.

4 Would you 'scape the awful senten
   From destruction flee;
 Seek the Lord by true repentance,
   Haste to Calvary.

243 WILL you open the door
       your heart to-night?
   Outside Jesus patiently stands;
 He is graciously waiting, how c
     you Him slight?   [hand
   He's knocking with nail-pierce

   Just open the door of your heart to-night,
     For Jesus now seeks you to win;
   He is waiting outside, swing the door open wid
     And gladly He'll enter in.

2 Will you open the door of yo
     heart to-night?
   Oh, soul, will you longer delay?
 When the Saviour can free you fro
     sin's awful blight,   [wa
   There is danger and death in yo

Will you open the door of your heart
to-night ?
God's Spirit is striving within ;
He may never again with your
stubborn will fight,
But leave you to perish in sin.

Will you open the door of your
heart to-night ?   [away ;
Do not send the dear Saviour
Lest He leave you for ever con-
demned in God's sight,
On the awful reckoning day.

44 IS there any sad heart that
is heavy laden ?
Any one here ? Any one here ?
Is there any poor soul who would
love the Saviour ?
Come and we will help you on
your way !

st as you are, the Lord will save you,
   Come without delay !
there any poor soul who would follow Jesus ?
me, and we will help you on your way !

Is there any who thirst for the living
water ?
Any one here ? Any one here ?
Is there any who sigh for the
crimson fountain ?
Come and we will help you on
your way !

Is there any who long to be own'd
by Jesus ?
Any one here ? Any one here ?
Is there any will say, " I believe
this moment " ?
Come and we will help you on
your way !

45 IF you are tired of the load
of your sin,
Let Jesus come into your heart ;
If you desire a new life to begin,
Let Jesus come into your heart.

Just now, your doubtings give o'er ;
Just now, reject Him no more ;
Just now, throw open the door ;
Let Jesus come into your heart.

If 'tis for purity now that you sigh,
Fountains for cleansing are flowing
near by.

If there's a tempest your voice
cannot still,   [can fill.
If there's a void this world ne'er

4 If friends, once trusted, have proven
untrue,   [you.
Find what a friend He will be unto
5 If you would join the glad songs of
the blest,   [rest.
If you would enter the mansions of

Just now, my doubtings are o'er ;
Just now, rejecting no more ;
Just now, I open the door
   And Jesus comes into my heart.

246 DRIFTING away from Christ
in thy youth,
Drifting away from mercy and truth,
Drifting to sin in tenderest youth,
Drifting away from God.

Brother, the Saviour has called you before ;
See ! you are nearing eternity's shore !
Soon you may perish, be lost evermore,
   Jesus now calls for you.

2 Drifting away from mother and home,
Drifting away in sorrow to roam,
Drifting where peace and rest cannot
come,
Drifting away from God.

3 Drifting away on sin's treach'rous
tide,
Drifting where death and darkness
abide,   [pride,
Drifting from heav'n away in your
Drifting away from God.

4 Drifting away from hope's blessed
shore,   [roar,
Drifting away where wild breakers
Drifting and   stranded, wreck'd,
evermore
Far from the light of God.

5 Why will ye drift on billows of shame,
Spurning His grace again and again ?
Soon you'll be lost ! in sin to remain,
Ever away from God.

247 DOST thou know at thy
bolted heart's door to-night,
The Saviour in meekness doth
stand,
And longs for admission ? Pray
listen now   [hand.
To the knock of the nail-pierced

Heed the knock of the nail-pierced hand,.....
Heed the knock of the nail-pierced hand ;....
Swing the door open wide, bid Him enter
and abide,
Heed the knock of the nail-pierced hand.....

2 You turn not away when a friend's
  at your door,
   Here's One there's none like in
   the land,
 Who asks to come in and for ever
   abide,
   Heed the knock of the nail-
   pierced hand.

3 All the pain and the shame of His
  death on the tree,
   A welcome from you should
   command,
 Since the weight of your sins in His
   body He bore,
   Heed the knock of the nail-
   pierced hand.

248 PASSING onward, quickly
  passing ;
   But I ask thee, Whither bound ?
 Is it to the many mansions,
   Where eternal rest is found ?
 Passing onward, passing onward,
   Tell me, sinner, whither bound ?

2 Passing onward, quickly passing ;
   Nought the wheels of time can
   stay ;   [going
 Sweet the thought that some are
   To the realms of perfect day.
 Passing onward, passing onward,
   Christ their Leader, Christ their
   Way.

3 Passing onward, quickly passing,
   Many on the downward road ;
 Careless of their souls immortal,
   Heeding not the call of God.
 Passing onward, passing onward,
   Trampling on the Saviour's blood.

4 Passing onward, quickly passing ;
   Time its course will swiftly run ;
 Still we hear the fond entreaty
   Of the ever gracious One :
 " Come and welcome, come and
   welcome,
   'Tis by Me that life is won."

249 HARK ! sinner, while God from
  on high doth entreat thee,
 And warning with language of
   mercy doth blend ;
 Attend to His voice, lest in judgment
   He meet thee ;
   " The harvest is passing, the
   summer will end."

2 How oft of thy danger and guilt
  hath told thee !
   How oft still the message of mer
   doth send !
 Haste, haste, while He waits in F
   arms to enfold thee !
   " The harvest is passing, t
   summer will end."

3 Despised and rejected, at length I
  may leave thee ;
   What anguish and horror t
   bosom will rend !
 Then haste thee, O sinner, while I
   will receive thee :
   " The harvest is passing, t
   summer will end."

4 Ere long and Jehovah will come
  His power !
   Our God will arise with His fo
   to contend ;
 Haste, haste thee, O sinner ! prepa
   for that hour :
   " The harvest is passing, t
   summer will end."

5 The Saviour will call thee in jud
  ment before Him,
   O, let all thy sins go, and ma
   Him thy friend !
 Now yield Him thy heart, and ma
   haste to adore Him !
   " Thy harvest is passing, th
   summer will end."

250 ONCE again the gospel messa
  From the Saviour you ha
   heard :
 Will you heed the invitation ?
   Will you turn and seek the Lord

   Come believing !...come believing !...
   Come to Jesus ! look and live !...
   Come believing !...come believing !...
   Come to Jesus ! look and live !

2 Many summers you have wasted,
   Ripened harvests you have see
 Winter snows by spring have melte
   Yet you linger in your sin.

3 Jesus for your choice is waiting ;
   Tarry not ; at once decide !
 While the Spirit now is striving,
   Yield and seek the Saviour's sid

4 Cease of fitness to be thinking ;
   Do not longer try to feel ;
 It is *trusting*, and not *feeling*,
   That will give the Spirit's seal.

Let your will to God be given,
  Trust in Christ's atoning blood ;
Look to Jesus now in heaven,
  Rest on His unchanging Word.

51 " ALMOST persuaded " now
    to believe ;
" Almost persuaded," Christ to
  receive ;
Seems now some soul to say ?—
" Go, Spirit, go Thy way :
Some more convenient day,
  On Thee I'll call."

" Almost persuaded : " come, come
  to-day !   [away !
" Almost persuaded : " turn not
Jesus invites you here,
Angels are ling'ring near,
Pray'rs rise from hearts so dear,
  O wanderer, come !

" Almost persuaded : " harvest is
  past !   [at last !
" Almost persuaded : " doom comes
" Almost " cannot avail ;
" Almost " is but to fail ;
Sad, sad, that bitter wail—
  " Almost "—*but lost.*

52 A VOICE is heard in the dewy
    dawn,
  And the call is sweet and low ;
Come now, My child, to the Shep-
    herd's fold,
  Where the living waters flow ;
But the gay heart answers in careless
    tones,
  As light as the morning chime :
" Let me live for the world just a
    little while,
  I will turn to God—sometime."

Beware ! beware ! At the pearly gate
God may answer your " Sometime," " Too
  late ! Too late ! "

The day is nearing the noontide glow,
  And the voice is heard again ;
It calls the soul to a nobler life,
  'Tis a patient, kind refrain ;
Enter now the Master's broad
    harvest field,
  In the strength of your early
    prime ;
Come, and bring to His work service
    good and true—
  Still the same reply—" Sometime!"

3 The feet are treading the western
    slope,
  And the air is growing chill ;
Oh, can it be God is waiting yet,
  That His voice is pleading still ?
That He'll flood with beauty the
    sunset sky,   [Clime ?
  Bright rays from the Golden
But the sinner, long-harden'd, has
    turn'd away,
  With the fatal word—"Sometime."

4 O soul, take heed, ere the shadows
    fall,
  And the day of grace be past,
For how shall a trembling sinner
    stand
  By the gates of death at last ?
Hear the Saviour's call ; at the
    Cross lay down
  Thy burden of guilt and crime ;
And the angels shall sing thee a
    sweeter song
  Than the sad refrain, " Sometime."

253 AFTER the storm that sweeps
    the sea ;
After the drifting to the lee,
After the rocks and sands are passed,
Cometh the joy of home at last.
    After all that here we see,
      What will there be, what will there be ?
    After all that here we see,
      After all, eternity.

2 After the winter long and drear ;
After the snow-clouds disappear ;
After the winds sweet odours bring,
Cometh the ever-welcome spring.

3 After the long and toilsome day ;
After the sun's fierce burning ray ;
After the toiler homeward goes,
Cometh the night and sweet repose.

4 After the march of time shall cease,
After earth-strife shall end in peace,
After the changeful disappears,
Cometh the long eternal years.

254 COME, soul, and find thy rest,
    No longer be distressed ;
Come to thy Saviour's breast ;
  O, don't stay away.
    Pray'rs are ascending now,
    Angels are bending now ;
    Both worlds are blending now ;
    Oh, don't stay away.

2 Dark is the world and cold,
Her cares cannot be told ;
Come to thy Saviour's fold ;
Oh, don't stay away.

3 Come with thy load of sin,
Christ died thy soul to win ;
Now He will take thee in ;
Oh, don't stay away.

4 Time, here, will soon be past,
Moments are flying fast ;
Judgment will come at last ;
Oh, don't stay away.

5 Come, oh ! we pray thee, come,
Come, and no longer roam ;
Come, now, and start for home ;
Oh, don't stay away.

255 RETURN, O wand'rer, to thy
home,
Thy Father calls for thee :
No longer now in exile roam,
In guilt and misery.
Return, return.

2 Return, O wand'rer, to thy home,
'Tis Jesus calls for thee ;
The Spirit and the Bride say "Come,"
Oh, now for refuge flee.
Return, return.

3 Return, O wand'rer, to thy home,
'Tis madness to delay ;
There are no pardons in the tomb,
And brief is mercy's day.
Return, return.

256 WHAT means this eager,
anxious throng,
Which moves with busy haste along ;
These wondrous gatherings day by
day ? [pray ?
What means this strange commotion,
In accents hushed the throng reply:
" Jesus of Nazareth passeth by."

2 Who is this Jesus ? Why should He
The city move so mightily ?
A passing stranger, has He skill
To move the multitude at will ?
Again the stirring notes reply :
" Jesus of Nazareth passeth by."

3 Jesus ! 'tis He who once below
Man's pathway trod, 'mid pain and
woe ;

And burdened ones, where'er
came, [and lam
Brought out their sick, and de
The blind rejoiced to hear the cry
" Jesus of Nazareth passeth by."

4 Again He comes ! From place to pla
His holy footprints we can trace.
He pauseth at our threshold—nay
He enters—condescends to stay,
Shall we not gladly raise the cry :
" Jesus of Nazareth passeth by ? "

5 Ho ! all ye heavy laden, come !
Here's pardon, comfort, rest, a
home.
Ye wanderers from a Father's fac
Return, accept His proffered grac
Ye tempted ones, there's refuge nig
" Jesus of Nazareth passeth by."

6 But if you still this call refuse,
And all His wondrous love abuse,
Soon will He sadly from you turn,
Your bitter prayer for pardon spur
"Too late ! too late !" will be the cry
" Jesus of Nazareth *has passed by*

257 THO' only a line, just a li
intervenes
Between your salvation and yo
Your soul will be lost if the line
not crossed,
God's Word to the sinner is tru
Oh, won't you step over, step over it now ?
Believing His Word to be true ;
Come then at the foot of the Cross humbly bow
And let the dear Saviour save you.

2 You may have gone far in the da
and the cold,
Like one in the wilderness lost ;
But would you come back to t
true Shepherd's fold,
There's only a line to be crossed

3 You may have been drifting t
world's stormy main, [tossec
By billow and tempest be
But would you return to the hom
port again,
There's only a line to be crossed

4 Has sin sown the seed of despair
your soul ?
O come without money or cost !
The Saviour is waiting to say, "
thou whole ; "
There's only a line to be crosse

58 THE Saviour is bending above
thee,
To hear what thy spirit will say,
  To the tender embrace,
  Of His mercy and grace,
Will the answer be " Yea, Lord,"
  or " Nay."
" I died for thee," sweetly He
  whispers,   [hands,"
" See, here are the wounds in My
  Thy finger bring near
  And touch without fear
The nail-prints as o'er thee He
  stands.

e Saviour is bending above thee,
To hear what thy spirit will say,
 the tender embrace of His mercy and grace,
Will the answer be "Yea, Lord," or "Nay " ?

Look up in the face of the Saviour,
  The thorn-crown'd yet beautiful
    brow ;
  He waits the reply
  Of thy tear-dimming eye,
Oh, what wilt thou answer Him now?
The Saviour is bending above thee,
  He asks for thy heart in return
  For the heart that He gave,
  To ransom and save ;
Oh, will not thy glad spirit burn ?

Thou hearest His offers of mercy,
  The promise of pardon and peace ;
  Come, wilt thou not say
  To His voice a glad " Yea,"
And bid all thy waverings cease ?
The Saviour is bending above thee,
  His quick ear awaits the glad word:
  " Lord Jesus, to-day,
  I whisper my ' Yea,'
And know that my answer is heard."

59 A FEW more years shall roll,
  A few more seasons come,
And we shall be with those that rest
  Asleep within the tomb.
  Then, oh, my Lord, prepare
    My soul for that great day ;
  Oh, wash me in Thy precious blood,
    And take my sins away.

A few more suns shall set
  O'er these dark hills of time,
And we shall be where suns are not,
  A far serener clime.
  Then, oh, my Lord, prepare
    My soul for that blest day
  Oh, wash me in Thy precious blood,
    And take my sins away.

3 A few more storms shall beat
  On this wild rocky shore,
And we shall be where tempests
  cease,
And surges swell no more.
  Then, oh, my Lord, prepare
    My soul for that calm day ;
  Oh, wash me in Thy precious blood,
    And take my sins away.

260 WHERE will you spend eter-
    nity ?
This question comes to you and me !
Tell me, what shall your answer be ?
Where will you spend eternity ?
  Eternity ! Eternity !
  Where will you spend eternity ?

2 Many are choosing Christ to-day,
Turning from all their sins away ;
Heav'n shall their happy portion be.
Where will you spend eternity ?
  Eternity ! Eternity !
  Where will you spend eternity ?

3 Leaving the strait and narrow way,
Going the downward road to-day,
Sad will their final ending be—
Lost thro' a long eternity !
  Eternity ! Eternity !
  Lost thro' a long eternity !

4 Repent, believe, this very hour,
Trust in the Saviour's grace and
  power,
Then will your joyous answer be,
Saved thro' a long eternity !
  Eternity ! Eternity !
  Saved thro' a long eternity !

261 NOW He will **save you**, now
    He will bless,
If all your vileness you but confess ;
He will receive you home to His
  breast,
If you are weary He'll give you rest.

2 Now is God's mercy offer'd to thee ;
Now His salvation, precious and free;
Will you not take it ?   Turn not
  aside
From the love offer'd and Him who
  died.

3 Now He beseeches you to believe ;
Now He is longing you to receive ;
Now light and darkness, heaven and
  hell,   [well.
Lie each before you, now choose ye

262 TIME is earnest, passing by ;
    Death is earnest, drawing nigh ;
Sinner, wilt thou trifling be ?
Time and death appeal to thee.

2 Life is earnest ; when 'tis o'er,
    Thou returnest never more ;
Soon to meet eternity,
Wilt thou never serious be ?

3 God is earnest ; kneel and pray,
    Ere thy season pass away ;
Ere be set His judgment throne—
Vengeance ready, mercy gone.

4 Oh, be earnest ; death is near ;
    Thou wilt perish, ling'ring here ;
Sleep no longer, rise and flee,
Lo, thy Saviour waits for thee.

REPENTANCE AND DECISION

263 LIKE a wayward child I
    wandered
From my Father's house away,
But I hear His voice entreating,
And I'm coming home to-day.

  Coming....home, coming....home,
  For I can no longer roam ;....
  I am sad and broken-hearted,
  And I'm coming, coming home !....

2 I have wandered in the darkness,
    All my path was lone and drear ;
But my Father did not leave me,
He was watching ever near.

3 O the rapture that awaits me
    When I reach my Father's door !
Once within its blest enclosure,
I am safe for evermore.

4 I will ask Him to forgive me
    For the wrong that I have done,
To receive, accept, and bless me,
Through His well-beloved Son.

264 OH, tender and sweet was the
    Master's voice,
As He lovingly called to me,
"Come over the line, it is only a step :
I am waiting, my child, for thee."

  " Over the line," hear the sweet refrain,
  Angels are chanting the heavenly strain ;
  " Over the line "—Why should I remain
  With a step between me and Jesus ?

2 But my sins are many, my faith is
    small,   [clear ;
Lo ! the answer came quick and
" Thou needst not trust in thyself
    at all,
Step over the line, I am here."

3 " But my flesh is weak," I tearfully
    said,
" And Thy way I cannot see ;
I fear if I try I may sadly fail,
    And thus may dishonour Thee."

4 Ah, the world is cold, and I cann
    go back,
Press forward I surely must ;
I will place my hand in His wound
    palm,
Step over the line, and *trust*.

  " Over the line," hear the sweet refrain,
  Angels are chanting the heavenly strain
  " Over the line "—I *will not* remain,
  I'll cross it and go to Jesus.

265 OH, hear my cry, be gracio
    now to me,
Come, great Deliv'rer, come !
My soul, bow'd down, is longi
    now for Thee,
Come, great Deliv'rer, come !

I've wander'd far away o'er mountains co
I've wander'd far away from home ;
Oh, take me now, and bring me to Thy fol
Come, great Deliv'rer, come !

2 I have no place, nor shelter from t
    night,
Come, great Deliv'rer, come !
One look from Thee would give r
    life and light,
Come, great Deliv'rer, come !

3 My path is lone, and weary are r
    feet,
Come, great Deliv'rer, come !
Mine eyes look up Thy loving sm
    to meet !
Come, great Deliv'rer, come !

4 Thou wilt not spurn contrition
    broken sigh,
Come, great Deliv'rer, come !
Regard my prayer, and hear r
    humble cry,
Come, great Deliv'rer, come !

266 HE tells me to trust and n
    fear,
He bids me each promise believ

His presence and glory seem near,
I open my heart to receive.

I am ra som'd I know,
For His Word tells me so,
So I trust, trust, trust !

My need He is pledged to supply,
I trust for each breath that I
breathe ;
And since I take *life* at His hands,
Why not *all* He wishes to give ?

Lord, I yield evermore,
For Thy promise is sure,
So I trust, trust, trust !

He offers me pardon and peace,
He offers me cleansing from sin ;
The fountain once open'd I see,
Dear Jesus, I dare to plunge in.

Now I know I am free,
For Thy blood cleanseth me,
While I trust, trust, trust !

Praise God, it is done—I am His !
The blood covers body and soul ;
I am pardon'd and cleans'd, I am
healed,
All glory, I'm ev'ry whit whole !

Praise His name, I believe,
And this moment receive,
While I trust, trust, trust !

67 THERE'S a gentle voice within calls away,....
'Tis a warning I have heard o'er
and o'er ;....
But my heart is melted now, oh,
obey,.... [more.
From my Saviour I will wander no

Yes, I will go ; Yes, I will go ;
To Jesus I will go and be saved.
Yes, I will go ; Yes, I will go ;
To Jesus I will go and be saved.

He has promised all my sins to
forgive,....
If I ask in simple faith for His
love,....
In His holy Word I learn how to live,
And to labour for His kingdom
above.

I will try to bear the Cross in my
youth,....
And be faithful in its cause till I
die ;....
If with cheerful step I walk in the
truth,.... [by.
I shall wear a starry crown by and

4 Still the gentle voice within calls
away,....
And its warning I have heard o'er
and o'er ;....
But my heart is melted now, I
obey,.... [more.
From my Saviour I will wander no

268 I'VE wandered far away from
God,
Now I'm coming home ;
The path of sin too long I've trod,
Lord, I'm coming home.

Coming home, coming home,
Never more to roam ;
Open wide Thine arms of love,
Lord, I'm coming home.

2 I've wasted many precious years,
Now I'm coming home ;
I now repent with bitter tears,
Lord, I'm coming home.

3 I'm tired of sin and straying, Lord,
Now I'm coming home ;
I'll trust Thy love, believe Thy Word,
Lord, I'm coming home.

4 My soul is sick, my heart is sore,
Now I'm coming home ;
My strength renew, my hope restore,
Lord, I'm coming home.

269 I HEAR Thy welcome voice,
That calls me, Lord, to Thee,
For cleansing in Thy precious blood,
That flowed on Calvary.

I am coming, Lord,
Coming now to Thee !
Trusting only in the blood
That flowed on Calvary.

2 Though coming weak and vile,
Thou dost my strength assure ;
Thou dost my vileness fully cleanse,
Till spotless all and pure.

3 All hail, atoning blood !
All hail, redeeming grace !
All hail, the gift of Christ, our Lord,
Our strength and righteousness !

270 THERE are angels hov'ring
'round,
There are angels hov'ring 'round,
There are angels, angels hov'ring
'round.

2 To carry the tidings home, etc.

3 To the new Jerusalem, etc.

4 Poor sinners are coming home, etc.

5 And Jesus bids them come, etc.

6 And children, too, may come, etc.

7 For Jesus loves to save, etc.

8 There's glory all around, etc.

271 CHRIST is knocking at my sad
heart,
    Shall I let Him in ?   [heart,
Patiently pleading with my sad
    Oh ! shall I let Him in ?
Cold and proud is my heart with sin ;
Dark and cheerless is all within ;
Christ is bidding me turn unto Him,
    Oh ! shall I let Him in ?

2 Shall I greet Him with loving word ?
    Shall I let Him in ?
Meekly accepting my gracious Lord,
    Oh ! shall I let Him in ?
He can infinite love impart ;
He can pardon this rebel heart ;
Shall I bid Him for ever depart,
    Or shall I let Him in ?

3 Yes, I'll open this heart's proud door,
    Yes, I'll let Him in ;
Gladly I'll welcome Him evermore,
    Oh ! yes, I'll let Him in !
Blessed Saviour, abide with me,
Cares and trials will lighter be ;
I am safe, if I'm only with Thee,
    O blessed Lord, come in !

272 JESUS is pleading with my
poor soul,
    Shall I be saved to-night ?
If I believe, He will make me whole,
    Shall I be saved to-night ?
Tenderly, sadly, I hear Him say,
    " How can you grieve Me from
    day to day ? "
Shall I go on in the old, old way,
    Or shall I be saved to-night ?

2 Jesus was nail'd to the Cross for me,
    Shall I be saved to-night ?
How can my heart so ungrateful be ?
    Shall I be saved to-night ?
Now He will save me by grace
    divine,
Now, if I will, I may call Him mine.
Can I the pleasures of earth resign ?
    Oh, shall I be saved to-night ?

3 Jesus is knocking at my poor hear
    Shall I be saved to-night ?
What if His Spirit should now depar
    Shall I be saved to-night ?
Over and over His voice I hear,
Sweetly it falls on my list'ning ea
Shall I reject Him, a Friend so dea
    Oh, shall I be saved to-night ?

4 What if that voice I should hear
more ?
    Shall I be saved to-night ?
Quickly I'll open this bolted door,
    Save me, O Lord, to-night !
Blessed Redeemer, come in, come i
Pity my sorrow, forgive my sin !
Now let Thy work in my soul begi
    For I will be saved to-night !

273 ONLY a step to Jesus !
    Then why not take it now
Come, and thy sin confessing,
    To Him thy Saviour bow.

    Only a step, only a step ;
    Come ! He waits for thee ;
    Come, and thy sin confessing,
    Thou shalt receive a blessing ;
    Do not reject the mercy
    He freely offers thee.

2 Only a step to Jesus !
    Believe, and thou shalt live ;
Lovingly now He's waiting,
    And ready to forgive.

3 Only a step to Jesus !
    A step from sin to grace ;
What has thy heart decided ?
    The moments fly apace.

4 Only a step to Jesus !
    O why not come, and say,
Gladly to Thee, my Saviour,
    I give myself away.

274 'TIS the promise of God fu
salvation to give
Unto Him who on Jesus His So
will believe.

    Hallelujah ! 'tis done,
    I believe on the Son ;
I am saved by the blood of the Crucified On

2 Tho' the pathway be lonely an
dangerous, too,
Surely Jesus is able to carry n
through.

Many loved ones have I in yon
  heavenly throng,
They are safe now in glory, and this
  is their song :

There are prophets and kings in
  that throng I behold,
And they sing while they march
  through the streets of pure gold :

There's a part in that chorus for you
  and for me,
And the theme of our praises for
  ever will be :

75 ONE sweetly solemn thought
    Comes to me o'er and o'er :
I'm nearer home to-day, to-day,
  Than I have been before.

    Nearer my home, nearer my home.
    Nearer my home to-day, to-day.
    Than I have been before.

Nearer my Father's house,
  Where many mansions be :
Nearer the great white throne to-day
  Nearer the crystal sea.

Nearer the bound of life,
  Where burdens are laid down :
Nearer to leave the cross to-day.
  And nearer to the crown.

Be near me when my feet
  Are slipping o'er the brink ;
For I am nearer home to-day,
  Perhaps, than now I think.

76 LORD, thro' the blood of the
    Lamb that was slain,
  Cleansing for me, cleansing for me !
From all the guilt of my sins now
  I claim
  Cleansing from Thee, cleansing
    from Thee !
Sinful and black tho' the past may
  have been,
Many the crushing defeats I have
  seen,   [lean,
Yet on Thy promise, O Lord, now I
  Cleansing for me, cleansing for me !

From all the doubts that have filled
  me with gloom,
  Cleansing for me !
From all the fears that would point
  me to doom,
  Cleansing for me !

Jesus, although I may not under-
  stand,   [my hand,
In childlike faith now I put forth
And through Thy Word and Thy
  grace I shall stand,
  Cleansed by Thee !

3 From all the care of what men
    think or say,
  Cleansing for me !
From ever fearing to speak, sing,
  or pray,
  Cleansing for me !
Lord, in Thy love and Thy power
  make me strong,
That all may know that to Thee I
  belong ;   [song—
When I am tempted, let this be my
  Cleansing for me !

277 LORD, I hear of show'rs of
      blessing,
  Thou art scattering full and free—
Show'rs the thirsty land refreshing.
  Let some droppings fall on me—
    Even me, even me,
  Let some droppings fall on me.

2 Pass me not, O God, my Father,
  Sinful though my heart may be :
Thou might'st leave me, but the rather
  Let Thy mercy light on me—
    Even me.

3 Pass me not, O mighty Spirit,
  Thou canst make the blind to see ;
Witnesser of Jesus' merit,
  Speak the word of power to me—
    Even me.

4 Love of God, so pure and changeless,
  Blood of Christ, so rich and free ;
Grace of God, so rich and boundless,
  Magnify it all in me—
    Even me.

5 Pass me not, Thy lost one bringing ;
  Bind my heart, O Lord, to Thee,
Whilst the streams of life are
  springing,
  Blessing others, oh, bless me !
    Even me.

278 DEPTH of mercy ! can there be
    Mercy still reserved for me ?
Can my God His wrath forbear ?—
Me, the chief of sinners, spare ?

2 I have long withstood His grace,
   Long provoked Him to His face ;
   Would not hearken to His calls,
   Grieved Him by a thousand falls.

3 Whence to me this waste of love ?
   Ask my Advocate above !
   See the cause in Jesus' face,
   Now before the throne of grace.

4 There for me the Saviour stands,
   Shows His wounds, and spreads His
      hands ;
   God is love, I know, I feel ;
   Jesus lives and loves me still.

5 If I rightly read Thy heart,
   If Thou all compassion art,
   Bow Thine ear, in mercy bow,
   Pardon and accept me now !

279 O JESUS, Thou art standing
         Outside the fast closed door,
   In lowly patience waiting
      To pass the threshold o'er.

2 O Jesus, Thou art knocking,
   And lo ! that hand is scarred,
   And thorns Thy brow encircle,
   And tears Thy face have marred !

3 Oh, love that passeth knowledge,
   So patiently to wait !
   Oh, sin that hath no equal,
   So fast to bar the gate !

4 O Jesus, Thou art pleading
   In accents meek and low—
   " I died for you, My children,
   And will you treat Me so ? "

5 O Lord, with shame and sorrow,
   We open now the door ;
   Dear Saviour, enter, enter,
   And leave us nevermore !

280 PASS me not, O gentle Saviour,
         Hear my humble cry ;
   While on others Thou art calling,
   Do not pass me by.
      Saviour, Saviour,
         Hear my humble cry ;
      While on others Thou art calling,
         Do not pass me by.

2 Let me at Thy throne of mercy
   Find a sweet relief ;
   Kneeling there in deep contrition,
   Help my unbelief.

3 Trusting only in Thy merits
   Would I seek Thy face ;
   Heal my wounded, broken spirit,
   Save me by Thy grace.

4 Thou, the spring of all my comfor[t]
   More than life to me—
   Whom have I on earth beside Thee[e]
   Whom in heav'n but Thee ?

281 I LAY my sins on Jesus,
         The spotless Lamb of God
   He bears them all, and frees us
   From the accursed load.
   I bring my guilt to Jesus,
   To wash my crimson stains
   White in His blood most precious[s]
   Till not a spot remains.

2 I lay my wants on Jesus,
   All fulness dwells in Him ;
   He heals all my diseases,
   He doth my soul redeem.
   I lay my griefs on Jesus,
   My burdens and my cares ;
   He from them all releases,
   He all my sorrows shares.

3 I rest my soul on Jesus,
   This weary soul of mine ;
   His right hand me embraces,
   I on His breast recline.
   I love the name of Jesus,
   Immanuel, Christ, the Lord ;
   Like fragrance on the breezes
   His name abroad is poured.

4 I long to be like Jesus,
   Meek, loving, lowly, mild ;
   I long to be like Jesus,
   The Father's Holy Child ;
   I long to be with Jesus,
   Amid the heav'nly throng,
   To sing with saints His praises,
   To learn the angels' song.

282 ALL my doubts I give to Jesus
         I've His gracious promise hear[d]
   I shall never be confounded,
   I am trusting in that Word.
      I am trusting, fully trusting,
         Sweetly trusting to His Word.
      I am trusting, fully trusting,
         Sweetly trusting to His Word.

2 All my sins I lay on Jesus !
   He doth wash me in His blood ;
   He will keep me pure and holy,
   He will bring me home to God.

All my fears I give to Jesus !
  Rests my weary soul on Him ;
Though my way be hid in darkness,
  Never can His light grow dim.

All my joys I give to Jesus !
  He is all I want of bliss ;
He of all the worlds is Master,
  He has all I need in this.

All I am I give to Jesus !
  All my body, all my soul !
All I have, and all I hope for,
  While eternal ages roll.

283 I WILL go, I cannot stay
  From the arms of love away ;
O for strength of faith to say,
  Jesus died for me.

  Can it be, O can it be,
  There is hope for one like me ?
  I will go with this my plea,
    Jesus died for me.

Tho' I long have tried in vain,
Tried to break the tempter's chain,
Yet to-day I'll try again,
  Jesus, help Thou me.

I am lost, and yet I know
Earth can never heal my woe ;
I will rise at once and go,
  Jesus died for me.

Something whispers in my soul,
Tho' my sins like mountains roll,
Jesus' blood will make me whole,
  Jesus died for me.

284 MY life, my love, I give to
    Thee,
Thou Lamb of God, who died for me:
O may I ever faithful be,
  My Saviour and my God !

  I'll live for Thee, I'll live for Thee,
  And O how glad my soul should be,
  That Thou didst give Thyself for me,
    My Saviour and my God !

I now believe Thou dost receive,
For Thou hast died that I might
  live ;   [Thee,
And now henceforth I'll trust in
  My Saviour and my God !

O Thou who died on Calvary,
To save my soul, and make me free ;
I consecrate my life to Thee,
  My Saviour and my God !

285 RING the bells of heaven !
    there is joy to-day,
  For a soul returning from the wild ;
See ! the Father meets him out upon
    the way,   [child.
  Welcoming His weary, wand'ring

  Glory ! Glory ! how the angels sing !
  Glory ! Glory ! how the loud harps ring !
  'Tis the ransomed army, like a mighty sea,
  Pealing forth the anthem of the free !

2 Ring the bells of heaven ! there is
    joy to-day,
  For the wand'rer now is reconciled ;
Yes, a soul is rescued from his sinful
    way,   [child.
  And is born a new, a ransom'd

3 Ring the bells of heaven ! spread
    the feast to-day !
  Angels swell the glad, triumphant
    strain !   [away !
Tell the joyful tidings ! bear it far
  For a precious soul is born again.

286 SAVIOUR, hear me, while
    before Thy feet
I the record of my sins repeat,
Stained with guilt, myself abhorring,
Fill'd with grief, my soul out-
    pouring,   [me,
Canst Thou still in mercy think of
Stoop to set my shackled spirit free ;
Raise my sinking heart, and bid me be
  Thy child forgiven ?

  Grace...there is my ev'ry debt to pay,
  Blood...to wash my ev'ry sin away,
  Pow'r...to keep me spotless day by day,
    In Christ for me.

2 Back with all the guilt my spirit bears
Past the haunting memories of years ;
Self and shame and fear despising,
Foes and taunting fiends surprising ;
Saviour, to Thy cross I press my way,
And a broken heart before it lay ;
Ere I leave, oh let me hear Thee say
  I am forgiven.

3 Yet why should I fear ? Hast Thou
    not died   [denied ?
That no seeking soul should be
To that heart, its sins confessing,
Canst Thou fail to give a blessing ?
By the love and pity Thou hast shown,
By the blood that did for me atone,
Boldly will I kneel before thy throne,
  A pleading soul.

4 All the rivers of Thy grace I claim,
Over ev'ry promise write my name ;
As I am I come believing,
As Thou art Thou dost, receiving,
Bid me rise, a freed and pardoned
slave,   [grave,
Master o'er my sin, the world, the
Charging me to preach Thy power
to save
To sin-bound souls.

287 LOVING Saviour, hear my cry,
Hear my cry, hear my cry ;
Trembling to Thine arms I fly,
Oh, save me at the Cross.
I have sinn'd, but Thou hast died,
Thou hast died, Thou hast died ;
In Thy mercy let me hide,
Oh, save me at the Cross.

> Lord Jesus, receive me,
> No more would I grieve Thee.
> Now, blessed Redeemer,
> Oh, save me at the Cross.

2 Though I perish I will pray,
I will pray, I will pray ;
Thou of Life the Living Way,
Oh, save me at the Cross.
Thou hast said Thy grace is free,
Grace is free, grace is free ;
Have compassion, Lord, on me,
Oh, save me at the Cross.

3 Wash me in Thy cleansing blood,
Cleansing blood, cleansing blood ;
Plunge me now beneath the flood,
Oh, save me at the Cross.
Only faith will pardon bring,
Pardon bring, pardon bring ;
In that faith to Thee I cling,
Oh, save me at the Cross.

288 LONG I have wandered afar
from my Lord,
Now I am coming home ;
Longing to be to His favour restored
Now I am coming home.

> Yes, I am coming, dear Lord, I'm coming,
> Just now I'm coming home ;
> Yes, I am coming, dear Lord, I'm coming,
> Just now I'm coming home.

2 Tired of the world with its folly and sin,
Now I am coming home ;
Believing the Saviour will welcome
me in,
Now I am coming home.

3 Knowing my Saviour can give m
His rest,
Now I am coming home ;
Longing to anchor my soul on H
breast,
Now I am coming home.

4 Humbly I crave but a poor servant'
place,
Now I am coming home ;
Only desiring to taste of His grac
Now I am coming home.

5 Oh, bless the Lord, my dear Saviou
I see,
Now I am coming home ;
Waiting to welcome a sinner like m
Now I am coming home.

289 I AM coming to the Cross,
I am poor, and weak, and blinc
I am counting all but dross,
I shall full salvation find.

> I am trusting, Lord, in Thee,
> Blest Lamb of Calvary ;
> Humbly at Thy Cross I bow,
> Save me, Jesus, save me now.

2 Long my heart has sighed for Thee,
Long has evil reigned within ;
Jesus sweetly speaks to me,
" I will cleanse you from all sin."

3 Here I give my all to Thee,   [store
Friends, and time, and earth
Soul and body Thine to be—
Wholly Thine for evermore.

290 YES, there is room for Jesus
Within this contrite heart !
Dear Saviour, wait no longer,
But grace divine impart.

> Room, O blessed Saviour,
> In my poor wand'ring heart ;
> Come in and reign for ever,
> New life and peace impart.

2 Yes, there is room for Jesus—
The Guest of heav'nly birth ;
His life He gave a ransom
For all the sons of earth.

3 Yes, there is room for Jesus,
Oh enter, Lord, and reign ;
The King and mighty Conqueror
O'er death and sin and pain.

4 I'll sing aloud the praises
Of Him who saves from doom ;
Dear Lord, through coming ages
My heart shall give Thee room.

91 THE great Physician now is near,
  The sympathising Jesus ;
He speaks the drooping heart to
    cheer,
  Oh, hear the voice of Jesus.

  Sweetest note in seraph song,
  Sweetest name on mortal tongue ;
  Sweetest carol ever sung,
    Jesus, blessed Jesus.

Your many sins are all forgiv'n,
  Oh, hear the voice of Jesus :
Go on your way in peace to heav'n,
  And wear a crown with Jesus.

All glory to the dying Lamb !
  I now believe in Jesus ;
I love the blessed Saviour's name,
  I love the name of Jesus.

His name dispels my guilt and fear,
  No other name but Jesus ;
Oh ! how my soul delights to hear
  The precious name of Jesus.

92 JUST as I am, without one
    plea,
But that Thy blood was shed for me,
And that Thou bidst me come to
    Thee,
  O Lamb of God, I come, I come.

Just as I am, and waiting not
To rid my soul of one dark blot ;
To Thee, whose blood can cleanse
    each spot,
  O Lamb of God, I come, I come.

Just as I am, Thou wilt receive,
Wilt welcome, pardon, cleanse,
    relieve ;
Because Thy promise I believe,
O Lamb of God, I come, I come.

Just as I am—Thy love unknown
Has broken ev'ry barrier down ;
Now to be Thine, yea, Thine alone,
  O Lamb of God, I come, I come.

93 JESUS, see me at Thy feet,
  Nothing but Thy blood can
    save me ;
Thou alone my need canst meet,
  Nothing but Thy blood can save me.

  No ! No ! Nothing do I bring,
  But by faith I'm clinging
  To Thy Cross, O Lamb of God !
  Nothing but Thy blood can save me.

2 See my heart, Lord, torn with grief,
  Nothing but Thy blood can save
    me ;
  Me unpardoned do not leave,
  Nothing but Thy blood can save
    me.

3 Dark, indeed, the past has been.
  Nothing but Thy blood can save
    me.
  Yet in mercy take me in,
  Nothing but Thy blood can save
    me.

4 As I am, oh, hear me pray,
  Nothing but Thy blood can save
    me ;
  I can come no other way,
  Nothing but Thy blood can save
    me.

5 All that I can do is vain,
  Nothing but Thy blood can save
    me ;
  I can ne'er remove a stain,
  Nothing but Thy blood can save
    me.

6 Lord, I cast myself on Thee,
  Nothing but Thy blood can save
    me ;
  From my guilt, oh, set me free,
  Nothing but Thy blood can save
    me.

294 O SPOTLESS Lamb, I come
    to Thee,
  No longer can I from Thee stay ;
  Break ev'ry chain, now set me free,
  Take all my sins away !

  Take all my sins away !
  Take all my sins away !
  O spotless Lamb, I come to Thee,
  Take all my sins away !

2 My hungry soul cried out for Thee,
  Come, and for ever seal my breast ;
  To Thy dear arms at last I flee,
  There only can I rest.

3 I plunge beneath Thy precious
    blood,
  My hand in faith takes hold of
    Thee ;
  Thy promises just now I claim
  Thou art enough for me.

CHRISTIAN LIFE AND SERVICE

295 TRYING to walk in the steps
of the Saviour,
Trying to follow our Saviour and
King ;   [example,
Shaping our lives by His blessed
Happy, how happy, the songs
that we bring.

How beautiful to walk in the steps of the
Saviour,
Stepping in the light, stepping in the light ;
How beautiful to walk in the steps of the
Saviour,
Led in paths of light.

2 Pressing more closely to Him who
is leading,
When we are tempted to turn
from the way ;
Trusting the arm that is strong to
defend us,
Happy, how happy, our praises
each day.

3 Walking in footsteps of gentle for-
bearance,
Footsteps of faithfulness, mercy,
and love ;
Looking to Him for the grace freely
promised,   [above.
Happy, how happy, our journey

4 Trying to walk in the steps of the
Saviour,   [our Guide ;
Upward, still upward, we'll follow
When we shall see Him, " the King
in His beauty,"
Happy, how happy, our place at
His side.

296 DO you ever feel downhearted
or discouraged ?
Do you ever think your work is
all in vain ?
Do the burdens thrust upon you
make you tremble,
And you fear that you shall ne'er
the vict'ry gain ?....

Have faith in God,..the sun will shine..
Tho' dark the cloud..may be to-day ;..
His heart hath planned..your path and mine!..
Have faith in God,..have faith alway...

2 Darkest night will always come
before the dawning,
Silver linings shine on God's side
of the cloud :

All your journey He has promise
to be with you,
Nought has come to you but wha
His love allowed.....

3 God is mighty ! He is able t
deliver ;   [hour
Faith can victor be in ev'ry tryir
Fear and care, and sin, and sorro
be defeated,
By our faith in God's almighty
conqu'ring pow'r.....

297 I CAN hear my Saviour callin
I can hear my Saviour callin
I can hear my Saviour calling,
" Take thy cross and follow, follo
Me."

Where He leads me I will follow,
Where He leads me I will follow,
Where He leads me I will follow,
I'll go with Him, with Him all the way.

2 I'll go with Him thro' the garden,
I'll go with Him, with Him all the way

3 I'll go with Him thro' the judgmen
I'll go with Him, with Him all th
way.

4 He will give me grace and glory,
And go with me, with me all the way

298 A TREMBLING soul, I sough
the Lord,
My sin confessed, my guilt deplored
How soft and sweet His word to m
"I took thy place, and died for thee.

No other hope,..no other plea ;..
He took my place,..and died for me ;..
O precious Lamb..of Calvary !..
He took my place,..and died for me....

2 Here rests my heart ; assuranc
sweet,
His blessed work He will complet
Since in His love so great and free,
He took my place, and died for me

3 When sorrow veils the smiling day
When evil foes beset my way,
Abundant grace in Him I see,
He took my place, and died for m

4 No room for doubt, no room for fear
When to my view the Cross appears
My joyful song shall ever be,
He took my place, and died for me

99 SOLDIERS of Zion, on we go,
Brave are the hearts that face
the foe ;
Vict'ry awaits us, for we know
We follow the Lord our King.
Not by the might of human arm,
Not by the pow'r of earth to harm,
But by the Spirit's holy charm,
Shall we the triumph sing.
Soldiers of Zion, on we go,
Brave are the hearts that face the foe.
Vict'ry awaits us, for we know
We follow the Lord our King.

Hark to the trump that sounds for
war,
See how the flag goes on before,
Look how the ranks swell more and
more,
As Jesus the King leads on.
Strong are the hosts of Sin and Death,
Stronger the might of Him who
saith, [breath ! "
" I will consume them with My
Then will the field be won.

Sure as the Truth will dawn the day
When giant Wrong will end his sway ;
Bondage and error flee away,
And earth to the Lord belong.
Courage, ye souls who fight and plod,
This is the path that worthies trod ;
Gird up your loins, elect of God :
Soon comes the victor's song.

00 JESUS comes with pow'r to
gladden,
When love shines in,
Ev'ry life that woe can sadden,
When love shines in.
Love will teach us how to pray,
Love will drive the gloom away,
Turn our darkness into day,
When love shines in.
When love shines in,...when love shines in,
How the heart is tuned to singing when love
shines in ;
When love shines in, when love shines in,
Joy and peace to others bringing, when love
shines in.

How the world will glow with beauty
When love shines in,
And the heart rejoice in duty,
When love shines in.
Trials may be sanctified,
And the soul in peace abide,
Life will all be glorified,
When love shines in.

3 Darkest sorrows will grow brighter,
When love shines in,
And the heaviest burden lighter,
When love shines in.
'Tis the glory that will throw
Light to show us where to go ;
O the heart shall blessing know
When love shines in.

4 We may have unfading splendour,
When love shines in,
And a friendship true and tender,
When love shines in.
When earth's vict'ries shall be won,
And our life in heav'n begun,
There will be no need of sun,
For love shines in.

301 O CHRIST, in Thee my soul
hath found,
And found in Thee alone,
The peace, the joy I sought so long
The bliss till now unknown.
Now none but Christ can satisfy,
None other name for me,....
There's love and life and lasting joy,
Lord Jesus, found in Thee.

2 I sigh'd for rest and happiness,
I yearned for them, not Thee ;
But while I pass'd my Saviour by,
His love laid hold on me.

3 I tried the broken cisterns, Lord,
But, ah ! the waters failed !
E'en as I stooped to drink, they fled,
And mock'd me as I wail'd.

4 The pleasures lost I sadly mourn'd,
But never wept for Thee,
Till grace the sightless eyes receiv'd,
Thy loveliness to see.

302 I SHALL see them again in
the light of the morning,
When the night has pass'd by with
its tears and its mourning,
Where the light of God's love is the
sun ever shining, [rest.
In the land where the weary ones

2 I shall know them again though ten
thousand surround them,
I shall hear their dear voice 'midst
the blessed ones round them ;
And the love that was theirs on the
earth shall detect them,
In the land where the weary ones
rest.

3 'Twas their lives in the past helped
    to fill me with gladness ;
And the future is heaven, the home
    with no sadness,
Where I see them to-day clad in
    bright robes of whiteness,
In the land where the weary ones
    rest.

4 Would I wish for them back from
    their bright home in heaven ?
No ! in patience I'll wait till the veil
    shall be riven,
And the Saviour restores me the
    friends He has given,
In the land where the weary ones
    rest.

303   OH ! the sowing time seems
          weary,
And full oft the workers cry,
To the Lord who rules the harvest,
For the reaping by and by.

What a reap..ing...reap..ing,
What a reaping it will be by and by...
    Ev'ry sorrow we have known,
    Ev'ry tear that we have sown,
What a reaping it will be by and by !...

2 In the sorrow and the suff'ring,
    When each breath is but a sigh ;
Tho' we sow in tears, remember
    There's a reaping by and by.

3 When our hearts are strained to
        breaking,
    Comfort other suff'rers nigh ;
And our harvest will be doubled
    In the reaping by and by.

4 For the love of Christ is flowing
    In a stream that's never dry ;
He will water all our sowing,
    For the reaping by and by.

304 THE way our fathers travelled
          is good enough for me ;
They followed in the footsteps that
    led from Calvary ;
It led them up to glory, that land of
    endless day ;
I expect to get to heaven by the
    same old way.

O this blessed old way, it is good enough for me,
It is good enough for me, it is good enough for
    me ;   [each day ;
My Saviour goes before me, I follow Him
I expect to get to heaven by the same old way.

2 The world may sneer and tell m
    I'll never reach the goal,
That good works are sufficient
    save a human soul ;
But while the world is talking, I st
    will watch and pray ;
I expect to get to heaven by th
    same old way.

3 When bowers of sin entice me to re
    my weary feet,
I find in Christ, my Saviour, a saf
    a sure retreat ;
He tells me to press onward, and ne
    look back, nor stay ;   [old wa
I expect to get to heaven by the san

4 Millions are now in glory, in shinir
    white arrayed,
Who travelled this same pathwa
    and often were dismayed ;
But happy now in glory, they sin
    both night and day ;
I expect to get to heaven by th
    same old way.

305   THERE'S a land that is fair
          than day,
And by faith we can see it afar ;
For the Father waits over the way
    To prepare us a dwelling-pla
    there.
In the sweet...by and by,...
    We shall meet on that beautiful shore.
In the sweet...by and by,...
    We shall meet on that beautiful shore.

2 We shall sing on that beautiful sho
    The melodious songs of the blest
And our spirits shall sorrow no mor
    Not a sigh for the blessing of rest

3 To our bountiful Father above,
    We will offer our tribute of prais
For the glorious gift of His love,
    And the blessings that hallow ou
    days.

306   ONWARD still, and upwar
          Follow evermore
Where our mighty Leader
    Goes in love before.
" Looking unto Jesus,"
    Reach a helping hand
To a struggling neighbour,
    Helping him to stand.
Marching on...ward,...up ..ward....
Marching steadily onward, Jesus leads the wa
Marching on...ward.. upward,
Onward unto glory, to the perfect...day.

2 Onward, ever onward,
Through the pastures green,
Where the streams flow softly,
Under skies serene ;
Or, if need be, upward,
O'er the rocky steep,
Trusting Him to guide us,
Strong to save and keep.

3 Upward, ever upward,
T'ward the radiant glow,
Far above the valley,
Where the mist hangs low.
On, with songs of gladness,
Till the march shall end,
Where ten thousand thousand
Hallelujahs blend.

07 OH, I have got good news for you
A story wonderful and true ;
'Twill make you happy, that I know,
It made me glad, and now I go—
To sing my great Redeemer's song,
To sing my great Redeemer's song,
To sing my great Redeemer's song,
With the happy saints above.

I once was far away from God,
On ruin's dark and fatal road,
And little dream'd I'd see the day
That I should tread the narrow way.

O'er this wild waste I loved to roam,
My back to God and heav'n and home,
When Jesus met me far astray,
And beckoned me to come away.

He said on Calv'ry's Cross He died,
A sacrifice for sin was made,
And all because He loved me so :
Then how could I do else than go ?

Now ev'rv one that's standing by
Oh, 'twas for you the Christ did die ;
This moment, too, He waits for thee,
Then just believe, and you'll be free.

Whene'er the record you believe,
You life eternal shall receive,
And soon from pain and sorrow free,
You'll join that glorious company.

08 IN the heav'nly pastures fair,
'Neath the tender Shepherd's
care, [to-day—
Let us rest beside the living stream
Calmly there in peace recline,
Drinking in the truth divine,
As His loving call we now with joy
obey.....

Glorious streams of life eternal,
Beauteous fields of living green,.....
Though reveal'd within the Word
Of our Shepherd and our Lord,
By the pure in heart alone can they be seen...

2 Far from all the noise and strife,
That disturbs our daily life,
Let us pause awhile in silence and adore;
Then the sound of His dear voice
Will our waiting souls rejoice,
As He nameth us His own for ever-
more.....

3 Oh, how good, and true, and kind,
Seeking His stray sheep to find,
If they wander into danger from His
side ;
Ever closely may we tread
Where His holy feet have led,
So at last with Him in heav'n we may
abide.....

309 FIRMLY stand for God in the
world's mad strife,
Tho' the bleak winds roar, and the
waves beat high ;
'Tis the Rock alone giveth strength
and life,
When the hosts of sin are nigh.
Let us stand on the Rock !
Firmly stand on the Rock :
On the Rock of Christ alone ;
If the strife we endure,
We shall stand secure,
'Mid the throng who surround the Throne.

2 Firmly stand for Right, with a
motive pure,
With a true heart bold, and a faith
e'er strong ; [sure,
'Tis the Rock alone giveth triumph
O'er the world's array of wrong.

3 Firmly stand for Truth ! it will
serve you best,
Tho' it waiteth long, it is sure at
last ; [rest.
'Tis the Rock alone giveth peace and
When the storms of life are past.

310 IN the dew of early youth,
None can help like Jesus ;
Seeking after pearls of truth,
None can help like Jesus ;
He's the source of living light,
He will guide your steps aright ;
None can help like Jesus,
No ! none like Jesus.

2 In the midday whirl of care,
　　None can help like Jesus ;
　When you heavy burdens bear,
　　None can help like Jesus ;
　He will give you sweetest rest,
　All who trust in Him are blest ;
　　None can help like Jesus,
　　No ! none like Jesus.

3 In the twilight's fading glow,
　　None can help like Jesus ;
　When your strength is ebbing slow,
　　None can help like Jesus ;
　He will shield from death's alarms,
　Fold you in His loving arms ;
　　None can help like Jesus,
　　No ! none like Jesus.

311　ALL around this very hour,
　　　　Falls there streams of heav'nly
　　　　　　pow'r ;
　Falling now so full and free,
　Praise the Lord, it's filling me.
　　Hallelujah ! feel the pow'r,
　　Falling like a mighty show'r ;
　　Coming now so full and free ;
　　Praise the Lord, it's filling me.

2 Send us show'rs of heav'nly grace ;
　Let Thy presence fill this place ;
　Speak the word and it shall be,
　That Thy showers fall on me.

3 Thou alone this pow'r canst give ;
　Without Thee I dare not live ;
　Give me pow'r to work for Thee,
　Let the stream reach even me.

312　JESUS, Thy blood and right-
　　　　eousness
　My beauty are, my glorious dress ;
　'Midst flaming worlds, in these
　　arrayed,
　With joy shall I life up my head.

2 Bold shall I stand in Thy great day ;
　For who aught to my charge shall lay ?
　Fully absolv'd through these I am
　From sin and fear, from guilt and
　　shame.

3 When from the dust of death I rise,
　To claim my mansion in the skies,
　Even then, this shall be all my plea,
　Jesus hath lived, hath died for me.

4 Jesus, be endless praise to Thee,
　Whose boundless mercy hath for me—
　For me, a full atonement made,
　An everlasting ransom paid.

5 O let the dead now hear Thy voic
　Now bid Thy banished ones rejoic
　Their beauty this, their glorio
　　dress,
　Jesus, Thy blood and righteousne

313　OVER the river they call me
　　　　Friends that are dear to m
　　　　　heart,....
　Soon shall I meet them in glory,
　　Never, no, never to part.
　　Over the river of Eden,
　　　Home to the mansions so fair ;
　　Angels will carry me safely,
　　　Jesus will welcome me there.

2 Over the river they call me ;
　　Hark ! 'tis their voices I hear,
　Borne on the wings of the twiligh
　Murmuring softly and clear.

3 Over the river they call me,
　　There is no sorrow nor night ;..
　There they are walking with Jesu
　Clothed in their garments
　　white.

4 Over the river they call me,
　　Watching with bright beami
　　eyes,...
　" Over the river I'm coming,"
　Gladly 'my spirit replies.

314　LET us sing a song that w
　　　　cheer us by the way,
　　In a little while we're going hom
　For the night will end in the ev
　　lasting day,
　　In a little while we're going hon
　　In a little while,...in a little while...
　　We shall cross the billow's foam ;
　　We shall meet at last,
　　When the stormy winds are past,
　　In a little while we're going home.

2 We will do the work that our han
　　may find to do,
　　In a little while we're going hom
　And the grace of God will our da
　　strength renew,
　　In a little while we're going hon

3 We will smooth the path for so
　　weary, wayworn feet,
　　In a little while we're going hom
　O may loving hearts spread arou
　　an influence sweet !
　　In a little while we're going hon

There's a rest beyond, there's relief
    from ev'ry care,
In a little while we're going home ;
And no tears shall fall in that city
    bright and fair,
In a little while we're going home.

15 ARE you heavy laden and
      with sorrow tried ?
Look in faith to Christ, your Helper,
    Friend, and Guide ;
Think of all your mercies, such a
    boundless store,
Tears will change to praises as you
    count them o'er.

ount..your mercies, such a boundless store,
ount..your mercies, pressed and running o'er,
ll..your mercies, count them o'er and o'er
ost in love and wonder at the boundless store.

Think of hidden dangers He has
    brought you through,
Of the cares and burdens He has
    borne for you,
Of His words of comfort in your
    deepest need,
Count the times when Jesus proved
    a Friend indeed.

Does your pathway darken when
    the clouds draw near ?
Count your many mercies, dry the
    flowing tear ;
Trust Him in the shadows dim and
    have no fear ;
" Heaven will be the sweeter for the
    dark down here."

As He looks from heaven down on
    you and me,
Know ye not He chooseth what each
    day shall be ?
Trust His loving wisdom, though the
    hot tears start,
Give to Him the incense of a grateful
    heart.

16 IT was down at the feet of
      Jesus,
O the happy, happy day !
That my soul found peace in
    believing,
And my sins were washed away.

Let me tell the old, old story
  Of His grace so full and free,
For I feel like giving Him the glory
  For His wondrous love to me.

2 It was down at the feet of Jesus,
    Where I found such perfect rest ;
Where the light first dawned on my
    spirit,
    And my soul was truly blest.

3 It was down at the feet of Jesus,
    Where I brought my guilt and sin ;
That He cancelled all my trans-
    gressions,
    And salvation entered in.

317 BLESSED is the service of our
      Lord and King,
Precious are the jewels we may help
    to bring ;
Down the passing ages words of
    counsel ring,
    He that winneth souls is wise.

He that winneth souls is wise ;...
In the home beyond the skies...
There's a crown of glory, oh, the wondrous prize
He that winneth souls is wise.

2 In the quiet home-life, showing
    love's bright ray,
More and more like Jesus, living
    ev'ry day,
We may guide a dear one to the
    heavenward way,
    He that winneth souls is wise.

3 Out upon the highway, going forth
    with prayer,
For the lost and straying seeking
    ev'rywhere,
Close beside the Shepherd, we His
    joy may share,
    He that winneth souls is wise.

4 Sow beside all waters, sow the
    gospel seed,
Here a word in season, there a loving
    deed ;
Sinners to the Saviour be it ours
    to lead,
    He that winneth souls is wise.

318 I'M a pilgrim, and I'm a
      stranger ;
I can tarry, I can tarry but a night !
Do not detain me, for I am going
To where the fountains are ever
    flowing.

I'm a pilgrim,..and I'm a stranger ;...
  I can tarry, I can tarry but a night ;...
I'm a pilgrim,..and I'm a stranger,...
  I can tarry, I can tarry but a night.

2 Of that city to which I journey,
   My Redeemer, my Redeemer is the
     light ;
   There is no sorrow, nor any sighing,
   Nor any tears there, nor any dying.

3 There the sunbeams are ever shining,
   O my longing heart, my longing
     heart is there ;
   Here in this country, so dark and
     dreary,
   I long have wander'd forlorn and
     weary.

319 THE dear old story of a
         Saviour's love
   Is sweeter as the days go by ;
   The glad assurance of a home above
   Is sweeter as the days go by.

   We'll fill..the days with joy..ful praise,
     We'll sing as the happy moments fly ;...
   The song of love to Him above
     Grows sweeter as the days go by.

2 The sunbeams shining from the
     living Light
   Are brighter as the days go by ;
   The stars of promise cheering
     sorrow's night
   Are brighter as the days go by.

3 Hope's anchor, holding in the
     stormy strife,
   Is stronger as the days go by ;
   We feel the throbbings of immortal
     life
   Grow stronger as the days go by.

4 The peace that Jesus gives to us
     anew
   Is deeper as the days go by ;
   The prospects opening to the
     Christian's view
   Are grander as the days go by.

320 CAN it be that Jesus bought
         me,
   And on the hallow'd Cross atoned
     for me,
   Loved me, chose me ere I knew Him?
   Oh, what a precious, precious
     Friend is He !

   Oh, it is wonderful, very, very wonderful,
     All His grace so rich and free !
   Oh, it is wonderful, very, very wonderful,
     All His love and grace to me !

2 Praise His name, He sought an
     found me,
   Sav'd me from wandering an
     brought me near ;
   Freely now His grace bestowing,
   Jesus is growing unto me mor
     dear.

3 It was months He had been waitin
   Waiting the dawning of th
     precious hour ;
   When I should at last be yielding,
   Yielding to Jesus ev'ry ransom'
     pow'r.

4 From that hour He has been seekin
   How He may fill me with H
     precious love ;
   How He may through grace tran
     form me,
   Meet for the fellowship of saint
     above.

5 As I think of all, I marvel
   Why in such patience He my goo
     has sought,
   And bestowed His grace upon me,
   And in my spirit such a chang
     has wrought.

6 So I cry with love o'erflowing :
   " Unto the Saviour be etern
     praise,
   Who redeemed me, soul and body,
   Filling with gladness all m
     earthly days."

321 NOR silver nor gold hath
         obtained my redemption,
   No riches of earth could hav
     saved my poor soul ;
   The blood of the Cross is my onl
     foundation,
   The death of my Saviour no
     maketh me whole.

   I am redeemed,...but not with silver,...
     I am bought,...but not with gold ;...
   Bought with a price,...the blood of Jesus,.
     Precious price of love untold.

2 Nor silver nor gold hath obtaine
     my redemption,
   The guilt on my conscience to
     heavy had grown ;
   The blood of the Cross is my onl
     foundation,
   The death of my Saviour coul
     only atone.

Nor silver nor gold hath obtained
my redemption,
The holy commandment forbade
me draw near;
The blood of the Cross is my only
foundation
The death of my Saviour removeth
my fear.

Nor silver nor gold hath obtained
my redemption,
The way into heaven could not
thus be bought;
The blood of the Cross is my only
foundation,
The death of my Saviour redemption hath wrought.

322 HOW sweet the name of
Jesus sounds
In a believer's ear;
It soothes his sorrows, heals his
wounds,
And drives away his fear.

It makes the wounded spirit whole,
And calms the troubled breast;
'Tis manna to the hungry soul,
And to the weary rest.

Dear Name, the Rock on which I
build,
My shield and hiding place,
My never-failing Treasury, filled
With boundless stores of grace.

Jesus, my Shepherd, Saviour, Friend,
My Prophet, Priest, and King,
My Lord, my Life, my Way, my
End,
Accept the praise I bring.

I would Thy boundless love pro-
claim
With every fleeting breath;
So shall the music of Thy Name
Refresh my soul in death.

323 WE are trav'ling on with our
staff in hand,
Walking in the good old way;
We are pilgrims bound for the
heav'nly land,
Walking in the good old way.
Walking in the blessedness of love untold,
Trav'ling to a country that will ne'er grow old,
Jesus, our Redeemer, we shall there behold,
Home in the realms of day.

2 We are trav'ling on through a
world of sin,
Walking in the good old way;
Though our foes are strong, we have
peace within,
Walking in the good old way.

3 We are trav'ling on in the Master's
name,
Walking in the good old way;
And we sing His praise with a loud
acclaim,
Walking in the good old way.

4 We are trav'ling on to the rolling
tide,
Walking in the good old way;
But we trust in Him who is still our
Guide,
Walking in the good old way.

324 WE may lighten toil and care,
Or a heavy burden share,
With a word, a kindly deed, or
sunny smile;
We may girdle day and night
With a halo of delight,
If we keep our hearts singing all the
while.
Keep your heart singing all the while,...
Make the world brighter with a smile,...
Keep the song ringing! lonely hours we may
beguile,
If we keep our hearts singing all the while.

2 If His love is in the soul,
And we yield to His control,
Sweetest music will the lonely hours
beguile;
We may drive the clouds away,
Cheer and bless the darkest day,
If we keep our hearts singing all the
while.

3 How a word of love will cheer,
Kindle hope and banish fear,
Soothe a pain, or take away the
sting of guile;
Oh, how much we all may do,
In the world we travel through,
If we keep our hearts singing all the
while.

325 "FEAR not, I am with thee;"
Blessed golden ray,
Light a star of glory,
Lighting up my way!

Through the clouds of midnight,
This bright promise shone,
" I will never leave thee,
Never will leave thee alone."

No...never alone,..No, never alone ;
He promised never to leave me,
Never to leave me alone.

2 Roses fade around me,
Lilies bloom and die,
Earthly sunbeams vanish—
Radiant still the sky !
Jesus, Rose of Sharon,
Blooming for His own,
Jesus, Heaven's sunshine,
Never will leave me alone.

3 Steps unseen before me,
Hidden dangers near ;
Nearer still my Saviour,
Whisp'ring, " Be of cheer ; "
Joys, like birds of spring-time,
To my heart have flown,
Singing all so sweetly,
" He will not leave me alone."

326 PRECIOUS Saviour, Thou hast
saved me ;
Thine, and only Thine I am ;
Oh, the cleansing blood has reach'd
me !
Glory, glory to the Lamb !

Glory, glory, hallelujah !
Glory, glory to the Lamb !
Oh, the cleansing blood has reach'd me !
Glory, glory to the Lamb !

2 Long my yearning heart was
striving
To obtain this precious rest ;
But when all my struggles ended,
Simply trusting, I was blest.

3 Consecrated to Thy service,
I will live and die for Thee ;
I will witness to Thy glory,
Of salvation, full and free.

4 Glory to the Lord who bought me !
Glory for His saving pow'r !
Glory to the Lord who keeps me !
Glory, glory, evermore !

327 HAVE you heard of that
heavenly home,
Just beyond the rough wilds where
we roam ;
Where the angels of light,

And the saints robed in white,
Lift their voices in song 'round t
throne ?

Where Je..sus is waiting for me,
Where Je..sus is waiting for me,
In those mansions so fair, He has gone
prepare,
Where Jesus is waiting for me....

2 How I long for that beautiful hom
Just beyond the dark vale and t
tomb !
For my loved ones are there,
In those palaces fair,
They are waiting for me by t
throne.

3 I will welcome the dawn of the da
When the trumpet shall call n
away,
To the sweet peaceful rest,
In the home of the blest,
In the light of that radiant thron

328 COME, ye that fear the Lord
Unto me, unto me ;
Come ye that fear the Lord,
Unto me !
I've something good to say
About the narrow way :
For Christ the other day
Saved my soul, saved my soul !
For Christ the other day
Saved my soul !

2 He gave me first to see
What I was, what I was ;
He gave me first to see
What I was !
He gave me first to see
My guilt and misery,
And then He set me free !
Bless His Name ! bless His Name
And then He set me free !
Bless His Name !

3 My old companions said,
" He's undone, he's undone ! "
My old companions said,
" He's undone ! "
My old companions said,
" He's surely going mad ! "
But Jesus makes me glad !
Bless His Name ! bless His Name
But Jesus makes me glad !
Bless His Name !

Some said, " He'll soon give o'er,
　You shall see, you shall see ! "
Some said, " He'll soon give o'er,
　You shall see ! "
But time has passed away,
Since I began to pray,
And I feel His love to-day !
　Bless His Name ! bless His Name !
And I feel His love to-day !
　Bless His Name !

:29 THERE'S an old-fashioned
　　story,
　And an old-fashioned song,
That has gladdened the weary
　Through the ages along ;
In the old upper chamber
　It was joyfully told ;
Oh, 'tis very old-fashioned,
　But as sweet as of old.

h, this old-fashion'd story and this old-
　fashion'd song
a joy to the weary all life's journey along,
or they know, hallelujah! in the city of gold ;
hey will sing it for ever, this sweet story of old.

There's a band of old soldiers,
　That to Jesus belong,
Who have told this old story,
　And have sung this old song ;
In the heat of the battle,
　In the face of the bold,
And to-day they will tell you
　'Tis as sweet as of old.

Oh, the old-fashioned story
　And the old-fashioned song,
O'er the broad earth are rolling,
　Winning souls all along ;
This sweet story of Jesus,
　And this glad song so old,
Shall be heard through the ages,
　In that bright upper fold.

:30 JESUS, Saviour, pilot me
　　Over life's tempestuous sea ;
Unknown waves before me roll,
Hiding rock and treach'rous shoal ;
Chart and compass come from Thee ;
Jesus, Saviour, pilot me.

As a mother stills her child,
Thou canst hush the ocean wild ;
Boist'rous waves obey Thy will,
When Thou say'st to them, " Be still,"
Wondrous Sov'reign of the sea,
Jesus, Saviour, pilot me.

3 When at last I reach the shore,
　And the fearful breakers roar
　'Twixt me and the peaceful rest,
　Then, while leaning on Thy breast,
　May I hear Thee say to me,
　" Fear not, I will pilot thee."

331 WOULD you know why Christ
　　　my Saviour
　Is my constant theme and song ?
Why to seek His loving favour
　Is my joy the whole day long ?

He redeem'd me,...He redeem'd me,..
　How the ransom'd choir repeat it o'er and
　　o'er ;...
He redeem'd me,...He redeem'd me,...
　Glory, glory be to Him for evermore....

2 Oh, the days are full of gladness
　　That I spend in His employ !
　I can banish care and sadness
　　In that song of heav'nly joy.

3 Come, beloved, bow before Him,
　　Seek the pardon of your King,
　That on earth you may adore Him,
　　And with saints in glory sing.

332 MY faith has found a resting-
　　　place,
　Not in device nor creed ;
I trust the ever-living One,
　His wounds for me shall plead.

　I need no other argument,
　I need no other plea ;
　It is enough that Jesus died,
　　And that He died for me.

2 Enough for me that Jesus saves,
　This ends my fear and doubt ;
A sinful soul I come to Him,
　He'll never cast me out.

3 My heart is leaning on the Word,
　The written Word of God ;
Salvation by my Saviour's name,
　Salvation through His blood.

4 My great Physician heals the sick,
　The lost He came to save ;
For me His precious blood He shed,
　For me His life He gave.

333 WHEN we have come to
　　　Jordan's tide,
　There'll be no dark river there ;
With Jesus standing close beside,
　There'll be no dark river there.

His boundless grace shall light the place,
With beams of glory fair ;
And in the sunshine from His face,
There'll be no dark river there.

> There'll be no dark river there,
> There'll be no dark river there ;
> Upon His breast we'll sweetly rest,
> There'll be no dark river there.

2 With angels bending from above,
There'll be no dark river there ;
In fellowship with Him we love,
There'll be no dark river there.
His word divine shall brightly shine,
His endless life we'll share ;
When all to Jesus we resign,
There'll be no dark river there.

3 And when we've crossed the mystic tide,
There'll be no dark river there ;
When we have reached the other side,
There'll be no dark river there.
And hand in hand we'll walk the strand
With loved ones bright and fair ;
For in that happy heav'nly land,
There'll be no dark river there.

4 Let this blest thought fresh courage give,
There'll be no dark river there ;
In that bright home of peace and love,
There'll be no dark river there.
The gates ajar, we see afar,
Beyond this world of care ;
Though Jordan's stream may us divide,
There'll be no dark river there.

334 OH, scatter seeds of loving deeds
Along the fertile field,
For grain will grow from what you sow,
And fruitful harvest yield.

> Then day by day..along your way..
> The seeds of pro..mise cast,..
> That ripened grain..from hill and plain,..
> Be gathered home..at last...

2 Tho' sown in tears thro' weary years,
The seed will surely live ;
Tho' great the cost, it is not lost,
For God will fruitage give.

3 The harvest home of God will come
And after toil and care,
With joy untold your sheaves of gol
Will all be garner'd there.

335 IN the Christian's home i
glory,
There remains a land of rest,
Where the Saviour's gone before me
To fulfil my soul's request.

> On the other side of Jordan,
> In the sweet fields of Eden,
> Where the Tree of Life is blooming,
> There is rest for you ;
> There is rest for the weary,
> There is rest for you !

2 He is fitting up my mansion,
Which eternally shall stand ;
There my stay shall not be transient
In that holy, happy land.

3 Pain nor sickness e'er can enter,
Grief nor woe my lot shall share ;
But in that celestial centre,
I a crown of life shall wear.

4 Death itself shall then be vanquished
And its sting shall be withdrawn
Shout with gladness, O ye ransomed
Hail with joy the happy morn !

5 Sing, O sing, ye heirs of glory !
Shout your triumphs as you go !
Zion's gates will open to you—
You shall find an entrance through.

336 LOVED with everlasting love
Led by grace that love to know
Spirit, breathing from above,
Thou hast taught me it is so.
Oh this full and perfect peace !
Oh this transport all divine !
In a love which cannot cease,
I am His, and He is mine.

> In a love, which cannot cease,
> I am His, and He is mine.

2 Heaven above is softer blue,
Earth around is sweeter green !
Something lives in every hue
Christless eyes have never seen ;
Birds with gladder songs o'erflow,
Flowers with deeper beautie
Since I know as *now* I know,   [shine
I am His, and He is mine.

> Since I know, as now I know,
> I am His, and He is mine.

Things that once were wild alarms
Cannot now disturb my rest ;
Closed in everlasting arms,
Pillowed on the loving breast,
Oh to lie for ever here,
Doubt and care and self resign,
While He whispers in my ear—
I am His, and He is mine.

<small>While He whispers in my ear—
I am His, and He is mine !</small>

His for ever, only His ;
Who the Lord and me shall part ?
Ah, with what a rest of bliss
Christ can fill the loving heart !
Heaven and earth may fade and flee,
First-born light in gloom decline ;
But, while God and I shall be,
I am His, and He is mine.

<small>But, while God and I shall be,
I am His, and He is mine !</small>

37 BLESSED Lily of the Valley,
oh, how fair is He !
He is mine,....I am His ;....
Sweeter than the angels' music is
His voice to me,
He is mine,....I am His !....
Where the lilies fair are blooming
by the waters calm,
There He leads me and upholds me
by His strong right arm ;
All the air is love around me, I can
feel no harm,
He is mine,....I am His.....

<small>il - - y of the Valley, He..is mine !
Lil - - y of the Valley, I am His !
weeter than the angels' music is His voice to me,
He is mine,..I am His !...</small>

Let me sing of all His mercies, of
His kindness true,
He is mine,....I am His ;....
Fresh at morn, and in the evening,
comes a blessing new,
He is mine,....I am His !....
With the deep'ning shadows comes a
whisper, " Safely rest !
Sleep in peace, for I am near thee,
naught shall thee molest ;
I will linger till the morning, Keeper,
Friend, and Guest,"
He is mine,....I am His.....

Though He lead me through the
valley of the shade of death,
He is mine,....I am His ;....

Should I fear when, oh, so tenderly,
He whispereth,
He is mine,....I am His ;....
For the sunshine of His presence
doth illume the night,
And He leads me through the valley
to the mountain height ;
Out of bondage, into freedom, into
cloudless light,
He is mine,....I am His.....

338 SOME day, I know not when
'twill be,
The angel of death will come to me ;
But this I know, if Christ be near,
Old Jordan's waves I will not fear.

2 My sins He long ago forgave,
And still I feel His pow'r to save ;
And if I keep the witness clear,
Old Jordan's waves I will not fear.

3 O'er me has sorrow's storm oft swept,
Safe from the danger me He's kept ;
If still I trust this Friend so dear,
Old Jordan's waves I will not fear.

4 My lov'd ones they have cross'd the tide,
But safely cross'd with Christ their
guide ;
They sweetly whisper in my ear,
Old Jordan's waves I do not fear.

5 So, if at death's cold brink I stand,
My hand clasped in the Saviour's hand;
I, too, shall shout in tones so clear,
Old Jordan's waves I do not fear.

339 TRUE-HEARTED, whole-
hearted, faithful and loyal,
King of our lives, by Thy grace
we will be ! [royal,
Under the standard exalted and
Strong in Thy strength we will
battle for Thee.

<small>Peal out the watchword ! silence it never !
Song of our spirit rejoicing and free ;
Peal out the watchword ! loyal for ever,
King of our lives, by Thy grace we will be !</small>

2 True-hearted, whole-hearted, fullest
allegiance
Yielding henceforth to our glorious
King :
Valiant endeavour and loving obed-
ience,
Freely and joyfully now would we
bring.

3 True-hearted, whole-hearted, Saviour
    all glorious !
  Take Thy great power and reign
    there alone ;
  Over our wills and affections vic-
    torious,
  Freely surrender'd and wholly
    Thine own.

340 A WORTHY soldier I would
      be
  Of Christ, who gave Himself for me,
    Obeying His command ;
  And with the gospel shield and sword,
  For truth and right, with Christ
    my Lord,
    God helping me, I'll stand.

    God helping me, I'll stand,....
    With His unyielding band ;
    All times and ev'rywhere for Christ,
    God helping me, I'll stand.

2 When over me shall grandly wave
  The banner of the martyred brave,
    God's faithful, steadfast band ;
  Beneath which none e'er fought in
    vain,
  All foes and dangers I'll disdain,
    God helping me, I'll stand.

3 Though I be weary in the fight,
  And Satan's legions, in their spite
    Attack on ev'ry hand, [Friend,
  I'll stand by Christ, my faithful
  And steadily, unto the end,
    God helping me, I'll stand.

341 IN the fight, say, does your
      heart grow weary ?
  Do you find your path is rough and
    thorny,
  And above the sky is dark and
    stormy ?
    Never mind : go on !
  Lay aside all fear, and onward
    pressing,
  Bravely fight, and God will give
    His blessing ;
  Though the war at times may prove
    distressing,
    Never mind : go on.

    When the road we tread is rough, let us
      bear in mind,
    In our Saviour strength enough we may
      always find ;
    Tho' the fighting may be tough, let our
      motto be :
      Go on,..go on..to vict'ry.

2 Faithful be, delaying not to follow
  Where Christ leads, though it ma
    be through sorrow ;
  If the strife should fiercer grow t
    morrow,
    Never mind : go on.
  Cheerful be, it will your burde
    lighten,
  One glad heart will always othe
    brighten ;
  Though the strife the coward's so
    may frighten,
    Never mind : go on !

3 When down-hearted, look away
    Jesus,
  Who for you did shed His bloo
    most precious ;
  Let us say, though all the wor
    should hate us,
    Never mind : go on !
  Do your best in fighting for yo
    Saviour,
  For His sake, fear not to lose men
    favour,
  If beside you should a comrad
    waver,
    Never mind : go on !

342 THERE'S a place in heav
      prepared for me,
  When the toils of this life are o'e
  Where the saints, robed in whit
    shall for ever be,
  Singing praises for evermore.

    Jesus promised me a home over there,
    Jesus promised me a home over there ;
    No more sickness, sorrow, pain or death
    Jesus promised me a home over there.

2 In my Father's home are mansio
    bright,
  Jesus says it, and I know 'tis tru
  There's a home for me in that lan
    of light :
  Brother, sister, there is one f
    you.

3 Many dear ones we loved are befo
    the throne,
  In that happy, happy home
    high ;
  I shall walk with them through t
    streets of gold,
  I shall wear a starry crown
    and by.

In that home above, beyond the skies,
Free from sickness, pain, and
 death I'll be,
There with Jesus to reign for evermore,
 Throughout all eternity.

343 TELL it to Jesus, He understands thee,
Reads all the secret intents of thy
 heart ;
Foes may misjudge and friends may
 mistake thee,
 He will not deal with thee but as
 thou art.

Tell it to Jesus, He understands thee,
 What is thy gain, and what is thy loss ;
While thou art His no harm can befall thee,
 Tell out thy heart at the foot of His Cross.

Tell it to Jesus, He understands thee,
 Knows all thy sorrows, and sees
 all thy tears ;
Knows all the hidden pow'rs that
 withstand thee,
 Knows all thy tremblings, thy
 doubts and thy fears.

Tell it to Jesus, He understands thee,
 He can explain ev'ry mystery of
 life ;
He can unravel tangles that try thee,
 He can speak peace 'midst thy
 turmoil and strife.

Tell it to Jesus, He understands thee,
 Seeks by His Spirit to perfect thy
 soul ;
Sorrows and trials He sends to refine
 thee,
 Tell Him thy case, not in part, but
 in whole.

Tell it to Jesus, He understands thee,
 Hide not thy faults, and excuse
 not thy sin ;
For in the day of account He will
 greet thee,
 Not as thou art from without, but
 within.

344 IS your life a channel of
 blessing ? [you ?
Is the love of God flowing thro'
Are you telling the lost of the
 Saviour ?
Are you ready His service to do ?

Make me a channel of blessing to-day,
Make me a channel of blessing, I pray ;
My life possessing, my service blessing,
Make me a channel of blessing to-day.

2 Is your life a channel of blessing ?
 Are you burdened for those that
 are lost ?
Have you urged upon those who are
 straying,
 The Saviour who died on the Cross?

3 Is your life a channel of blessing ?
 Is it daily telling for Him ?
Have you spoken the word of
 salvation
 To those who are dying in sin ?

4 We cannot be channels of blessing
 If our lives are not free from all
 sin ;
We will barriers be and a hindrance
 To those we are trying to win.

345 THE blood has always precious
 been,
 'Tis precious now to me ;
Through it alone my soul has rest,
 From fear and doubt set free.

Oh, wondrous is the crimson tide
 Which from my Saviour flowed ;
And still in heav'n my song shall be,
 The precious, precious blood.

2 I will remember now no more,
 God's faithful Word has said,
The follies and the sins of him
 For whom My Son has bled.

3 Not all my well-remembered sins
 Can startle or dismay ;
The precious blood atones for all,
 And bears my guilt away.

4 Perhaps this feeble frame of mine
 Will soon in sickness lie,
But, resting on the precious blood,
 How peacefully I'll die.

346 SOW flowers, and flowers will
 blossom
 Around you wherever you go ;
Sow weeds, and of weeds reap the
 harvest,
 You'll reap whatsoever you sow.

You'll reap whatsoever you sow,...
You'll reap whatsoever you sow,...
The harvest is certainly coming,
You'll reap whatsoever you sow.

2 Sow blessings, and blessings will
  ripen,
    Sow hatred, and hatred will grow;
  Sow mercy, and reap sweet compassion,
    You'll reap whatsoever you sow.

3 Sow love, and its sweetness up-
  rising
    Shall fill all your heart with its glow;
  Sow hope, and receive its fruition,
    You'll reap whatsoever you sow.

4 In faith sow the Word of the Master,
    A blessing He'll surely bestow ;
  And souls shine like stars for your
  crowning,
    You'll reap whatsoever you sow.

5 Preach Christ in His wonderful
  fulness,
    That all His salvation may know;
  Reap life through the ages eternal,
    You'll reap whatsoever you sow.

347 I HAVE a Friend, a precious
  Friend,
    O how He loves me ;
  He says His love will never end,
    O how He loves me.

    O how He loves me !
    O how He loves me !
    I know not why, I only cry,
    O how He loves me !

2 Why He should come, I cannot tell,
    O how He loves me ;
  In my poor broken heart to dwell,
    O how He loves me.

3 He died to save my soul from death,
    O how He loves me ;
  I'll praise Him while He gives me
  breath,
    O how He loves me.

4 He walks with me along life's road,
    O how He loves me ;
  He carries ev'ry heavy load,
    O how He loves me.

5 He has a home prepared for me,
    O how He loves me ;
  With Him I'll spend eternity,
    O how He loves me.

348 FOR ever with the Lord !
    Amen, so let it be !
  Life from the dead is in that word ;
    'Tis immortality.
  Here in the body pent,
    Absent from Him I roam ;
  Yet nightly pitch my moving tent,
    A day's march nearer home.
        Nearer home, nearer home,
        A day's march nearer home.

2 My Father's house on high,
    Home of my soul, how near
  At times to faith's foreseeing eye,
    Thy golden gates appear !
  My thirsty spirit faints
    To reach the land I love,
  The bright inheritance of saints—
    Jerusalem above.

3 For ever with the Lord !
    Father, if 'tis Thy will,
  The promise of that faithful word,
    E'en here to me fulfil.
  Be Thou at my right hand,
    Then can I never fail ;
  Uphold Thou me, so I shall stand,
    Fight, and I must prevail.

4 So when my latest breath
    Shall rend the vail in twain,
  By death I shall escape from death
    And life eternal gain.
  Knowing as I am known,
    How shall I love that word !
  And oft repeat before the throne,
    For ever with the Lord !

349 I'VE cast my heavy burden
    down on Canaan's happ
  shore,
    I'm living where the healin
    waters flow ;....
  I'll wander in the wilderness o
  doubt and sin no more ;
    I'm living where the healin
    waters flow.....
  Living on the shore. I'm living on the shore,
  I'm living where the healing waters flow...

2 With Israel's trusting children I'r
    rejoicing on my way,
    I'm living where the healin
    waters flow ;....
  The cloudy, fiery pillar is m
  guiding light to-day ;
    I'm living where the healin
    waters flow.....

My hung'ring soul is satisfied with
 manna from above,
 I'm living where the healing
  waters flow ;....
No more I thirst, the rock I've found,
 that fount of endless love ;
 I'm living where the healing
  waters flow.....

I'm singing "Hallelujah," safely
 anchored is my soul,
 I'm living where the healing
  waters flow ;....
I'm resting on His promises, the
 blood has made me whole ;
 I'm living where the healing
  waters flow.....

50 WHEN Israel out of bondage
   came,
 A sea before them lay ;
The Lord reach'd down His mighty
  hand,
 And rolled the sea away.

Then forward still, 'tis Jehovah's will,
 Tho' the billows dash and spray ;
With a conqu'ring tread we will push ahead,
 He'll roll the sea away.

Before me was a sea of sin,
 So great I feared to pray ;
My heart's desire the Saviour read,
 And rolled the sea away.

When sorrows dark, like stormy
  waves,
 Were dashing o'er my way ;
Again the Lord in mercy came,
 And rolled the sea away.

And when I reach the sea of death,
 For needed grace I'll pray ;
I know the Lord will quickly come,
 And roll the sea away.

51 I ONCE was a stranger
   To grace and to God,
I knew not my danger
 And felt not my load ;
Though friends spoke in rapture
 Of Christ on the tree,
Jehovah Tsidkenu
 Was nothing to me.

Like tears from the daughters
 Of Zion that roll,
I wept when the waters
 Went over His soul ;

Yet thought not that my sins
 Had nailed to the tree,
Jehovah Tsidkenu—
 'Twas nothing to me.

3 When free grace awoke me
 By light from on high,
Then legal fears shook me,
 I trembled to die ;
No refuge, no safety,
 In self could I see,
Jehovah Tsidkenu
 My Saviour must be.

4 My terrors all vanished
 Before the sweet name,
My guilty fears banished,
 With boldness I came
To drink at the fountain,
 Life-giving and free,
Jehovah Tsidkenu
 Is all things to me.

5 E'en treading the valley,
 The shadow of death,
This watchword shall rally
 My faltering breath ;
For when from life's fever
 My God sets me free,
Jehovah Tsidkenu
 My death-song shall be.

352 LOW in the grave He lay,
   Jesus, my Saviour !
 Waiting the coming day—
  Jesus, my Lord !

Up from the grave He arose,....
With a mighty triumph o'er His foes ;...
He arose a Victor from the dark domain,
And He lives for ever with His saints to reign;
 He arose !...He arose !...
 Hallelujah ! Christ arose !

2 Vainly they watch His bed—
  Jesus, my Saviour !
Vainly they seal the dead—
  Jesus, my Lord !

3 Death cannot keep his prey—
  Jesus, my Saviour !
He tore the bars away—
  Jesus, my Lord !

353 WHO can wash a sinner's
   guilt away ?
 There is no one like the Saviour,
  hallelujah !

Who can turn his darkness into day ?
There is no one like the Saviour,
hallelujah !

Oh, glory, glory hallelujah !
There is no one like the Saviour, hallelujah !
While we live or die, in the earth or sky,
There is no one like the Saviour, hallelujah !

2 When we're lowly bent with grief
and care,
There is no one like the Saviour,
hallelujah !
He speaks and the sunbeams linger
there,
There is no one like the Saviour,
hallelujah.

3 When we're tempest tossed upon
life's deep,
There is no one like the Saviour,
hallelujah !
He speaks, and the wild waves
hush to sleep,
There is no one like the Saviour,
hallelujah !

4 When we feel the icy touch of death,
There is no one like the Saviour,
hallelujah !
He will take us at our closing breath,
There is no one like the Saviour,
hallelujah.

5 Over in that blest home of the soul,
There is no one like the Saviour,
hallelujah !
This shall be our song while ages roll,
There is no one like the Saviour,
hallelujah.

354 WHEN I see life's golden sunset lighting up the rosy west,
When the shadows backward o'er
my way are cast,
I shall look upon that moment as
the one supremely blest ;
I'm going home at last.

I'm going home at last,....
I'm going home at last ;....
When my work on earth is ended and my
race below is run,
I'm going home at last.

2 Tho' the road at times was weary
over which my feet have trod,
Tho' through many tribulations
I have passed ;
Yet I soon will reach my mansion
in the city of our God ;
I'm going home at last.

3 When I pass down through th[e]
valley and the shadow of th[e]
dead,
To my blessed Saviour's hand
will hold fast ;
He has promised to go with me, [a]
my soul will have no dread ;
I'm going home at last.

355 WHEN the troubles gather
And the billows roll,
Dark the way before you,
Cares oppress the soul ;
There is blessed sunshine
Just beyond your view ;
Oft 'tis but a trial
You are going through.

See the sunlight, shining bright and clear ;
Blessed sunlight drives away all fear ;
Look above you, clouds will disappear ;
Put your trust in Jesus, He is ever near.

2 Though you cannot fathom
Why you're called to bear
All the heavy burdens
That you cannot share ;
Keep the Cross before you
In the darkest day ;
Put your trust in Jesus
All along the way.

3 Go, with faith, to conquer
Trials that appear ;
Know that Christ your Saviour
With His help is near.
Ne'er give up the battle,
Hard though it may be,
For your Lord has promised
You the victory.

4 Though severe the conflict,
And the anguish deep ;
Though the trial's heavy
That may o'er you sweep ;
God is always near you,
Giving strength to bear
All the heavy burdens
When they shall appear.

5 Tried and found not wanting,
Will the Master say ;
Tried, yet ever faithful
All along life's way ;
Tried as in the furnace
Of refining fire,
You shall see the triumph
Of your heart's desire.

56 THEY tell me there are dangers
 In the path my feet must tread,
But they cannot see the glory
 That is shining round my head.

Oh, 'tis Jesus leads my footsteps,
He has made my heart His own,
For I would not dare to journey
Thro' the wide, wide world alone.

They tell me life has trials,
 And the fairest hopes will flee,
But I trust my all to Jesus,
 For I know He cares for me.

I know my heart is sinful,
 And my love is all too small,
But with Jesus' arms around me
 I shall win and conquer all.

57 COME, ye that love the Lord,
 And let your joys be known ;
Join in a song with sweet accord,
 And thus surround the throne.

We're marching to Zion,
Beautiful, beautiful Zion ;
We're marching upward to Zion,
The beautiful city of God.

Let those refuse to sing
 Who never knew our God ;
But children of the heav'nly King
 Must speak their joys abroad.

The hill of Zion yields
 A thousand sacred sweets ;
Before we reach the heav'nly fields,
 Or walk the golden streets.

Then let our songs abound
 And ev'ry tear be dry ;
We're marching through Immanuel's
 ground,
To fairer worlds on high.

58 STANDING like a lighthouse
 on the shores of time,
Looking o'er the waves of darkness,
 sin, and crime,
Open up your windows, there's a
 work sublime :
Let the Gospel light shine out.

Let the Gospel light shine out...
Let the Gospel light shine out...
While your lamp is burning, keep the win-
 dows clean,
Let the Gospel light shine out.

There are human shipwrecks lying
 all around !
O what moral darkness everywhere
 is found !

Warn some other vessels off from
 dang'rous ground :
Let the Gospel light shine out.

3 Do not let the bushel cover up your
 light ;
Keep your lamp in order, trimmed
 and burning bright ;
Try to be a blessing, brighten up
 the night :
Let the Gospel light shine out.

4 Try to live for Jesus till this life is o'er,
For along this pathway you will pass
 no more ;
Till He bids you welcome on the
 other shore,
Let the Gospel light shine out.

359 WOULD you always cheerful be?
 Let the blessed sunlight in ;
Would you bid the darkness flee ?
 Let the blessed sunlight in.

Let the blessed sunlight, sunlight in,
Let the blessed sunlight in ;...
Would you never weary when the days are
 dreary,
Let the blessed sunlight in...

2 Would you brighten dreary days ?
 Let the blessed sunlight in ;
Would you fill your heart with praise?
 Let the blessed sunlight in.

3 Would you ease a burden'd heart ?
 Let the blessed sunlight in ;
Would you joy and strength impart?
 Let the blessed sunlight in.

4 Would you speed the truth abroad ?
 Let the blessed sunlight in ;
Would you bring the world to God ?
 Let the blessed sunlight in.

360 I'VE found a Friend in Jesus,
 He's everything to me,
He's the Fairest of Ten Thousand
 to my soul ;   [I see
The Lily of the Valley, in Him alone
All I need to cleanse and make me
 fully whole ;
In sorrow He's my comfort, in
 trouble He's my stay,   [roll.
He tells me ev'ry care on Him to
He's the Lily of the Valley, the
 Bright and Morning Star,
He's the Fairest of Ten Thousand
 to my soul.

In sorrow He's my comfort, in trouble He's
my stay,
He tells me ev'ry care on Him to roll.
He's the Lily of the Valley, the Bright and
Morning Star,
He's the Fairest of Ten Thousand to my soul.

2 He all my grief has taken, and all
my sorrows borne,
In temptation He's my strong and
mighty tower ;
I've all for Him forsaken, I've all my
idols torn
From my heart, and now He keeps
me by His pow'r.
Though all the world forsake me,
and Satan tempt me sore,
Through Jesus I shall safely reach
the goal ;
He's the Lily of the Valley, the
Bright and Morning Star,
He's the Fairest of Ten Thousand
to my soul.

3 He'll never, never leave me, nor yet
forsake me here,
While I live by faith and do His
blessed will ;
A wall of fire about me, I've nothing
now to fear,
With His manna He my hungry
soul shall fill ;
Then sweeping up to glory I'll see
His blessed face,   [flow ;
Where rivers of delight shall ever
He's the Lily of the Valley, the
Bright and Morning Star,
He's the Fairest of Ten Thousand
to my soul.

361 ONE little hour for watching
with the Master,
Eternal years to walk with Him
in white ;
One little hour to bravely meet
disaster,
Eternal years to reign with Him
in light.
Then souls, be brave, and watch until the
morrow !
Awake ! arise ! your lamps of purpose trim !
Your Saviour speaks across the night of sorrow :
Can ye not watch one little hour with Him ?

2 One little hour to suffer scorn and
losses,
Eternal years beyond earth's
cruel frowns ;

One little hour to carry heavy cross
Eternal years to wear unfadi
crowns.

3 One little hour for weary toils an
trials,   [ful res
Eternal years for calm and peac
One little hour for patient se
denials,   [bles
Eternal years of life where life

362 SAVED by grace alone, God
own Word believing ;
It is glory all the way !
Walking in the light, daily gra
receiving :
It is glory all the way !
Glo - - ry ! glo - - ry ! it is glory all the way.
Glo - - ry ! glo - - ry ! it is glory all the way.

2 Not a care have I since my Savio
It is glory all the way !   [careth
Guided by His eye, while with n
He fareth,
It is glory all the way !

3 Sever'd from the world His de
name confessing :
It is glory all the way !
Taking up the Cross, sharing in th
blessing :
It is glory all the way !

4 Sinner, put your trust in this lovin
Saviour :
It is glory all the way !
Freely He forgives all our pa
behaviour :
It is glory all the way !

363 I KNOW I love Thee bette
Lord,
Than any earthly joy,
For Thou hast given me the peac
Which nothing can destroy.
The half has never yet been told,....
Of love so full and free ;
The half has never yet been told,....
The blood it cleanseth me.....

2 I know that Thou art nearer still
Than any earthly throng,
And sweeter is the thought of The
Than any lovely song.

3 Thou hast put gladness in my hear
Then well may I be glad ;
Without the secret of Thy love
I could not but be sad.

O Saviour, precious Saviour mine !
  What will Thy presence be,
If such a life of joy can crown
  Our walk on earth with Thee ?

64   WHEN my life work is ended
      and I cross the swelling tide,
When the bright and glorious
  morning I shall see ;
I shall know my Redeemer when I
  reach the other side,
And His smile will be the first to
  welcome me.

I shall know...Him, I shall know Him,
  As redeem'd by His side I shall stand.
I shall know...Him, I shall know Him
  By the print of the nails in His hand.

Oh, the soul-thrilling rapture when
  I view His blessed face
    And the lustre of His kindly beam-
      ing eye ;
How my full heart will praise Him
  for the mercy, love, and grace,
    That prepares me for a mansion
    in the sky.

Oh, the dear ones in glory, how they
  beckon me to come,
    And our parting at the river I
    recall ;
To the sweet vales of Eden they will
  sing my welcome home,
    But I long to meet my Saviour
    first of all.

Thro' the gates to the city in a robe
  of spotless white,
    He will lead me where no tears
    shall ever fall ;
In the glad song of ages I shall
  mingle with delight,
    But I long to meet my Saviour
    first of all.

65   THE prize is set before us,
    To win, His words implore us ;
The eye of God is o'er us,
  From on high, from on high !
His loving tones are calling,
While sin is dark, appalling ;
'Tis Jesus gently calling,
  He is nigh, He is nigh.

By-and-by we shall meet Him,
By-and-by we shall greet Him,
And with Jesus reign in glory, by-and-by.

2 We'll follow where He leadeth,
  We'll pasture where He feedeth,
  We'll yield to Him who pleadeth,
    From on high, from on high !
Then nought from Him shall sever,
Our hope shall brighten ever,
And faith shall fail us never,
  He is nigh, He is nigh.

3 Our home is bright above us,
No trials dark to move us,
But Jesus dear to love us,
  There on high, there on high !
We'll give Him best endeavour,
And praise His name for ever,
His precious ones can never,
  Never die, never die.

366   WHEN all my labours and
      trials are o'er,
And I am safe on that beautiful
  shore,
Just to be near the dear Lord I adore,
  Will thro' the ages be glory for me.

Oh, that will be...glory for me,...
Glory for me,...glory for me,...
When by His grace I shall look on His face,
That will be glory, be glory for me.

2 When by the gift of His infinite
    grace,
I am accorded in heaven a place,
Just to be there and to look on His
  face,
  Will thro' the ages be glory for me.

3 Friends will be there I have lov'd
    long ago ;
Joy like a river around me will flow ;
Yet, just a smile from my Saviour, I
  know,
  Will thro' the ages be glory for me.

367   THOU my everlasting portion,
      More than friend or life to
      me,
All along my pilgrim journey,
  Saviour, let me walk with Thee

Close to Thee, close to Thee,
Close to Thee, close to Thee,
All along my pilgrim journey,
Saviour, let me walk with Thee.

2 Not for ease or worldly pleasure,
  Nor for fame my prayer shall be ;
Gladly will I toil and suffer,
  Only let me walk with Thee.

Close to Thee, close to Thee,
Close to Thee, close to Thee,
Gladly will I toil and suffer,
Only let me walk with Thee.

3 Lead me through this vale of shadows,
　Bear me o'er life's fitful sea ;
Then the gate of life eternal
　May I enter, Lord, with Thee.

Close to Thee, close to Thee,
Close to Thee, close to Thee ;
Then the gate of life eternal
May I enter, Lord, with Thee.

368　SINCE Christ my soul from sin
　　　　set free,
This world has been a heav'n to me,
And 'mid earth's sorrow and its woe,
'Tis heav'n my Jesus here to know.

Oh hallelujah, yes, 'tis heav'n,
'Tis heav'n to know my sins forgiv'n ;
On land or sea, what matters where,
Where Jesus is, 'tis heav'n there.

2 Once heaven seemed a far-off place,
Till Jesus showed His smiling face ;
Now it's begun within my soul,
'Twill last while endless ages roll.

3 What matter where on earth we
　dwell ?
On mountain top, or in the dell ?
In cottage or in mansion fair,
Where Jesus is, 'tis heaven there.

369　TAKE the world, but give me
　　　　Jesus,
All its joys are but a name,
But His love abideth ever,
　Thro' eternal years the same.

Oh, the height and depth of mercy !
　Oh ! the length and breadth of love !
Oh, the fulness of redemption,
　Pledge of endless life above.

2 Take the world, but give me Jesus,
Sweetest comfort of my soul ;
With my Saviour watching o'er me
I can sing, though billows roll.

3 Take the world, but give me Jesus,
Let me view His constant smile ;
Then throughout my pilgrim journey
Light will cheer me all the while.

4 Take the world, but give me Jesus,
In His Cross my trust shall be,
Till, with clearer, brighter vision,
Face to face my Lord I see.

370　SAVIOUR, lead me, lest
　　　　stray,....
Gently lead me all the way ;....
I am safe when by Thy side,....
I would in Thy love abide.....

Lead me, lead me,
　Saviour, lead me, lest I stray ;....
Gently down the stream of time,....
　Lead me, Saviour, all the way.....

2 Thou, the refuge of my soul,....
When life's stormy billows roll,...
I am safe when Thou art nigh,....
All my hopes on Thee rely.....

3 Saviour, lead me then at last,....
When the storm of life is past,....
To the land of endless day,....
Where all tears are wiped away....

371　A WONDERFUL Saviour
　　　　Jesus, my Lord,
A wonderful Saviour to me ;
He hideth my soul in the cleft of t
　rock,
　Where rivers of pleasure I see.

He hideth my soul in the cleft of the rock,
　That shadows a dry thirsty land ;
He hideth my life in the depths of His love
　And covers me there with His hand.

2 A wonderful Saviour is Jesus, m
　Lord,
He taketh my burden away ;
He holdeth me up, and I shall n
　be mov'd,
He giveth me strength as my da

3 With numberless blessings eac
　moments He crowns
　And fill'd with His fulness divin
I sing in my rapture, oh, glory to Go
For such a Redeemer as mine !

4 When cloth'd in His brightne
　transported I rise,
To meet Him in clouds of the sk
His perfect salvation, His wonderf
　love,　　　　　　　　　　[hig
I'll shout with the millions (

372　JERUSALEM the golden,
　　　　With milk and honey bles
Beneath thy contemplation
　Sink heart and voice opprest ;
I know not, oh ! I know not,
　What joys await us there,
What radiancy of glory,
　What bliss beyond compare.

They stand, those halls of Zion,
    All jubilant with song ;
And bright with many an angel,
    And all the martyr throng ;
The Prince is ever in them,
    The daylight is serene,
The pastures of the blessed
    Are deck'd in glorious sheen.

There is the throne of David,
    And there, from care releas'd,
The shout of them that triumph,
    The song of them that feast ;
And they who, with their Leader,
    Have conquer'd in the fight,
For ever and for ever
    Are cloth'd in robes of white.

Oh, sweet and blessed country,
    The home of God's elect !
Oh, sweet and blessed country,
    That eager hearts expect !
Jesus, in mercy bring us
    To that dear land of rest,
Who art, with God the Father,
    And Spirit, ever blest.

373 O THE grace of God is bound-
      less,
    It is like a mighty sea,
And it rolls on through the ages,
    Bearing love to you and me ;
But the Lord's so great in goodness,
    That He opens heav'n to view,
And not only gives us mercy,
    But He gives us glory too.

    There's grace...and glory too,...
    There's grace...and glory too ;...
    There's grace below for weal or woe,
    And then there's glory too.

2 There is grace for each temptation,
    There is strength for ev'ry day,
There's a lift for ev'ry burden
    That we carry on the way,
There's a refuge from the tempest,
    There is help for all we do.
And when we shall end the journey,
    We will find there's glory too.

3 For the grace that God has given,
    I will praise Him in my song :
I will love Him and will serve Him
    While my days of life prolong ;
And when I shall get to heaven,
    And my journey I review,
Then I'll bless His name for ever,
    That there's grace and glory too.

374 IN the shadow of His wings
      There is rest, sweet rest ;
There is rest from care and labour,
There is rest for friend and neighbour;
    In the shadow of His wings
    There is rest, sweet rest ;
    In the shadow of His wings
    There is rest.....

    There is rest ! sweet rest !
    There is peace ! sweet peace !
    There is joy, glad joy,
    In the shadow of His wings !...

2 In the shadow of His wings
    There is peace, sweet peace ;
Peace that passeth understanding,
Peace, sweet peace, that knows no
    ending ;
    In the shadow of His wings
    There is peace, sweet peace,
    In the shadow of His wings
    There is peace.....

3 In the shadow of His wings
    There is joy, glad joy ;
There is joy to tell the story,
Joy exceeding, full of glory ;
    In the shadow of His wings
    There is joy, glad joy,
    In the shadow of His wings
    There is joy.....

375 TO that summer land up
      yonder,
    Where the angels ever sing
Hallelujahs to the Saviour,
    Sweet hosannahs to the King ;
We are marching swiftly onward,
    Guided by a Father's hand,
Thro' this world of sin and sorrow,
    To that happy summer-land.

    Oh,...the joy when we get there,...
    Golden crowns of life to wear,...
    In that happy land so fair,
    In that summer land up yonder.

2 To that summer land up yonder
    Some are going ev'ry day,
And the time is drawing nearer
    When we, too, shall go away ;
We are going straight to Jesus,
    There to join the ransom'd band,
We will praise His name for ever,
    In that happy summer land.

3 In that summer land up yonder,
    There's a place prepared for all
Who are trusting in the Saviour,
    Who will listen to His call ;

And the happy time is coming
  When the Lord shall give command,
And we'll leave this world for ever,
  For that happy summer land.

376 WHEN you start for the land
    of heavenly rest,
  Keep close to Jesus all the way ;
For He is the Guide, and He knows
    the way best,
  Keep close to Jesus all the way.

Keep close to Jesus, keep close to Jesus,
  Keep close to Jesus all the way ;
By day or by night never turn from the right,
  Keep close to Jesus all the way.

2 Never mind the storms or trials as
    you go.
  Keep close to Jesus all the way ;
'Tis a comfort and joy His favour
    to know,
  Keep close to Jesus all the way.

3 To be safe from the darts of the evil
    one,
  Keep close to Jesus all the way ;
Take the shield of faith till the
    vict'ry is won,
  Keep close to Jesus all the way.

4 We shall reach our home in heaven
    by and by,
  Keep close to Jesus all the way ;
Where to those we love we'll never
    say " good-bye,"
  Keep close to Jesus all the way.

377 WHAT a fellowship, what a
    joy divine,
  Leaning on the everlasting arms ;
What a blessedness, what a peace
    is mine,
  Leaning on the everlasting arms.

Lean - - ing, lean - - ing,
  Safe and secure from all alarms,
Lean - - ing, lean - - ing,
  Leaning on the everlasting arms.

2 Oh, how sweet to walk in this pilgrim
    way,
  Leaning on the everlasting arms ;
Oh, how bright the path grows from
    day to day,
  Leaning on the everlasting arms.

3 What have I to dread, what have I
    to fear,
  Leaning on the everlasting arms ?
I have blessed peace with my Lord
    so near,
  Leaning on the everlasting arms.

378 THERE comes to my hea
    one sweet strain,....
A glad and a joyous refrain,....
I sing it again and again,   [lov
  Sweet peace, the gift of God

Peace, peace, sweet peace,
  Wonderful gift from above ;
Oh, wonderful, wonderful peace,
  Sweet peace, the gift of God's love.

2 By Christ on the Cross peace w
    made,....
My debt by His death was all paid,.
No other foundation is laid
  For peace, the gift of God's love.

3 When Jesus, as Lord, I ha
    crown'd,....
My heart with this peace di
    abound,....
In Him the rich blessing I found,
  Sweet peace, the gift of God
    love.

4 In Jesus for peace I abide,....
  And as I keep close to His side,.
There's nothing but peace dot
    betide,
  Sweet peace, the gift of God's lov

379 I HAVE a song I love to sin
    Since I have been redeemed
Of my Redeemer, Saviour, King,
  Since I have been redeemed.

Since I...have been redeemed,...
Since I...have been redeemed,...
  I will glory in His Name.
Since I...have been redeemed,...
  I will glory in the Saviour's Name.

2 I have a Christ that satisfies,
    Since I have been redeemed ;
To do His will my highest prize,
    Since I have been redeemed.

3 I have a witness bright and clear,
    Since I have been redeemed,
Dispelling ev'ry doubt and fear
    Since I have been redeemed.

4 I have a joy I can't express,
    Since I have been redeemed ;
All through His blood and righ
    eousness,
    Since I have been redeemed.

5 I have a home prepared for me,
    Since I have been redeemed ;
Where I shall dwell eternally,
    Since I have been redeemed.

80 TILL I learned to love Thy name,
Lord, Thy grace denying,
I was lost in sin and shame,
Dying, dying, dying !

This is now my constant theme,
This my favourite story,
Jesus' blood avails for me,
Glory glory, glory !

Nothing could the world impart,
Darkness held no morrow ;
In my soul, and in my heart,
Sorrow, sorrow, sorrow !

When I learned to love Thy name,
O, Thou meek and lowly ;
Rapture kindled to a flame,
Holy, holy, holy !

Henceforth shall creation ring
With salvation's story ;
Till I rise with Thee to sing,
Glory, glory, glory !

Hallelujah ! grace is free,
I will tell the story,
Jesus' blood hath made me free.
Glory, glory, glory !

81 THERE is sunshine in my soul
to-day,
More glorious and bright,
Than glows in any earthly sky,
For Jesus is my light.

Oh, there's sun - - shine, blessed sun - - shine,
While the peaceful, happy moments roll ;...
When Jesus shows His smiling face,
There is sunshine in my soul.

There is music in my soul to-day,
A carol to my King,
And Jesus, listening, can hear
The song I cannot sing.

There is springtime in my soul
to-day,
For when the Lord is near
The dove of peace sings in my heart,
The flowers of grace appear.

There is gladness in my soul to-day,
And hope, and praise, and love,
For blessings which He gives me
now,
For joys " laid up " above.

82 I HAVE entered the valley of
blessing so sweet,
And Jesus abides with me there ;

And His Spirit and blood make my
cleansing complete,
And His perfect love casteth out
fear.

Oh, come to this valley of blessing so sweet,
Where Jesus will fulness bestow,
Oh, believe and receive and confess Him,
That all His salvation may know.

2 There is peace in the valley of
blessing so sweet,
And plenty the land doth impart ;
There is rest for the weary-worn
traveller's feet,
And joy for the sorrowing heart.

3 There is love in the valley of blessing
so sweet,
Such as none but the blood-
washed may feel,
When heaven comes down redeemed
spirits to greet,
And Christ sets His covenant seal.

4 There's a song in the valley of
blessing so sweet,
And angels would fain join the
strain,
As with rapturous praises we bow
at His feet,
Crying, " Worthy the Lamb that
was slain ! "

383 TO the work ! to the work !
we are servants of God,
Let us follow the path that our
Master has trod,
With the balm of His counsel our
strength to renew,
Let us do with our might what our
hands find to do.

Toiling on,...toiling on,...
Toiling on,...toiling on,...
Let us hope,...let us watch and pray,...
And labour till the Master comes.

2 To the work ! to the work ! let the
hungry be fed ;
To the Fountain of Life let the weary
be led ;
In the Cross and its banner our glory
shall be,
While we herald the tidings, " Salvation is free ! "

3 To the work ! to the work ! there
is labour for all,
For the kingdom of darkness and
error shall fall,

And the name of Jehovah exalted
shall be
In the loud swelling chorus, " Salvation is free ! "

4 To the work ! to the work ! pressing
on to the end,
For the harvest will come, and the
reapers descend ;
And the home of the ransomed our
dwelling will be,
And our chorus for ever, " Salvation
is free ! "

384 I HEAR my dying Saviour
say :
Follow Me ! come, follow Me !
For thee I gave My life away,
Follow Me ! come, follow Me !
I know how heart and flesh may fail,
I've borne the fury of the gale ;
Do thou, My child, o'er hill and dale,
Follow Me ! come, follow Me !

2 Tho' thou hast sinned I pardoned
thee ;
Follow Me ! come, follow Me !
From inbred sin I'll set thee free ;
Follow Me ! come, follow Me !
Oh, look to Me, dismiss thy fears,
And trust Me thro' all coming years !
My hand shall wipe away thy tears,
Follow Me ! come, follow Me !

3 Come, cast upon Me all thy cares !
Follow Me ! come, follow Me !
Thy heavy load Mine arm upbears,
Follow Me ! come, follow Me !
In all thy changeful life I'll be [sea,
Thy God and Guide o'er land and
Thy bliss through all eternity,
Follow Me ! come, follow Me !

385 O, HOW sweet the glorious
message,
Simple faith may claim ;
Yesterday, to-day, for ever,
Jesus is the same.
Still He loves to save the sinful,
Heal the sick and lame ;
Cheer the mourner, still the tempest,
Glory to His name !

Yesterday, to-day, for ever, Jesus is the same,
All may change, but Jesus never ! glory to His
name.
Glory to His name, glory to His name,
All may change, but Jesus never ! glory to His
name !

2 He who was the Friend of sinners,
Seeks thee, lost one, now ;
Sinner, come, and at His footstool
Penitently bow.   [the
He who said, " I'll not condemn
Go, and sin no more,"
Speaks to thee that word of pardon
As in days of yore.

3 Him who pardoned erring Peter,
Never need'st thou fear ;
He that came to faithless Thomas,
All thy doubts will clear.
He who let the loved disciple
On His bosom rest,
Bids thee, still, with love as tender
Lean upon His breast.

4 He who, 'mid the raging billows,
Walk'd upon the sea ;
Still can hush our wildest tempest,
As on Galilee.
He who wept and prayed in anguish
In Gethsemane,
Drinks with us each cup of trembling
In our agony.

5 As of old He walk'd to Emmaus,
With them to abide ;
So thro' all life's way He walketh
Ever near our side.
Soon again shall we behold Him,
Hasten, Lord, the day !
But 'twill still be "this same Jesus,
As He went away.

386 AMID the trials which I meet
Amid the thorns that pierce
my feet,
One thought remains supremely
sweet,
Thou thinkest, Lord, of me !

Thou thinkest, Lord, of me,....
Thou thinkest, Lord, of me,....
What need I fear since Thou art near
And thinkest, Lord, of me !

2 The cares of life come thronging
fast,
Upon my soul their shadow cast ;
Their gloom reminds my heart at
last,
Thou thinkest, Lord, of me !

3 Let shadows come, let shadows go,
Let life be bright or dark with woe,
I am content, for this I know,
Thou thinkest, Lord, of me !

387 ENTHRONED is Jesus now,
　　Upon His heav'nly seat ;
The kingly crown is on His brow,
　　The saints are at His feet.

There with the glorified, safe by our Saviour's
We shall be satisfied by and by ;　　　　[side,
by .. and by, ... by .. and by ....
We shall be satisfied by and by.

In shining white they stand,
　　That great and countless throng ;
A palmy sceptre in each hand,
　　On ev'ry lip a song.

They sing the Lamb of God,
　　Once slain on earth for them ;
The Lamb, thro' whose atoning blood
　　Each wears his diadem.

Thy grace, O Holy Ghost,
　　Thy blessed help supply,
That we may join that radiant host,
　　Triumphant in the sky.

388 SOUND the battle cry !
　　See ! the foe is nigh ;
Raise the standard high,
　　For the Lord ;
Gird your armour on,
　　Stand firm, ev'ry one ;
Rest your cause upon
　　His holy word.

Rouse, then, soldiers ! rally round the banner !
Ready, steady, pass the word along,
Onward, forward, shout aloud Hosannah !
Christ is Captain of the mighty throng.

2 Strong to meet the foe,
　　Marching on we go,
While our cause we know
　　Must prevail ;
Shield and banner bright,
　　Gleaming in the light ;
Battling for the right,
　　We ne'er can fail.

3 Oh ! Thou God of all,
　　Hear us when we call ;
Help us one and all,
　　By Thy grace ;
When the battle's done,
　　And the vict'ry won,
May we wear the crown
　　Before Thy face.

389 I'VE reached the land of corn
　　and wine,
And all its riches freely mine ;

Here shines undimmed one blissful
　　day,
For all my night has passed away.

Oh, Beulah Land, sweet Beulah Land,
As on the highest mount I stand,
I look away across the sea,
Where mansions are prepared for me,
And view the shining glory shore,
My heaven, my home, for evermore.

2 My Saviour comes and walks with
　　me,
And sweet communion here have we ;
He gently leads me by His hand,
For this is heaven's borderland.

3 A sweet perfume upon the breeze
Is borne from ever-vernal trees,
And flowers that never-fading grow,
Where streams of life for ever flow.

4 The zephyrs seem to float to me
Sweet sounds of heaven's melody,
As angels with the white-robed
　　throng
Join in the sweet redemption song.

390 JESUS, keep me near the Cross,
　　There a precious fountain,
Free to all, a healing stream,
　　Flows from Calvary's mountain.

In the Cross, in the Cross
Be my glory ever,
Till my raptur'd soul shall find
Rest beyond the river.

2 Near the Cross, a trembling soul,
　　Love and mercy found me ;
There the bright and morning star
　　Shed its beams around me.

3 Near the Cross ! oh, Lamb of God,
　　Bring its scenes before me ;
Help me walk from day to day,
　　With its shadow o'er me.

4 Near the Cross I'll watch and wait,
　　Hoping, trusting ever,
Till I reach the golden strand,
　　Just beyond the river.

391 HIS grace was sufficient for me !
　　When in trembling and fear,
　　To His side I drew near,
And to cleanse me from sin,
Made my heart pure within,
His grace was sufficient for me.

For me,...for me,...
His grace is sufficient for me ;...
For me,...for me,...
His grace is sufficient for me.

2 His grace was sufficient for me !
  And whatever my lot,
  I can hear His " fear not ! "
  I am safe in His care,
  Who can guard from each snare,
  His grace is sufficient for me.

3 His grace is sufficient for me !
  All my needs He'll provide,
  And my steps homeward guide ;
  And in death I shall sing,
  As I rest 'neath His wing,
  His grace is sufficient for me.

4 His grace is sufficient for me !
  When in mansions of bliss,
  Still my theme shall be this ;
  And for aye I shall sing,
  To the praise of my King,
  Whose grace is sufficient for me.

392 WITH 'His dear and loving
  care,
Will the Saviour lead us on
To the hills and valleys fair,
  Over Jordan ?
Yes, we'll rest our weary feet, .
By the crystal waters sweet,
When the peaceful shore we greet,
  Over Jordan.

  Over Jordan ! over Jordan !
Yes, we'll rest our weary feet, by the crystal
  waters sweet,
  Over Jordan ! over Jordan !
When the peaceful shore we'll greet, over
  Jordan.

2 Through the rocky wilderness
  Will the Saviour lead us on,
  To the land we shall possess,
    Over Jordan ?
  Yes, by night the wondrous ray,
  Cloudy pillar by the day,
  They shall guide us on our way,
    Over Jordan.

3 With His strong and mighty hand,
  Will the Saviour lead us on,
  .To that good and pleasant land,
    Over Jordan ?
  Yes, where vine and olive grow,
  And the brooks and fountains flow,
  Thirst nor hunger shall we know,
    Over Jordan.

4 In the promised land to be,
  Will the Saviour lead us on,
  Till fair Canaan's shore we see,
    Over Jordan ?

Yes, to dwell with Thee at last,
Guide and lead us as Thou hast,
Till the parted wave be past,
  Over Jordan.

393 ONCE it was the blessing,
    Now it is the Lord ;
  Once it was the feeling,
    Now it is His Word ;
  Once His gifts I wanted,
    Now the Giver own ;
  Once I sought for healing,
    Now Himself alone.
    All in all for ever,
    Jesus will I sing ;
    Everything in Jesus,
    And Jesus ev'rything.

2 Once 'twas painful trying,
    Now 'tis perfect trust ;
  Once a half salvation,
    Now the uttermost ;
  Once 'twas ceaseless holding,
    Now He holds me fast ;
  Once 'twas constant drifting,
    Now my anchor's cast.

3 Once 'twas busy planning,
    Now 'tis trustful prayer ;
  Once 'twas anxious caring,
    Now He has the care ;
  Once 'twas what I wanted,
    Now what Jesus says ;
  Once 'twas constant asking,
    Now 'tis ceaseless praise.

4 Once it was my working,
    His it hence shall be ;
  Once I tried to use Him,
    Now He uses me ;
  Once the pow'r I wanted,
    Now the Mighty One ;
  Once for self I labour'd,
    Now for Him alone.

5 Once I hoped in Jesus,
    Now I know He's mine ;
  Once my lamps were dying,
    Now they brightly shine ;
  Once for death I waited,
    Now His coming hail ;
  And my hopes are anchor'd
    Safe within the veil.

394 THE King of Love my Shep
    herd is,
  Whose goodness faileth never ;
I nothing lack if I am His,
  And He is mine for ever.

Where streams of living water flow,
My ransom'd soul He leadeth,
And where the verdant pastures grow
With food celestial feedeth.

Perverse and foolish, oft I strayed,
But yet in love He sought me,
And on His shoulder gently laid,
And home rejoicing brought me.

In death's dark vale I fear no ill,
With Thee, dear Lord, beside me ;
Thy rod and staff my comfort still
Thy Cross before to guide me.

And so thro' all the length of days
Thy goodness faileth never ;
Good Shepherd, may I sing Thy praise
Within Thy house for ever.

95 I AM not skill'd to understand
What God hath will'd, what God hath plann'd ;
I only know at His right hand
Stands One who is my Saviour !

I take Him at His word indeed :
" Christ died for sinners," this I read ;
For in my heart I find a need
Of Him to be my Saviour !

That He should leave His place on high,
And come for sinful man to die,
You count it strange ?—so once did I,
Before I knew my Saviour !

And oh, that He fulfilled may see
The travail of His soul in me,
And with His work contented be,
As I with my dear Saviour !

Yea, living, dying, let me bring
My strength, my solace from this spring,
That He who lives to be my King,
Once died to be my Saviour !

96 I AM dwelling in the mountain
Where the golden sunlight gleams,
O'er a land whose wondrous beauty
Far exceeds my fondest dreams ;
Where the air is pure, ethereal,
Laden with the breath of flow'rs,
That are blooming by the fountain,
'Neath the never-fading bow'rs.

Is not this the land of Beulah ?
Blessed, blessed land of light,
Where the flowers bloom for ever,
And the sun is always bright.

2 I am drinking at the fountain,
Where I ever would abide ;
For I've tasted life's pure river,
And my soul is satisfied ;
There's no thirsting for life's pleasures,
Nor adorning, rich and gay,
For I've found a richer treasure,
One that fadeth not away.

3 Oh, the Cross has wondrous glory,
Oft I've proved this to be true ;
When I'm in the way so narrow,
I can see a pathway through,
And how sweetly Jesus whispers :
Take the Cross, thou need'st not fear,
For I've tried the way before thee,
And the glory lingers near.

397 MY times are in Thy hand ;
My God, I wish them there ;
My life, my friends, my soul I leave
Entirely to Thy care.

2 My times are in Thy hand,
Whatever they may be,
Pleasing or painful, dark or bright,
As best may seem to Thee.

3 My times are in Thy hand ;
Why should I doubt or fear ?
My Father's hand will never cause
His child a needless tear.

4 My times are in Thy hand ;
Jesus, the Crucified !
Those hands my cruel sins had pierced
Are now my guard and guide.

5 My times are in Thy hand ;
I'll always trust in Thee ;
And, after death, at Thy right hand
I shall for ever be.

398 THY way, not mine, O Lord,
However dark it be ;
Oh, lead me by Thine own right hand,
Choose Thou the path for me.

2 Smooth let it be or rough,
It will be still the best ;
Winding or straight, it can but lead
Right onward to Thy rest.

3 I dare not choose my lot ;
   I would not if I might ;
But choose Thou for me, O my God,
   So shall I walk aright.

4 Take Thou my cup, and it
   With joy or sorrow fill,
As ever best to Thee may seem ;
   Choose Thou my good or ill.

5 Choose Thou for me my friends,
   My sickness or my health ;
Choose Thou my every care for me,
   My poverty or wealth.

6 Not mine, not mine the choice,
   In things or great or small ;
Be Thou to me my Guide, my
   Strength,
My Wisdom, and my All.

399 I AM trusting Thee, Lord
   Jesus,
   Trusting only Thee !
Trusting Thee for full salvation,
   Great and free.

2 I am trusting Thee for pardon,
   At Thy feet I bow,
For Thy grace and tender mercy,
   Trusting now.

3 I am trusting Thee for cleansing,
   In the crimson flood ;
Trusting Thee to make me holy,
   By Thy blood.

4 I am trusting Thee to guide me,
   Thou alone shalt lead,
Ev'ry day and hour supplying
   All my need.

5 I am trusting Thee for power,
   Thine can never fail ;   [give me,
Words which Thou Thyself shalt
   Must prevail.

6 I am trusting Thee, Lord Jesus,
   Never let me fall !
I am trusting Thee for ever,
   And for all.

400 SING the wondrous love of
   Jesus,
   Sing His mercy and His grace ;
In the mansions, bright and blessed,
   He'll prepare for us a place.....
When we all...get to heaven
   What a day of rejoicing that will be !...
When we all...see Jesus,
   We'll sing and shout the victory.....

2 While we walk the pilgrim pathwa
   Clouds will overspread the sky ;
But when trav'lling days are over
   Not a shadow, not a sigh.....

3 Let us, then, be true and faithful,
   Trusting, serving ev'ry day ;
Just one glimpse of Him in glory
   Will the toils of life repay.....

4 Onward to the prize before us !
   Soon His beauty we'll behold ;
Soon the pearly gates will open,
   We shall tread the streets of gold

401 DOES Jesus care when m
   heart is pained,
   Too deeply for mirth or song ;
      As the burdens press,
      And the cares distress,
   And the way grows weary an
      long ?
O, yes, He cares ; I know He cares ;
His heart is touched with my grief
When the days are weary, the long nigh
   dreary,
I know my Saviour cares.....

2 Does Jesus care when my way
      dark
   With a nameless dread and fear
      As the daylight fades
      Into the deep night shades,
   Does He care enough to be near

3 Does Jesus care when I've tried an
      failed,
   To resist some temptation strong
      When in my deep grief
      I find no relief,
   Tho' my tears flow all the nig
      long ?

4 Does Jesus care when I've sa
   " good-bye,"
   To the dearest on earth to me,
      And my sad heart aches
      Till it nearly breaks—
   Is this aught to Him ? Does I
      see ?

402 I KNOW not what awaits m
   God kindly veils mine eye
And o'er each step of my onwa.
   way
He makes new scenes to rise ;
And ev'ry joy He sends me, com
   A sweet and glad surprise.

Where He may lead I'll follow,
My trust in Him repose ;
And ev'ry hour in perfect peace
I'll sing, He knows, He knows.

2 One step I see before me,
'Tis all I need to see,   [shines
The light of heaven more brightly
When earth's illusions flee ;
And sweetly through the silence
came
His loving, " Follow Me."

3 O blissful lack of wisdom,
'Tis blessed not to know ;
He holds me with His own right hand
And will not let me go ;
And lulls my troubled soul to rest
In Him who loves me so.

4 So on I go not knowing,
I would not if I might ;
I'd rather walk in the dark with God
Than go alone in the light ;
I'd rather walk by faith with Him,
Than go alone by sight.

403   LOVED ! then the way will
not be drear ;
For One we know is ever near,
Proving it to our hearts so clear
That we are loved.

2 Loved with an everlasting love
By Him who left His home above,
To bring us life, and light, and love,
Because He loved.

3 Loved when our sky is clouded o'er,
And days of sorrow press us sore ;
Still will we trust Him evermore,
For we are loved.

4 Loved, when we leave our native
soil,
In heathen lands to live and toil ;
Under His shadow nought can foil—
Still we are loved.

5 Time, that affects all things below,
Can never change the love He'll
show ;   [flow,
The heart of Christ with love will
And we are loved.

6 Loved in the past of yesterday,
And all along our future way,
And in the present of to-day—
For ever loved.

7 Loved when we sing the glad new
song
To Christ, for whom we've waited
long,   [throng—
With all the happy, ransomed
And ever loved.

404   UPON the western plain
There comes the signal strain,
'Tis loyalty, loyalty, loyalty to Christ ;
Its music rolls along,
The hills take up the song,
Of loyalty, loyalty, yes, loyalty to
Christ.

" On to victory ! on to victory ! "
Cries our great Commander : " On !..."
We'll move at His command, we'll soon possess
the land,
Thro' loyalty, loyalty, yes, loyalty to Christ.

2 O hear, ye brave, the sound
That moves the earth around,
'Tis loyalty, loyalty, loyalty to Christ ;
Arise to dare and do,
Ring out the watchword true,
Of loyalty, loyalty, yes, loyalty to
Christ.

3 Come, join our loyal throng,
We'll rout the giant wrong,
'Tis loyalty, loyalty, loyalty to Christ ;
Where Satan's banners float,
We'll send the bugle note,
Of loyalty, loyalty, yes, loyalty to
Christ.

4 The strength of youth we lay
At Jesus' feet to-day,
'Tis loyalty, loyalty, loyalty to Christ ;
His Gospel we'll proclaim,
Throughout the world's domain,
Of loyalty, loyalty, yes, loyalty to
Christ.

405   I AM thinking to-day of that
beautiful land
I shall reach when the sun goeth
down ;
When thro' wonderful grace by my
Saviour I stand,
Will there be any stars in my
crown ?

Will there be any stars, any stars in my crown,
When at evening the sun goeth down ?
When I wake with the blest in the mansions
of rest,
Will there be any stars in my crown ?

2 In the strength of the Lord let me
    labour and pray,
  Let me watch as a winner of souls ;
That bright stars may be mine in
    the glorious day,
  When His praise like the sea-
    billow rolls.

3 Oh, what joy will it be when His
    face I behold,
  Living gems at His feet to lay
    down ;
It would sweeten my bliss in the city
    of gold,
  Should there be any stars in my
    crown.

406 WE would see Jesus—for the
        shadows lengthen
      Across this little landscape of
        our life ;
  We would see Jesus, our weak faith
    to strengthen,
      For the last weariness—the final
        strife.

2 We would see Jesus—the great Rock
    Foundation,
      Whereon our feet were set with
        sovereign grace ;
  Not life, not death, with all their
    agitation,
      Can thence remove us, if we see
        His face.

3 We would see Jesus—other lights
    are paling,
      Which for long years we have
        rejoiced to see ;
  The blessings of our pilgrimage are
    failing,
      We would not mourn them, for
        we go to Thee.

4 We would see Jesus—this is all we're
    needing,
      Strength, joy, and willingness
        come with the sight ;
  We would see Jesus, dying, risen,
    pleading,
      Then welcome day, and farewell
        mortal night !

407 SAVIOUR, more than life to
        me,
  I am clinging, clinging, close to Thee;
  Let Thy precious blood applied,
  Keep me ever, ever near Thy side.

Ev'ry day,...ev'ry hour,...
Let me feel Thy cleansing power ;
May Thy tender love to me
Bind me closer, closer, Lord, to Thee.

2 Through this changing world below
  Lead me gently, gently as I go ;
  Trusting Thee I cannot stray,
  I can never, never lose my way.

3 Let me love Thee more and more,
  Till this fleeting, fleeting life is o'er
  Till my soul is lost in love,
  In a fairer, brighter world above.

408 MY happy soul rejoices,
      The sky is bright above ;
  I'll join the heav'nly voices,
    And sing redeeming love.

  For there's pow'r in Jesus' blood,
  Pow'r in Jesus' blood ;
  There's pow'r in Jesus' blood
  To wash me white as snow.

2 I heard the blessed story
    Of Him who died to save ;
  The love of Christ swept o'er me,
    My all to Him I gave.

3 His gracious words of pardon
    Were music to my heart ;
  He took away my burden,
    And bade my fears depart.

4 I plunged beneath this fountain,
    That cleanseth white as snow ;
  It pours from Calv'ry's mountain,
    With blessings in its flow.

5 Oh, crown Him King for ever !
    My Saviour and my Friend ;
  By Zion's crystal river
    His praise shall never end.

409 AS the shadows of the night
      round are falling,
    I am thinking of that day by an
      by ;
  When the trumpet of the Lord shall
    be calling,
    As the day breaks o'er the hills.

I'll go singing, I'll go shouting on my journey
    home,
Till the day breaks, till the day breaks,
There'll be singing, there'll be shouting, when
    we all get home,
When the day breaks o'er the hills....

2 When we gather home at last there'll
    be singing,
    Such as angels round the throne
      never heard ;

For the song of souls redeemed shall
    go ringing,
  As the day breaks o'er the hills.

I shall rise to be with Jesus for ever,
I shall meet the ones who passed
    on before;
We shall meet to part no more,
    never, never,
  When the day breaks o'er the hills.

410 IN the harvest field there is
    work to do,
For the grain is ripe, and the
    reapers few;
And the Master's voice bids the
    workers true
  Heed the call that He gives to-day.

Labour on !...labour on !...
Keep the bright reward in view;
or the Master has said, He will strength renew;
Labour on till the close of the day !

Crowd the garner well with its
    sheaves all bright,
Let the song be glad, and the heart
    be light;
Fill the precious hours, ere the
    shades of night
  Take the place of the golden day.

In the gleaner's path may be rich
    reward,
Tho' the time seems long, and the
    labour hard;
For the Master's joy, with His chosen
    shared,
  Drives the gloom from the darkest
    day.

Lo ! the harvest home in the realms
    above
Shall be gained by each who has
    toil'd and strove,
When the Master's voice, in its
    tones of love,
  Calls away to eternal day.

411 THE sands of time are sinking,
    The dawn of heaven breaks;
The summer morn I've sighed for,
    The fair sweet morn awakes;
Dark, dark hath been the midnight,
    But dayspring is at hand,
And glory, glory dwelleth,
    In Immanuel's land.

2 O Christ He is the fountain,
    The deep, sweet well of love;
The streams on earth I've tasted,
    More deep I'll drink above;
There to an ocean fulness
    His mercy doth expand,
And glory, glory dwelleth
    In Immanuel's land.

3 With mercy and with judgment,
    My web of time He wove,
And aye the dews of sorrow
    Were lustred by His love;
I'll bless the hand that guided,
    I'll bless the heart that planned,
When throned where glory dwelleth
    In Immanuel's land.

4 The bride eyes not her garment,
    But her dear bridegroom's face;
I will not gaze at glory,
    But on my King of grace;
Not at the crown He gifteth,
    But on His pierced hand;
The Lamb is all the glory
    Of Immanuel's land.

5 I've wrestled on towards heaven,
    'Gainst storm, and wind, and tide;
Now like a weary traveller
    That leaneth on his guide.
Amid the shades of ev'ning,
    While sinks life's ling'ring sand,
I hail the glory dawning
    In Immanuel's land.

412 ONCE I thought I walk'd with
    Jesus,
    Yet such changeful moods I had;
Sometimes trusting, sometimes
    doubting,
    Sometimes joyful, sometimes sad.
Oh, the peace my Saviour gives,
Peace I never knew before;
For my way has brighter grown,
Since I learn'd to trust Him more.

2 For He called me closer to Him,
    Bade my doubting tremors cease;
And when I had fully trusted,
    Filled my soul with perfect peace.

3 Now I'm trusting ev'ry moment,
    Less than this is not enough;
And my Saviour bears me gently
    O'er the places once so rough.

4 Blessed Saviour, Thou dost keep me
    By Thy pow'r from day to day,
And my heart is full of gladness,
    For Thou'lt keep me all the way.

413 WHEN peace, like a river,
    attendeth my way,
When sorrows, like sea-billows,
    roll ;
Whatever my lot, Thou hast taught
    me to know,
    " It is well, it is well with my
    soul."

    It is well...with my soul,...
    It is well, it is well with my soul.

2 If Satan should buffet, if trials
    should come,
    Let this blest assurance control,
That Christ hath regarded my help-
    less estate,
And hath shed His own blood for
    my soul.

3 My sin—oh, the bliss of this glorious
    thought—
My sin—not in part, but the whole,
Is nail'd to His Cross, and I bear it
    no more ;
    Praise the Lord, praise the Lord,
    O my soul !

4 For me, be it Christ, be it Christ
    hence to live !
    If Jordan above me shall roll,
No pang shall be mine, for in death
    as in life,
Thou wilt whisper Thy peace to
    my soul.

5 But Lord, 'tis for Thee, for Thy
    coming we wait,
    The sky, not the grave, is our goal ;
Oh, trump of the angel ! oh, voice
    of the Lord !
    Blessed Hope ! blessed rest of my
    soul !

414 DO you fear the foe will in the
    conflict win ?
Is it dark without you, darker still
    within ?
Clear the darkened windows, open
    wide the door,
    Let a little sunshine in.

    Let the blessed sunshine in,...
    Let the blessed sunshine in ;...
    Clear the darkened windows, open wide the
      door,
    Let a little sunshine in.

2 Does your faith grow fainter in the
    cause you love ?
Are your prayers unanswered by
    your God above ?

Clear the darkened windows, ope
    wide the door,
    Let a little sunshine in.

3 Would you go rejoicing on the up-
    ward way,
Knowing naught of darkness, dwell-
    ing in the day ?
Clear the darkened windows, ope
    wide the door,
    Let a little sunshine in.

415 THE dear loving Saviour hath
    found me,
And shattered the fetters that bound
    me,
Tho' all was confusion around me,
    He came and spake peace to my
    soul ;
The blessed Redeemer that bought
    me,
In tenderness constantly sought me
The way of salvation He taught me,
    And made my heart perfectly
    whole.

    He saves me, He saves me,
    His love fills my soul, hallelujah !
    Oh, glory, oh, glory.
    His Spirit abideth within ;
    He saves me, He saves me,
    His love fills my soul, hallelujah !
    Oh, glory, oh, glory,
    His blood cleanseth me from all sin.

2 He sought me so long ere I knew
    Him,
But finally winning me to Him,
I yielded my all to pursue Him,
    And asked to be filled with His
    grace ;
Although a vile sinner before Him,
Through faith I was led to implore
    Him,
And now I rejoice and adore Him,
    Restored to His loving embrace.

3 I never, no never will leave Him,
Grow weary of service, and grieve
    Him,
I'll constantly trust and believe Him
    Remain in His presence divine ;
Abiding in love ever flowing,
In knowledge and grace ever
    growing,
Confiding implicitly, knowing
    That Jesus the Saviour is mine.

16 LEAD, kindly Light, amid
    th' encircling gloom,
    Lead Thou me on ;
The night is dark, and I am far from
    home ;
    Lead Thou me on ;
Keep Thou my feet ; I do not ask
    to see   [for me.
The distant scene—one step enough
I was not ever thus, nor prayed
    that Thou
    Shouldst lead me on ;
I loved to choose and see my path ;
    but now
    Lead Thou me on ;
I loved the garish day, and spite of
    fears,
Pride ruled my will : remember not
    past years !
So long Thy power hath blessed
    me, sure it still
    Will lead me on,
O'er moor and fen, o'er crag and
    torrent, till
    The night is gone :
And with the morn those angel-
    faces smile,
Which I have loved long since, and
    lost awhile.

17 BLESSED assurance, Jesus is
    mine,
Oh, what a foretaste of glory divine !
Heir of salvation, purchase of God,
Born of His Spirit, washed in His
    blood.

    This is my story, this is my song,
    Praising my Saviour all the day long ;
    This is my story, this is my song,
    Praising my Saviour all the day long.

Perfect submission, perfect delight,
Visions of rapture now burst on my
    sight ;
Angels descending, bring from above
Echoes of mercy, whispers of love.

Perfect submission, all is at rest,
I in my Saviour am happy and blest ;
Watching and waiting, looking above,
Fill'd with His goodness, lost in
    His love.

18 LIKE a river glorious
    Is God's perfect peace,
Over all victorious
    In its bright increase ;

Perfect, yet it floweth
    Fuller every day ;
Perfect, yet it groweth
    Deeper all the way.
    Stayed upon Jehovah,
      Hearts are fully blest ;
    Finding, as He promis'd,
      Perfect peace and rest.

2 Hidden in the hollow
    Of His blessed hand,
Never foe can follow
    Never traitor stand ;
Not a surge of worry,
    Not a shade of care,
Not a blast of hurry
    Touch the spirit there.

3 Ev'ry joy or trial
    Falleth from above,
Traced upon our dial
    By the Son of Love.
We may trust Him fully
    All for us to do,
They who trust Him wholly,
    Find Him wholly true.

419 ELIJAH made a sacrifice
    To offer to Jehovah ;
It had been wet with water thrice,
    Baal's sacrifice was over.
Elijah pray'd : the fire came down
And licked the water all around ;
So doubting ones believed, and found
    Elijah's God was living.
    Elijah's God still lives to-day,
    To take the guilt of sin away ;
    And when I pray my heart's desire,
    Upon my soul He sends the fire.

2 Elijah's God still lives to-day,
    And answers still by fire ;
My friend, just let Him have His way
    He'll grant your heart's desire.
Consume the sacrifice you make,
And bid your slumb'ring soul awake;
The chain of in-bred sin will break ;
    Elijah's God is living.

3 Elijah's God still lives to-day,
    And answers still in power,
As when Elijah pray'd for rain,
    God answered with a shower.
If you would have your soul
    refreshed,
With rain that falls from heaven,
You must " pray through " like all
    the rest,
    And showers shall be given.

420 MY hope is built on nothing less
Than Jesus' blood and righteousness;
I dare not trust the sweetest frame,
But wholly lean on Jesus' Name.

On Christ, the solid Rock, I stand;
All other ground is sinking sand,
All other ground is sinking sand.

2 When darkness seems to veil His face,
I rest on His unchanging grace;
In ev'ry high and stormy gale,
My anchor holds within the veil.

3 His oath, His covenant and blood,
Support me in the 'whelming flood;
When all around my soul gives way,
He then is all my hope and stay.

421 FACE to face with Christ, my Saviour,
Face to face—what will it be?
When with rapture I behold Him,
Jesus Christ, who died for me.

Face to face shall I behold Him,
Far beyond the starry sky;
Face to face in all His glory,
I shall see Him by and by!

2 Only faintly now I see Him,
With the darkling veil between,
But a blessed day is coming,
When His glory shall be seen.

3 What rejoicing in His presence,
When are banished grief and pain;
When the crooked ways are straightened,
And the dark things shall be plain.

4 Face to face! O! blissful moment!
Face to face—to see and know;
Face to face with my Redeemer,
Jesus Christ, who loves me so.

422 IN the good old way where the saints have gone,
And the King leads on before us,
We are travelling home to the heavenly hills,
With the day-star shining o'er us.

Travelling home to the mansions fair,
Crowns of rejoicing and life to wear;
O what a shout when we all get there,
Safe in the glory land!

2 In the good old way, like the ransomed throng,
Unto Zion now returning,

We are travelling home at the King's command,
And our lamps are trimmed and burning.

3 In the good old way, with a steadfast faith,
In the bonds of love and union,
What a joy is ours! for the King we see,
And with Him we hold communion.

4 Tho' our feet must stand on the cold, cold brink
Of the Jordan's stormy river,
With the King we'll cross to the other side,
And we'll sing His praise for ever.

423 ANYWHERE with Jesus can safely go,
Anywhere He leads me in this world below,
Anywhere without Him dearest joy would fade,
Anywhere with Jesus I am not afraid.

Anywhere! anywhere!
Fear I cannot know.
Anywhere with Jesus
I can safely go.

2 Anywhere with Jesus I am not alone,
Other friends may fail me, He still my own;
Though His hand may lead me over drearest ways,
Anywhere with Jesus is a house of praise.

3 Anywhere with Jesus I can go to sleep,
When the darkling shadows round about me creep;
Knowing I shall waken never more to roam,
Anywhere with Jesus will be home sweet home.

424 THE cross that He gave may be heavy,
But it ne'er outweights His grace;
The storm that I feared may surround me,
But it ne'er excludes His face.

e cross is not greater than His grace,...
e storm cannot hide His blessed face ;...
.m satisfied to know that with Jesus here
. can conquer ev'ry foe.   [below,

The thorns in my path are not
    sharper
Than composed His crown for me ;
The cup that I drink not more bitter
    Than He drank in Gethsemane.

The light of His love shineth
    brighter,
As it falls on paths of woe ;
The toil of my work groweth lighter
    As I stoop to raise the low.

His will I have joy in fulfilling,
    As I'm walking in His sight ;
My all to the blood I am bringing,
    It alone can keep me right.

5   WHEN the storms of life are
    raging,
    Tempests wild on sea and land,
I will seek a place of refuge
    In the shadow of God's hand.

He will hide..me,..He will hide..me,..
    Where no harm..can e'er betide me :
He will hide..me,..safely hide..me
    In the sha - - dow of His hand.

Though He may send some affliction,
    'Twill but make me long for
    home ;
For in love and not in anger,
    All His chastenings will come.

Enemies may strive to injure,
    Satan all his arts employ ;
He will turn what seems to harm me
    Into everlasting joy.

So, while here the cross I'm bearing,
    Meeting storms and billows wild,
Jesus for my soul is caring,
Naught can harm His Father's
    child.

6   'TIS so sweet to trust in Jesus,
    Just to take Him at His
    Word ;
Just to rest upon His promise,
    Just to know, " Thus saith the
    Lord."

Jesus, Jesus, how I trust Him !
    How I've prov'd Him o'er and o'er !
Jesus, Jesus, precious Jesus !
    Oh, for grace to trust Him more.

2 Oh, how sweet to trust in Jesus,
    Just to trust His cleansing blood ;
Just in simple faith to plunge me
    'Neath the healing, cleansing flood.

3 Yes, 'tis sweet to trust in Jesus,
    Just from sin and self to cease ;
Just from Jesus simply taking
    Life and rest, and joy and peace.

4 I'm so glad I learned to trust Thee,
    Precious Jesus, Saviour, Friend ;
And I know that Thou art with me,
    Wilt be with me to the end.

427   TRUSTING in Jesus, my
    Saviour divine,
I have the witness that still He is
    mine ;
Great are the blessings He giveth
    to me,
Oh, I am happy as mortal can be.

I am redeemed,..and I know it full well,..
Saved by His grace,..I with Him shall dwell ;..
I am redeemed,..and the child of His love,..
Heir to a glo - - rious crown above...

2 Once I was far from my Saviour and
    King,
Now He has taught me His mercy
    to sing ;
Peace in believing He giveth to me ;
Oh, I am happy as mortal can be.

3 Trusting in Jesus, oh, what should
    I fear ?
Nothing can harm me when He is
    so near ;
Sweet is the promise He giveth to
    me ;
Oh, I am happy as mortal can be.

4 If while a stranger I journey below,
Fill'd with His fulness such rapture
    I know,
What will the bliss of eternity be,
When in His beauty the King I
    shall see ?

428   JESUS, lover of my soul,
    Let me to Thy bosom fly,
While the nearer waters roll,
    While the tempest still is high ;
Hide me, O my Saviour, hide,
    Till the storm of life is past ;
Safe into the haven guide ;
    Oh, receive my soul at last.

2 Other refuge have I none ;
  Hangs my helpless soul on Thee ;
Leave, ah ! leave me not alone,
  Still support and comfort me.
All my trust on Thee is stay'd,
  All my help from Thee I bring ;
Cover my defenceless head
  With the shadow of Thy wing.

3 Thou, O Christ ! art all I want ;
  More than all in Thee I find ;
Raise the fallen, cheer the faint,
  Heal the sick, and lead the blind.
Just and holy is Thy name,
  I am all unrighteousness ;
Vile and full of sin I am,
  Thou art full of truth and grace.

4 Plenteous grace with Thee is found,
  Grace to cover all my sin ;
Let the healing streams abound,
  Make and keep me pure within ;
Thou of life the fountain art,
  Freely let me take of Thee ;
Spring Thou up within my heart,
  Rise to all eternity.

429 WORK, for the night is
    coming !
  Work thro' the morning hours ;
Work while the dew is sparkling ;
  Work 'mid springing flowers ;
Work while the day grows brighter,
  Under the glowing sun ;
Work, for the night is coming,
  When man's work is done.

2 Work, for the night is coming !
  Work through the sunny noon ;
Fill the bright hours with labour,
  Rest comes sure and soon.
Give to each flying minute
  Something to keep in store ;
Work, for the night is coming,
  When man works no more.

3 Work, for the night is coming !
  Under the sunset skies ;
While their bright tints are glowing,
  Work; for daylight flies.
Work till the last beam fadeth,
  Fadeth to shine no more ;
Work, while the night is dark'ning,
  When man's work is o'er.

430 JESUS, and shall it ever be,
  A mortal man asham'd of Thee ?

Asham'd of Thee, whom ang
  praise !
Whose glories shine thro' endl
  days !

2 Asham'd of Jesus ! sooner far
Let evening blush to own a star ;
He sheds the beams of light divi
O'er this benighted soul of mine.

3 Asham'd of Jesus ! just as soon
Let midnight be asham'd of noo
'Twas midnight with my soul, till
Bright Morning Star, bade darkn
  flee.

4 Asham'd of Jesus ! that dear Frie
On whom my hopes of hea
  depend !
No ! when I blush, be this my sha
That I no more revere His name.

431 SOLDIERS of Jesus ! soldi
    of the Cross !
Follow your Captain, counting
  but loss ;
If you fight the battle, you shall g
  renown ;
And if you are faithful you sh
  wear a crown.

March on ! March on ! soldiers of Imman
  March on ! March on ! singing as we go
Glory ! glory to the Lamb of Calvary !
  In His might we conquer ev'ry foe.

2 Soldiers of Jesus ! gird ye to
  fray ;   [da
Stand in your armour, in this
Where the battle rages, there m
  ye be found,
Where the need is greatest, tha
  holy ground.

3 Soldiers of Jesus ! lift your stand
  high !   [to di
Write on your banners, " Jesus ca
By the Cross of Jesus we the vict
  win,   [all
For the blood of Jesus cleanseth fr

4 Soldiers of Jesus ! when the batt
  done,
Foes all are vanquished, and
  vict'ry won ;
Then with shouts of triumph
  shall hail the King,
When the vaults of heaven with
  praises ring.

Soldiers of Jesus! of the Lamb once
    slain,   [to reign;
Know ye that Jesus soon will come
Lift your heads in gladness, victory
    is nigh!
Send a shout of welcome thro' the
    earth and sky.

Come, Lord Jesus! come and take Thy people
    home!
Come, oh come! we long Thy face to see!
Come, Lord Jesus, claim the kingdom and the
    pow'r;
Set the earth from all its bondage free.

32 MORE about Jesus would I
        know,
More of His grace to others show;
More of His saving fulness see,
More of His love, who died for me.

    More, more about Jesus,
    More, more about Jesus;
    More of His saving fulness see,
    More of His love who died for me.

More about Jesus let me learn,
More of His holy will discern;
Spirit of God, my teacher be,
Showing the things of Christ to me.

More about Jesus, in His Word,
Holding communion with my Lord;
Hearing His voice in ev'ry line,
Making each faithful saying mine.

More about Jesus, on His throne,
Riches in glory all His own;
More of His Kingdom's sure increase,
More of His coming, Prince of Peace.

33 MY heart is resting, O my God,
        I will give thanks and sing;
My heart is at the secret source
Of ev'ry precious thing.

Now the frail vessel Thou hast made,
    No hand but Thine shall fill;
For the waters of this world have
    failed,
    And I am thirsty still.

I thirst for springs of heav'nly life,
    And here all day they rise;
I seek the treasure of Thy love,
    And close at hand it lies.

And a new song is in my mouth,
    To long loved music set—
Glory to Thee for all Thy grace
    I have not tasted yet.

5 "Thou art my portion," saith my
    Ten thousand voices say,   [soul,
And the music of their glad Amen
    Will never die away.

434 SOMETIME we'll stand before
        the judgment bar,
    The quick, the risen dead;
The Lord will then make known the
    record there;
    Our names will all be read.

I'll be present when the roll is called,
    Pure and spotless thro' the crimson flood;
I will answer when they call my name;
    Sav'd thro' Jesus' blood.

2 I'll then receive a bright and starry
    As only God can give;   [crown,
And when I've been with Him ten
    thousand years,
    I'll have no less to live.

3 Then we shall meet to never part
    again,
    Our toil will then be o'er;
We'll lay our burdens down at Jesus'
    And rest for evermore.   [feet,

435 RESCUE the perishing,
        Care for the dying,
Snatch them in pity from sin and the
    Weep o'er the erring ones, [grave;
    Lift up the fallen,
Tell them of Jesus, the mighty to save.

    Rescue the perishing, care for the dying;
    Jesus is merciful, Jesus will save.

2 Tho' they are slighting Him,
    Still He is waiting,
Waiting the penitent child to receive;
    Plead with them earnestly,
    Plead with them gently;
He will forgive if they only believe.

3 Down in the human heart,
    Crush'd by the tempter,   [restore;
Feelings lie buried that grace can
    Touched by a loving heart,
    Wakened by kindness,
Cords that were broken will vibrate
    once more.

4 Rescue the perishing,
    Duty demands it;
Strength for Thy labour the Lord will
    Back to the narrow way,   [provide.
    Patiently win them;   [died.
Tell the poor wand'rer a Saviour has

436 BEHOLD, what love, what
        boundless love,
The Father hath bestowed
On sinners lost, that we should be
  Now called the sons of God !

  Behold, what manner of love !...
  What manner of love the Father hath
    bestowed upon us,
  That we, that we should be call'd,...
  Should be call'd the sons of God.

2 No longer far from Him, but now
    By " precious blood " made nigh ;
Accepted in the " well-beloved,"
  Near to God's heart we lie.

3 What we in glory soon shall be,
    " It doth not yet appear ; "
But when our precious Lord we see,
  We shall His image bear.

4 With such a blessed hope in view,
    We would more holy be ;
More like our risen, glorious Lord,
  Whose face we soon shall see.

437 PEACE, perfect peace, in this
        dark world of sin ?
The blood of Jesus whispers peace
  within.

2 Peace, perfect peace, by thronging
    duties pressed ?
To do the will of Jesus, this is rest.

3 Peace, perfect peace, with sorrows
    surging round ?
On Jesus' bosom naught but calm
  is found.

4 Peace, perfect peace, with loved
    ones far away ?
In Jesus' keeping we are safe and
  they.

5 Peace, perfect peace, our future all
    unknown ?
Jesus we know, and He is on the
  throne.

6 Peace, perfect peace, death shadow-
    ing us and ours ?
Jesus has vanquished death and all
  its powers.

7 It is enough ; earth's struggles soon
    shall cease,
And Jesus call us to Heaven's perfect
  peace.

438 I'VE seen the face of Jesus—
        He smiled in love on me ;
It filled my heart with rapture,
  My soul with ecstasy.
The scars of deepest anguish
  Were lost in glory bright ;
I've seen the face of Jesus—
  It was a wondrous sight !

  Oh ! glorious face of beauty,
    Oh ! gentle touch of care ;
  If here it is so blessed,
    What will it be up there ?

2 And since I've seen His beauty,
    All else I count. but loss ;
The world, its fame and pleasure,
  Is now to me but dross.
His light dispelled my darkness,
  His smile was, oh, so sweet !
I've seen the face of Jesus—
  I can but kiss His feet.

3 I've heard the voice of Jesus—
    He told me of His love,
And called me His own treasure,
  His undefiled, His dove.
It came like softest music
  Across an ocean calm,
And seemed to play so sweetly
  Some wondrous holy psalm.

4 I felt the hand of Jesus—
    My brow it throbbed with care ;
He placed it there so softly,
  And whispered, " Do not fear."
Like clouds before the sunshine,
  My cares have rolled away ;
I'm sitting in His presence—
  It is a cloudless day.

5 I know He's coming shortly
    To take us all above ;
We'll sing redemption's story,
  The story of His love ;
We ll hear His voice and music,
  We'll feel His hand of care ;
He'll never rest—He says so—
  Until He has us there.

439 MY Jesus, I love Thee, I know
        Thou art mine,
For Thee all the pleasures of sin
  resign ;
My gracious Redeemer, my Saviour
  art Thou,
If ever I loved Thee, my Jesus, 'ti
  now.

I love Thee because Thou hast first
   loved me,
And purchased my pardon when
   nailed to the tree ;
I love Thee for wearing the thorns
   on Thy brow,   [now.
If ever I loved Thee, my Jesus, 'tis

I will love Thee in life, I will love
   Thee in death,
And praise Thee as long as Thou
   lendest me breath ;
And say, when the death-dew lies
   cold on my brow,   [now.
If ever I loved Thee, my Jesus, 'tis

40   OH, I love to read of Jesus
         and His love,
How He left His Father's mansion
   far above ;
   How He came on earth to live,
   How He came His life to give ;
Oh, I love to read of Jesus and His
   love !

It's just like Him " to take my sins away,
To make me glad and free, to keep me day
   by day ;
It's just like Him " to give His life for me,
That I might go to heaven, and ever with
   Him be.

Oh, I love to read of Jesus as He
   went   [intent ;
Ev'rywhere, to do His Father's will
   How He gave the blind their sight,
   How He gave the wrong'd ones
     right,
How He swift deliv'rance to the
   captive sent !

Oh, I love to read of Jesus on the
   tree,
For it shows how great the love that
   died for me ;
   And the blood that from His side
   Flow'd, when on the Cross He
     died,
Paid my debt, and evermore doth
   make me free.

Oh, my dear and precious Saviour,
   at Thy feet,
Here I give myself and all I have
   complete ;
   I will serve Thee all my days
   With a heart all fill'd with praise,
And I'll thank Thee face to face
   when we shall meet !

441   'TIS the old time religion,
     'Tis the old time religion,
   'Tis the old time religion,
    It's good enough for me.

   'Tis the old time religion,
   'Tis the old time religion,
   'Tis the old time religion,
   It's good enough for me.

2 It was good for our mothers,
   It's good enough for me.

3 Makes me love ev'rybody,
   It's good enough for me.

4 It has saved our fathers,
   It's good enough for me.

5 It was good for the Prophet Daniel,
   It's good enough for me.

6 It was good for the Hebrew children,
   It's good enough for me.

7 It was tried in the fiery furnace,
   It's good enough for me.

8 It was good for Paul and Silas,
   It's good enough for me.

9 It will do when I am dying,
   It's good enough for me.

10 It will take us all to heaven,
   It's good enough for me.

442   HAVE you ever heard the
         story
   Of the Babe of Bethlehem,
Who was worshipp'd by the angels
   And the wise and holy men ;
How He taught the learned doctors
   In the temple far away ?
Oh, I'm glad, so glad to tell you,
   He is just the same to-day.

   He is just....the same to-day,....
   He is just....the same to-day,....
   Seeking those who are astray,
   Saving souls along the way ;
   Thank God, He is just the same to-day.

2 Have you ever heard the story,
   How He walked upon the sea,
To His dear disciples tossing
   On the waves of Galilee ;
How the waves in angry motion
   Quickly would His will obey ?
Oh, I'm glad, so glad to tell you,
   He is just the same to-day.

3 Have you ever heard of Jesus
   Praying in Gethsemane,
And the ever-thrilling story
   How He died upon the tree ;

Cruel thorns His forehead piercing,
As His spirit passed away ?
This He did for you, my brother,
And He's just the same to-day.

443 HAVE you on the Lord believed ?
Still there's more to follow ;
Of His grace have you received ?
Still there's more to follow ;
Oh, the grace the Father shows !
Still there's more to follow !
Freely He His grace bestows,
Still there's more to follow !

More and more, more and more,
Always more to follow !
Oh, His matchless, boundless love !
Still there's more to follow !

2 Have you felt the Saviour near ?
Still there's more to follow ;
Does His blessed presence cheer ?
Still there's more to follow ;
Oh, the love that Jesus shows !
Still there's more to follow !
Freely He His love bestows !
Still there's more to follow !

3 Have you felt the Spirit's power ?
Still there's more to follow ;
Falling like the gentle shower ?
Still there's more to follow ;
Oh, the power the Spirit shows !
Still there's more to follow !
Freely He His power bestows !
Still there's more to follow !

444 THERE are songs of joy that
I love to sing,
When my heart was blithe as a bird
in spring ;
But the song I have learn'd is so
full of cheer,   [darkness drear.
That the dawn shines out in the

O, the new,...new song !...O, the new,... new
   song !...
I can sing...it now...with the ran - - som'd
   throng ;
Power and dominion to Him that shall reign,...
Glory and praise to the Lamb that was slain.

2 There are strains of home that are
dear as life,
And I list to them oft 'mid the din
of strife ;
But I know of a home that is wondrous fair,   [singing there.
And I sing the psalms they are

3 Can my lips be mute, or my he
be sad,
When the gracious Master hath ma
me glad ?
When He points where the ma
mansions be,
And sweetly says, " There is one
thee ? "

4 I shall catch the gleam of its jasp
wall,
When I come to the gloom of t
even-fall ;
For I know that the shadows, drea
and dim,
Have a path of light that will le
to Him.

445 ALL the way my Saviour lea
me :
What have I to ask beside ?
Can I doubt His tender mercy,
Who through life has been n
Guide ?

2 Heav'nly peace, divinest comfort,
Here by faith in Him to dwell !
For I know, whate'er befall me,
Jesus doeth all things well.

3 All the way my Saviour leads me
Cheers each winding path I trea
Gives me grace for ev'ry trial,
Feeds me with the living bread.

4 Tho' my weary steps may falter,
And my soul athirst may be,
Gushing from the rock before me,
Lo ! a spring of joy I see.

5 All the way my Saviour leads me
Oh, the fulness of His love !
Perfect rest to me is promis'd,
In my Father's house above.

6 When my spirit, cloth'd immortal,
Wings its flight to realms of day
This my song through endless ages
Jesus led me all the way.

446 ON for Jesus ! steady be yo
arm and brave ;
Onward, onward ; take the shi
and sword ;
On for Jesus ! standard of yo
Captain wave,
Pressing onward, trusting in F
Word.

Marching, marching on,...
We're marching onward still for Jesus ;
Marching, marching on ...
Beneath the banner of the free ;
" On for Jesus ! " this shall be the battle-cry,
Ne'er retreating, ever pressing on ;
On for Jesus ! marching on to victory,
As we shout the glad redemption song.

On for Jesus ! tiresome tho' the
    conflict be,
Tho' the hosts of sin are pressing
    hard ;
On for Jesus ! striving for the
    victory,
    Endless life will soon be your
    reward.

On for Jesus ! till the sound of
    strife is o'er !
When the great Commander calls
    for thee,
Thou shalt wear a crown of life for
    evermore,
    And with Jesus reign eternally.

47 I HAVE a Friend, and He
    came to seek me,
I was afar on the ocean wave ;
Into the fold of His love He brought
    me ;
    Peace to my soul from that hour
    He gave.

Glory, glory, Jesus is my Saviour,
I'll sing and praise Him in the glad, new song ;
Glory, glory, I will give Him glory,
Then mine eyes behold Him, in the blood-
    wash'd throng.

O how my heart with its joy is
    bounding,   [He ;
O what a Saviour and Friend is
Full of compassion and rich in
    blessing,
    O how He loves and cares for me.

I have a Friend that will ne'er
    forsake me,   [pow'r ;
I shall be kept by His mighty
Safe in the arms of His love that
    folds me,   [hour.
    Moment by moment and hour by

I have a hope that is sure and stead-
    fast—   [I stand ;
Firm as the rock where by faith
I have the pledge of a rest eternal,
    Waiting for me in the soul's bright
    land.

448 ABIDING, oh, so wondrous
    sweet !
I'm resting at the Saviour's feet ;
I trust in Him—I'm satisfied,
I'm resting on the Crucified !

    Abid - - ing, abid - - ing,
        Oh ! so wondrous sweet !...
    I'm rest - - ing, rest - - ing
        At the Saviour's feet....

2 He speaks, and by His word is giv'n
His peace, a rich fortaste of heav'n !
Not as the world He peace doth give,
'Tis thro' this hope my soul shall
    live.

3 I live ; not I ; through Him alone
By whom the mighty work is done ;
Dead to myself, alive to Him,
I count all lost His rest to gain.

4 Now rest, my heart, the work is done,
I'm saved thro' the Eternal Son !
Let all pow'rs my soul employ,
To tell the world my peace and joy.

449 THERE stands a Rock on
    shores of time,
    That rears to heav'n its head
    sublime;
    That Rock is cleft, and they are
    blest
Who find within this cleft a rest.

Some build their hopes on the ever drifting
    sand,
Some on their fame, or their treasure, or their
    land ;
Mine's on a Rock that for ever will stand,
    Jesus, the " Rock of Ages."

2 That Rock's a cross, its arms out-
    spread,
Celestial glory bathes its head ;
To its firm base my all I bring,
And to the Rock of Ages cling.

3 That Rock's a tower, whose lofty
    height,   [light.
Illum'd with heav'n's unclouded
Opes wide its gate beneath the
    dome,   [at home.
Where saints find rest with Christ

450 WHEN the pearly gates are
    opened
    To a sinner " saved by grace,"
When thro' everlasting mercy,
    I behold my Saviour's face ;

When I enter in the mansions
  Of the city bright and fair,
I shall have a royal welcome,
  For I'll be no stranger there.

I shall be...no stranger there,
Jesus will...my place prepare ;
He will meet me,...He will greet me,...
I shall be...no stranger there.

2 Thro' time's ever-changing seasons,
    I am pressing toward the goal ;
  'Tis my heart's sweet native country,
    'Tis the home-land of my soul ;
  Many lov'd ones, cloth'd with
      beauty,
    In those wondrous glories share ;
  When I rise, redeem'd, forgiven,
    I shall be no stranger there.

3 There my dear Redeemer liveth,
    Blessed Lamb upon the throne ;
  By the crimson marks upon them,
    He will surely claim His own.
  So, whenever sad or lonely,
    Look beyond the earthly care ;
  Weary child of God, remember,
    You will be no stranger there.

451 I WANDERED in the shades
        of night,
    Till Jesus came to me,
  And, with the sunlight of His love,
    Bade all my darkness flee.

Sunlight, sunlight, in my soul to-day...
Sunlight, sunlight all along the way,...
Since the Saviour found me, took away my sin,..
I have had the sunlight of His love within.

2 Though clouds may gather in the
      sky,
    And billows round me roll,
  However dark the world may be,
    I've sunlight in my soul.

3 While walking in the light of God,
    I sweet communion find ;
  I press with holy vigour on,
    And leave the world behind.

4 I cross the wide extended fields,
    I journey o'er the plain ;
  And in the sunlight of His love,
    I reap the golden grain.

5 Soon shall I see Him as He is,
    The Light that came to me ;
  Behold the brightness of His face,
    Throughout eternity.

452 TRAV'LING on the sea of lif
          we're homeward bound,
    Drifting wrecks and struggling sou
      are all around ;
    But we do not fear the voyage, f
      we know
    That the Saviour steers us as w
      onward go.

We're homeward bound for glory,...homewa
    bound for glory ;...
  There we'll meet with lov'd ones gone befor
We're homeward bound for glory,..homewa
    bound for glory,...
All the storms of life will soon be o'er.

2 Jesus guides our storm-toss'd barqu
      across the seas,
    He will bring us safely to the port
      peace ;
    He's the Pilot ; He is standing
      the helm,
    And no angry winds or waves ca
      overwhelm.

3 Come on board the gospel vessel, d
      not stay,
    And we'll help you as we journe
      on the way ;
    Soon to harbour at our Father
      blest abode,
    We will worship in the city of ou
      God.

453 ONE more day's work f
          Jesus ;
    One less of life for me !
      But heaven is nearer,
      And Christ is dearer,
    Than yesterday to me ;
      His love and light
      Fill all my soul to-night.

One more day's work for Jesus,
One more day's work for Jesus,
One more day's work for Jesus,
    One less of life for me.

2 One more day's work for Jesus ;
    How glorious is my King !
      'Tis joy, not duty,
      To speak His beauty,
    My soul mounts on the wing
      At the mere thought
      How Christ my life has bough

3 One more day's work for Jesus ;
    How sweet the work has been ;
      To tell the story,
      To show the glory,

When Christ's flock enter in !
How it did shine
In this poor heart of mine.

One more day's work for Jesus—
Oh, yes, a weary day ;
But heav'n shines clearer,
And rest comes nearer,
At each step of the way ;
And Christ in all—
Before His face I fall.

Oh, blessed work for Jesus !
Oh, rest at Jesus' feet !
There toil seems pleasure,
My wants are treasure,
And pain for Him is sweet ;
Lord, if I may,
I'll serve another day.

54 TO my blessed Lord and
Saviour, as He walks before
me here,   [day ;....
I am getting nearer, nearer ev'ry
And He says I shall be like Him,
when before Him I appear,
And I'm getting nearer, nearer
ev'ry day.

ev'ry day, praise the Lord, I'm getting nearer,
and the way, praise the Lord, is getting clearer;
rom my Lord no more I'll roam, for I see the
lights of home,
nd I'm getting nearer, nearer ev'ry day....

To the pure and perfect stature of
our great and living Head,
I am getting nearer, nearer ev'ry
day ;....
To the perfect will of Jesus, in the
way that I am led,   [day.
I am getting nearer, nearer ev'ry

To the time when I shall gladly lay
my cross and burdens down,
I am getting nearer, nearer, ev'ry
day ;....
To the time when from my Saviour
I'll receive a robe and crown,
I am getting nearer, nearer, ev'ry
day.

To that blest eternal city that lies
just across the foam,
I am getting nearer, nearer, ev'ry
day ;....
Often thro' faith's open vision I can
see the spires of home,
And I'm getting nearer, nearer
ev'ry day.

455 BRIGHTLY beams our
Father's mercy
From His lighthouse evermore ;
But to us He gives the keeping
Of the lights along the shore.

Let the lower lights be burning !
Send a gleam across the wave !
Some poor fainting, struggling seaman
You may rescue, you may save !

2 Dark the night of sin has settled,
Loud the angry billows roar ;
Eager eyes are watching, longing,
For the lights along the shore.

3 Trim your feeble lamp, my brother,
Some poor sailor, tempest-tossed,
Trying now to make the harbour,
In the darkness *may be lost.*

456 TELL me the story of Jesus
Write on my heart ev'ry
word,
Tell me the story most precious,
Sweetest that ever was heard ;
Tell how the angels, in chorus,
Sang as they welcomed His birth,
Glory to God in the highest !
Peace and good tidings to earth.

Tell me the story of Jesus,
Write on my heart ev'ry word ;
Tell me the story most precious,
Sweetest that ever was heard.

2 Fasting, alone in the desert,
Tell of the days that He passed,
How for our sins He was tempted,
Yet was triumphant at last ;
Tell of the years of His labour,
Tell of the sorrow He bore,
He was despised and afflicted,
Homeless, rejected, and poor.

3 Tell of the Cross where they nailed
Him,
Writhing in anguish and pain ;
Tell of the grave where they laid
Him,
Tell how He liveth again ;
Love in that story so tender,
Clearer than ever I see ;
Stay, let me weep while you whisper,
Love paid the ransom for me.

457 IT pays to serve Jesus—I
speak from my heart ;
He'll always be with us, if we do our
part ;

There's naught in this wide world
can pleasure afford,
There's peace and contentment in
serving the Lord.

I love Him far better than in days of yore,
I'll serve Him more truly than ever before,
I'll do as He bids me whatever the cost,
I'll be a true soldier—I'll die at my post.

2 And oft when I'm tempted to turn
from the track   [wanders back
I think of my Saviour—my mind
To the place where they nailed Him
on Calvary's tree,   [for thee."
I heard a voice saying, " I suffered

3 A place I remember where I was
set free,   [heaven to me ;
'Twas where I found pardon—a
There Jesus spoke sweetly to my
weary soul,   [heart whole.
My sins were forgiven, He made my

4 How rich is the blessing that the world
cannot give,
I'm satisfied fully for Jesus to live ;
Tho' friends may forsake me and
trials arise,   [never dies.
I am trusting in Jesus, His love

5 There is no one like Jesus can cheer
me to-day,   [fade away ;
His love and His kindness can ne'er
In winter, in summer, in sunshine
and rain,
His love and affection are always
the same.

6 Will you have this blessing that
Jesus bestows,
A free, full salvation from sin's
bitter throes ?
O come to the Saviour, to Calvary
flee,   [for thee.
The fountain is opened, is flowing

458   TO Jesus ev'ry day I find my
heart is closer drawn ;
He's fairer than the glory of the gold
and purple dawn ;
He's all my fancy pictured in its
fairest dreams and more ;
Each day He grows still sweeter than
He was the day before.

The half...cannot be fancied...this side...the
golden shore ;...
O there...He'll be still sweeter than He ever
was before.

2 His glory broke upon me when I s
Him from afar ;
He's fairer than the lily, bright
than the morning star ;
He fills and satisfies my long
spirit o'er and o'er ;
Each day He grows still swee
than He was the day before.

3 My heart is sometimes heavy, b
He comes with sweet relief ;
He folds me to His bosom when
droop with blighting grief ;
I love the Christ who all my burde
in His body bore ;
Each day He grows still swee
than He was the day before.

459   WHEN we walk with the Lo
In the light of His word,
What a glory He sheds on our way !
While we do His good will
He abides with us still,
And with all who will trust and obe

Trust and obey ; for there's no other way
To be happy in Jesus, but to trust and obey

2 Not a shadow can rise,
Not a cloud in the skies,
But His smile quickly drives it awa
Not a doubt nor a fear,
Not a sigh nor a tear,
Can abide while we trust and obey.

3 Not a burden we bear,
Not a sorrow we share,
But our toil He doth richly repay ;
Not a grief nor a loss,
Not a frown nor a cross,
But is blest if we trust and obey.

4 But we never can prove
The delights of His love
Until all on the altar we lay ;
For the favours He shows
And the joy He bestows,
Are for them who will trust and obe

5 Then in fellowship sweet
We will sit at His feet,
Or we'll walk by His side in the way
What He says we will do,
Where He sends we will go,
Never fear, only trust and obey.

460   ONWARD, Christian soldier
marching as to war,
Looking unto Jesus, who is go
before ;

Christ, the Royal Master, leads
  against the foe ;   [go.
Forward into battle see His banners
nward, Christian soldiers ! marching as to war,
ooking unto Jesus, who is gone before.

At the name of Jesus Satan's host
  doth flee ;   [victory !
On then, Christian soldiers, on to
Hell's foundations quiver at the
  shout of praise ;
Brothers, lift your voices, loud your
  anthems raise.

Like a mighty army moves the
  Church of God ;
Brothers, we are treading where the
  saints have trod ;
We are not divided, all one body we,
One in hope and doctrine, one in
  charity.

Crowns and thrones may perish,
  kingdoms rise and wane ;
But the church of Jesus constant
  will remain ;
Gates of hell can never 'gainst that
  Church prevail ;
We have Christ's own promise, and
  that cannot fail.

Onward then, ye people, join our
  happy throng ;
Blend with ours your voices in the
  triumph song :
" Glory, praise, and honour, unto
  Christ the King "—
This, through countless ages, men
  and angels sing.

61 WHEN a sinner comes, as a
  sinner may,
There is joy,....there is joy ;....
When he turns to God in the gospel
  way,
There is joy,....there is joy.

  There is joy among the angels,
    And their harps with music ring ;...
  When a sinner comes repenting,
    Bending low before the King.

When a soul is born in the kingdom
  bright,
There is joy,...there is joy ;....
When it walks by faith in the gospel
  light,
There is joy,....there is joy.

3 When a pilgrim comes to the river
  wide,
There is joy,....there is joy ;....
When he dwells secure on the other
  side,
There is joy,....there is joy.

462 THE Lord hath made this
  world of ours
Most beautiful and bright ;
The golden sun to rule by day,
The moon and stars by night ;
But souls are wand'ring far from
  Him,
In darkened paths astray ;
So make me, Saviour, more and
A light along the way.   [more,

A light along the way, make me, dear Lord,
    I pray !
Love's happy rays show forth Thy praise, a
    light along the way ;
A light along the way, make me, dear Lord, I
    pray ;
Love's happy rays show forth Thy praise, a
    light along the way.

2 So many need a helping hand,
  A kindly word of cheer,
To tell them of the mighty Friend
  Whose grace is always near.
O make me prompt to hear Thy
  voice,
  And ready to obey,
That I may be, to saddened hearts,
  A light along the way.

3 Some lives shine out like beacons
  grand,
  Some seem but candles small,
But if we truly shine for Him,
  The Lord hath need of all.
O may His Spirit fill my soul,
  And lead me day by day,
That, though unworthy, I shall be
  A light along the way.

463 SOWING in the morning,
  sowing seeds of kindness,
Sowing in the noontide, and the
  dewy eve ;
Waiting for the harvest, and the
  time of reaping,
We shall come rejoicing, bringing
  in the sheaves.

Bringing in the sheaves, bringing in the sheaves,
We shall come, rejoicing, bringing in the sheaves.

2 Sowing in the sunshine, sowing in
   the shadows,
   Fearing neither clouds nor winter's
      chilling breeze ;
By and by the harvest, and the
   labour ended,
   We shall come rejoicing, bringing
      in the sheaves.

3 Go then, ever weeping, sowing for
   the Master,
   Tho' the loss sustained our spirit
      often grieves ;
When our weeping's over, He will
   bid us welcome,
   We shall come rejoicing, bringing
      in the sheaves.

464 THO' dark the path my feet
      may tread, it is a joy to know
   There'll be no shadows on the
      other side ;
We should not fear the wildest
   storm, but sing as on we go,
   There'll be no shadows on the
      other side.

There'll be no shadows, no...shadows,
   Jesus is the sunshine of that land so fair ;
There'll be no shadows, no...shadows,
   Pain and death can never enter there....

2 Life's brightest day may have its
      clouds, but still our hearts
      should sing,   [side ;
   There'll be no shadows on the other
'Twill not be long till cares are o'er,
   and we are with the King,
   There'll be no shadows on the
      other side.

3 We're marching homeward to a land
      where weary feet may rest ;
   There'll be no shadows on the
      other side ;
No pain or sorrow e'er can touch the
   regions of the blest :
   There'll be no shadows on the
      other side.

465 TAKE the name of Jesus
      with you,
   Child of sorrow and of woe ;
It will joy and comfort give you—
   Take it then where'er you go.

Precious name,...oh, how sweet !...
   Hope of earth and joy of heaven ;
Precious name,...oh, how sweet !...
   Hope of earth and joy of heaven.

2 Take the name of Jesus ever,
   As a shield from ev'ry snare ;
If temptations round you gather,
   Breathe that holy name in praye[r]

3 Oh, the precious name of Jesus !
   How it thrills our souls with joy
When His loving arms receive us,
   And His songs our tongues emplo[y]

4 At the name of Jesus bowing,
   Falling prostrate at His feet ;
King of kings, in heaven we'[ll]
   crown Him,
When our journey is complete.

466 I SHALL wear a golden crow[n]
      When I get home ;
   I shall lay my burdens down,
      When I get home ;
Clad in robes of glory,
   I shall sing the story,
   Of the Lord who bought me,
      When I get home.

When I..get..home,..when I..get..home ..
   All sorrow will be over when I get home ;
When I..get..home,..when I..get..home,..
   All sorrow will be over, when I get home.

2 All the darkness will be past,
      When I get home ;
   I shall see the light at last,
      When I get home ;
Light from heaven streaming,
   O'er my pathway beaming,
   Ever guides me onward,
      Till I get home.

3 I shall see my Saviour's face,
      When I get home ;
   Sing again of saving grace,
      When I get home ;
I shall stand before Him ;
   Gladly I'll adore Him,
   Ever to be with Him,
      When I get home.

467 THE Lord is my Shepherd,
      shall not want,
   He maketh me down to lie
In pastures green, He leadeth m[e]
   The quiet waters by.

His yoke is easy, His burden is light,
   I've found it so, I've found it so ;
He leadeth me by day and by night
   Where living waters flow.

My soul crieth out, "Restore me
   again,
And give me the strength to take
The narrow path of righteousness,
   E'en for His own name's sake."

Yea, though I should walk in the
   valley of death,
   E'en yet will I fear no ill ;
For Thou art with me and Thy rod
   And staff they comfort still.

68   WE are building in sorrow,
     and building in joy,
   A temple the world cannot see ;
But we know it will stand if we
   found it on a rock,
   Thro' the ages of eternity.

We are building day by day as the moments
   glide away,
Our temple which the world may not see ;...
v'ry vict'ry won by grace will be sure to find
   its place
     In our building for eternity....

Ev'ry deed forms a part in this
   building of ours,
   That is done in the name of the
     Lord ;
For the love that we show, and the
   kindness we bestow,   [reward.
He has promis'd us a bright

Then be watchful and wise, let the
   temple we rear
   Be one that no tempest can shock ;
For the Master has said, and He
   taught us in His Word,
We must build upon the solid
   rock.

69   HOME to Zion we are bound,
     Happy in the love of Jesus ;
Peace abiding we have found,
   Happy in the love of Jesus.

     Happy, happy,
Singing all the way, happy all the day ;
     Happy, happy,
Happy in the love of Jesus.

Trusting, we will forward go,
   Happy in the love of Jesus ;
Treading changeful paths below,
   Happy in the love of Jesus.

Soon we'll reach the homeland fair,
   Happy in the love of Jesus ;
And shall dwell for ever there,
   Happy in the love of Jesus.

470   YONDER'S the land where the
     lov'd ones are,
   Soon will the mist roll away !
Joy soon to rest in that realm afar,
   Soon will the mist roll away !
There in the loving smile of Christ
   to abide,
   Visions of glory day by day !
Faith fondly whispers while in
   shadows we hide,
   Soon will the mist roll away !

Yonder's the land where the lov'd ones are,
   Soon will the mist roll away !
Joy soon to rest in that realm afar,
   Soon will the mist roll away !

2 Dark looms the path, but the promise
   heed,
   Soon will the mist roll away !
Jesus alone can relieve thy need,
   Soon will the mist roll away !
Clear will the purpose of the Lord
   be to thee,
   Hasten the Master to obey ;
Blissful the vision that beyond we
   shall see,
   Soon will the mist roll away !

3 Bear thou the cross till the crown
   is won,
   Soon will the mist roll away !
Work till the will of the Lord be
   done,
   Soon will the mist roll away !
All will be reconciled to thee by and
   by,
   Faith guideth on to perfect day ;
Soon shall the glory dawn upon
   ev'ry eye,
   Soon will the mist roll away !

471   OUR souls cry out, hallelujah !
     And our faith enraptured
     sings,
While we throw to the breeze the
   standard,
   Of the mighty King of kings.

On the vict'ry side, on the vict'ry side,
   In the ranks of the Lord are we ;
On the vict'ry side we will boldly stand,
   Till the glory land we see.

2 Our souls cry out, hallelujah !
   For the Lord Himself comes near,
And the shout of a royal army
   On the battle-field we hear.

3 Our souls cry out, hallelujah !
    For the tempter flies apace
And the chains he has forged are
        breaking,   [grace.
    Thro' the pow'r of redeeming

4 Our souls cry out, hallelujah !
    And our hearts beat high with
        praise,   [conquer,
Unto Him, in whose name we'll
    And our song of triumph raise.

472 I BELIEVE in the story never
        old,
        I believe it !   [told,
    I believe in the Saviour long fore-
        I believe it !   [than gold,
    I believe He's more precious far
        I believe it !   [name.
    I am saved by believing on His

I am saved by believing on His name,...
I am saved, for His Word is just the same,...
'Tis the same " whosoever," for His love
    changeth never,
I am saved by believing on His name.

2 I believe in the tidings of His birth,
        I believe it !   [earth,
    I believe in the song of peace on
        I believe it !   [mirth,
    I believe 'twas a time of joy and
        I believe it !
    I am saved by believing on His name.

3 I believe that the shepherds heard
        I believe it !   [the song,
    I believe that they saw the heav'nly
        I believe it !   [throng,
    I believe that the glory shone around,
        I believe it !
    I am saved by believing on His name.

4 I believe that the wise men saw His
        I believe it !   [star,
    I believe that they followed from
        I believe it !   [afar,
    I believe that they found the
        Saviour there,
        I believe it !
    I am saved by believing on His name.

5 I believe that He came to seek and
        I believe it !   [save,
    I believe that eternal life He gave,
        I believe it !   [grave,
    I believe I shall live beyond the
        I believe it !
    I am saved by believing on His name.

473 SUFFICIENT for me, suf
        cient for me,
    His grace so abundant and free
In sorrow or pain this joy sh
    remain :
    His grace is sufficient for me.....

474 THERE is a land of pu
        delight,
    Where saints immortal reign,
Infinite day excludes the night,
    And pleasures banish pain.

We're feeding on the Living Bread,
We're drinking at the Fountain-head ;
And who-so drinketh, Jesus said,
Shall never, never thirst again.
What, never thirst again ?
No, never thirst again !
And who-so drinketh, Jesus said,
Shall never, never thirst again !

2 There everlasting Spring abides,
    And never-with'ring flowers :
Death, like a narrow sea, divides
    This heavenly land from ours.

3 O could we make our doubts remov
    Those gloomy thoughts that ris
And see the Canaan that we love
    With unbeclouded eyes.

4 Could we but climb where Mos
        stood,
    And view the landscape o'er,
Not Jordan's stream, nor death
        cold flood,
    Should fright us from the shore.

The following Chorus may be substituted :—
We're marching through Immanuel's grou
And soon shall hear the trumpet sound,
And then we shall with Jesus reign,
And never, never part again.
What, never part again ?
No, never part again !
And then we shall with Jesus reign,
And never, never part again !

475 THOU Shepherd of Israel, a
        mine,
    The joy and desire of my heart,
For closer communion I pine,
    I long to reside where Thou art.

2 The pasture I languish to find,
    Where all who their Sheph
        obey,
Are fed on His bosom reclined,
    And screened from the heat of t
        day.

Ah, show me that happiest place,
   That place of Thy people's abode,
Where saints in an ecstasy gaze,
   And hang on a crucified God.

Thy love for a sinner declare,
   Thy passion and death on the tree,
My spirit to Calvary bear,
   To suffer and triumph with Thee.

'Tis there, with the lambs of Thy flock,
   There only I covet to rest ;
To lie at the foot of the Rock,
   Or rise to be hid in Thy breast.

'Tis there I would always abide,
   And never a moment depart,
Concealed in the cleft of Thy side,
   Eternally hid in Thy heart

76 HOW good is the God we adore,
   Our faithful, unchangeable Friend,
Whose love is as great as His power,
   And knows neither measure nor end.

'Tis Jesus, the First and the Last,
   Whose Spirit shall guide us safe home ;
We'll praise Him for all that is past,
   And trust Him for all that's to come.

77 A FEW more marchings weary,
   Then we'll gather home !
A few more storm-clouds dreary,
   Then we'll gather home !
A few more days the cross to bear,
And then with Christ a crown to wear ;
   A few more marchings weary,
   Then we'll gather home !

> O'er....time's rapid river,
> Soon....we'll rest for ever.
> No more marchings weary
> When we gather home !

2 A few more nights of weeping,
   Then we'll gather home !
A few more watches keeping,
   Then we'll gather home !
A few more vict'ries over sin,
A few more sheaves to gather in ;
   A few more marchings weary,
   Then we'll gather home !

3 A few more sweet links broken,
   Then we'll gather home !
A few more kind words spoken,
   Then we'll gather home !
A few more partings on the strand
And then away to Canaan's land ;
   A few more marchings weary,
   Then we'll gather home !

478 FROM Egypt's cruel bondage fled,
   Obedient to our Lord's command,
And by His Word and Spirit led,
   We're on the way to Canaan's Land !

> We're on the way, a pilgrim band ;
> We're on the way to Canaan's land ;
> Divinely guided day by day,
> We're on the way, we're on the way.

2 Through wildernesses wide and drear,
   Our Lord will guide our steps aright ;
Behold, to prove His presence here,
   The cloud by day, the fire by night !

3 His pow'r the smitten rock controls,
   A crystal stream our need supplies;
He feeds our hungry, fainting souls
   With daily manna from the skies !

4 In hostile lands we feel no fear ;
   No foe our onward march can stay ;
In ev'ry conflict He is near,
   Whose presence cheers us on the way.

5 Ere long, the river crossed, we'll meet   [hand ;
   The ransomed host at His right
And there receive a welcome sweet,
   From our dear Lord, to Canaan's Land !

479 THE sunshine I have found
   will fill each day with joy,
   And ev'ry moment sweetly bless ;
The rays that gently fall upon my
   daily path   [eousness.
   Are given by the Sun of Right-

> So if the sky is dark, and if the day is dreary,
>   The sun is shining somewhere, this I know,
>   I know,
> And so to keep my heart from ever growing
>   weary,
> I'll carry my sunshine with me ev'rywhere
>   I go.

2 Look up and praise the Lord ! the
    flowers need the rain
      That falls upon them day by day,
    Just as our thirsty souls would seek
      the cooling springs
      If we were walking in a desert way.

3 But for the child of God there
    always is a ray,
      That struggles thro' the clouds
      above ;
    That shines across his path and helps
      his wav'ring faith
      To rest securely in a Father's
      love.

4 It is the light that shines, when
    Jesus speaks to me,
      And tells me I am saved by grace ;
    The sunshine I have found is free to
      all who seek
      The sunshine of my blessed
      Saviour's face.

480 AM I a soldier of the Cross,....
      A follower of the Lamb ?....
And shall I fear to own His cause,
  Or blush to speak His name ?

      We will stand...the storm,....
      We will anchor by-and-by....

2 Must I be carried to the skies,....
  On flow'ry beds of ease,....
While others fought to win the
  prize,
And sailed through bloody seas ?

3 Are there no foes for me to face ?....
  Must I not stem the flood ?....
Is this vile world a friend to grace,
  To help me on to God ?

4 Since I must fight if I would reign,....
  Increase my courage, Lord !....
I'll bear the toil, endure the pain,
  Supported by Thy word.

481 JESUS, my all, to heav'n is
      gone,
He whom I fix my hopes upon ;
His track I see, and I'll pursue
The narrow way till Him I view.

2 The way the holy prophets went,
The road that leads from banish-
  ment ;
The King's highway of holiness
I'll go, for all His paths are peace.

3 This is the way I long have sough
And mourn'd because I found it no
Till late I heard my Saviour say,
"Come hither, child ; I am the Way

482 SOLDIERS of Christ, arise—
      And put your armour on ;
Strong in the strength which G
  supplies
  Through His eternal Son !

2 Strong in the Lord of hosts,
  Stand in His mighty pow'r ;
Who in the strength of Jesus trus
  Is more than conqueror !

3 Stand then in His great might,
  With all His strength endued ;
And take, to arm you for the fight
  The panoply of God.

4 To keep your armour bright,
  Attend with constant care ;
Still marching in your Captai
  sight,
  And watching unto pray'r.

5 Jesus hath died for you—
  What can His love withstand ?
Believe, hold fast your shield, a
  who
  Shall pluck you from His hand

6 Then, having all things done,
  And ev'ry conflict past—
Accepted each through Christ alo
  You shall be crowned at last.

483 · I WAITED for the Lord my G
      And patiently did bear ;
At length to me He did incline
  My voice and cry to hear.

2 He took me from a fearful pit,
  And from the miry clay,
And on a rock He set my feet,
  Establishing my way.

3 He put a new song in my mouth,
  Our God to magnify ;
Many shall see it, and shall fear,
  And on the Lord rely.

4 O blessed is the man whose trust
  Upon the Lord relies ;
Respecting not the proud, nor suc
  As turn aside to lies.

5 In Thee let all be glad, and joy,
  Who seeking Thee abide ;
Who Thy salvation love, say still,
  The Lord be magnified.

484 CHRISTIAN! seek not yet
    repose ;
Hear thy guardian angel say,
Thou art in the midst of foes ;
    Watch and pray.

Principalities and powers,
    Must'ring their unseen array,
Wait for thy unguarded hours :
    Watch and pray.

Gird thy heavenly armour on ;
    Wear it ever, night and day ;
Ambushed lies the evil one :
    Watch and pray.

Hear the victors who o'ercame ;
    Still they mark each warrior's
    way ;
All with one sweet voice exclaim,
    " Watch and pray."

Hear, above all, hear thy Lord,
    Him thou lovest to obey ;
Hide within thy heart His Word—
    " Watch and pray."

Watch as if on that alone
    Hung the issue of the day ;
Pray that help may be sent down :
    Watch and pray.

485 THERE is a Name I love to
    hear,
I love to sing its worth ;
It sounds like music in mine ear,
    The sweetest Name on earth.

It tells me of a Saviour's love,
    Who died to set me free ;
It tells me of His precious blood,
    The sinner's perfect plea.

It bids my trembling soul rejoice,
    And dries each rising tear ;
It tells me in a " still, small voice,"
    To trust and never fear.

Jesus, the Name I love so well,
    The Name I love to hear,
No saint on earth its worth can tell,
    No heart conceive how dear.

This Name shall shed its fragrance
    Along this thorny road,   [still
Shall sweetly smooth the rugged hill
    That leads me up to God.

And there, with all the blood-
    bought throng,
    From sin and sorrow free,
I'll sing the new eternal song
    Of Jesus' love to me.

486 THE Lord's my Shepherd, I'll
    not want,
He makes me down to lie
In pastures green ; He leadeth me
    The quiet waters by.

2 My soul He doth restore again,
    And me to walk doth make
Within the paths of righteousness,
    Ev'n for His own Name's sake.

3 Yea, though I walk in death's dark
    vale,
    Yet will I fear none ill ;
For Thou art with me ; and Thy
    rod
    And staff me comfort still.

4 My table Thou hast furnished
    In presence of my foes ;
My head Thou dost with oil anoint,
    And my cup overflows.

5 Goodness and mercy all my life
    Shall surely follow me,
And in God's house for evermore
    My dwelling-place shall be.

487 TO Calvary, Lord, in spirit
    now
Our weary souls repair,
To dwell upon Thy dying love,
    And taste its sweetness there.

2 Sweet resting place of every heart,
    That feels the plague of sin,
Yet knows that deep, mysterious
    joy,
    The peace of God within.

3 There through Thine hour of deepest
    woe,
    Thy suffering spirit passed ;
Grace there its wondrous victory
    gained,
    And love endured its last.

4 Dear suffering Lamb, Thy bleeding
    wounds,
    With cords of love divine,
Have drawn our willing hearts to
    Thee,
    And linked our life with Thine.

5 Our longing eyes would fain behold
    That bright and blessed brow,
Once wrung with bitterest anguish,
    wear
    Its crown of glory now.

488 COURAGE, brother! do not
     stumble,
   Though thy path be dark as night;
There's a star to guide the humble,
   Trust in God, and do the right.

2 Let the road be rough and dreary,
     And its end far out of sight;
Foot it bravely, strong or weary;
     Trust in God, and do the right.

3 Perish policy and cunning!
     Perish all that fears the light!
Whether losing, whether winning,
     Trust in God, and do the right.

4 Trust no party, sect, or faction,
     Trust no leaders in the fight;
But in every word and action,
     Trust in God, and do the right.

5 Trust no lovely forms of passion,
     Fiends may look like angels bright,
Trust no custom, school, or fashion,
     Trust in God, and do the right.

6 Simple rule, and safest guiding,
     Inward peace, and inward might;
Star upon our path abiding,
     Trust in God, and do the right.

7 Some will hate thee, some will love
     thee,
   Some will flatter, some will slight;
Cease from man, and look above
     thee,
   Trust in God, and do the right.

489 JESUS calls us; o'er the
     tumult
Of our life's wild, restless sea,
Day by day His sweet voice soundeth
Saying, " Christian, follow me! "

2 As of old, apostles heard it
     By the Galilean lake,
Turned from home, and toil, and
     kindred,
   Leaving all for His dear sake.

3 Jesus calls us from the worship
     Of the vain world's golden store;
From each idol that would keep us,
   Saying, " Christian, love Me
     more."

4 In our joys and in our sorrows,
     Days of toil and hours of ease;
Still He calls, in cares and pleasures,
   " Christian, love Me more than
     these."

5 Jesus calls us; by Thy mercies,
     Saviour, may we hear Thy call
Give our hearts to Thy obedience
   Serve and love Thee best of all.

490 IN the cross of Christ I glo
     Tow'ring o'er the wrecks
     time;
All the light of sacred story
   Gathers round its head sublime

2 When the woes of life o'ertake me
     Hopes deceive and fears annoy
Never shall the Cross forsake me,
   Lo! it glows with peace and joy

3 When the sun of bliss is beaming
     Light and love upon my way;
From the Cross the radiance strea
     ing,
   Adds new lustre to the day.

4 Bane and blessing, pain and pleasu
     By the Cross are sanctified;
Peace is there that knows
     measure,
   Joys that through all time abide

491 GLORIOUS things of thee
     spoken,
Zion, city of our God;
He whose word cannot be broken
   Formed thee for His own abode

2 On the rock of ages founded,
     What can shake thy sure repos
With salvation's walls surrounded
   Thou mayest smile at all thy fo

3 See! the streams of living waters,
     Springing from eternal love,
Well supply thy sons and daughter
   And all fear of want remove.

4 Saviour, if of Zion's city,
     I, through grace, a member am,
Let the world deride or pity,
   I will glory in Thy name.

5 Fading is the worldling's pleasure
     All his boasted pomp and show
Solid joys and lasting treasure,
   None but Zion's children know.

492 THROUGH the night of do
     and sorrow
Onward goes the pilgrim band,
Singing songs of expectation,
   Marching to the Promised Lan

Clear before us through the darkness
  Gleams and burns the guiding
    light,
Brother clasps the hand of brother,
  Stepping fearless through the
    night.

One the strain that lips of thousands
  Lift as from the heart of one ;
One the conflict, one the peril,
  One the march in God begun ;

One the gladness of rejoicing,
  On the far, eternal shore,
Where the one Almighty Father
  Reigns in love for evermore.

Onward, therefore, pilgrim brothers,
  Onward with the Cross our aid !
Bear its shame, and fight its battle,
  Till we rest beneath its shade.

Soon shall come the great awakening,
  Soon the rending of the tomb ;
Then the scattering of all shadows,
  And the end of toil and gloom.

93 GO, labour on, spend, and be
      spent,
  Thy joy to do the Father's will ;
It is the way the Master went,
  Should not the servant tread it
    still ?

Go, labour on : 'tis not for nought,
  Thy earthly loss is heavenly gain ;
Men heed thee, love thee, praise thee
  not,   [men ?
  The Master praises : what are

Men die in darkness at your side,
  Without a hope to cheer the tomb ;
Take up the torch, and wave it wide,
  The torch that lights time's
    thickest gloom.

Toil on, and in thy toil rejoice,
  For toil comes rest, for exile home ;
Soon shall thou hear the Bride-
  groom's voice,   [come ! "
  The midnight peal, " Behold I

94 LO ! round the throne at God's
      right hand
The saints in countless myriads
  stand ;
Of ev'ry tongue redeemed to God,
Arrayed in garments washed in
  blood.

2 Through tribulation great they came,
  They bore the cross, despised the
    shame ;   [rest,
  From all their labours now they
  In God's eternal glory blest.

3 Hunger and thirst they feel no more,
  Nor sin, nor pain, nor death deplore ;
  The tears are wiped from every eye,
  And sorrow yields to endless joy.

4 They see their Saviour face to face,
  And sing the triumphs of His grace ;
  Him day and night they ceaseless
    praise,
  To Him their loud Hosannas raise.

5 O may we tread the sacred road
  That holy saints and martyrs trod ;
  Wage to the end the glorious strife,
  And win, like them, the crown of life.

495 I THIRST, Thou wounded
        Lamb of God,
  To wash me in Thy cleansing blood ;
  To dwell within Thy wounds, then
    pain
  Is sweet, and life or death is gain.

2 Take my poor heart, and let it be
  For ever closed to all but Thee !
  Seal Thou my breast, and let me
    wear
  That pledge of love for ever there.

3 How can it be, Thou heavenly King,
  That Thou shouldst us to glory bring?
  Make slaves the partners of Thy
    throne,
  Decked with a never-fading crown?

4 Hence our hearts melt, our eyes o'er-
    flow,   [know,
  Our words are lost : nor will we
  Nor will we think of aught beside,
  " My Lord, my Love is crucified ! "

496 THOU sweet beloved will of
        God,   [hill,
  My anchor ground, my fortress
  My spirit's silent, fair abode,
  In Thee I hide me, and am still.

2 O will, that willest good alone,
    Lead Thou the way, Thou guidest
      best ;
  A little child, I follow on,   [breast.
    And trusting, lean upon Thy

3 Oh, lightest burden, sweetest yoke !
  It lifts, it bears my happy soul ;
It giveth wings to this poor heart ;
  My freedom is Thy grand control.

4 Upon God's will I lay me down,
  As child upon its mother's breast;
No silken couch, nor softest bed,
  Could ever give me such deep
    rest.

5 Thy wonderful grand will, my God,
  With triumph now I make it
    mine ;
And faith shall cry a joyous " Yes !"
  To every dear command of Thine.

497 BRETHREN in Christ, and
  well beloved,
To Jesus and His servants dear,
Enter and show yourselves approved;
  Enter and find that God is here.

2 Welcome from earth : lo, the right
    hand
  Of fellowship to you we give !
With open hearts and hands we
    stand,
  And you in Jesus' name receive.

3 Say, are your hearts resolved as ours ?
  Then let them burn with sacred
    love ;   [powers,
Then let them taste the heav'nly
  Partakers of the joys above.

4 Thou God that answerest by fire,
  The Spirit of burning now impart ;
And let the flames of pure desire
  Rise from the altar of our heart.

5 In part we only know Thee here,
  But wait Thy coming from above :
And we shall then behold Thee near,
  And we shall all be lost in love.

498 WE sing the praise of Him who
  died,
Of Him who died upon the Cross ;
The sinner's hope let men deride,
  For this we count the world but
    loss.

2 Inscribed upon the Cross we see,
  In shining letters, " God is love ; "
He bears our sins upon the tree,
  He brings us mercy from above.

3 The Cross ! it takes our guilt awa
  It holds the fainting spirit up ;
It cheers with hope the gloomy da
  And sweetens every bitter cup.

4 It makes the coward spirit brave,
  And nerves the feeble arm
    fight ;
It takes its terror from the grave,
  And gilds the bed of death wi
    light.

5 The balm of life, the cure of woe,
  The measure and the pledge
    love ;
The sinner's refuge here below,
  The angels' theme in heaven abov

499 FROM all that dwell bel
  the skies,
Let the Creator's praise arise ;
Let the Redeemer's name be sung
  Through every land, by every tong

2 Eternal are Thy mercies, Lord ;
  Eternal truth attends Thy Word ;
Thy praise shall sound from sho
  to shore,
  Till suns shall rise and set no mor

500 COME, Holy Spirit, calm o
  minds,
And fit us to approach our God
Remove each vain, each world
    thought,
  And lead us to Thy blest abode.

2 Hast Thou imparted to our souls
  A living spark of heavenly fire ?
Oh, kindle now the sacred flame,
  And make us burn with pu
    desire !

3 Impress upon our wandering hear
  The love that Christ to sinners bo
Help us to look on Him we pierce
  And our redeeming God adore.

4 A brighter faith and hope impart,
  And let us now Thy glory see ;
Oh, soothe and cheer each burden
    heart,
  And bid our spirits rest in Thee

501 WHILE shepherds watch
  their flocks by night,
All seated on the ground ;
The angel of the Lord came down
  And glory shone around.

" Fear not ! " said he—for mighty
    dread
  Had seized their troubled mind—
" Glad tidings of great joy I bring
  To you and all mankind.

" To you in David's town this day,
  Is born of David's line
The Saviour, who is Christ the Lord,
  And this shall be the sign :

" The heavenly babe you there shall
    find
  To human view displayed,
All meanly wrapped in swathing
    bands,
  And in a manger laid."

Thus spake the seraph—and forth-
    with
  Appeared a shining throng
Of angels praising God, who thus
  Addressed their joyful song :

" All glory be to God on high !
  And to the earth be peace ;
Good-will henceforth from heaven
    to men
  Begin, and never cease ! "

502 OPPRESSED by noonday's
    scorching heat,
  To yonder Cross I flee,
Beneath its shelter take my seat—
  No shade like this to me !

Beneath that Cross clear waters
    burst,
  A fountain sparkling free,
And there I quench my desert
    thirst—
  No spring like this to me !

For burdened ones, a resting-place
  Beneath that Cross I see ;
Here I cast off my weariness—
  No rest like this for me !

A stranger here, I pitch my tent
  Beneath this spreading tree ;
Here shall my pilgrim life be spent—
  No home like this for me !

503 LORD, I have made Thy Word
    my choice,
  My lasting heritage ;
There shall my noblest powers
    rejoice,
  My warmest thoughts engage.

2 I'll read the histories of Thy love,
  And keep Thy laws in sight,
While through Thy promises I rove
  With ever fresh delight.

3 'Tis a broad land of wealth unknown,
  Where springs of life arise,
Seeds of immortal bliss are sown,
  And hidden glory lies.

4 The best relief that mourners have,
  It makes our sorrows blest ;
Our fairest hope beyond the grave,
  And our eternal rest.

504 HAPPY the souls to Jesus
    joined,
  And saved by grace alone ;
Walking in all His ways, they find
  Their heaven on earth begun.

2 The Church triumphant in Thy love,
  Their mighty joys we know ;
They sing the Lamb in hymns above,
  And we in hymns below.

3 Thee in Thy glorious realm they
    praise,
  And bow before Thy throne ;
We in the kingdom of Thy grace—
  The kingdoms are but one.

4 The holy to the holiest leads ;
  From thence our spirits rise ;
And he that in Thy statues treads
  Shall meet Thee in the skies.

505 FATHER of mercies ! in Thy
    Word
  What endless glory shines !
For ever be Thy name adored
  For these celestial lines.

2 Here may the wretched sons of want
  Exhaustless riches find ;
Riches above what earth can grant,
  And lasting as the mind.

3 Here the Redeemer's welcome voice
  Spreads heav'nly peace around ;
And life and everlasting joys
  Attend the blissful sound.

4 Oh, may these heavenly pages be
  My ever dear delight,
And still new beauties may I see,
  And still increasing light.

5 Divine Instructor, gracious Lord !
  Be Thou for ever near ;
Teach me to love Thy sacred Word,
  And view my Saviour there.

506 GOD is our refuge and our strength,
In straits a present aid ;
Therefore, although the earth remove,
We will not be afraid.

2 Though hills amidst the seas be cast;
Though waters roaring make,
And troubled be ; yea, though the hills
By swelling seas do shake.

3 A river is, whose streams do glad
The city of our God ;
The holy place, wherein the Lord
Most high hath His abode.

4 God in the midst of her doth dwell,
Nothing shall her remove ;
The Lord to her an helper will,
And that right early prove.

5 Be still, and know that I am God ;
Among the heathen I
Will be exalted ; I on earth
Will be exalted high.

507 OH, sing a new song to the Lord,
For wonders He hath done ;
His right hand and His holy arm
Him victory hath won.

2 The Lord God His salvation
Hath caused to be known ;
His justice in the heathen's sight
He openly hath shown.

3 He mindful of His grace and truth
To Israel's house hath been ;
And the salvation of our God
All ends of th' earth have seen.

4 Let all the earth unto the Lord
Send forth a joyful noise ;
Lift up your voice aloud to Him,
Sing praises and rejoice.

5 With harp, with harp, and voice of psalms,
Unto Jehovah sing ;
With trumpets, cornets, gladly sound
Before the Lord the King.

508 WHEN all Thy mercies, O my God,
My rising soul surveys,
Transported with the view, I'm lost
In wonder, love, and praise.

2 Unnumbered comforts on my sou
Thy tender care bestowed,
Before my infant heart conceived
From whom these comforts flowe

3 When worn with sickness oft ha
Thou
With health renewed my face ;
And when in sins and sorrows sunk
Revived my soul with grace.

4 Ten thousand thousand precio
gifts
My daily thanks employ ;
Nor is the least a cheerful heart
That tastes those gifts with joy.

5 Through every period of my life
Thy goodness I'll pursue ;
And after death, in distant worlds
the glorious theme renew.

6 Through all eternity to Thee
A joyful song I'll raise ;
But oh, eternity's too short
To utter all Thy praise.

509 HOW bright these glorio
spirits shine !
Whence all their white array ?
How came they to the blissful sea
Of everlasting day ?

2 Lo, these are they from sufferin
great
Who came to realms of light,
And in the blood of Christ ha
washed
Those robes which shine so brig

3 Now, with triumphal palms th
stand
Before the throne on high,
And serve the God they lov
The glories of the sky.   [amid

4 Hunger and thirst are felt no mo
Nor suns with scorching ray ;
God is their sun, whose cheeri
Diffuse eternal day.   [bea

5 'Mong pastures green He'll lead F
flock,
Where living streams appear ;
And God the Lord from every eye
Shall wipe off every tear.

6 To Him who sits upon the throne,
The God whom we adore,
And to the Lamb that once w
Be glory evermore !   [sla

10 GOD moves in a mysterious way
His wonders to perform ;
He plants His footsteps in the sea,
And rides upon the storm.

Deep in unfathomable mines
Of never-failing skill,
He treasures up His bright designs
And works His sovereign will.

Ye fearful saints, fresh courage take !
The clouds ye so much dread
Are big with mercy ; and shall break
In blessing on your head.

Judge not the Lord by feeble sense,
But trust Him for His grace ;
Behind a frowning providence
He hides a smiling face.

His purposes will ripen fast,
Unfolding every hour ;
The bud may have a bitter taste,
But sweet will be the flower.

Blind unbelief is sure to err,
And scan His work in vain ;
God is His own interpreter,
And He will make it plain.

11 JESUS, the very thought of Thee,
With sweetness fills my breast ;
But sweeter far Thy face to see,
And in Thy presence rest.

Nor voice can sing, nor heart can frame,
Nor can the memory find
A sweeter sound than Thy blest name,
O Saviour of mankind. [name,

O Hope of ev'ry contrite heart,
O Joy of all the meek,
To those who fall, how kind Thou art !
How good to those who seek !

But what to those who find ? Ah, this,
Nor tongue nor pen can show ;
The love of Jesus, what it is
None but His loved ones know.

Jesus, our only joy be Thou,
As Thou our prize wilt be ;
Jesus, be Thou our glory now,
And through eternity.

512 I LOVE to tell the story,
How Christ the King of Glory,
Left heav'n above to come and rescue me ;
For sinners He received them,
His blood was shed to save them—
So Jesus died for sinners just like me.

Yes, yes, yes, O yes !
Jesus died to set poor sinners free ;
You say, " How do I know it ? "
John three sixteen will show it ;
That big word " whosoever " just means me.

2 So now I'll try to please Him,
My life I'll give to serve Him ;
His true and faithful servant I will be ;
And when called home to glory,
I'll sing the good old story,
That Jesus died for sinners just like me.

3 Then, brother, won't you love Him ?
And, sister, won't you trust Him ?
I know He died for you as well as me ;
We need our sins forgiven
That we may go to heaven,
To live with Christ, who died for you and me.

513 IN my soul oft rises, bringing pain and woe,
The alarming question, " Am I saved or no ? "
Then the Word brings comfort, it doth fully show,
Tho' my faith may waver, Christ, the Rock, stands fast.

The Rock stand fast, the Rock stands fast !
Tho' my faith may waver, Christ, the Rock, stands fast !
The Rock stands fast, the Rock stands fast !
Glory be to God ! Christ, the Rock, stands fast !

2 When, before me marshalled, all my sins arise, [of paradise,
Swords of flame that bar the gates
Tho' oppressed with doubtings, still my soul replies :
" Tho' my faith may waver, Christ, the Rock, stands fast ! "

3 While life's storm is raging, heaping up hope's wrecks,
While delights allure and sore temptations vex,

I will cry, tho' fears and doubts my
    soul perplex :
" Tho' my faith may waver, Christ,
    the Rock, stands fast ! "

514 IF our Lord should come
    to-night,
    With the bright angelic host,
Would He find us in His vineyard,
    Ev'ry servant at his post ?
Thro' the precious, cleansing blood
    Are our garments clean and white ?
Are we dwelling in the light,
    Should our Lord appear to-night ?

Are we watching, are we waiting
    In the raiment pure and white ?
Should we joy at His appearing
    If our Lord should come to-night ?...

2 If our Lord should come to-night,
    Come as King and Judge of all,
Are there any here assembled
    Who would tremble at His call
Is there one, oh, is there one
    Far from Jesus and the light,
Unrepentant, lost, undone,
    If the Judge should come to-
        night ?

3 Christ as King and Judge will come
    'Tis recorded in His book ;
He will bid us stand before Him,
    Not a soul will He o'erlook !
Are we ready, ev'ry one ?
    Are we in the raiment white,
If the Judge of all mankind
    Should appear this very night ?

THE SECOND COMING

515 'TIS almost time for the Lord
    to come,
    I hear the people say ;
The stars of heav'n are growing dim,
    It must be the breaking of the day.

O it must be the breaking of the day,
O it must be the breaking of the day,
The night is almost gone, the day is coming on ;
    O it must be the breaking of the day.

2 The signs foretold in the sun and
        moon,
    In earth, and sea, and sky,
Aloud proclaim to all mankind,
    The coming of the Master draweth
        nigh.

3 It must be time for the waiting
        Church
    To cast her pride away,
With girded loins and burning
        lamps,
    To look for the breaking of the
        day.

4 Go quickly out in the streets and
        lanes,
    And in the broad highway,
And call the maim'd, the halt, and
        blind,
    To be ready for the breaking of
        the day.

516 WHEN the Bridegroom cometh
    by and by,....
    When the Bridegroom cometh by
        and by,....

Will your lamps be burning brigh
Will your robes be pure and whit
When the Bridegroom cometh
    and by ?

Oh be ready ! Oh be ready !
Ready when the Bridegroom comes ;...
    Oh be ready ! Oh be ready !
Ready when the Bridegroom comes.

2 When the Bridegroom cometh
    and by,....
When the Bridegroom cometh
    and by,....
Oh be ready for that day,
    With your sins all washed away
When the Bridegroom cometh
    and by.

3 When the Bridegroom cometh
    and by,....
When the Bridegroom cometh
    and by,....
Will your wearied heart rejoice
    At the sound of Jesus' voice,
When the Bridegroom cometh
    and by ?

4 When the Bridegroom cometh
    and by,....
When the Bridegroom cometh
    and by,....
Will the sorrows of the past
    All be changed to joy at last,
When the Bridegroom cometh
    and by ?

When the Bridegroom cometh by and by,....
When the Bridegroom cometh by and by,....
When the Lord shall call His own,
Can you stand before the throne,
When the Bridegroom cometh by and by?
When the Bridegroom cometh by and by,....
When the Bridegroom cometh by and by,....
Will you join the ransomed host,
Or be found among the lost,
When the Bridegroom cometh by and by?

17 WHEN Jesus comes to reward His servants,
Whether it be noon or night,
Faithful to Him He will find us watching,
With our lamps all trimmed and bright?

, can we say we are ready, brother—
Ready for the soul's bright home?
y, will He find you and me still watching,
Waiting, waiting, when the Lord shall come?

If at the dawn of the early morning,
He shall call us one by one,
When to the Lord we restore our talents,
Will He answer thee, "Well done?"

Have we been true to the trust He left us?
Do we seek to do our best?
If in our hearts there is naught condemns us,
We shall have a glorious rest.

Blessed are those whom the Lord finds watching,
In His glory they shall share;
If He should come at the dawn or midnight,
Will He find us watching there?

18 WILL our lamps be filled and ready,
When the Bridegroom comes?
And our lights be clear and steady,
When the Bridegroom comes?
In the night,....that solemn night,....
Will our lamps be burning bright,
When the Bridegroom comes?

Oh be ready! Oh be ready!
Oh be ready when the Bridegroom comes!
Oh be ready! Oh be ready!
Oh be ready when the Bridegroom comes!

2 Shall we hear a welcome sounding
When the Bridegroom comes?
And a shout of joy resounding,
When the Bridegroom comes?
In the night,....that solemn night,....
Will our lamps be burning bright,
When the Bridegroom comes?

3 Don't delay our preparation
Till the Bridegroom comes;
Lest there be a separation,
When the Bridegroom comes.
In the night,....that solemn night,....
Will our lamps be burning bright,
When the Bridegroom comes?

4 It may be a time of sorrow,
When the Bridegroom comes,
If our oil we hope to borrow
When the Bridegroom comes;
In the night,....that solemn night,....
Will our lamps be burning bright,
When the Bridegroom comes?

5 Oh, there'll be a glorious meeting,
When the Bridegroom comes;
And a hallelujah greeting,
When the Bridegroom comes.
In that night,....that solemn night,....
With our lamps all burning bright,
When the Bridegroom comes.

519 THE Lord is coming by and by,
Be ready when He comes;
He comes from His fair home on high,
Be ready when He comes;
He is the Lord our righteousness,
And comes His chosen ones to bless,
And at His Father's throne confess;
Be ready when He comes.

Will you be ready when the Bridegroom comes?....
Will you be ready when the Bridegroom comes?....
Will your lamp be trim'd and bright,
Be it morning, noon, or night?
Will you be ready when the Bridegroom comes?

2 He soon will come to earth again,
Be ready when He comes;
Begin His universal reign,
Be ready when He comes;

With hallelujahs heav'n will ring,
When Jesus does redemption bring ;
O trim your lamps to meet your
  King !
Be ready when He comes.

3 Behold ! He comes to one and all,
  Be ready when He comes ;
He quickly comes with trumpet call,
  Be ready when He comes ;
To judgment called at His command,
Drawn thither by His mighty hand,
Before His throne we all must stand ;
  Be ready when He comes.

520 IT may be at morn, when the
  day is awaking,
When sunlight thro' darkness and
  shadow is breaking,
That Jesus will come in the fulness
  of glory,
  To receive from the world " His
    own."

O Lord Jesus, how long ?
How long ere we shout the glad song ?...
  Christ returneth ! Hallelujah !
    Hallelujah ! Amen !
    Hallelujah ! Amen !

2 It may be at midday, it may be at
  twilight,
It may be, perchance, that the
  blackness of midnight
Will burst into light in the blaze of
  His glory,
When Jesus receives " His own."

3 While hosts cry Hosanna from
  heav'n descending,
With glorified saints, and the angels
  attending,
With grace on His brow, like a halo
  of glory,
Will Jesus receive " His own."

4 Oh, joy ! oh, delight ! should we go
  without dying,
No sickness, no sadness, no dread,
  and no crying ;
Caught up thro' the clouds with our
  Lord into glory,
When Jesus receives " His own."

521
    REJOICE, ye saints, the time
      draws near   [appear,
When Christ will in the clouds
And for His people call.

Trim your lamps and be ready,
Trim your lamps and be ready,
Trim your lamps and be ready for the m‖
  night cry.
For the midnight cry, for the midnight cry,
Trim your lamps and be ready for the m‖
  night cry.

2 The trumpet sounds, the thunde‖
  roll ;
The heavens passing as a scroll,
  The earth will burn with fire.

3 Poor sinners then on earth will cr‖
While lightnings flash from out t‖
  sky,
  " O mountains, on us fall ! "

4 Come, brethren all, and let us try
To warn poor sinners, and to cry,
  " Behold, the Bridegroom comes‖

522   JESUS is coming ! sing t‖
    glad word !
  Coming for those He redeem'd ‖
    His blood,
  Coming to reign as the glorified Lor‖
    Jesus is coming again !

Jesus is coming, is coming again !
Jesus is coming again ;...
Shout the glad tidings o'er mountain and plai‖
  Jesus is coming again !

2 Jesus is coming ! the dead shall aris‖
  Lov'd ones shall meet in a joyf‖
    surprise,   [skie
  Caught up together to Him in t‖
    Jesus is coming again !

3 Jesus is coming ! His saints
    release !
  Coming to give to the warring ear‖
    peace ;   [shall ceas‖
  Sinning, and sighing, and sorr‖
    Jesus is coming again !

4 Jesus is coming ! the promise
    true :
  Who are the chosen, the faithful, t‖
    few,   [review
  Waiting and watching, prepared f‖
    Jesus is coming again !

523   I'M waiting for Thee, Lord,
    Thy beauty to see, Lord,
I'm waiting for Thee, for Thy comi‖
  again ;
Thou art gone over there, Lord,
A place to prepare, Lord,
Thy home I shall share at Thy comi‖
  again.

'Mid danger and fear, Lord,
I'm oft weary here, Lord,
The day must be near of Thy coming
 again ;
'Tis all sunshine there, Lord,
No sighing nor care, Lord,
But glory so fair at Thy coming again.

Whilst Thou art away, Lord,
I stumble and stray, Lord ;
Oh, hasten the day of Thy coming
 again !
This is not my rest, Lord ;
A pilgrim confest, Lord,
I wait to·be blest at Thy coming again.

Our loved ones before, Lord,
Their troubles are o'er, Lord,
I'll meet them once more at Thy
 coming again ;
The blood was the sign, Lord,
That marked them as Thine, Lord,
And brightly they'll shine at Thy
 coming again.

E'en now let my ways, Lord,
Be bright with Thy praise, Lord,
For brief are the days ere Thy coming
 again.
I'm waiting for Thee, Lord,
Thy beauty to see, Lord, [again.
To triumph for me like Thy coming

524 OH, for the peace which floweth
 like a river,
 Making life's desert places bloom
  and smile !
Oh, for the faith to grasp heav'n's
 bright " for ever,"
 Amid the shadows of earth's
  " little while ! "

A little while for patient vigil
 keeping,
 To face the storm, to battle with
  the strong ;
A little while to sow the seed with
 weeping,
 Then bind the sheaves and sing
  the harvest song !

A little while to keep the oil from
 failing,
 A little while faith's flickering
  lamp to trim ;
And then the Bridegroom's coming
 footsteps hailing,
 To haste to meet Him with the
  bridal hymn !

4 And He who is Himself the Gift and
 Giver ; [smile—
 The future glory and the present
With the bright promise of the glad
 " for ever."
 Will light the shadows of the
  " little while ! "

525 " TILL He come ! " Oh, let
 the words
Linger on the trembling chords ;
Let the " little while " between
In their golden light be seen ;
Let us think how heaven and home
Lie beyond that " Till He come ! "

2 When the weary ones we love
Enter on their rest above—
Seems the earth so poor and vast ?
All our life-joy overcast ?
Hush ! be ev'ry murmur dumb ;
It is only " Till He come ! "

3 Clouds and conflicts round us press ;
Would we have one sorrow less ?
All the sharpness of the Cross,
All that tells the world is loss—
Death, and darkness, and the tomb :
Only whisper, " Till He come ! "

4 See, the feast of love is spread,
Drink the wine and break the bread :
Sweet memorials—till the Lord
Call us round His heavenly board ;
Some from earth, from glory some,
Severed only " Till He come."

526 THOU art coming, O my
 Saviour !
Thou art coming, O my King !
Ev'ry tongue Thy name confessing,
 Well may we rejoice and sing !
Thou art coming ! rays of glory
 Thro' the veil Thy death has rent,
Gladden now our pilgrim pathway,
 Glory from Thy presence sent.

Thou art coming ! Thou art coming !
 We shall meet Thee on Thy way !
Thou art coming ! we shall see Thee,
 And be like Thee on that day !
Thou art coming ! Thou art coming !
 Jesus, our beloved Lord.
Oh, the joy to see Thee reigning,
 Worshipped, glorified, adored.

2 Thou art coming, not a shadow,
 Not a mist, and not a tear,
Not a sin, and not a sorrow,
 On that sunrise, grand and clear ;

Thou art coming ! Jesus, Saviour,
Nothing else seems worth a
thought ;
Oh, how marvellous the glory,
And the bliss Thy pain hath
bought.

3 Thou art coming ! we are waiting
With a " hope " that cannot fail ;
Asking not the day or hour,
Anchor'd safe within the veil ;
Thou art coming ! at Thy table
We are witnesses for this,
As we meet Thee in communion,
Earnest of our coming bliss.

527   HAVE ye heard the song from
the golden land ?
Have ye heard the glad new song ?
Let us bind our sheaves with a
willing hand,
For the time will not be long.

The Lord of the harvest will soon appear ;
His smile, His voice we shall see and hear !
The Lord of the harvest will soon appear,
And gather the reapers home !

2 They are looking down from the
golden land—
Our belov'd are looking down ;
They have done their work, they
have borne their cross,
And receiv'd their promis'd crown.

3 Oh ! the song rolls on from the golden
land,
And our hearts are strong to-day ;
For it nerves our souls with its music
sweet,
As we toil in the noontide ray.

4 Oh ! the song rolls on from the
golden land,
From its vales of joy and flow'rs ;
And we feel and know by a living
faith
That its tones will soon be ours.

528   WHEN the trumpet of the
Lord shall sound,
And time shall be no more,
And the morning breaks, eternal,
bright and fair,
When the saved of earth shall gather
Over on the other shore,
And the roll is called up yonder,
I'll be there.

When the roll...is called up yon - - der,
When the roll...is called up yon - - der,
When the roll...is called up yon - - der,
When the roll is called up yonder, I'll be there

2 On that bright and cloudle
morning,
When the dead in Christ shall rise,
And the glory of His resurrectio
share ;
When His chosen ones will gather
To their home beyond the skies,
And the roll is called up yonde
I'll be there.

3 Let us labour for the Master
From the dawn till setting sun,
Let us talk of all His wondrow
love and care ;
Then, when all of life is over,
And our work on earth is done,
And the roll is called up yonde
I'll be there.

529   THERE'S an hour which
man knoweth,
Nor the angels round the throne
When the Lord shall come in glo
from the sky ;   [Hir
All the saints shall rise to me
For He calleth for His own,
They shall hear the trumpet soun
ing by and by.

Are you ready ?...ready ?...looking for the King
Ready, while you labour, watch, and pray ?
Are you ready ? ready ? looking for the King
Ready for the happy Crowning Day ?

2 What a blessed transformation
In the twinkling of an eye,
When the mortal shall immortal li
put on !   [Hir
Those who love Him shall be li
When He cometh from on high,
At the noontide, at the midnigh
or at dawn.

3 Though our sins have been a
scarlet,
Let us seek the streams that flo
From the Cross that rose on Ca
vary's rugged height ;
He is able still to keep us,
And present us white as snow,
When He comes again as clouds o
dazzling light.

530 WHEN the King comes back
　　from the far-off land,
And the trumpet sounds to meet
　　Him ;
Oh ! the joy that thrills thro' the
　　raptur'd band　　　　[Him.
Of the saints as they rise to greet

O hasten, Lord, that happy day,
　The Kingdom of Thy glory ;
For our spirits yearn for Thy blest return,
　As we muse on the Gospel story.

When the morning breaks on the
　　hills of time,
And the shadows all are fleeing,
When the Bride awakes to the
　　marriage chime,
And her faith is lost in seeing.

When the fight is o'er, and the
　　victory won,
And the vanquish'd foe is flying ;
When the Captain calls with His
　　own " Well done ! "
To the crown of the life undying.

Oh ! to share the grace of the holy
　　place
Where the angel hosts adore Him ;
Where our eyes shall gaze on the
　　Bridegroom's face,
As we stand all fair before Him !

Speed, speed that hour when Thy
　　blood-bought pow'r
Shall reveal Thy full salvation ;
And the world resound to her utmost
　　bound
With the song of the new creation.

All blessing, glory, honour be,
　And praise that ceaseth never,
To Him that sits upon the throne,
　And to the Lamb for ever !

531 HAPPY home-coming of our
　　King,
We'll meet our loved ones gone
　　before ;　　　　　[bring
And sweet the greeting they will
To us upon the golden shore.

Happy home-coming, blessed home-coming,
Glorious home-coming of our Saviour-King
That a glad meeting on that great morning
At the home-coming of our Saviour-King !

Blessed home-coming of our King ;
　We'll join the everlasting psalm
Of joy that angel voices sing :
　" The song of Moses and the
　　Lamb."

3 Glorious home-coming of our King ;
　　With Jesus we will live for aye
　Where songs of love and gladness
　　ring
　In tune thro' heav'n's eternal day.

532 AS once to earth the Saviour
　　came,
Sometime He'll come again ;
The sky with heavenly light aflame,
Sometime He'll come again.

Sometime,....sometime,
　Christ shall come to reign ;
Prepare my soul to meet Him,
　Sometime He'll come again.

2 Tell ev'rywhere, with great delight,
　　Sometime He'll come again ;
　Upon the clouds of glory bright,
　　Sometime He'll come again.

3 O'er all the earth the tidings ring,
　　Sometime He'll come again ;
　Not as a babe, but as a king,
　　Sometime He'll come again.

4 When dawns that blessed morning
　　fair,
　Sometime He'll come again ;
　His saints will meet Him in the air,
　　Sometime He'll come again.

5 Oh, let us live and do our best,
　　Sometime He'll come again ;
　Then He will take us home to rest,
　　Sometime He'll come again.

533 HAIL to the Lord's Anointed,
　　Great David's greater Son ;
Hail in the time appointed,
　His reign on earth begun !
He comes to break oppression,
　To set the captive free ;
To take away transgression,
　And rule in equity.

2 He shall come down like showers
　　Upon the fruitful earth ;
　And love, joy, hope, like flowers,
　　Spring in His path to birth.
　Before Him on the mountains
　　Shall Peace, the herald, go ;
　And righteousness in fountains
　　From hill to valley flow.

3 Kings shall fall down before Him,
　　And gold and incense bring ;
　All nations shall adore Him,
　　His praise all people sing.

For He shall have dominion
  O'er river, sea, and shore,
Far as the eagle's pinion
  Or dove's light wing can soar.

534 HARK! hark! hear the glad
      tidings;
Soon, soon Jesus will come,
Robed, robed in honour and glory,
To gather His ransomed ones home.
      Yes, yes, oh yes,
    To gather His ransomed ones home.

2 Joy! joy! sound it more loudly;
  Sing, sing glory to God;
Soon, soon Jesus is coming,
  Publish the tidings abroad:
      Yes, yes, oh yes,
    Publish the tidings abroad.

3 Bright, bright seraphs attending;
  Shouts, shouts filling the air;
Down, down, swiftly from heaven
Jesus our Lord will appear:
      Yes, yes, oh yes,
    Jesus our Lord will appear.

4 Still, still rest on the promise;
  Cling, cling fast to His word;
Wait, wait—if He should tarry,
  We'll patiently wait for the Lord:
      Yes, yes, oh yes,
    Patiently wait for the Lord.

535 WHY stand ye idly gazing
      T'wards heaven's blessed
      height?   [again;
This same Jesus is coming back

The shining angels told it,
  Arrayed in spotless white;
This same Jesus is coming ba
  again.

This same Jesus, this same Jesus!
  Oh, tell the joyful tidings to all the sons
    men!
Oh, let us work and pray, rejoicing ev'ry day
  This same Jesus is coming back again.

2 Receiving His good Spirit,
  We'll know His presence near;
This same Jesus is coming ba
  again;
He fills us with His blessing,
  He gives us love and cheer;
This same Jesus is coming ba
  again.

3 Our lowly talents doubling,
  More faithful may we be;
This same Jesus is coming ba
  again;
And spread abroad His Gospel
  With happy hearts and free;
This same Jesus is coming ba
  again.

4 In ev'ry time of trial
  We'll trust His changeless love
This same Jesus is coming ba
  again;
The mighty King of Glory
  Still reigns for us above:
This same Jesus is coming ba
  again.

THE HOLY SPIRIT

536 OH, spread the tidings round,
      Wherever man is found,
Wherever human hearts and human
      woes abound;
Let ev'ry Christian tongue proclaim
      the joyful sound:
    The Comforter has come!

The Comforter has come, the Comforter has
  come!
  The Holy Ghost from heaven, the Father's
    promise giv'n;
Oh, spread the tidings sound wherever man is
  found—
    The Comforter has come!

2 The long, long night is past,
  The morning breaks at last;
And hush'd the dreadful wail and
  fury of the blast.

As o'er the golden hills the d
  advances fast!
    The Comforter has come!

3 Lo, the great King of kings,
  With healing in His wings
To ev'ry captive soul a full deliv
  ance brings;
And thro' the vacant cells the so
  of triumph rings:
    The Comforter has come!

4 O boundless love divine!
  How shall this tongue of mine
To wond'ring mortals tell the mat
  less grace divine— ·[image shin
That I, a child of hell, should in I
    The Comforter has come!

Sing till the echoes fly
Above the vaunted sky,
And all the saints above to all below
  reply,
In strains of endless love, the song
  that ne'er will die :
    The Comforter has come !

37 OPEN my eyes that I may see
    Glimpses of truth Thou hast
    for me ;   [key
Place in my hands the wonderful
That shall unclasp and set me free.
Silently now I wait for Thee,
Ready, my God, Thy will to see ;
Open my eyes, illumine me,
    Spirit divine !

Open my ears that I may hear
Voices of truth Thou sendest clear ;
And while the wave notes fall on
  my ear,
Ev'rything false will disappear.
Silently now I wait for Thee,
Ready, my God, Thy will to see ;
Open my ears, illumine me,
    Spirit divine !

Open my mouth and let me bear
Gladly the warm truth ev'rywhere ;
Open my heart and let me prepare
Love with Thy children thus to
  share.
Silently now I wait for Thee.
Ready, my God, Thy will to see ;
Open my heart, illumine me,
    Spirit divine !

38 THE Holy Ghost has come—
    We feel His presence here !
Our hearts would now no longer
  roam,
  But bow in filial fear.

This tenderness of love,
  The hush of solemn power—
'Tis heaven descending from above
  To fill this favour'd hour !

Earth's darkness all has fled,
  Heav'n's light serenely shines ;
And ev'ry heart divinely led,
  To holy thought inclines.

No more let sin deceive,
  Nor earthly cares betray ;
Oh, let us never, never grieve
  The Comforter away !

539 OUR blest Redeemer, ere He
    breath'd
  His tender, last farewell,
A Guide, a Comforter bequeath'd
  With us to dwell.

2 He came sweet influence to impart,
  A gracious, willing Guest,
Where He can find one humble
  heart
    Wherein to rest.

3 And His that gentle voice we hear,
  Soft as the breath of even,
That checks each thought, that
  calms each fear,
    And speaks of heaven.

4 And ev'ry virtue we possess,
  And ev'ry conquest won,
And ev'ry thought of holiness
    Are His alone.

5 Spirit of purity and grace,
  Our weakness pitying see ;
O make our hearts Thy dwelling-
  place,
    And worthier Thee.

6 O praise the Father, praise, the Son ;
  Blest Spirit, praise to Thee ;
All praise to God, the Three in One,
  The One in Three.

540 COME, gracious Spirit, heav'nly
    Dove,
With light and comfort from above ;
Be Thou our Guardian, Thou our
  Guide,
O'er ev'ry thought and step preside.

2 The light of truth to us display,
That we may know and choose Thy
  way ;
Plant holy fear in ev'ry heart,
That we from God may ne'er depart.

3 Conduct us safe conduct us far
From ev'ry sin and hurtful snare ;
Lead us to Christ, the Living Way,
Nor let us from His pastures stray.

4 Lead us to holiness, the road
That we must take to dwell with
  God ;
Lead us to God, our final rest,
To be with Him for ever blessed !

541 HOLY Spirit, faithful Guide,
　　Ever near the Christian's side,
Gently lead us by the hand,
Pilgrims in a desert land :
Weary souls for e'er rejoice
While they hear that sweetest voice,
Whisper softly, " Wand'rer, come,
Follow Me, I'll guide thee home."

2 Ever present, truest Friend,
　　Ever near Thine aid to lend ;
Leave us not to doubt and fear,
Groping on in darkness here ;
When the storms are raging sore,
Hearts grow faint and hopes give o'er,
Whisper softly, " Wand'rer, come,
Follow Me, I'll guide thee home."

3 When our days of toil shall cease,
　　May our hearts be filled with peace ;
Drawing near in praise and pray'r,
Knowing that our names are there ;
Pleading naught but Jesus' blood,
He'll be with us in the flood,
Whisper softly, " Wand'rer, come,
Follow Me, I'll guide thee home."

542 COME, Holy Ghost, our hearts
　　inspire,
Let us Thine influence prove ;
Source of the old prophetic fire,
Fountain of light and love.

2 Come, Holy Ghost, for, moved by
　　Thee,
The prophets wrote and spoke ;
Unlock the truth, Thyself the Key,
Unseal the sacred book.

3 Expand Thy wings, celestial Dove,
　　Brood o'er our nature's night ;
On our disordered spirits move,
And let there now be light.

4 God, thro' Himself, we then shall
　　know,
If Thou within us shine ; [below,
And sound, with all Thy saints
The depths of love divine.

543 JESUS, Thine all-victorious
　　love
Shed in my heart abroad ;
Then shall my feet no longer rove,
Rooted and fixed in God.

2 Oh, that in me the sacred fire
　　Might now begin to glow,
Burn up the dross of base desire,
And make the mountains flow.

3 Thou who at Pentecost didst fall,
　　And all my sins consume,
Come, Holy Ghost, for Thee I call,
Spirit of burning, come !

4 Refining fire, go through my hear
　　Illuminate my soul ;
Scatter Thy life through every pa
And sanctify the whole.

5 My steadfast soul from falling fre
　　Shall then no longer move ;
While Christ is all the world to me
And all my heart is love.

544 SPIRIT Divine, attend o
　　prayers,
And make our hearts Thy home
Descend with all Thy gracio
　　powers,
Oh, come, great Spirit, come !

2 Come as the light—to us reveal
　　Our need of Thee below ;
And lead us in those paths of life
Where all the righteous go.

3 Come as the fire—and purge o
　　hearts
With sacrificial flame ;
Let our whole self an offering be
To our Redeemer's name.

4 Come as the dew—and sweetly ble
　　This consecrated hour ;
May barrenness rejoice to own
Thy fertilising power.

5 Come as the Dove—and spread Th
　　wings,
The wings of peaceful love ;
And let Thy Church on ear
　　become
Blest as the Church above.

6 Come as the wind—with rushi
　　sound
And Pentecostal grace ;
That all of women born may see
The glory of Thy face.

545 GRACIOUS Spirit, Lo
　　divine,
Let Thy light within me shine ;
All my sin and fear remove,
Fill me with Thy heavenly love.

2 Speak Thy matchless grace to me,
　　From my sin, oh, set me free ;
Lead me to the Lamb of God,
Wash me in His precious blood.

Faith, and hope, and charity,
Comforter, descend from Thee :
Thou th' anointing Spirit art ;
These Thy gifts to me impart.

Life and peace to me impart,
Seal salvation on my heart ;
Breathe Thyself into my breast,
Earnest of immortal rest.

46 GRACIOUS Spirit, dwell with
me :
I myself would gracious be ;
And with words that help and heal,
Would Thy life in mine reveal ;
And, with actions bold and meek,
Would for Christ my Saviour speak.

Tender Spirit, dwell with me :
I myself would tender be ;
Shut my heart up like a flower
At temptation's darksome hour ;
Open it when shines the sun,
And His love by fragrance own.

Mighty Spirit, dwell with me :
I myself would mighty be,
Mighty so as to prevail
Where unaided man must fail ;
Ever by a mighty hope
Pressing on and bearing up.

Holy Spirit, dwell with me :
I myself would holy be ;
Separate from sin, I would
Choose and cherish all things good ;
And whatever I can be,
Give to Him who gave me Thee.

47 JOYS are flowing like a river
    Since the Comforter has
    come ;
He abides with us for ever, [home.
  Makes the trusting heart His

Blessed quietness, holy quietness,
  What assurance in my soul !
On the stormy sea, He speaks peace to me,
  How the billows cease to roll.

Bringing life and health and glad-
  ness,·
  All around this heavenly Guest ;
Banished unbelief and sadness,
  Changed our weariness to rest.

Like the rain that falls from heaven,
  Like the sunlight from the sky,
So the Holy Ghost is given,
  Coming on us from on high.

4 See a fruitful field is growing,
  Blessed fruits of righteousness,
And the streams of life are flowing
  In the lonely wilderness.

5 What a wonderful salvation,
  Where we always see His face ;
What a perfect habitation,
  What a quiet resting place !

548 HERE from the world we turn,
    Jesus to seek ;
Here may His loving voice
  Graciously speak !
Jesus, our dearest Friend,
While at Thy feet we bend,
Oh, let Thy smile descend !
  'Tis Thee we seek.

2 Come, Holy Comforter,
  Presence divine,
Now in our longing hearts
  Graciously shine !
Oh, for Thy mighty pow'r !
Oh, for a blessed show'r,
Filling this hallowed hour
  With joy divine !

3 Saviour, Thy work revive !
  Here may we see
Those who are dead in sin
  Quick'ned by Thee :
Come to our hearts to-night,
Make ev'ry burden light,
Cheer Thou our waiting sight ;
  We long for Thee.

549 THEY were in an upper
    chamber,
  They were all with one accord,
When the Holy Ghost descended,
  As was promised by our Lord.

O Lord, send the pow'r just now ;
O Lord, send the pow'r just now ;
O Lord, send the pow'r just now,
  And baptize ev'ry one.

2 Yes, this pow'r from heav'n de-
    scended
  With the sound of rushing wind ;
Tongues of fire came down upon
    them,
  As the Lord said He would send.

3 Yes, this " old-time " pow'r was
    given
  To our fathers who were true ;
This is promised to believers,
  And we all may have it too.

550 JESUS for me, Jesus for me,
All the time ev'rywhere, Jesus
for me.

551 THY Holy Spirit, Lord, alone,
Can turn our hearts from sin ;
His power alone can sanctify
And keep us pure within.

> O Spirit of Faith and Love,
> Come in our midst, we pray,
> And purify each waiting heart ;
> Baptise us with pow'r to-day.

2 Thy Holy Spirit, Lord, alone
Can deeper love inspire ;
His power alone within our souls
Can light the sacred fire.

3 Thy Holy Spirit, Lord, can bring
The gifts we seek in pray'r ;
His voice can words of comfort spe
And still each wave of care.

4 Thy Holy Spirit, Lord, can give
The grace we need this hour ;
And while we wait, O Spirit, come
In sanctifying power.

> O Spirit of Love, descend,
> Come in our midst, we pray
> And like a rushing mighty wind,
> Sweep over our souls to-day.

552 THOU art enough for me,
Thou art enough for me ;
Oh, precious living, loving Lord,
Yes, Thou art enough for me !

PRAYER AND CONSECRATION

553 ALAS ! and did my Saviour
bleed !
And did my Sovereign die ?
Would He devote that sacred head
For such a worm as I ?

> Help me, dear Saviour, Thee to own,
> And ever faithful be ;
> And when Thou sittest on Thy throne,
> O Lord, remember me.

2 Was it for crimes that I had done
He groaned upon the tree ?
Amazing pity ! grace unknown !
And love beyond degree !

3 Well might the sun in darkness hide,
And shut his glories in,
When Christ, the mighty Maker,
died
For man, the creature's sin.

4 Thus might I hide my blushing face,
While His dear cross appears,
Dissolve my heart in thankfulness,
And melt mine eyes to tears.

5 But drops of grief can ne'er repay
The debt of love I owe ;
Here, Lord, I give myself away ;
'Tis all that I can do.

554 SEARCH me, O God ! my
actions try,
And let my life appear,
As seen by Thine all-searching eye—
To mine my ways make clear.

2 Search all my sense, and know
heart,
Who only canst make known,
And let the deep, the hidden par
To be fully shown.

3 Throw light into the darkened ce
Where passion reigns within ;
Quicken my conscience till it feels
The loathsomeness of sin.

4 Search all my thoughts, the sec
springs,
The motives that control ;
The chambers where polluted thi
Hold empire o'er the soul.

5 Search, till Thy fiery glance
cast
Its holy light through all,
And I by grace am brought at las
Before Thy face to fall.

6 Thus prostrate I shall learn of Th
What now I feebly prove,
That God alone in Christ can be
Unutterable love !

555 FROM ev'ry stormy wind t
blows,
From ev'ry swelling tide of woes,
There is a calm, a sure retreat,
'Tis found beneath the Mercy-sea

2 There is a place where Jesus shed
The oil of gladness on our heads ;
A place that all beside more swee
It is the blood-stain'd Mercy-sea

There is a scene where spirits blend,
Where friend holds fellowship with
   friend ;
Tho' sund'red far, by faith we meet,
Around one common Mercy-seat.

56 LONG my wilful heart said
      "no"
To Jesus' tender pleading ;
Now I long His love to know,
My stubborn will is yielding.

Yes, dear Lord, yes, dear Lord,
  Here I give my all to Thee ;
I believe, I believe the blood avails for me.

Bringing all I am and have
  In humble consecration,
Trusting in the blood, I claim
  This uttermost salvation.

Giving o'er my doubts and fears
  And all my useless trying,
Trusting not my pray'rs or tears,
  But on Thy Word relying.

Yes, dear Lord, in life or death
  With Thee all good possessing,
Not by feeling but by faith
  I take the promised blessing.

57 I HAVE heard my Saviour
      calling,
I have heard my Saviour calling,
I have heard my Saviour calling,
"Take thy cross and follow, follow
  Me."

Where He leads me I will follow,
Where He leads me I will follow,
Where He leads me I will follow,
  I'll go with Him, with Him all the way.

Tho' He leads me through the
   valley,   [way.
I'll go with Him, with Him all the
Tho' He leads me thro' the garden,
I'll go with Him, with Him all the
  way.

Tho' He leads me to the conflict,
I'll go with Him, with Him all the
  way.

Tho' He leads through fiery trials,
I'll go with Him, with Him all the
  way.

58 JESUS, I my cross have taken,
      All to leave and follow Thee ;
Destitute, despised, forsaken,
  Thou from hence my all shalt be.

I will follow Thee, my Saviour,
  Thou didst shed Thy blood for me,
And though all the world forsake Thee,
  By Thy grace I'll follow Thee.

2 Perish ev'ry fond ambition,
  All I've sought, and hoped, and
    known ;
Yet how rich is my condition !
  God and heaven are still mine own.

3 Let the world despise and leave me :
  They have left my Saviour too—
Human hearts and looks deceive
   me—
  Thou art not, like them, untrue.

4 And whilst Thou shalt smile upon me
  God of wisdom, love and might,
Foes may hate, and friends disown
   me :
  Show Thy face and all is bright.

5 Man may trouble and distress me,
  'Twill but drive me to Thy breast ;
Life with trials hard may press me,
  Heaven will bring me sweeter rest.

6 Oh ! 'tis not in grief to harm me,
  While Thy love is left to me ;
Oh ! 'twere not in joy to charm me,
  Were that joy unmixed with Thee.

559 WHAT a Friend we have in
       Jesus,
  All our sins and griefs to bear ;
What a privilege to carry
  Ev'rything to God in pray'r.
Oh, what peace we often forfeit,
  Oh, what needless pain we bear—
All because we do not carry
  Ev'rything to God in pray'r.

2 Have we trials and temptations ?
  Is there trouble anywhere ?
We should never be discouraged,
  Take it to the Lord in pray'r.
Can we find a friend so faithful,
  Who will all our sorrows share ?
Jesus knows our ev'ry weakness,
  Take it to the Lord in pray'r.

3 Are we weak and heavy laden,
  Cumbered with a load of care ?
Precious Saviour, still our refuge—
  Take it to the Lord in pray'r.
Do thy friends despise, forsake thee ?
  Take it to the Lord in pray'r ;
In His arms He'll take and shield
   thee,
  Thou wilt find a solace there.

560 SWEET hour of pray'r, sweet
    hour of pray'r,
That calls me from a world of care,
And bids me, at my Father's throne,
Make all my wants and wishes known
In seasons of distress and grief
My soul has often found relief,
And oft escaped the tempter's snare,
By thy return, sweet hour of pray'r.

2 Sweet hour of pray'r, sweet hour of
    pray'r,
The joy I feel, the bliss I share
Of those whose anxious spirits burn
With strong desires for thy return !
With such I hasten to the place
Where God, my Saviour, shows His
    face,
And gladly take my station there,
And wait for thee, sweet hour of
    pray'r.

3 Sweet hour of pray'r, sweet hour of
    pray'r,
Thy wings shall my petition bear
To Him whose truth and faithfulness
Engage the waiting soul to bless ;
And since He bids me seek His face,
Believe His Word, and trust His
    grace,
I'll cast on Him my ev'ry care,
And wait for thee, sweet hour of
    pray'r.

561 I AM Thine, O Lord, I have
    heard Thy voice,
And it told Thy love to me ;
But I long to rise in the arms of
    faith,
And be closer drawn to Thee.

Draw me near - - er,...nearer blessed Lord,
  To the Cross where Thou hast died ;
Draw me nearer, nearer, nearer, blessed Lord,
  To Thy precious, bleeding side.

2 Consecrate me now to Thy service,
    Lord,
By the pow'r of grace divine ;
Let my soul look up with a steadfast
    hope,
And my will be lost in Thine.

3 Oh, the pure delight of a single hour
That before Thy throne I spend,
When I kneel in prayer, and with
    Thee, my God,
I commune as friend with friend.

4 There are depths of love that
    cannot know
Till I cross the narrow sea ;
There are heights of joy that I ma
    not reach
Till I rest in peace with Thee.

562 WHAT tho' the clouds a
    hovering o'er me,
And I seem to walk alone,
Longing, 'mid my cares and crosse
    For the joys that now are flown
If I've Jesus, " Jesus only,"
    Then my sky will have a gem ;
He's the Sun of brightest splendou
    And the Star of Bethlehem.

2 What though all my earthly journe
    Bringeth naught but weary hour
And in grasping for life's roses,
    Thorns I find instead of flowers
If I've Jesus, " Jesus only,"
    I possess a cluster rare ;
He's the " Lily of the Valley,"
    And the " Rose of Sharon " fair

3 What though all my heart is year
    For the loved of long ago—   [ir
Bitter lessons sadly learning
    From the shadowy page of woe
If I've Jesus, " Jesus only,"
    He'll be with me to the end ;
And, unseen, by mortal vision,
    Angel bands will o'er me bend.

4 When I soar to realms of glory,
    And an entrance I await,
If I whisper, " Jesus only ! "
    Wide will ope the pearly gate ;
When I join the heavenly chorus,
    And the angel hosts I see,
Precious Jesus, " Jesus only,"
    Will my theme of rapture be.

563 COME ye yourselves apart an
    rest awhile,   [throng
Weary I know it, of the press ar
Wipe from your brow the sweat ar
    dust of toil,   [be stron
And in My quiet strength aga

2 Come ye aside from all the wor
    holds dear,   [never know
For converse which the world h
Alone with Me and with My Fath
    here,   [alon
With Me and with My Father n

Come, tell Me all that you have said
   and done,
  Your victories and failures, hopes
    and fears ;   [and won ;
I know how hardly souls are wooed
  My choicest wreaths are always
    wet with tears.

Come ye and rest ! the journey is
   too great,
  And ye will faint beside the way
    and sink ;
The bread of life is here for you to
   eat,   [to drink.
  And here for you the wine of love

Then, fresh from converse with your
   Lord, return
  And work till daylight softens into
    even ;   [ye learn
The brief hours are not lost in which
  More of your Master and His rest
    in heaven.

64 GO bury thy sorrow,
    The world hath its share ;
 Go bury it deeply,
   Go hide it with care ;
  Go think of it calmly,
    When curtain'd by night ;
  Go tell it to Jesus,
    And all will be right.

2 Go tell it to Jesus,
   He knoweth thy grief ;
  Go tell it to Jesus,
   He'll send thee relief ;
  Go gather the sunshine
   He sheds on the way ;
  He'll lighten thy burden,
   Go, weary one, pray.

3 Hearts growing a-weary
   With heavier woe,
  Now droop 'mid the darkness—
   Go comfort them, go !
  Go bury thy sorrow,
   Let others be blest ;
  Go give them the sunshine ;
   Tell Jesus the rest.

65 HARK, my soul ! it is the
    Lord !
'Tis thy Saviour, hear His Word ;
Jesus speaks, and speaks to thee,
" Say, poor sinner, lov'st thou
  Me ? "

2 " I deliv'red thee when bound,
  And, when bleeding, healed thy
    wound ;
  Sought thee wand'ring, set thee right
  Turned thy darkness into light.

3 " Can a woman's tender care
  Cease towards the child she bare ?
  Yes, she may forgetful be,
  Yet will I remember thee.

4 " Mine is an unchanging love,
  Higher than the heights above,
  Deeper than the depths beneath,
  Free and faithful, strong as death.

5 " Thou shalt see My glory soon,
  When the work of grace is done ;
  Partner of My throne shalt be :
  Say, poor sinner, lov'st thou Me ? "

6 Lord, it is my chief complaint
  That my love is weak and faint ;
  Yet I love Thee and adore ;
  O for grace to love Thee more !

566 SWEET the moments, rich in
    blessing,
  Which before the Cross I spend ;
Life and health, and peace possess-
   ing,
  From the sinner's dying Friend !

2 Here I rest, for ever viewing,
  Mercy poured in streams of blood ;
  Precious drops, my soul bedewing,
   Plead, and claim my peace with
    God.

3 Truly blessed is this station,
  Low before His Cross to lie,
  While I see divine compassion
  Beaming in His languid eye.

4 Here it is I find my heaven,
  While upon the Lamb I gaze ;
  Love I much?—I've much forgiven :
  I'm a miracle of grace.

5 Love and grief my heart abiding,
  With my tears His feet I'll bathe ;
  Constant still in 'aith abiding—
  Life deriving from His death.

567 SPEAK to my soul, Lord
    Jesus,
  Speak now in tend'rest tone ;
Whisper in loving kindness :
  " Thou art not left alone."

Open my heart to hear Thee,
Quickly to hear Thy voice ;
Fill Thou my soul with praises,
Let me in Thee rejoice.

Speak Thou in softest whispers,
Whispers of love to me ;
" Thou shalt be always conq'ror,
Thou shalt be always free."
Speak Thou to me each day, Lord,
Always in tend'rest tone ;
Let me now hear Thy whisper,
" Thou art not left alone."

2 Speak to Thy children ever,
Lead in the holy way ;
Fill them with joy and gladness,
Teach them to watch and pray.
May they in consecration
Yield their whole lives to Thee ;
Hasten Thy coming kingdom,
Till our dear Lord we see.

3 Speak now as in the old time
Thou didst reveal Thy will ;
Let me know all my duty,
Let me Thy law fulfil.
Lead me to glorify Thee,
Help me to show Thy praise,
Gladly to do Thy bidding,
Honour Thee all my days.

568 I NEED Thee ev'ry hour,
Most gracious Lord ;
No tender voice like Thine
Can peace afford.

I need Thee, oh, I need Thee,
Ev'ry hour I need Thee ;
Oh, bless me now, my Saviour,
I come to Thee.

2 I need Thee ev'ry hour,
Stay Thou near by ;
Temptations lose their pow'r
When Thou art nigh.

3 I need Thee ev'ry hour,
In joy or pain ;
Come quickly and abide,
Or life is vain.

4 I need Thee ev'ry hour,
Teach me Thy will ;
And Thy rich promises
In me fulfil.

5 I need Thee ev'ry hour,
Most Holy One ;
Oh, make me Thine indeed,
Thou blessed Son !

569 NEARER, my God, to Thee
Nearer to Thee ;
E'en though it be a cross
That raiseth me ;
Still all my song shall be,
Nearer, my God, to Thee,
Nearer to Thee.

2 Though like a wanderer,
The sun gone down,
Darkness be over me,
My rest a stone ;
Yet in my dreams I'd be
Nearer, my God, to Thee,
Nearer to Thee.

3 There let the way appear,
Steps unto heav'n ;
All that Thou sendest me,
In mercy giv'n ;
Angels to beckon me
Nearer, my God, to Thee,
Nearer to Thee.

4 Then with my waking thoughts,
Bright with Thy praise,
Out of my stony griefs
Bethel I'll raise ;
So by my woes to be
Nearer, my God, to Thee,
Nearer to Thee.

5 Or if on joyful wing,
Cleaving the sky,.
Sun, moon, and stars forgot,
Upward I fly ;
Still all my song shall be,
Nearer, my God, to Thee,
Nearer to Thee.

570 THY life was given for Me
Thy blood, O Lord, was sh
That I might ransomed be,
And quickened from the dead.
Thy life, Thy life was given for m
What have I given for Thee ?

2 Long years were spent for me
In weariness and woe,
That through eternity
Thy glory I might know.
Long years, long years were spent
Have I spent one for Thee ?   [m

3 Thy Father's home of light,
Thy rainbow circled throne,
Were left for earthly night—
For wand'rings sad and lone.
Yea, all, yea, all was left for me :
Have I left aught for Thee ?

Thou, Lord, hast borne for me
　　More than my tongue can tell
Of bitterest agony,
　　To rescue me from hell.
Thou sufferedst all for me, for me :
　　What have I borne for Thee ?

And Thou has brought to me,
　　Down from Thy home above,
Salvation full and free,
　　Thy pardon and Thy love.
Great　gifts,　great　gifts　Thou
　　broughtest me :
　　What have I brought to Thee ?

Oh, let my life be given,
　　My years for Thee be spent ;
World-fetters all be riven,
　　And joy with suffering blent ;
To Thee, to Thee my all I bring,
My Saviour and my King !

71 ONCE I was dead *in* sin, and
　　hope within me died,
But now I'm dead *to* sin, with Jesus
　　crucified.

　　And can it be that " He loved me,
　　　And gave Himself for me ? "

O height I cannot reach ! O depth
　　I cannot sound !
O love, O boundless love, in my
　　Redeemer found !

O cold, ungrateful heart, that can
　　from Jesus turn,
When living fires of love should on
　　His altar burn !

I live—and yet not I, but Christ
　　that lives in me ;
Who from the law of sin and death
　　hath made me free.

72 PRAY'R is the key,
　　With the bending knee,
To open the morn's first hours ;
　　See the incense rise
　　To the starry skies,
Like perfume from the flow'rs.

　　Not a soul so sad,
　　Not a heart so glad,
When cometh the shades of night,
　　But the daybreak song
　　Will the joy prolong,
And some darkness turn to light.

3　Take the golden key
　　In your hand and see,
As the night tide drifts away,
　　How its blessed hold
　　Is a crown of gold,
Through the weary hours of day.

4　When the shadows fall,
　　And the vesper call
Is sobbing its low refrain,
　　'Tis a garland sweet
　　To the toil-worn feet,
And an antidote for pain.

5　Soon the year's dark door
　　Shall be shut no more ;
Life's tears shall be wiped away,
　　As the pearl gates swing,
　　And the gold harps ring,
And the sun unsheathes for aye.

573 WHEN I survey the wondrous
　　　Cross
　　On which the Prince of Glory
　　　died,
　　My richest gain I count but loss,
　　　And pour contempt on all my
　　　pride.

2 Forbid it, Lord, that I should boast,
　　Save in the death of Christ, my
　　　God ;
　　All the vain things that charm me
　　　most,
　　I sacrifice them to His blood.

3 See, from His head, His hands, His
　　　feet,
　　Sorrow and love flow mingled
　　　down ;
　　Did e'er such love and sorrow meet,
　　Or thorns compose so rich a crown?

4 Were the whole realm of nature
　　　mine,
　　That were an offering far too
　　　small ;
　　Love so amazing, so divine,
　　Demands my soul, my life, my all.

574 WOULD you live for Jesus, and
　　　be always pure and good ?
　　Would you walk with Him within
　　　the narrow road ?
　　Would you have Him bear your
　　　burden, carry all your load ?
　　Let Him have His way with Thee.

His power can make you what you ought to be !
His blood can cleanse your heart and make
  you free ;
His love can fill your soul, and you will see
'Twas best for Him to have His way with thee.

2 Would you have Him make you
    free, and follow at His call ?
  Would you know the peace that
    comes by giving all ?
  Would you have Him save you, so
    that you need never fall ?
    Let Him have His way with thee.

3 Would you in His kingdom find a
    place of constant rest ?
  Would you prove Him true each
    providential test ?
  Would you in His service labour
    always at your best ?
    Let Him have His way with thee.

575 ALL, all to Jesus, I consecrate
      anew ;
    He is my portion for ever.
  Only His glory henceforth will I
    pursue ;
    He is my portion for ever.

Take, take the world, with all its gilded toys,
Take, take the world, I covet not its joys.
Mine is a wealth no moth nor rust destroys :
  Jesus my portion for ever.

2 All, all to Jesus, my trusting heart
    can say ;
    He is my portion for ever.
  Led by His mercy, I'm walking ev'ry
    day ;
    He is my portion for ever.

3 Tho' He may try me, this blessed
    truth I know :
    He is my portion for ever.
  He will not leave me, His promise
    tells me so :
    He is my portion for ever.

4 All, all to Jesus, I cheerfully resign ;
    He is my portion for ever.
  I have the witness that He, my
    Lord, is mine :
    He is my portion for ever.

The following Chorus may be substituted :—
Make Jesus Christ the centre of your life,
He'll reign supreme where only sin was rife ;
He'll speak the word, and end the deadly
  strife ;
    Make Him the centre for ever.

576 MY spirit, soul, and body,
      Jesus, I give to Thee,
  A consecrated off'ring,
    Thine evermore to be.

  My all is on the altar,
    Lord, I am all Thine own ;
  Oh, may my faith ne'er falter,
    Lord, keep me Thine alone.

2 O Jesus, mighty Saviour,
    I trust in Thy great name ;
  I look for Thy salvation,
    Thy promise now I claim.

3 Now, Lord, I yield my members,
    From sin's dominion free,
  For warfare and for triumph,
    As weapons unto Thee.

4 I'm Thine, O blessed Jesus,
    Washed in Thy precious blood
  Sealed by Thy Holy Spirit,
    A sacrifice to God.

577 PRAY, always pray ; the Holy
      Spirit pleads
  Within thee all thy daily, hourly
    needs.

2 Pray, always pray ; beneath sin's
    heaviest load,
  Prayer sees the blood from Jesu'
    side that flowed.

3 Pray, always pray ; though weary,
    faint, and lone ;
  Prayer nestles by the Father's
    sheltering throne.

4 Pray, always pray ; amid the world's
    turmoil,
  Prayer keeps the heart at rest, and
    nerves for toil.

5 Pray, always pray ; if joys thy
    pathway throng,
  Prayer strikes the harp, and sings
    the angels' song.

6 Pray, always pray ; if loved ones
    pass the veil,
  Prayer drinks with them of springs
    that cannot fail.

7 All earthly things with earth shall
    fade away ;
  Prayer grasps eternity ; pray, always
    pray.

78 SAVIOUR! Thy dying love
    Thou gavest me,
Nor should I aught withhold,
  My Lord, from Thee ;
In love my soul would bow,
My heart fulfil its vow,
Some off'ring bring Thee now,
    Something for Thee.

At the blest Mercy-seat,
  Pleading for me,
My feeble faith looks up,
  Jesus, to Thee ;
Help me the cross to bear,
Thy wondrous love declare,
Some song to raise, or prayer,
    Something for Thee.

Give me a faithful heart—
  Likeness to Thee—
That each departing day
  Henceforth may see
Some work of love begun,
Some deed of kindness done,
Some wanderer sought and won,
    Something for Thee.

All that I am and have—
  Thy gifts so free—
In joy, in grief, through life,
  O Lord, for Thee !
And when Thy face I see,
My ransomed soul shall be,
Through all eternity,
    Something for Thee.

79 COME, ye disconsolate ! wher-
    e'er ye languish,
Come to the Mercy-seat, fervently
    kneel ;
Here bring your wounded hearts,
    here tell your anguish,
Earth has no sorrow that heav'n
    cannot heal.

Joy of the desolate ! light of the
    straying,   [pure !
Hope of the penitent, fadeless and
Here speaks the Comforter, tenderly
    saying,   [cannot cure.
Earth has no sorrow that heav'n

Here see the bread of life; see
    waters flowing
Forth from the throne of God,
    pure from above ;
Come to the feast of love ; come
    ever knowing,   [can remove.
Earth has no sorrow but heav'n

580 MY faith looks up to Thee,
    Thou Lamb of Calvary,
    Saviour divine ;
Now hear me while I pray,
Take all my guilt away ;
Oh, let me from this day
    Be wholly Thine !

2 May Thy rich grace impart
Strength to my fainting heart,
    My zeal inspire !
As Thou hast died for me,
Oh, may my love to Thee,
Pure, warm, and changeless be
    A living fire !

3 While life's dark maze I tread,
And griefs around me spread,
    Be Thou my Guide ;
Bid darkness turn to day,
Wipe sorrow's tears away,
Nor let me ever stray
    From Thee aside.

4 When ends life's transient dream,
When death's cold, sullen stream
    Shall o'er me roll ;
Blest Saviour, then, in love,
Fear and distrust remove ;
Oh, bear me safe above,
    A ransomed soul !

581 ALL to Jesus I surrender,
    All to Him I freely give ;
I will ever love and trust Him,
  In His presence daily live.
    I surrender all....
    I surrender all....
  All to Thee, my blessed Saviour,
    I surrender all.

2 All to Jesus I surrender,
  Humbly at His feet I bow ;
Worldly pleasures all forsaken,
  Take me, Jesus, take me now.

3 All to Jesus, I surrender,
  Make me, Saviour, wholly Thine ;
Let me feel the Holy Spirit,
  Truly know that Thou art mine.

4 All to Jesus I surrender,
  Lord, I give myself to Thee ;
Fill me with Thy love and power,
  Let Thy blessing fall on me.

5 All to Jesus I surrender,
  Now I feel the sacred flame ;
O the joy of full salvation !
  Glory, glory to His name !

582 'TIS the blessed hour of prayer,
When our hearts lowly bend,
And we gather to Jesus, our Saviour
and Friend ;
If we come to Him in faith, His
protection to share ;
What a balm for the weary ! O how
sweet to be there !

Blessed hour of prayer,
Blessed hour of prayer ;
What a balm for the weary !
O how sweet to be there.

2 'Tis the blessed hour of prayer, when
the Saviour draws near,
With a tender compassion His
children to hear ;
When He tells us we may cast at
His feet ev'ry care ;
What a balm for the weary ! O how
sweet to be there !

3 'Tis the blessed hour of prayer, when
the tempted and tried
To the Saviour who loves them their
sorrow confide ;
With a sympathising heart He
removes ev'ry care ;
What a balm for the weary ! O how
sweet to be there.

4 At the blessed hour of prayer,
trusting Him we believe
That the blessings we're needing
we'll surely receive,
In the fulness of this trust we shall
lose ev'ry care ;
What a balm for the weary ! O how
sweet to be there.

583 TEACH us to pray !
O Father, we look up to Thee,
And this our one request shall be,
Teach us to pray, teach us to pray.

2 Teach us to pray !
A form of words will not suffice ;
The heart must bring its sacrifice ;
Teach us to pray, teach us to pray.

3 Teach us to pray !
To whom shall we, Thy children,
turn ?
Teach us the lesson we should learn ;
Teach us to pray, teach us to pray.

4 Teach us to pray !
To Thee alone our hearts look up ;
Prayer is our only door of hope ;
Teach us to pray, teach us to pray.

584 NEARER, still nearer, clo
to Thy heart,
Draw me, my Saviour, so precio
Thou art ; [brea
Fold me, O fold me close to T
Shelter me safe in that " Haven
Rest," [Rest
Shelter me safe in that " Haven

2 Nearer, still nearer, nothing
bring, [Kin
Naught as an off'ring to Jesus, n
Only my sinful, now contrite heart
Grant me the cleansing Thy blo
doth impart.

3 Nearer, still nearer, Lord, to
Thine,
Sin, with its follies, I gladly resign
All of its pleasures, pomp and
pride, [crucifie
Give me but Jesus, my Lo

4 Nearer, still nearer, while life sh
last, [pas
Till all its struggles and trials a
Then thro' eternity, ever I'll be
Nearer, my Saviour, still nearer
Thee.

585 SOFTLY now the light of da
Fades upon our sight away ;
Free from care, from labour free,
Lord, we would commune with Th

2 Thou whose all-pervading eye
Naught escapes, without, within ;
Pardon each infirmity,
Open fault and secret sin.

3 Soon for us the light of day
Shall for ever pass away ;
Then from sin and sorrow free,
Take us, Lord, to dwell with Thee.

586 I AM praying, blessed Saviou
To be more and more li
Thee ;
I am praying that Thy Spirit
Like a dove may rest on me.

Thou who knowest all my weakness,
Thou who knowest all my care,
While I plead each precious promise,
Hear, oh, hear and answer pray'r.

2 I am praying, blessed Saviour,
For a faith so clear and bright,
That its eye will see Thy glory
Through the deepest, dark
night.

I am praying to be humbled
By the pow'r of grace divine,
To be clothed upon with meekness,
And to have no will but Thine.

I am praying, blessed Saviour,
And my constant pray'r shall be,
For a perfect consecration,
That shall make me more like Thee

87 TAKE my life, and let it be
Consecrated, Lord, to Thee;
Take my moments and my days,
Let them flow in ceaseless praise.

Take my hands, and let them move
At the impulse of Thy love;
Take my feet, and let them be
Swift and beautiful for Thee.

Take my voice, and let me sing
Always, only, for my King;
Take my lips, and let them be
Filled with messages from Thee.

Take my silver and my gold,
Not a mite would I withhold;
Take my intellect, and use
Ev'ry power as Thou shalt choose.

Take my will and make it Thine,
It shall be no longer mine;
Take my heart, it *is* Thine own;
It shall be Thy royal throne.

Take my love; my Lord, I pour
At Thy feet its treasure store;
Take myself, and I will be
Ever, *only*, ALL for Thee!

88 LORD Jesus Christ, we seek
Thy face;
Within the vail we bow the knee,
Oh, let Thy glory fill the place,
And bless us while we wait on
Thee.

We thank Thee for the precious
blood
That purged our sins and brought
us nigh,
All cleansed and sanctified to God,
Thy holy Name to magnify.

Shut in with Thee, far, far above
The restless world that wars below;
We seek to learn and prove Thy
love,   [know.
Thy wisdom and Thy grace to

4 Thy brow that once with thorns
was bound,
Thy hands, Thy side we fain
would see;
Draw near, Lord Jesus, glory
crowned,
And bless us while we wait on
Thee.

589 THO' the foes of right oppress,
Keep on praying;
Christ the Lord, is near to bless,
All prevailing.
Let not fear your heart appal,
Naught of evil can befall,
Stronger is your God than all,
Keep on praying.

Keep on praying, keep on praying,
Thro' the Saviour's blessed name, all prevailing.

2 Christian, has your faith grown
weak?
Keep on praying;
Do the tears roll down your cheek?
Keep on praying.
Soon you never more will sigh,
Tears no more shall dim your eye;
Pray to Him who's always nigh,
Never failing.

3 Pilgrim, have you weary grown?
Keep on praying;
God is yet upon His throne,
Keep on praying.
He will hear your faithful cry,
He to help is ever nigh,
You shall conquer by and by,
Keep on praying.

4 Praises shall with prayers ascend,
Keep on praying;
Pray and praise till life shall end,
Keep on praying.
Till you reach the golden gate,
Where the ransom'd souls await,
Claiming there your triumph great
Keep on praying.

590 MORE holiness give me,
More strivings within;
More patience in suff'ring,
More sorrow for sin;
More faith in my Saviour,
More sense of His care;
More joy in His service,
More purpose in prayer.

2 More gratitude give me,
More trust in the Lord ;
More pride in His glory,
More hope in His Word ;
More tears for His sorrows,
More pain at His grief ;
More meekness in trial,
More praise for relief.

3 More purity give me,
More strength to o'ercome ;
More freedom from earth stains,
More longings for home ;
More fit for the kingdom,
More use would I be ;
More blessed and holy,
More, Saviour, like Thee.

591 I'M over in Canaan where
riches abound,
Living on the vict'ry side ;
Each day going on to possess higher
ground,
Living on the vict'ry side.

Sing glo - ry, hallelujah !...
I'm living on the vict'ry side ;
Since Christ my soul hath sanctified,
I'm living on the vict'ry side.

2 No longer by fears am I fettered
and bound,
Living on the vict'ry side.
Sweet freedom in service for Christ
I have found,
Living on the vict'ry side.

3 I walk in the sunshine of God's holy
light,
Living on the vict'ry side ;
The will of my Lord is my joy and
delight,
Living on the vict'ry side.

4 The Lord whom I trust is my
strength and my song,
Living on the vict'ry side ;
No foes can alarm since to Him I
belong,
Living on the vict'ry side.

592 ARE you weary, are you
heavy-hearted ?
Tell it to Jesus, tell it to Jesus.
Are you grieving over joys departed?
Tell it to Jesus alone.

Tell it to Jesus, tell it to Jesus.
He is a Friend that's well known
You have no other such a friend or brother,
Tell it to Jesus alone.

2 Do the tears flow down your chee**k**
unbidden ?
Tell it to Jesus, tell it to Jesus.
Have you sins that to man's ey**e**
are hidden ?
Tell it to Jesus alone.

3 Do you fear the gath'ring clouds **of**
sorrow ?
Tell it to Jesus, tell it to Jesus.
Are you anxious what shall b**e**
to-morrow ?
Tell it to Jesus alone.

4 Are you troubled with the thoug**ht**
of dying ?
Tell it to Jesus, tell it to Jesus.
For Christ's coming kingdom a**re**
you sighing ?
Tell it to Jesus alone.

593 EVER Thine, Thine alone,
Henceforth, Saviour, I wi**ll**
be ;
This my joy, my life's ambition,
Day by day to grow like Thee.

594 PRAYER is the soul's since**re**
desire,
Uttered or unexpressed,
The motion of a hidden fire
That trembles in the breast.

2 Prayer is the burden of a sigh,
The falling of a tear,
The upward glancing of an eye,
When none but God is near.

3 Prayer is the simplest form **of**
speech
That infant lips can try ;
Prayer, the sublimest strains th**at**
reach
The Majesty on high.

4 Prayer is the Christian's vital breat**h**
The Christian's native air ;
His watchword at the gates **of**
death,
He enters heaven with prayer.

5 Prayer is the contrite sinner's voic**e**
Returning from his ways ;
While angels in their songs rejoice,
And cry, " Behold, he prays ! "

6 O Thou by whom we come to God,
The Life, the Truth, the Way !
The path of prayer Thyself hast tro**d**,
Lord, teach us how to pray !

595 MORE love to Thee, O Christ!
    More love to Thee;
Hear Thou the pray'r I make
    On bended knee.
This is my earnest plea—
More love, O Christ, to Thee!
    More love to Thee!

2 Once earthly joy I crav'd,
    Sought peace and rest;
Now Thee alone I seek,
    Give what is best.
This all my pray'r shall be—
More love, O Christ, to Thee!
    More love to Thee!

3 Let sorrow do its work,
    Come grief or pain;
Sweet are Thy messengers,
    Sweet their refrain,
When they can sing with me—
More love, O Christ, to Thee!
    More love to Thee!

4 Then shall my latest breath
    Whisper Thy praise;
This be the parting cry
    My heart shall raise;
This still its prayer shall be—
More love, O Christ, to Thee!
    More love to Thee!

596 O TEACH me more of Thy
    blest ways,
Thou Holy Lamb of God!
And fix and root me in Thy grace,
    As one redeemed by blood.

Oh, tell me often of Thy love,
    Of all Thy grief and pain,
And let my heart with joy confess
    That thence comes all my gain.

For this, oh, may I freely count
    Whate'er I have but loss,
The dearest object of my love,
    Compared with Thee, but dross.

Engrave this deeply on my heart,
    With an eternal pen,
That I may, in some small degree,
    Return Thy love again.

597 APPROACH, my soul, the
    mercy-seat,
Where Jesus answers prayer;
There humbly fall before His feet,
    For none can perish there.

2 Thy promise is my only plea,
    With this I venture nigh;
Thou callest burdened souls to Thee,
    And such, O Lord, am I!

3 Bowed down beneath a load of sin,
    By Satan sorely prest;
By wars without, and fears within—
    I come to Thee for rest.

4 Be Thou my shield and hiding-place;
    That, sheltered near Thy side,
I may my fierce accuser face,
    And tell him Thou hast died.

5 Oh, wondrous love—to bleed and
    die,
To bear the Cross and shame,
That guilty sinners such as I
    Might plead Thy gracious name.

598 I'VE found the "Pearl of
    greatest price,"
My heart doth sing for joy:
And sing I must, for Christ I have—
    Oh, what a Christ have I!

2 My Christ He is the "Lord of lords,"
    The Sovereign " King of kings,"
The risen " Sun of Righteousness,
    With healing in His wings."

3 My Christ He is " the Tree of Life,"
    That in God's Eden grows,
The living "clear as crystal"
    stream
Whence life for ever flows.

4 Christ is my Meat, Christ is my
    Drink,
My Medicine and my Health;
My Portion, mine Inheritance,
    Yea, all my Boundless Wealth.

599 OH, for a heart to praise my
    God,
A heart from sin set free;
A heart that always feels the blood
    So freely shed for me;

2 A heart resigned, submissive, meek,
    My great Redeemer's throne,
Where only Christ is heard to speak,
    Where Jesus reigns alone;

3 A humble, holy, contrite heart,
    Believing, true, and clean,
Which neither life, nor death can
    part
From Him that dwells within.

4 A heart in every thought renewed,
 And full of love divine,
Perfect, and right, and pure, and
  good,
 A copy, Lord, of Thine !

5 Thy nature, gracious Lord, impart ;
 Come quickly from above ;
Write Thy new name upon my
  heart—
 Thy new, best name of love.

600 WHAT various hindrances we
  meet
 In coming to the Mercy Seat !
Yet who, that knows the worth of
  prayer,
 But wishes to be often there ?

2 Prayer makes the darkened clouds
  withdraw,
 Prayer climbs the ladder Jacob saw ;
Gives exercise to faith and love,
 Brings ev'ry blessing from above.

3 Restraining prayer, we cease to
  fight,
 Prayer makes the Christian's armour
  bright ;
And Satan trembles when he sees
 The weakest saint upon his knees.

4 While Moses stood with arms spread
  wide,
 Success was found on Israel's side :
But when through weariness they
  failed,
 That moment Amalek prevailed.

5 Have you no words ? ah ! think
  again, [plain,
 Words flow apace when you com-
And fill your fellow-creatures' ear
 With the sad tale of all your care.

6 Were half the breath thus vainly
  spent,
 To heaven in supplication sent,
Your cheerful song would oftener
  be, [me ! "
 " Hear what the Lord has done for

601 JESUS, Thou joy of loving
  hearts,
 Thou fount of life, Thou light of
  men ! [imparts
From the best bliss that earth
 We turn unfilled to Thee again.

2 Thy truth unchang'd hath ev‹
  stood,
 Thou savest those that on The‹
  call ; [goo‹
To them that seek Thee Thou a
 To them that find Thee, All in al‹

3 We taste Thee, O Thou livir
  bread, [still
 And long to feast upon The‹
We drink of Thee, the fountaii
  head, [to fi‹
 And thirst our souls from Th‹

4 Our restless spirits yearn for Thee,
 Where'er our changeful lot
  cast, [se‹
Glad when Thy gracious smile w
 Blest when our faith can hol
  Thee fast.

5 O Jesus, ever with us stay !
 Make all our moments calm an
  bright ;
Chase the dark night of sin away ;
 Shed o'er the world Thy ho‹
  light.

602 LORD, speak to me, that
  may speak
 In living echoes of Thy tone ;
As Thou hast sought, so let me seel
 Thy erring children lost and lon

2 Oh, lead me, Lord, that I may lead
 The wandering and the waverir
  feet ;
Oh, feed me, Lord, that I may feed
 Thy hungering ones with mann
  sweet.

3 Oh, teach me, Lord, that I ma
  teach [impar
 The precious things Thou do
And wing my words, that the
  may reach [hear
 The hidden depths of many

4 Oh, give Thine own sweet rest ‹
  me, [pow
 That I may speak with soothii
A word in season, as from Thee,
 To weary ones in needful hour.

5 Oh, fill me with Thy fulness, Lor
 Until my very heart o'erflow
In kindling thought, and glowii
  word, [sho
 Thy love to tell, Thy praise

Oh, use me, Lord, use even me,
 Just as Thou wilt, and how, and
  where :
Until Thy blessed face I see,
 Thy rest, Thy joy, Thy glory share.

03 WHO shall roll the stone
   away ?
Who shall break the seal ?
Who can drive the clouds away,
 Wounded hearts to heal ?

 Only God can lift the weight
  That keeps fast the glory gate !
 Even now, Lord, while we pray,
  Thou can'st roll the stones away !

Who can lead the weary soul
 To the Saviour's Cross ?
Who can make us joyfully
 Count all else but loss ?

3 Who can banish unbelief,
 As in prayer we bow ?
Who can ope the silent lips ?
 God can—here and now !

4 Who can cleanse our sins away,
 By His precious blood ?
Only one can these things do—
 Christ the Son of God.

5 Who will come to Jesus now ?
 Now, this very hour ?
He will save you willingly,
 Keep you by His pow'r !

604 IS your name written there,
   On the page white and fair ?
In the book of His kingdom,
 Is your name written there ?

TESTIMONY AND ASSURANCE

05 NAUGHT have I gotten but
   what I received ;
Grace hath bestowed it since I have
 believed,
Boasting excluded, pride I abase ;
I'm only a sinner saved by grace !

 Only a sinner saved by grace !
 Only a sinner saved by grace !
 This is my story—to God be the Glory—
 I'm only a sinner saved by grace.

Once I was foolish, and sin ruled
 my heart,   [depart ;
Causing my footsteps from God to
Jesus hath found me, happy my
 case—
I now am a sinner saved by grace !

Tears unavailing, no merit had I :
Mercy had saved me, or else I must
 die ;
Sin had alarm'd me, fearing God's
 face ;   [grace !
But now I'm a sinner saved by

Suffer a sinner whose heart over-
 flows,   [knows ;
Loving his Saviour, to tell what he
Once more to tell it, would I em-
 brace—
I'm only a sinner saved by grace !

06 I LOVE to tell the story
   Of unseen things above,
Of Jesus and His glory,
 Of Jesus and His love !

I love to tell the story !
 Because I know it's true !
It satisfies my longings
 As nothing else would do.

 I love to tell the story !
 'Twill be my theme in glory
 To tell the Old, Old Story
  Of Jesus and His love.

2 I love to tell the story !
 More wonderful it seems
Than all the golden fancies
 Of all our golden dreams ;
I love to tell the story !
 It did so much for me !
And that is just the reason
 I tell it now to thee.

3 I love to tell the story !
 'Tis pleasant to repeat
What seems, each time I tell it,
 More wonderfully sweet.
I love to tell the story !
 For some have never heard
The message of salvation
 From God's own Holy Word.

4 I love to tell the story !
 For those who know it best
Seem hungering and thirsting
 To hear it, like the rest.
And when in scenes of glory,
 I sing the NEW, NEW SONG,
'Twill be—the OLD, OLD STORY
 That I have loved so long.

607 I WAS a sinner, but now I'm
         free,   [me ;
His wondrous grace has rescued
Once I was blind, but now I see,
    A brand from the burning, He
    rescued me.

He rescued me His own to be,
  A brand from the burning, He set me free ;
Oh, how I'll praise Him thro' eternity,
  A brand from the burning, He rescued me.

2 Once I was wayward, afar would
       stray,   [me ;
His wondrous grace has rescued
Now I am on the "King's highway,"
    A brand from the burning, He set
    me free.

3 Once evil led me, but now God
       reigns,   [me ;
His wondrous grace has rescued
Broken for e'er are sin's dark
       chains,   [me free.
    A brand from the burning, He set

608 O BROTHER, have you told
         how the Lord forgave ?
    Let us hear you tell it over once
    again ;
Thy coming to the Cross, where He
    died to save,   [again.
    Let us hear you tell it over once
Are you walking now in His blessed
    light ?
    Are you cleansed from ev'ry
    guilty stain ?
Is He your joy by day and your
    song by night ?   [again.
    Let us hear you tell it over once

    Let us hear...you tell it o - ver,...
    Tell it o - - ver once again....
    Tell the sweet and blessed story,
    It will help you on to glory,
    Let us hear you tell it over once again.

2 When toiling up the way was the
       Saviour there ?   [again ;
    Let us hear you tell it over once
Did Jesus bear you up in His tender
       care ?   [again.
    Let us hear you tell it over once
Never have you found such a Friend
    as He,
Who can help you 'midst the toil
    and pain ;
O all the world should hear what
    He's done for thee !   [again.
    Let us hear you tell it over once

3 Was ever on your tongue such
       blessed theme ?   [agai
    Let us hear you tell it over on
'Tis ever sweeter far than t
       sweetest dream ;   [aga
    Let us hear you tell it over on
There are aching hearts in t
    world's great throng,
    Who have sought for rest, a
    all in vain ;
Hold Jesus up to them by yc
    word and song ;   [aga
    Let us hear you tell it over on

4 The battles you have fought, a
       the vict'ries won,   [agai
    Let us hear you tell it over on
'Twill help them on the way w
    have just begun,   [aga
    Let us hear you tell it over on
We are striving now with the ho
    of sin,   [shall reig
    Soon with Christ our Saviour
Ye ransomed of the Lord, try a s
    to win ;   [aga
    Let us hear you tell it over on

609 NOW just a word for Jesus,
         Your dearest Friend so tru
Come cheer our hearts and tell us
What He has done for you.

    Now just a word for Jesus—
      'Twill help us on our way ;
    One little word for Jesus,
      O speak, or sing, or pray.

2 Now just a word for Jesus,
    You feel your sins forgiv'n,
And by His grace are striving
    To reach a home in heav'n.

3 Now just a word for Jesus,
    A cross it cannot be
To say I love my Saviour,
    Who gave His life for me.

4 Now just a word for Jesus,
    Let not the time be lost ;
The heart's neglected duty
    Brings sorrow to its cost.

5 Now just a word for Jesus,
    And if your faith be dim,
Arise in all your weakness,
    And leave the rest to Him.

610 I HAVE a Shepherd, One
         love so well ;
How He has blessed me tongue c
    never tell ;

On the Cross He suffered, shed His
blood and died,
That I might ever in His love confide.

llowing Jesus, ever day by day,
·thing can harm me when He leads the way ;
·rkness or sunshine, whate'er befall,
sus, the Shepherd, is my All in all.

Pastures abundant doth His hand
provide,
Still waters flowing ever at my side ;
Goodness and mercy follow on my
track,   [I lack.
With such a Shepherd nothing can

When I would wander from the path
astray,   [the way ;
Then He will draw me back into
In the darkest valley I need fear no
ill,   [me still.
For He, my Shepherd, will be with

When labour's ended and the
journey done,
Then He will lead me safely to my
home ;
There I shall dwell in rapture sure
and sweet,
With all the loved ones gathered
round His feet.

1 I'M not ashamed to own my
Lord,
Or to defend His cause ;
Maintain the honour of His Word,
The glory of His Cross.

At the Cross, at the Cross, where I first saw
the light,
And the burden of my heart roll'd away,...
It was there by faith I received my sight,
And now I am happy all the day.

Jesus, my Lord ! I know His name—
His name is all my trust,
Nor will He put my soul to shame,
Nor let my hope be lost.

Firm as His throne His promise
stands,
And He can well secure
What I've committed to His hands,
Till the decisive hour.

Then will He own my worthless
name
Before His Father's face ;
And, in the new Jerusalem,
Appoint my soul a place.

612 I WAS wrecked on a rocky
and desolate shore,   [sea ;
Sinking slowly beneath the wild
When all of my struggles and efforts
were o'er,   [me.
Christ threw out the life-line to

He threw out the life-line to me,...
He threw out the life-line to me,...
From Calvary's tree, far over the sea,
Christ threw out the life-line to me.

2 The billows were dashing, the waves
rolling high,   [see ;
No help from the land could I
When hope had all vanished, and
danger was nigh,   [me.
Christ threw out the life-line to

3 When all was confusion 'midst dark
billows' roll,   [see,
No light thro' the gloom could I
By trusting Him fully He rescued
my soul,   [me.
Christ threw out the life-line to

4 And now as I wander I sing as I go,
His mercy is boundless and free,
And tell the glad story, that others
may know,   [me.
Christ threw out the life-line to

5 Your sins like the billows around you
may rise,
And dangers your frail barque
pursue ;
There's One who will heed you, and
hear your faint cries,
He'll throw out the life-line to you.

613 MY path was always rough
and drear,
My soul was always sad ;
But now my path is smooth and
bright,
My soul for ever glad.

It was Je - - sus, my Saviour, who wrought
this change in me ;
It was Je - - sus, my Saviour, blest Lamb
of Calvary,
I came to Him just as I was, from sin He
set me free ;
It was Je - - sus, my Saviour, who wrought
this change in me.

2 My soul was stained with many sins,
I lived in fear and dread ;
But now my soul is free from stain,
And all my fears have fled.

3 O wand'ring one in paths of sin,
  The Saviour calls to thee ;
He longs to give you peace and rest,
  From sin to set you free.

614 I WAS once far away from
  the Saviour,
  And as vile as a sinner could be ;
And I wondered if Christ the
  Redeemer
  Could save a poor sinner like me.

2 I wander'd on in the darkness,
  Not a ray of light could I see ;
And the thought fill'd my heart
  with sadness, [me.
  There's no hope for a sinner like

3 And then, in that dark lonely hour,
  A voice sweetly whisper'd to me,
Saying, " Christ the Redeemer has
  pow'r
  To save a poor sinner like thee."

4 I listened, and lo ! 'twas the
  Saviour [me ;
  That was speaking so kindly to
I cried, " I'm the chief of sinners,
  Thou canst save a poor sinner like
  me ! "

5 I then fully trusted in Jesus ;
  And oh, what a joy came to me !
My heart was filled with His praises,
  For saving a sinner like me.

6 No longer in darkness I'm walking,
  For the light is now shining on
  me ;
And now unto others I'm telling
  How He saved a poor sinner like
  me.

7 And when life's journey is over,
  And I the dear Saviour shall see,
I'll praise Him for ever and ever,
  For saving a sinner like me.

615 I'M happy in Jesus, my
  Saviour, my King,
And all the day long of His goodness
  I sing ;
To Him in my weakness I lovingly
  cling,
  For He is so precious to me.

  For He is so precious to me,...
  For He is so precious to me,...
  'Tis heaven below my Redeemer to know.
  For He is so precious to me....

2 He stood at the door amid sunshi
  and rain,
So patiently waiting an entrance
  gain ;
What shame that so long He e
  treated in vain,
  For He is so precious to me.

3 I stand on the mountain of sunshi
  at last,
No cloud in the heavens a shad
  to cast ;
His smile is upon me, the valley
  past,
  For He is so precious to me.

4 I praise Him because He appoint
  a place,
Where, some day, thro' faith in H
  marvellous grace,
My eyes shall behold Him, shall lo
  on His face,
  For He is so precious to me.

616 O WHAT a change ! from t
  darkness of night,
Into the blaze of the clear shini
  light ;
Out of my weakness to power a
  might, [chang
  O what a change ! O what

  O what a change in my heart there has be
  O what a change since the Saviour came
  O what a change, to be free from all sin,
  O what a change ! O what a change !

2 O what a change ! From my hung
  for bread,
Into a place where God's childr
  are fed ;
Into the blessing of life from t
  dead, [chang
  O what a change ! O what

3 O what a change ! From my burd
  of care,
Into His love He invites me to sha
  Into His joy from the sorrow I be
  O what a change ! O what
  change !

4 O what a change ! In the flash
  an eye,
When we shall meet with our L
  by and by ;
Into a realm where we never sh
  die, [chang
  O what a change ! O what

17 I KNOW not why God's
wondrous grace
To me He hath made known,
Nor why, unworthy of such love,
He bought me for His own—

But "I know whom I have believed,
And am persuaded that He is able
To keep that which I've committed
Unto Him against that day."

I know not how this saving faith
To me He did impart,
Nor how believing in His Word
Wrought peace within my heart—

I know not how the Spirit moves—
Convincing men of sin—
Revealing Jesus through the Word,
Creating faith in Him—

I know not what of good or ill
May be reserved for me,
Of weary ways or golden days
Before His face I see—

I know not when my Lord may
come,
At night or noonday fair—
Nor if I'll walk the vale with Him,
Or " meet Him in the air."

18 TO the feet of my Saviour in
trembling and fear,
A penitent sinner I came ;
He saw, and in mercy He bade me
draw near ;
All glory and praise to His name.

e touched me and thus made me whole,..
ringing comfort and rest to my soul ;...
glad happy day, all my sins rolled away !
r He touched me and thus made me whole....

I knew not the tender compassion
and love
That Jesus, my Saviour, had
shown ;
Tho' burdened with grief, His dear
hand brought relief ;
He healed me and called me His
own.

" My grace is sufficient," I heard
His dear voice,   [soul ;
" O come and find rest for your
From sin you to save My life freely
I gave ;   [whole."
I died that you might be made

4 O Jesus, dear Jesus, Thy name I
adore,
For saving and keeping my soul ;
Thy praises I'll sing, my Redeemer
and King,
Thy dear loving hand made me
whole.

5 O come, my dear brother, He's
waiting for you,
Your sin-burdened heart to con-
sole ;
Your weary head rest on His dear,
loving breast ;
He suffered and died for your
soul.

619 I FLED from Egypt's bondage,
I heard that help was near ;
I cast my care on Jesus,
And He dispersed my fear ;
I pass'd between the billows,
Walled up on ev'ry hand,
I trusted to my Captain,
And sought the promised land.

I am over, yes, over ;
On Canaan's shore I stand ;
I am over, yes, over,
In the promised land.

2 I sang a song of triumph,
I shouted o'er and o'er,
And then pursued my journey
For Canaan's happy shore ;
I came to Sinai's mountain,
I trod the desert sand,
I drank at Horeb's fountain,
Seeking the promised land.

3 The spies brought back their
message,
Some wept, some said, " We can ;"
The land was all 'twas promised,
But who would lead the van ?
At last, my heart despairing
Of ent'ring with this band,
I cried aloud to Jesus
To show the promised land.

4 Then, after weary marches,
And many a longing sigh,
I found the river crossing,
And saw the land was nigh.
The Lord look'd down in mercy,
By faith I touched His hand,
I followed close beside Him,
And found the promised land.

5 And now my song of gladness,
  I'm singing day by day,
For fellowship with Jesus
  Makes calm and bright my way.
I fear not for the morrow,
  For His almighty hand
I know shall lead and keep me
  In this the promised land.

620 THERE'S a song in my heart
    that my lips cannot sing,
'Tis praise in the highest to Jesus
    my King ;
Its music each moment is thrilling
    my soul,
For I was a sinner, but Christ made
    me whole.

A sinner made whole ! a sinner made whole !
The Saviour hath bought me and ransomed
    my soul !
My heart it is singing, the anthem is ringing,
For I was a sinner, but Christ made me whole.

2 I shall stand one day faultless and
    pure by His throne,
  Transformed from my image, con-
    formed to His own ;
  Then I shall find words for the song
    in my soul,
  For I was a sinner, but Christ made
    me whole.

3 All the music of heaven, so perfect
    and sweet,
  Will blend with my song, and will
    make it complete ;
  Thro' ages unending the echoes will
    roll,
  For I was a sinner, but Christ made
    me whole.

621 TELL what the Lord has done
    for you,
Speak just a word, speak just a
    word ;   [true,
Stand for the right, be brave and
Speak just a word for Jesus.

Speak just a word, speak just a word,
  Gladly His love proclaim :
Tell what the Lord has done for you,
  Speak just a word for Jesus.

2 Early begin to bear the cross,
  Speak just a word, speak just a
    word ;
  They who deny Him suffer loss,
  Speak just a word for Jesus.

3 Tell if the Lord has cleansed yo⟩
    sin,
  Speak just a word, speak just ⟩
    word ;
  It may to Him some others win,
  Speak just a word for Jesus.

4 Fear not the world, nor heed ⟩
    frown,
  Speak just a word, speak just ⟩
    word ;
  They who endure shall wear t⟩
    crown,
  Speak just a word for Jesus.

622 OH, happy day, that fixed m⟩
    choice,
  On Thee, my Saviour and m⟩
    God !
Well may this glowing heart r⟩
    joice,
  And tell its raptures all abroad.

  Happy day, happy day,
When Jesus washed my sins away !
  He taught me how to watch and pray⟩
  And live rejoicing ev'ry day.
  Happy day, happy day,
When Jesus washed my sins away.

2 'Tis done, the great transactio⟩
    done !
  I am my Lord's and He is mine⟩
He drew me, and I followed on,
  Charmed to confess the voi⟩
    divine.

3 Now rest, my long-divided heart,
  Fixed on this blissful centre, res⟩
Nor ever from thy Lord depart,
  With Him of every good possesse⟩

4 High heaven that heard the solen⟩
    vow,
  That vow renewed shall dai⟩
    hear,
Till in life's latest hour I bow,
  And bless in death a bond so de⟩

623 HE brought me out of t⟩
    miry clay,
He set my feet on the Rock to sta⟩
He puts a song in my soul to-day,
  A song of praise, Hallelujah !

624 I CAME to Jesus, weary, wo⟩
    and sad,
  He took my sins away,
  He took my sins away;

His wondrous love has made my
heart so glad,
He took my sins away.

He took my sins away, He took my sins away
And keeps my footsteps day by day ;
I'm so glad He saved my guilty soul
And took my sins away.

The load of sin was more than I
could bear,
He took it all away,
He took it all away ;
And now on Him I roll my ev'ry
care,
He took my sins away.

3 No condemnation have I in my
heart,
He took my sins away,
And keeps me day by day ;
His perfect peace He did to me
impart,
He took my sins away.

4 If you will come to Jesus Christ
to-day,
He'll take your sins away,
He'll take your sins away ;
And keep you happy in the narrow
way,
He'll take your sins away.

MISSIONARY

25 I HEAR ten thousand voices
singing
Their praises to the Lord on high ;
Far distant shores and hills are
ringing
With anthems of their nation's joy:
" Praise ye the Lord ! for He has
given
To lands in darkness hid His light;
As morning rays light up the heaven,
His Word has chased away our
night."

On China's shores I heard His praises
From lips that once kissed idol
stones ;
Soon as His banner He upraises,
The Spirit moves the breathless
bones ;
" Speed, speed Thy Word o'er land
and ocean ;
The Lord in triumph has gone
forth ;
The nations hear with strange
emotion ;
From East to West, from South
to North."

The song has sounded o'er the waters
And India's plains re-echo joy ;
Beneath the moon sit India's
daughters,
Soft singing as the wheel they
ply—
" Thanks to Thee, Lord, for hopes
of glory,
For peace on earth to us revealed ;
Our cherished idols fall before Thee,
Thy Spirit has our pardon sealed."

626 FROM Greenland's icy moun-
tains,
From India's coral strand,
Where Afric's sunny fountains
Roll down their golden sand ;
From many an ancient river,
From many a palmy plain,
They call us to deliver
Their land from error's chain.

2 What though the spicy breezes
Blow soft o'er Ceylon's isle,
Though ev'ry prospect pleases,
And only man is vile ;
In vain with lavish kindness
The gifts of God are strewn,
The heathen in his blindness
Bows down to wood and stone.

3 Can we, whose souls are lighted
With wisdom from on high,
Can we to men benighted
The lamp of life deny ?
Salvation ! O Salvation !
The joyful sound proclaim,
Till each remotest nation
Has learnt Messiah's name.

4 Waft, waft, ye winds, His story,
And you, ye waters, roll,
Till, like a sea of glory,
It spreads from pole to pole ;
Till o'er our ransomed nature,
The Lamb for sinners slain,
Redeemer, King, Creator,
In bliss returns to reign.

627 OVER the mountains so bleak
and so cold,
Far from the beautiful city of gold,

Lost ones are straying, because you and I
Never have told them a Saviour stood nigh.

Oh, won't somebody tell them,
Tell them of Calvary's tree ;
Tell them the story of Jesus,
What a great Saviour is He !

2 Lost ones are groping in sin's awful night,
Falling and dying away from the right ;
Many the message of Christ never heard,
Lost ones for whom no one ever has cared.

3 Speed with the message, oh, speed in His name,
Hasten the story of Christ to proclaim !
Hasten to bring back the fallen and lost ;
Speed with the message, whatever the cost.

628 THERE'S a call comes ringing o'er the restless wave,
Send the light !...Send the light !...
There are souls to rescue, there are souls to save,
Send the light !...Send the light !...

Send the light...the blessed Gospel light,
Let it shine...from shore to shore !...
Send the light !...and let its radiant beams
Light the world...for evermore.

2 We have heard the Macedonian call to-day,
Send the light !...Send the light !...
And a golden off'ring at the Cross we lay,
Send the light !...Send the light !...

3 Let us pray that grace may ev'rywhere abound,
Send the light !...Send the light !...
And the Christ-like spirit ev'rywhere be found,
Send the light !...Send the light !...

4 Let us not grow weary in the work of love,
Send the light !...Send the light !...
Let us gather jewels for a crown above.
Send the light !...Send the light !...

629 BLOW ye the trumpet, blow
The gladly solemn sound ;
Let all the nations know
To earth's remotest bound
The year of jubilee is come,
Return, ye ransom'd sinners, hon

2 Jesus, our great High Priest,
Has full atonement made,
Ye weary spirits, rest,
Ye mourning souls, be glad ;
The year of jubilee is come,
Return, ye ransom'd sinners, hon

3 Exalt the Lamb of God,
The sin-atoning Lamb,
Redemption by His blood
Through all the world proclair
The year of jubilee is come,
Return, ye ransom'd sinners, hon

630 COMING, coming, yes, they a
Coming, coming from afar,
From the wild and scorching deser
Afric's sons of colour deep ;
Jesus' love has drawn and won the
At His Cross they bow and wee

2 Coming, coming, yes, they are,
Coming, coming, from afar ;
From the fields and crowded citi
China gathers to His feet ;
In His love Shem's gentle childre
Now have found a safe retreat.

3 Coming, coming, yes, they are,
Coming, coming, from afar ;
From the Indus and the Ganges,
Steady flows the living stream,
To love's ocean, to His bosom,
Calvary their wond'ring theme.

4 Coming, coming, yes, they are,
Coming, coming from afar ;
From the steppes of Russia dreary
From Slavonia's scattered lands
They are yielding soul and spirit
Into Jesus' loving hands.

5 Coming, coming, yes, they are,
Coming, coming from afar ;
From the frozen realms of midnigl
Over many a weary mile,
To exchange their souls' long wint
For the summer of His smile.

6 Coming, coming, yes, they are,
Coming, coming from afar.

All to meet in plains of glory,
  All to sing His praises sweet ;
What a chorus, what a meeting,
  With the family complete !

31 HOW many sheep are straying,
    Lost from the Saviour's fold !
Upon the lonely mountain
  They shiver with the cold ;
Within the tangled thickets,
  Where poison vines do creep,
And over rocky ledges
  Wander the poor, lost sheep.

Oh, come, let us go and find them ;
In the paths of death they roam,
; the close of the day, 'twill be sweet to say,
  " I have brought some lost one home."

Oh, who will go to find them ?
  Who, for the Saviour's sake
Will search with tireless patience
  Through brier and through brake ?
Unheeding thirst or hunger,
  Who still, from day to day,
Will seek, as for a treasure,
  The sheep that go astray ?

Say, will *you* seek to find them ?
  From pleasant bowers of ease,
Will you go forth determined
  To find the " least of these ? "
For still the Saviour calls them,
  And looks across the wold ;
And still He holds wide open
  The door into His fold.

How sweet 'twould be at evening,
  If you and I could say,
" Good Shepherd, we've been seek-
    ing
The sheep that went astray !
Heart-sore and faint with hunger,
  We heard them making moan,
And lo ! we come at nightfall,
  And bear them safely home."

32 SOMEONE shall go at the
    Master's word
Over the seas to the lands afar,
Telling to those who have never
    heard
  What His wonderful mercies are.
  Shall it be you—Shall it be I
Who shall haste to tell what we
    know so well ?
    Shall you ? Shall I ?

2 Someone will gather the sheaves for
    Him,
  Someone shall bind them with
    joyful hand ;
Someone shall toil through the
    shadows dim,
  For the morn in the heavenly land.
  Shall it be you—Shall it be I
Who shall bind the corn for the
    golden morn ?
    Shall you ? Shall I ?

3 Someone shall travel with eager feet
  Over the mountain and through
    the wild,
Bringing the news of redemption
    sweet
  To each wandering sinful child.
  Shall it be you—Shall it be I
Who shall sound the tale over hill
    and dale ?
    Shall you ? Shall I ?

4 Someone shall carry His banner high,
  Waving it out where the foe holds
    sway ;
Some in His service shall live and die,
  And with Jesus shall win the day !
  Shall it be you—Shall it be I
Who His name shall bear, and His
    triumph share ?
    Shall you ? Shall I ?

633 SPEED away ! speed away on
    your mission of light,
To the lands that are lying in dark-
    ness and night ;
'Tis the Master's command : go ye
    forth in His name,   [claim.
The wonderful Gospel of Jesus pro-
Take your lives in your hand, to the
    work while 'tis day,
Speed away ! speed away ! speed
    away !

2 Speed away ! speed away with the
    life-giving Word,
To the nations that know not the
    voice of the Lord ;
Take the wings of the morning and
    fly o'er the wave,
In the strength of your Master the
    lost ones to save.
He is calling once more—not a
    moment's delay !
Speed away ! speed away ! speed
    away !

3 Speed away ! speed away with the
message of rest
To the souls by the tempter in
bondage opprest ;
For the Saviour has purchased their
ransom from sin,
And the banquet is ready : oh,
gather them in !
To the rescue make haste, there's
no time for delay :
Speed away ! speed away ! speed
away !

634 FAR, far away in heathen
darkness dwelling,
Millions of souls for ever may be
lost ;
Who, who will go, Salvation's story
telling—
Looking to Jesus, counting not
the cost ?

" All power is given unto Me !
All power is given unto Me !
Go ye into all the world and preach the Gospel ;
and lo I am with you alway."

2 See, o'er the world, wide open doors
inviting ;   [in !
Soldiers of Christ, arise and enter
Christians, awake ! your forces all
uniting,
Send forth the Gospel, break the
chain of sin !

3 " Why will ye die ? " the voice of
God is calling :   [His Name ;
" Why will ye die ? " re-echo in
Jesus hath died to save from death
appalling :
Life and salvation therefore go
proclaim.

4 God speed the day when those of
every nation,
" Glory to God " triumphantly
shall sing :
Ransomed, redeemed, rejoicing in
salvation,
Shout " Hallelujah, for the Lord
is King ! "

635 IT may not be on the moun-
tain's height,
Or over the stormy sea ;
It may not be at the battle's front
My Lord will have need of me ;

But if by a still small voice He ca
To paths that I do not know,
I'll answer, " dear Lord, with m
hand in Thine,
I'll go where You want me to go

I'll go where You want me to go, dear Lor
Over mountain, or plain, or sea,
I'll say what You want me to say, dear Lo
I'll be what You want me to be.

2 Perhaps to-day there are lovi
words   [speak
Which Jesus would have m
There may be now in the path of s
Some wand'rer whom I shou
seek,   [Guid
O Saviour, if Thou wilt be m
Tho' dark and rugged the way,
My voice shall echo the messa
sweet,
I'll say what You want me to sa

3 There's surely somewhere a low
place,
In earth's harvest field so wide,
Where I may labour thro' life'
short day
For Jesus the crucified ;
So, trusting my all to Thy tend
care,
And knowing Thou lovest me,
I'll do Thy will with a heart sincer
I'll be what You want me to be

636 WE'VE a story to tell to t
nations,
That shall turn their hearts
the right ;
A story of truth and sweetness,
A story of peace and light.

For the darkness shall turn to dawning,
And the dawning to noonday bright,
And Christ's great kingdom shall come
earth,
The Kingdom of Love and Light.

2 We've a song to be sung to t
nations.
That shall lift their heart to t
Lord ;
A song that shall conquer evil
And shatter the spear and swor

3 We've a message to give to t
nations,
That the Lord who reigneth abo
Hath sent us His Son to save us,
And show us that God is love.

We've a Saviour to show to the
   nations,
  Who the path of sorrow hath trod,
That all of the world's great peoples
  Might come to the truth of God.

37 HEAR the wail across the sea,
     Comes from millions unto
     thee,
Weary ones who might be free,
  Did they but know of Calvary.

   Wailing, wailing o'er the sea ;
    Wailing, wailing unto thee ;
   Wailing, wailing to be free :
    Go, tell them all of Calvary !

Wailing of the prophet cursed,
  Of fanatics, wildest, worst,
Help us, Lord, their chains to burst,
  And set them free by Calvary.

Wailings reach this favoured shore,
  Wailings ceasing nevermore ;
Men are dying evermore—
  Go, tell them all of Calvary.

38 FAR and near the fields are
     teeming
  With the waves of ripen'd grain ;
Far and near their gold is gleaming,
  O'er the sunny slope and plain.

   Lord of harvest, send forth reapers !
    Hear us, Lord, to Thee we cry ;
   Send them now the sheaves to gather,
    Ere the harvest time pass by.

Send them forth with morn's first
    beaming,
  Send them in the noontide's glare ;
When the sun's last rays are gleam-
    ing,
  Bid them gather ev'rywhere.

O Thou, whom thy Lord is sending,
  Gather now the sheaves of gold,
Heav'nward then at ev'ning wending
  Thou shalt come with joy untold.

39 OH, where are the reapers that
     garner in
The sheaves of the good from the
  fields of sin ?
With sickles of truth must the work
  be done,   [home.''
And no one may rest till the ''harvest

Where are the reapers ? O who will come
  d share in the glory of the '' harvest home ?''
 , who will help us to garner in
 e sheaves of good from the fields of sin ?

2 Go out in the byeways and search
   them all,
  The wheat may be there, tho' the
    weeds are tall ;
  Then search in the highway, and
    pass none by,   [high.
  But gather from all for the home on

3 The fields are all rip'ning, and far
   and wide,
  The world is awaiting the harvest
    tide ;   [great,
  But reapers are few, and the work is
  And much will be lost should the
    harvest wait.

4 So come with your sickles, ye sons
   of men,   [grain ;
  And gather together the golden
  Toil on till the Lord of the harvest
    come,
  Then share in the joy of the ''harvest
    home.''

640 THE whole wide world for
     Jesus—
  This shall our watchword be,
Upon the highest mountain,
  Down by the widest sea ;
The whole wide world for Jesus !
  To Him all men shall bow,
In city or in prairie—
  The world for Jesus now !

The whole wide world, the whole wide world—
Proclaim the Gospel tidings thro' the whole
  wide world ;
Lift up the Cross for Jesus, His banner be
  unfurl'd—
Till ev'ry tongue confess Him thro' the whole
  wide world !

2 The whole wide world for Jesus
  Inspires us with the thought
That ev'ry son of Adam
  Should by His blood be bought ;
The whole wide world for Jesus !
  O faint not by the way !
The Cross shall surely conquer
  In this our glorious day.

3 The whole wide world for Jesus—
  The marching order sound ;
Go ye and preach the Gospel
  Wherever man is found.
The whole wide world for Jesus !
  Our banner is unfurl'd ;
We battle now for Jesus,
  And faith demands the world !

4 The whole wide world for Jesus—
  In the Father's house above
Are many wondrous mansions—
  Mansions of light and love ;
The whole wide world for Jesus !
  Ride forth, O conqu'ring King,
Thro' all the mighty nations
  The world to glory bring !

641 OUR Saviour's voice is soft
      and sweet
  When, bending from above,
He bids us gather round His feet,
  And calls us by His love.

2 But while our thankful hearts
      rejoice
  That thus He bids us come,
" Jesus," we cry with pleading voice,
  " Bring heathen wand'rers home."

3 They never heard the Saviour's name
  They have not learn'd His way ;
They do not know His grace who
      came
  To take their sins away.

4 Dear Saviour, let the joyful sound
  In distant lands be heard ;
And oh ! wherever sin is found,
  Send forth Thy pardoning Word.

5 And if our lips may breathe a prayer,
  Though raised in trembling fear,
Oh ! let Thy grace our hearts
      prepare
  And choose some herald here.

642 TELL it out among the heathen
      that the Lord is King !
  Tell it out !...Tell it out !...
Tell it out among the nations, bid
  them shout and sing !
  Tell it out !...Tell it out !...
Tell it out with adoration that He
  shall increase,
That the mighty King of Glory is
  the King of Peace :
Tell it out with jubilation, tho' the
  waves may roar,
That He sitteth on the water floods,
  our King for evermore !

Tell it out among the heathen that the
  Lord is King !
    Tell it out !...Tell it out !...
Tell it out among the nations, bid them
  shout and sing !
    Tell it out !...Tell it out !

2 Tell it out among the heathen th
  the Saviour reigns !
  Tell it out !...Tell it out !...
Tell it out among the nations, b
  them burst their chains !
  Tell it out !...Tell it out !...
Tell it out among the weeping on
  that Jesus lives ;
Tell it out among the weary on
  what rest He gives ;
Tell it out among the sinners th
  He came to save ;
Tell it out among the dying that I
  triumphed o'er the grave.

3 Tell it out among the heathen, Jes
  reigns above !
  Tell it out !...Tell it out !...
Tell it out among the nations th
  He reigns in love !
  Tell it out !...Tell it out !...
Tell it out among the highways a
  the lanes at home ;
Let it ring across the mountains
  and the ocean foam !
Like the sound of many waters
  our glad shout be,
Till it echo and re-echo from t
  islands of the sea !

643 HARVEST fields are waiting
      White the waving grain ;
Christ the Master calleth,
  Soon the day will wane.
Hasten at His bidding,
  Join the reaper band ;
Help them at their labour,
  Work with willing hand.

Har - - vest fields are wait - - ing,
  La - - bour while you may ;...
Time...is swiftly fly - - ing,
  Come and work to-day.

2 Harvest fields are waiting,
  Do not linger long ;
Borne upon the breezes
  Comes the reaper's song.
Patiently, O toiler,
  Pluck the golden grain,
Ere the shades of evening
  Fall o'er hill and plain.

3 Harvest fields are waiting,
  Who will come to-day,
Join the band of reapers,
  Bear the sheaves away ?

Soon the day of toiling,
Will be ever past ;
May the Master's greeting
Be " Well done " at last !

44 LET the song go round the earth—
Jesus Christ is Lord !
Sound His praises, tell His worth,
Be His name adored ;
Ev'ry clime and ev'ry tongue
Join the grand, the glorious song !

Let the song go round the earth !
From the Eastern sea,
Where the daylight has its birth,
Glad, and bright, and free ;
China's millions join the strains,
Waft them on to India's plains.

Let the song go round the earth !
Lands where Islam's sway
Darkly broods o'er home and hearth,
Cast their bonds away !
Let His praise from Afric's shore
Rise and swell her wide lands o'er !

Let the song go round the earth !
Where the summer smiles ;
Let the notes of holy mirth
Break from distant isles !
Inland forests dark and dim,
Snow-bound coasts give back the hymn.

Let the song go round the earth !
Jesus Christ is King !
With the story of His worth
Let the whole world ring !
Him creation all adore
Evermore and evermore !

45 LO ! the golden fields are smiling,
Wherefore idle shouldst thou be ?
Great the harvest, few the workers,
And the Lord hath need of thee.
Go and work, the time is waning,
Let thy earnest heart reply
To the call so oft repeated,
" Blessed Master, here am I."

Hark ! the song, the song of busy workers,
In the fields so fair to see ;
Go and fill thy place among them,
For the Lord hath need of thee.

Take the balm of consolation
That so oft has cheered thy heart ;

Let some weary brother toiler,
In thy comfort share a part,
Go and lift the heavy burden
He has struggled long to bear ;
Go, and kneeling down beside him,
Blend thy faith with his in prayer.

3 Go and gather souls for Jesus,
Precious souls thy love may win ;
Lead them to the door of mercy ;
Tell them how to enter in.
Go and gather souls for Jesus ;
Work while strength and breath remain ;
What are years of constant labour
To the joy thou yet shall gain ?

4 Go, then, work ! the Master calleth ;
Go, no longer idle be ;
Waste no more thy precious moments,
For the Lord hath need of thee.
Once He gave His life thy ransom,
That thy soul with Him might live ;
Now the service He demandeth
Can thy heart refuse to give ?

646 JESUS shall reign where'er the sun
Does his successive journeys run ;
His kingdom spread from shore to shore,
Till moons shall wax and wane no more.

2 To Him shall endless prayer be made,
And endless praises crown His head ;
His name like sweet perfume shall rise
With ev'ry morning sacrifice.

3 People and realms of ev'ry tongue
Dwell on His love with sweetest song ;
And infant voices shall proclaim
Their early blessings on His name.

4 Blessings abound where'er He reigns,
The pris'ner leaps to loose his chains ;
The weary find eternal rest,
And all the sons of want are blest.

5 Let ev'ry creature rise and bring
Peculiar honours to our King ;
Angels descend with songs again ;
And earth repeat the loud Amen !

647 HE expecteth, He expecteth!
　　Down the stream of time,
Still the words come softly ringing,
　　Like a chime.

2 Oft-times faint, now waxing louder,
　　As the hour draws near,
When the King in all His glory
　　Shall appear.

3 He is waiting with long patience
　　For His crowning day,
For that kingdom which shall never
　　Pass away.

4 And till ev'ry tribe and nation
　　Bow before His throne
He expecteth loyal service
　　From His own.

5 He expecteth—but He heareth
　　Still the bitter cry
From earth's millions, " Come and
　　help us,
　　　　For we die."

6 He expecteth—does He see us
　　Busy here and there,
Heedless of those pleading accents
　　Of despair?

7 Shall we—dare we disappoint Him?
　　Brethren, let us rise!
He who died for us is watching
　　From the skies;

8 Watching till His royal banner
　　Floateth far and wide,
Till He seeth of His travail
　　Satisfied!

648 " HE was not willing that any
　　should perish; "
Jesus enthroned in the glory
　　above,　　　　　[sorrows,
Saw our poor fallen world, pities our
Poured out His life for us, won-
　　derful love!
Perishing, perishing! thronging our
　　pathway,
　　Hearts break with burdens too
　　heavy to bear,
Jesus would save, but there's no one
　　to tell them,　　　[despair.
No one to lift them from sin and

2 " He was not willing that any
　　should perish; "
Cloth'd in our flesh with its sorrow
　　and pain;

Came He to seek the lost, comfo
　　the mourner,
　　Heal the heart broken by sorro
　　and shame.
Perishing, perishing! Harvest
　　passing,
　　Reapers are few, and the nig
　　draweth near;
Jesus is calling thee, haste to t
　　reaping,
Thou shalt have souls, precio
　　souls for thy hire.

3 Plenty for preasure, but little f
　　Jesus;
　　Time for the world with i
　　troubles and toys;
No time for Jesus' work, feeding t
　　hungry,
　　Lifting lost souls to eternity's joy
Perishing, perishing! Hark, ho
　　they call us:
　　Bring us our Saviour, oh, tell
　　of Him;
We are so weary, so heavily laden,
　　And with long weeping our ey
　　have grown dim.

4 " He was not willing that a
　　should perish; "
　　Am I His follower, and can I li
Longer at ease with a soul goi
　　downward,
　　Lost for the lack of the help
　　might give?
Perishing, perishing! Thou wa
　　not willing;
　　Master, forgive, and inspire
　　anew;　　　　　[ev
Banish our worldliness, help us
　　Live with eternity's values
　　view.

649 O'ER those gloomy hills
　　darkness,
　　Look, my soul, be still, and gaze
All the promises do travail
　　With a glorious day of grace;
Blessed jubilee! blessed jubilee!
　　Let thy glorious morning dawn.

2 Let the Indian, let the Negro,
　　Let the rude barbarian see
That divine and glorious conquest
　　Once obtained on Calvary;
Let the Gospel, let the Gospel
　　Loud resound from pole to pol

Kingdoms wide that sit in darkness,
  Let them have the glorious light;
And from eastern coast to western
  May the morning chase the night;
And redemption, and redemption,
  Freely purchased, win the day.

Fly abroad, eternal Gospel,
  Win and conquer, never cease;
May Thy lasting, wide dominions
  Multiply and still increase;
May Thy sceptre, may Thy sceptre,
  Sway th' enlightened world around.

50 O JESUS, Thou Shepherd
      divine;
  Keep us in the safe, narrow way;
And out of the cold lead into Thy fold
  Some poor wand'ring soul, we pray.

51 LORD, Thou hast gone two
      thousand years,
  Yet they have never heard
Tidings of Thy redeeming love,
  Or seen Thy holy Word.   [lain,
Sleeping and still Thy Church has
  Heedless of the high command—
" Go forth to ev'ry tribe and tongue,
  To ev'ry distant land."

  Send them, O Lord, to speak of Thee,
    Tell - - ing of Thy love and grace;
  Send them, O Lord, to tell of Thee,
    To ev'ry tribe and race.

Once o'er this bright and favour'd
    land
  Lay there the pall of night;
Gloom of a savage heathendom,
  With foul and bloody rite.
Brave ones arose and came to us,
  Bringing o'er the tidings sweet,
Then cruel men bent low to Thee,
  And worshipped at Thy feet.

So would we do for other lands
  Lying in deepest death,

Sinking to meet their awful doom
  With ev'ry passing breath.
Hear, Jesus, hear our fervent pray'r,
  Wake Thy sleeping Church to
    know
Her hour of privilege and power,
  And bid her rise and go.

652 THOU whose almighty word
      Chaos and darkness heard,
      And took their flight,
  Hear us, we humbly pray,
  And where the Gospel day
  Sheds not its glorious ray,
      Let there be light !

2 Thou who didst come to bring
  On Thy redeeming wing
      Healing and sight;
  Health to the sick in mind,
  Sight to the inly blind,
  O now to all mankind
      Let there be light !

3 Spirit of truth and love,
  Life-giving, holy Dove,
      Speed forth Thy flight;
  Move on the water's face,
  Spreading the beams of grace,
  And in earth's darkest place
      Let there be light !

4 Blessed and holy Three,
  Glorious Trinity,
      Wisdom, Love, Might;
  Boundless as ocean's tide,
  Rolling in fullest pride,
  Through the earth far and wide,
      Let there be light !

653 JESUS is the Way—the only
      Way,
  Lovingly He calleth, thus the
    Scriptures say,   [day—
  Whosoever will let Him come to-
  The blessed Jesus is the only Way.

CHILDREN

54 JESUS wants me for a sunbeam
      To shine for Him each day;
  In ev'ry way try to please Him,
    At home, at school, at play.

  A sunbeam, a sunbeam,
  Jesus wants me for a sunbeam,
  A sunbeam, a sunbeam,
  I'll be a sunbeam for Him.

2 Jesus wants me to be loving,
    And kind to all I see;
  Showing how pleasant and happy
    His little one can be.

3 I will ask Jesus to help me
    To keep my heart from sin;
  Ever reflecting His goodness,
    And always shine for Him.

4 I'll be a sunbeam for Jesus,
　I can, if I but try,
Serving Him moment by moment,
　Then live with Him on high.

655 IN a world where sorrow
　　　Ever will be known,
Where are found the needy,
　And the sad and lone ;
How much joy and comfort
　You can all bestow,
If you scatter sunshine
　Ev'rywhere you go.

Scat - - ter sunshine all along your way,...
Cheer, and bless, and brighten
　Ev'ry passing day.

2 Slightest actions often
　Meet the sorest needs,
For the world wants daily
　Little kindly deeds ;
Oh, what care and sorrow
　You may help remove,
With your songs and courage,
　Sympathy and love.

3 When the days are gloomy,
　Sing some happy song,
Meet the world's repining
　With a courage strong ;
Go with faith undaunted
　Through the ills of life,
Scatter smiles and sunshine
　O'er its toil and strife.

656 I LOVE to hear the story
　　　Which angel voices tell,
How once the King of Glory
　Came down on earth to dwell ;
I am both weak and sinful,
　But this I surely know,
The Lord came down to save me,
　Because He loved me so.

2 I'm glad my blessed Saviour
　Was once a child like me,
To show how pure and holy
　His little ones might be ;
And if I try to follow
　His footsteps here below,
He never will forget me,
　Because He loved me so.

3 To sing His love and mercy,
　My sweetest songs I'll raise,
And, though I cannot see Him,
　I know He hears my praise ;

For He has kindly promised
　That I shall surely go
To sing among the angels,
　Because He loved me so.

657 THERE'S a Friend for litt
　　　children
Above the bright blue sky,
A Friend that never changes,
　Whose love will never die ;
Unlike our friends by nature,
　Who change with changing yea
This Friend is always worthy
　The precious name He bears.

2 There's a rest for little children
　Above the bright blue sky,
Who love the blessed Saviour,
　And to His Father cry ;
A rest from ev'ry trouble,
　From sin and danger free ;
There ev'ry little pilgrim
　Shall rest eternally.

3 There's a home for little children
　Above the bright blue sky,
Where Jesus reigns in glory,
　A home of peace and joy ;
No home on earth is like it,
　Nor can with it compare ;
For ev'ryone is happy,
　Nor can be happier there.

4 There's a crown for little children
　Above the bright blue sky,
And all who look to Jesus
　Shall wear it by and by ;
A crown of brightest glory,
　Which He shall sure bestow
On all who love the Saviour,
　And walk with Him below.

5 There's a song for little children
　Above the bright blue sky,
And a harp of sweetest music
　For their hymn of victory ;
And all above is pleasure,
　And found in Christ alone ;
O come, dear little children,
　That all may be your own !

658 THE world looks very beauti
　　　And full of joy to me ;
The sun shines out in glory
　On ev'rything I see ;
I know I shall be happy
　While in the world I stay,

For I will follow Jesus
    All the way.
      For I will follow Jesus
      All the way.

I'm but a youthful pilgrim,
    My journey's just begun ;
They say I'll meet with sorrow
    Before my journey's done ;
The world is full of trouble,
    And trials, too, they say ;
But I will follow Jesus
    All the way.

Then, like a little pilgrim,
    Whatever I may meet,
I'll take it—joy or sorrow—
    And lay at Jesus' feet ;
He'll comfort me in trouble,
    He'll wipe my tears away ;
With joy I'll follow Jesus
    All the way.

Then trials cannot vex me,
    And pain I need not fear,
For when I'm close by Jesus,
    Grief cannot come too near ;
Not even death can harm me,
    When death I meet one day ;
To heav'n I'll follow Jesus
    All the way.

59   WHEN He cometh, when He
       cometh
    To make up His jewels,
All His jewels, precious jewels,
    His loved and His own.
    Like the stars of the morning,
    His bright crown adorning,
    They shall shine in their beauty,
    Bright gems for His crown.

He will gather, He will gather
    Bright gems for His kingdom,
All the pure ones, all the bright ones,
    His loved and His own.

Little children, little children
    Who love their Redeemer,
Are the jewels, precious jewels,
    His loved and His own.

30   JESUS bids us shine
      With a clear, pure light,
Like a little candle
    Burning in the night ;
In this world is darkness
    So we must shine,
You in your small corner,
    And I in mine.

2 Jesus bids us shine,
    First of all for Him ;
Well He sees and knows it
    If our light is dim ;
He looks down from heaven
    To see us shine,
You in your small corner,
    And I in mine.

3 Jesus bids us shine,
    Then, for all around,
Many kinds of darkness
    In this world abound ;
Sin and want and sorrow,
    So we must shine,
You in your small corner,
    And I in mine.

661   GOD make my life a little light,
      Within the world to glow ;
A little flame that burneth bright
    Wherever I may go.

2 God make my life a little flower,
    That giveth joy to all ;
Content to bloom in native bower,
    Although the place be small.

3 God make my life a little song,
    That comforteth the sad ;
That helpeth others to be strong,
    And makes the singer glad.

4 God make my life a little staff,
    Whereon the weak may rest ;
That so what health and strength I
      have
    May serve my neighbours best.

5 God make my life a little hymn
    Of tenderness and praise,
Of faith that never waxeth dim,
    In all His wondrous ways.

662   JESUS found me wand'ring,
      Far from Him astray,
Tenderly He led me
    To the shining way ;
Words of peace He whispered,
    Bade my fears depart ;
Oh ! 'twas sweet to hear Him
    Whisp'ring in my heart !

Whisp'ring, whisp'ring, oh, what joy is mine !
Whisp'ring, whisp'ring, words of love divine.
No strain of earthly music such rapture can
    impart :
I'm glad I ever heard Him whisp'ring in my
    heart.

2 I can hear Him whisper,
　When my soul is tried,
" Fear not, I am with thee ;
　I am at thy side."
When the foe assails me
　Jesus takes my part ;
I rejoice to hear Him
　Whisp'ring in my heart.

3 Would you hear the Saviour's
　Gentle voice within ?
Now, while He is calling,
　Leave the path of sin.
Peace that passeth knowledge
　Freely He'll impart ;
You to-day may hear Him
　Whisp'ring in your heart.

663 SAFE in the arms of Jesus,
　　Safe on His gentle breast,
There by His love o'ershaded,
　Sweetly my soul shall rest.
Hark ! 'tis the voice of angels,
　Borne in a song to me,
Over the fields of glory,
　Over the jasper sea.

　　Safe in the arms of Jesus,
　　　Safe on His gentle breast,
　　There by His love o'ershaded,
　　　Sweetly my soul shall rest.

2 Safe in the arms of Jesus,
　Safe from corroding care,
Safe from the world's temptations,
　Sin cannot harm me there.
Free from the blight of sorrow,
　Free from my doubts and fears ;
Only a few more trials,
　Only a few more tears !

3 Jesus, my heart's dear refuge,
　Jesus has died for me ;
Firm on the Rock of Ages
　Ever my trust shall be.
Here will I wait with patience,
　Wait till the night is o'er ;
Wait till I see the morning
　Break on the golden shore.

664 SHALL we gather at the river,
　　Where bright angel feet have
　　　trod,
With its crystal tide for ever
　Flowing from the throne of God ?

　　Yes, we'll gather at the river,
　　The beautiful, the beautiful river,
　　Gather with the saints at the river
　　That flows from the throne of God.

2 On the margin of the river,
　Washing up its silver spray,
We will walk and worship ever,
　All the happy golden day.

3 Ere we reach the shining river,
　Lay we ev'ry burden down ;
Grace our spirits will deliver,
　And provide a robe and crown.

4 At the smiling of the river,
　Mirror of the Saviour's face,
Saints whom death will never sev
　Lift their songs of saving grace.

5 Soon we'll reach the shining rive
　Soon our pilgrimage will cease ;
Soon our happy hearts will quive
　With the melody of peace.

665 SHINING for Jesus ev'rywhe
　　I go ;
Shining for Jesus in this world
　woe ;　　　　　　　[gro
Shining for Jesus, more like Him
　Shining all the time for Jesus.

　　Shining all the time, shining all the time,
　　　Shining for Jesus, beams of love divi
　　Glorifying Him ev'ry day and hour,
　　　Shining all the time for Jesus.

2 Shining for Jesus when the way
　bright ;
Shining for Jesus in the dark
　night ;　　　　　　　[ligh
Shining for Jesus, making burd
　Shining all the time for Jesus.

3 Shining for Jesus in a world of si
Shining for Jesus, bringing lost o
　in ;
Shining for Jesus, glorifying Him
　Shining all the time for Jesus.

4 Shining for Jesus while He gives
　grace ;　　　　　　　[rac
Shining for Jesus while I run t
Shining for Jesus till I see His fac
　Shining all the time for Jesus.

666 MIGHTY army of the you
　　Lift the voice of cheerful so
Send the welcome word along,
　Jesus lives !
Once He died for you and me,
Bore our sins upon the tree,
Now He lives to make us free,
　Jesus lives !

It not till the shadows lengthen, till you
  older grow ;   [go,
lly now and sing for Jesus, ev'rywhere you
t your joyful voices high, ringing clear thro'
  earth and sky,
s the blessed tidings fly, Jesus lives !

Tongues of children, light and free,
Tongues of youth all full of glee,
Sing to all on land and sea,
    Jesus lives !
Light for you and all mankind,
Sight for all by sin made blind,
Life in Jesus all may find,
    Jesus lives !

Jesus lives, oh blessed words !
King of kings, and Lord of lords !
Lift the Cross and sheathe the swords,
    Jesus lives !
See, He breaks the prison wall,
Throws aside the dreadful pall,
Conquers death at once for all,
    Jesus lives !

7   JESUS is our Shepherd,
    Wiping ev'ry tear ;
Folded in His bosom,
  What have we to fear ?
Only let us follow
  Whither He doth lead,
To the thirsty desert,
  Or the dewy mead.

2 Jesus is our Shepherd,
  Well we know His voice !
How its gentle whisper
  Makes our heart rejoice !
Even when He chideth,
  Tender is His tone ;
None but He shall guide us,
  We are His alone.

3 Jesus is our Shepherd,
  For the sheep He bled ;
Ev'ry lamb is sprinkled
  With the blood He shed.
Then on each He setteth
  His own secret sign,
" They that have My Spirit,
  These," saith He, " are Mine."

4 Jesus is our Shepherd,
  Guarded by His arm,
Though the wolves may raven,
  None can do us harm ;
When we tread death's valley,
  Dark with fearful gloom,
We will fear no evil,
  Victors o'er the tomb.

668   GOLDEN harps are sounding,
    Angel voices ring,
Pearly gates are opened,
  Opened for the King ;
Christ, the King of Glory,
  Jesus, King of Love,
Is gone up in triumph
  To His home above.

    All His work is ended
      Joyfully we sing,
    Jesus has ascended !
      Glory to our King !

2 He who came to save us,
  He who bled and died,
Now is crown'd with glory
  At His Father's side ;
Never more to suffer,
  Never more to die—
Jesus, King of Glory,
  Is gone up on high.

3 Praying for His children
  In that blessed place,
Calling them to glory,
  Sending them His grace ;
His bright home preparing,
  Little ones, for you,
Jesus ever liveth,
  Ever loveth too.

669   SAVIOUR, blessed Saviour,
    Listen while we sing,
Hearts and voices raising
  Praises to our King.
All we have to offer,
  All we hope to be ;
Body, soul, and spirit,
  All we yield to Thee.

    Looking unto Jesus,
      Never need we yield,
    Over all the armour,
      Faith, the battle shield.

2 Nearer, ever nearer,
  Christ, we draw to Thee,
Deep in adoration,
  Bending low the knee.
Thou, for our redemption,
  Cam'st on earth to die ;
Thou, that we might follow,
  Hast gone up on high.

3 Great, and ever greater,
  Are Thy mercies here ;
True, and everlasting,
  Are the glories there ;

Where no pain or sorrow,
  Toil, or care is known ;
Where the angel legions
  Circle round Thy throne.

4 Onward, ever onward,
  Journeying o'er the road
Worn by saints before us,
  Journeying on to God.
Leaving all behind us,
  May we hasten on ;
Backward never looking,
  Till the prize is won.

5 Higher, then, and higher,
  Bear the ransomed soul,
Earthly toils forgotten,
  Saviour, to its goal ;
Where, in joys unthought of,
  Saints with angels sing,
Never weary raising
  Praises to their King.

670 JESUS loves me ! this I know,
  For the Bible tells me so ;
Little ones to Him belong,
They are weak, but He is strong.
> Yes, Jesus loves me !
> Yes, Jesus loves me !
> Yes, Jesus loves me !
>   The Bible tells me so.

2 Jesus loves me ! He who died
Heaven's gate to open wide ;
He will wash away my sin,
Let His little child come in.

3 Jesus loves me ! He will stay
Close beside me, all the way !
If I love Him, when I die
He will take me home on high.

671 I AM so glad that our Father
  in heav'n
Tells of His love in the Book He has
  giv'n ;
Wonderful things in the Bible I see ;
This is the dearest, that Jesus loves
  me.
> I am so glad that Jesus loves me,
> Jesus loves even me.

2 Jesus loves me and I know I love
  Him ;
Love brought Him down my lost
  soul to redeem ;
Yes, it was love made Him die on
  the tree ;   [me.
Oh, I am certain that Jesus loves

3 In this assurance I find sweetest re
Trusting in Jesus I know I am ble
Satan dismayed from my soul d
  now flee,   [
When I just tell Him that Jesus lo

4 Oh, if there's only one song I
  sing,   [Ki
When in His beauty I see the gr
This shall my song in eternity be
" Oh, what a wonder that Je
  loves me ! "

(Second Tune—" The Glory Song

672 I AM so glad that our Fat
  in heav'n
Tells of His love in the Book He
  giv'n ;
Wonderful things in the Bible I s
This is the dearest, that Jesus lo
  me.
> I am so glad...Jesus loves me,...
> Jesus loves me,...Jesus loves me ;...
> Wonderful things in the Bible I see,
> This is the dearest, that Jesus loves me

2 Jesus loves me and I know I l
  Him ;
Love brought Him down my
  soul to redeem ;
Yes, it was love made Him die
  the tree ;   [
Oh, I am certain that Jesus lo
> I am so glad...Jesus loves me,...
> Jesus loves me,...Jesus loves me ;...
> Yes, it was love made Him die on the tr
> Oh, I am certain that Jesus loves me.

3 In this assurance I find sweetest r
Trusting in Jesus I know I am ble
Satan dismayed from my soul
  doth flee,   [
When I just tell him that Jesus lo
> I am so glad...Jesus loves me,...
> Jesus loves me,...Jesus loves me ;...
> Satan dismayed from my soul now doth
> When I just tell him that Jesus loves m

4 Oh, if there's only one song I
  sing,   [K
When in His beauty I see the g
This shall my song in eternity
" Oh, what a wonder that Jesus lo
  me ! "
> I am so glad...Jesus loves me,...
> Jesus loves me,...Jesus loves me ;...
> This shall my song in eternity be,
> " Oh, what a wonder that Jesus loves m

'3 TAKE up the battle-cry all
along the line,
Victory by and by, victory divine ;
With your Commander nigh, foes in
vain combine,
Raise aloft the banner, let it bear
the sign—
 ll the world for Jesus," let the chorus ring ;
 ll the world for Jesus," crown Him King.
 ll the world for Jesus," let the watchword be
'orward go in Jesus' name to victory."

Truth's armour you may claim, faith
will be your shield,
Fighting on in Jesus' Name, mighty
pow'r you wield ;
Glory for God your aim, naught can
make you yield,
Shout aloud the triumph sure to be
revealed.

Soldiers, with courage go, go forsaking all ;
Onward, then, to meet the foe, soon
the foe shall fall ;
Send mighty blow on blow—let no
fear appal,   [call.
In the Name of Jesus sound afar the

'4 AROUND the throne of God
in heav'n
Thousands of children stand,
Children whose sins are all forgiv'n,
A holy, happy band :
Singing Glory, glory, glory ;
Singing Glory, glory, glory.

What brought them to that world
above
That heav'n so bright and fair,
Where all is peace, and joy, and love ?
How came those children there ?
Singing Glory, glory, glory ;
Singing Glory, glory, glory.

Because the Saviour shed His blood
To wash away their sin ;   [flood,
Bathed in that pure and precious
Behold them white and clean !
Singing Glory, glory, glory ;
Singing Glory, glory, glory.

On earth they sought the Saviour's
grace,
On earth they loved His Name ;
So now they see His blessed face,
And stand before the Lamb.
Singing Glory, glory, glory ;
Singing Glory, glory, glory.

675 I THINK when I read that
sweet story of old,
When Jesus was here among men,
How He call'd little children as
lambs to His fold,
I should like to have been with
Him then.
I wish that His hands had been
placed on my head,
That His arms had been thrown
around me ;
And that I might have seen His kind
look when He said,   [Me."
" Let the little ones come unto

2 Yet still to His footstool in prayer I
may go,
And ask for a share in His love ;
And if I thus earnestly seek Him
below,
I shall see Him and hear Him
above ;
In that beautiful place He has gone
to prepare   [given ;
For all who are washed and for-
And many dear children are gather-
ing there,
" For of such is the kingdom of
heaven."

3 But thousands and thousands who
wander and fall
Never heard of that heavenly
home ;
I should like them to know there is
room for them all,
And that Jesus has bid them to
come.   [time,
I long for that blessed and glorious
The fairest and brightest and best,
When the dear little children of every
clime
Shall crowd to His arms and be
blest.

676 THERE'S a message of love,
Come down from above,
To invite little children to heav'n ;
In God's blessed book
Poor sinners may look,
And see how all sin is forgiv'n.
For there they may read
How Jesus did bleed,
His life everlasting to give ;
He cleanseth the soul,
He maketh us whole,
That with Him in heav'n we may live

2   And then, when they die,
      He takes them on high,
To be with Him in heav'n above !
    For so kind is His heart,
    That He never will part,
From a child that has tasted His love.
    And oh ! what a delight
    In heav'n so bright,
When they see the dear Saviour's face,
    On His beauty to gaze,
    And sing to His praise,
And rejoice in His own boundless grace.

677 WE are little children, very young indeed,
But the Saviour's promise each of us may plead.
    If we seek Him early,
    If we come to-day,
    We can be His little friends,
    He has said we may.

2 Little friends of Jesus, what a happy thought !
What a precious promise in the Bible taught !

3 Little friends of Jesus, walking by His side,
With His arm around us, ev'ry step to guide.

4 We must love Him dearly with a constant love,
Then we'll go and see Him in our home above.

678 WE are but little children weak,
    Nor born in any high estate ;
What can we do for Jesus' sake,
Who is so high and good and great?

2 O day by day, each Christian child
Has much to do, without, within ;
A death to die for Jesus' sake,
A weary war to wage with sin.

3 When deep within our swelling hearts
    The thoughts of pride and anger rise,
When bitter words are on our tongues
And tears of passion in our eyes.

4 Then we may stay the angry blow,
    Then we may check the hasty word ;
Give gentle answers back again,
And fight a battle for our Lord.

5 With smiles of peace and looks [of] love [ma]
Light in our dwellings we m
Bid kind good humour brighten the
And still do all for Jesus' sake.

6 There's not a child so small and we
But has his little cross to take ;
His little work of love and praise
That he may do for Jesus' sake

679 YIELD not to temptation,
    For yielding is sin,
Each vict'ry will help you
    Some other to win ;
Fight manfully onward,
    Dark passions subdue,
Look ever to Jesus,
    He'll carry you through.
    Ask the Saviour to help you,
    Comfort, strengthen and keep you ;
    He is willing to aid you,
    He will carry you through.

2 Shun evil companions,
    Bad language disdain,
God's name hold in rev'rence,
    Nor take it in vain ;
Be thoughtful and earnest,
    Kind hearted and true,
Look ever to Jesus,
    He'll carry you through.

3 To him that o'ercometh
    God giveth a crown ;
Thro' faith we shall conquer,
    Tho' often cast down ;
He who is our Saviour,
    Our strength will renew,
Look ever to Jesus,
    He'll carry you through.

680 THERE is a happy land,
    Far, far away,
Where saints in glory stand,
    Bright, bright as day.
O how they sweetly sing,
    " Worthy is our Saviour King
Loud let His praises ring,
    Praise, praise for aye.

2 Come to this happy land,
    Come, come away ;
Why will ye doubting stand ?
    Why still delay ?
O we shall happy be,
    When, from sin and sorrow free
Lord, we shall live with Thee,
    Blest, blest for aye.

3 Bright in that happy land
   Beams ev'ry eye ;
Kept by a Father's hand,
   Love cannot die :
On, then, to glory run ;
Be a crown and kingdom won ;
And, bright above the sun,
   Reign, reign for aye.

681 WHITHER, pilgrims, are you
      going,
   Going each with staff in hand ?
We are going on a journey,
   Going at our King's command.
Over hills, and plains, and valleys,
We are going to His palace,
We are going to His palace,
   Going to the better land.

Tell us, pilgrims, what you hope for,
   In that far-off, better land ?
Spotless robes and crowns of glory,
   From a Saviour's loving hand.
We shall drink of life's clear river,
We shall dwell with God for ever,
We shall dwell with God for ever,
   In that bright, that better land.

Pilgrims, may we travel with you
   To that bright and better land ?
Come and welcome, come and wel-
     come,
   Welcome to our pilgrim band.
Come, oh ! come, and do not leave
     us ;
Christ is waiting to receive us,
Christ is waiting to receive us,
   In that bright, that better land.

682 OUR God will guide us right,
    and, walking in the light,
   We shall win a crown of glory on
    that day,....
When Jesus calls His own together
   round the throne,
   Who keep along the middle of the
    King's highway.
The King's highway ! the King's highway !
, turn aside from ev'rything that leads
  astray !
r God will guide us right, and walking in the
  light,   [highway.
'll keep along the middle of the King's
Wherever you may be, whatever you
    may see
   That would lead you into evil, say
   you " Nay ! "....

I will not turn aside, whatever may
   betide :
   I'll keep along the middle of the
    King's highway.

3 The meadows may be green where
   " byepath stile " is seen :
   " Turn aside ! " the little flowers
    seem to say ;....
Be sure you give no heed, they're
   trying to mislead ;
   Just keep along the middle of the
    King's highway.

4 For, on enchanted ground, there's
   danger all around,
   And a thousand pleasant voices
    bid you stay ;....
With fingers stop your ears, and
   never mind their jeers ;
   Just keep along the middle of the
    King's highway.

683 WHEN mothers of Salem
    Their children brought to Jesus,
The stern disciples drove them back,
   And bade them depart ;
But Jesus saw them ere they fled,
And sweetly smiled, and kindly said,
   " Suffer little children to come
    unto Me."

2 " For I will receive them,
   And fold them in My bosom ;
I'll be a Shepherd to those lambs,
   Oh, drive them not away !
For if their hearts to Me they give,
They shall with Me in glory live ;
   Suffer little children to come unto
    Me."

3 How kind was our Saviour
   To bid those children welcome !
But there are many thousands who
   Have never heard His Name ;
The Bible they have never read ;
They know not that the Saviour said,
   " Suffer little children to come
    unto Me."

4 Oh ! soon may the heathen
   Of ev'ry tribe and nation
Fulfil the blessed word, and cast
   Their idols all away ;
Oh ! shine upon them from above,
And show Thyself a God of love ;
   Teach the little children to come
    unto Thee.

SPECIAL SOLOS

684 I ONCE heard a sweet story of
    wonderful love,
And it lifted the cross that I bore ;
Made me think of the home and the
    dear ones above :
I am longing to hear it once more.

I am longing to hear it once more ;...
The story repeat o'er and o'er ;...
It is rapture divine to know He is mine ;
I am longing to hear it once more.

2 Tho' afar I had wandered in darkness
    and sin,   [poor,
And tho' helpless, and weary, and
This sweet story left light, hope, and
    gladness within :
I am longing to hear it once more.

3 That sweet story of Jesus who died
    on the tree
Will be told on eternity's shore ;
How He came as a ransom for you
    and for me :
I am longing to hear it once more.

685 WEARY child, thy sin forsaking,
    Close thy heart no more ;
From thy dream of pleasure waking,
    Open wide the door.

While the lamp of life is burning,
And the heart of God is yearning,
To His loving arms returning,
Give thy wand'ring o'er.

2 To the Saviour's tender pleading
    Close thy heart no more ;
Now the call of mercy heeding,
    Open wide the door.

3 To the Gospel invitation
    Close thy heart no more ;
To receive a full salvation,
    Open wide the door.

4 To the joy that fadeth never
    Close thy heart no more ;
To the peace abiding ever
    Open wide the door.

686 JESUS is all the world to me,
    My life, my joy, my all ;
He is my strength from day to day,
    Without Him I would fall.
When I am sad, to Him I go,
No other one can cheer me so ;
When I am sad He makes me glad,
    He's my Friend.

2 Jesus is all the world to me,
    My Friend in trials sore ;
I go to Him for blessings, and
    He gives them o'er and o'er.
He sends the sunshine and the rai
He sends the harvest's golden grai
Sunshine and rain, harvest of gra
    He's my Friend.

3 Jesus is all the world to me,
    And true to Him I'll be ;
O, how could I this Friend deny,
    When He's so true to me ?
Following Him I know I'm right,
He watches o'er me day and nigh
Following Him by day and night.
    He's my Friend.

4 Jesus is all the world to me,
    I want no better friend ;
I trust Him now, I'll trust Him wh
    Life's fleeting days shall end ;
Beautiful life with such a Friend ;
Beautiful life that has no end ;
Eternal life, eternal joy,
    He's my Friend.

687 THERE'S a sweet old sto
    which I long to hear,
When the night is long and drear
When I feel the power of the temp
    near,
And my soul is sad and weary.

'Tis the old, old story of His love,...
'Tis the sweet, old message from above
For no other I can find that can calm
    troubled mind,
Like the sweet old story of His love !...

2 There's a sweet old story that I lo
    to read,
When my spirit dreads the morro
When, to help me onward, streng
    or cheer I need,
Or when comfort I would borro

3 There's a sweet old story that I lo
    to tell
To the heart by grief o'ertaken
To the friendless brothers who
    darkness dwell,
And to those by hope forsaken.

688 WHAT shall I bring to t
    Saviour ?
What shall I lay at His feet?

I have no glittering jewels,
  Gold or frankincense so sweet.....

    Gifts to the Saviour I'm bringing,
    Love's richest treasures to lay
    Low at His feet with rejoicing,
    Ere yonder sunset to-day....

What shall I bring to the Saviour ?
  Lips His dear praises to sing ;
Feet that will walk in the pathway
  Leading to Jesus, our King.....

What shall I bring to the Saviour ?
  Love that is purest and best ;
Life in its sweetness and beauty,
  All for His service so blest.....

89 HOW oft I prayed for power,
      And tarried by the way ;
I wanted some great blessing
  To use each busy day.

    But now He uses me,...
    Praise God, He uses me,...
    The blessed Holy Spirit uses me,...
    But now He uses me....
    Praise God, He uses me,...
    The blessed Holy Spirit uses me.

I did not get the blessing
  Until the Blesser came,
Nor was I fit for service,
  Till filled with love's warm flame.

To-day my richest blessing
  Is doing His sweet Word,
My highest joy each moment,
  Is to be used of God.

90 BEFORE a Cross uplifted high,
      I stood alone one day ;
My soul was burdened with a guilt
  No tears could wash away.

    Love,...mighty and wonderful,
    Love,...so boundless and free !...
    Love,...that suffered upon the Cross,
    The love that died for me.

In grief and pain I wept aloud,
  In helpless agony ;
When from the Cross I heard One
    speak,
  " I gave My life for thee."

That voice, so sweet, entranced my
    soul,
  It gave me hope and cheer ;
Tho' trembling, I drew near the cross
  For I had naught to fear.

4 And there upon the cruel Cross
  My Saviour died that day ;
I looked, believed, and from my soul
  The burden roll'd away.

691 JESUS all my grief is sharing,
      He my mansion is preparing ;
When I'm trembling and despairing,
  He will surely hear my call ;
When the storms around me sweep-
    ing,
Tho' in helplessness I'm sleeping,
I am safe in His own keeping,
  This to me is best of all ;
  Best of all, best of all ;
I am safe in His own keeping,
  This to me is best of all.

2 Jesus loves and watches o'er me,
  With His grace He will restore me ;
Angel guards He sends before me,
  Lest in fatal snares I fall ; [me,
With His friends He hath enrolled
By His might He will uphold me,
In His arms He will enfold me,
  This to me is best of all ;
  Best of all, best of all ;
In His arms He will enfold me.
  This to me is best of all.

3 Jesus loves and He will guide me,
  All I need He will provide me ;
In His bosom He will hide me
  When the woes of life appal ;
He will hear my feeblest sighing,
Needful grace to me supplying,
He'll be with me when I'm dying,
  This to be is best of all ;
  Best of all, best of all ;
He'll be with me when I'm dying,
  This to me is best of all.

692 I'VE a home fair and bright in
      yonder City,
  To its gates I am marching along ;
When my fighting for Jesus here is
    over,
  I shall then take my place with
    the throng
That face to face behold the
    Saviour,
  In whose praise is raised its song.

    Up in the golden City
    There's a mansion to me will be giv'n ;
  I have riches I know that the world can't
    bestow,
    I'm an heir of the wealth of heav'n.

2 It is true, on the way to yonder City,
  I've to cross o'er a cold rolling
  flood;
  But I trust Him to guide me by
  whose pity
  I've been led to the sin-cleanseing
  blood;   [me,
  As He has said, He'll never leave
  I will trust my Friend, my God.

3 Do you know there's no place in
  yonder City
  For a soul that is burdened with
  guilt ?
  Do you know that no sin can ever
  enter ?
  Hasten then to the blood that was
  spilt
  To cleanse from sin, and with me
  journey
  To the City God has built.

693   HE is not a disappointment!
          Jesus is far more to me
Than in all my glowing day-dreams
  I had fancied He could be;
And the more I get to know Him,
  so the more I find Him true,
And the more I know that others
  should be led to know Him too.

2 He is not a disappointment ! He has
    saved my soul from sin;
  All the guilt and all the anguish,
    which oppressed my heart within,
  He has banished by His presence,
    and His blessed kiss of peace
  Has assured my heart for ever that
    His love will never cease.

3 He is not a disappointment! He is
    coming by and by.
  In my heart I have the witness that
    His coming draweth nigh.
  All the scoffers may despise me, and
    no change around may see,
  But He tells me He is coming, and
    that's quite enough for me.

4 He is not a disappointment! He is
    all in all to me—
  Blessed Saviour, Sanctifier, the un-
    changing Christ is He !
  He has won my heart's affections,
    and He meets my every need;
  He is not a disappointment, for He
    satisfies indeed.

694   HAVE you read the story
          the Cross,
  Where Jesus bled and died ;
  Where your debt was paid by H
    precious blood   [side
  That flowed from His wound
  He died an atoning death for thee,
  He died an atoning death ;
  Oh, wondrous love ! it was for thee
  He died an atoning death !

2 Have you read how they placed t
    crown of thorns
  Upon His lovely brow ?
  When He prayed, forgive them, o
    forgive,
  They know not what they do.

3 Have you read how He saved t
    dying thief
  When hanging on the tree ?
  Who looked with pitying eyes a
    said,
  Dear Lord, remember me.

4 Have you read that He looked
    heaven and said,
  'Tis finished—'twas for thee ?
  Have you ever said, I thank The
    Lord,
  For giving Thy life for me.

695   WHEN I shall reach my hor
          in glory,
  And see my Saviour face to fac
  This shall be all my song and stor
  A sinner saved by grace.
  Saved by grace,...saved by grace,...
  For ever I'll tell the sto - - ry,
  How Jesus saved...me by His grace,...
  And brought me to His glory.

2 I'll tell how by His blood He boug
    me,   [rac
  With all our lost and ransom
  And how so tenderly He sought m
  And saved me by His grace.

3 I'll tell them how His Spirit seal
    me,   [trac
  And cleansed me from each sin
  And how when sick and worn I
    healed
  And saved me by His grace.

4 I'll sing how lovingly He led me
    At last to yonder heavenly plac
  And how He shepherded and fed m
  And kept me by His grace.

Yes, when I reach my home in glory,
　　And see my Saviour face to face;
This shall be all my song and story,
　　A sinner saved by grace.

96 THE works and ways of God
　　　　　on high
I cannot solve—I do not try;
But though I cannot these unfold,
One thing I know—to this I'll hold,
Though all the world beside deny—
A sinner saved by grace am I.
　　I cannot tell you why, nor how,
　　　For oh! I do not understand;
　　I only say, "I know! I know!"
　　　On this unshaken ground I stand.

I know that my Redeemer lives,
I know, I know that He forgives!
I know that I, who once was dead,
Am now alive in Christ, my Head.
Let all the world beside deny—
"I know I live!" shall be my cry.

Now at His word the darkness flies,
And beams of sunlight flood my eyes,
I do not know; enough for me
That I who once was blind now see!
Let all the world beside deny—
"I know I see!" shall be my cry.

Beyond this mortal vale there stands
A house for me not made with hands;
E'en now I see beyond the dome,
And occupy my heavenly home;
Let all the world beside deny—
I know I have a home on high.

97 IN the heart of London city,
　　　'Mid the dwellings of the poor,
These bright golden words were
　　　uttered:
　　I have Christ! what want I more?
　　I have Christ!...what want I more?...
　　I have Christ!...what want I more?...
　　I have Christ!...what want I more?...
Spoken by a lonely woman,
　　Dying on a garret floor,
Having not one earthly comfort:
　　I have Christ! what want I more?

Oh, her words will live for ever,
　　I repeat them o'er and o'er;
God delights to hear me saying:
　　I have Christ! what want I more?

Oh, my dear, my fellow-sinners,
　　High and low, and rich and poor,
Can you say, with deep thanksgiving:
　　I have Christ! what want I more?

5 Look away from earth's attractions,
　　All its joys will soon be o'er;
Trust Him now, and say with glad-
　　　ness:
　　I have Christ! what want I more?

698 MY Father is rich in houses
　　　　　and lands,
He holdeth the wealth of the world in
　　His hands!
Of rubies and diamonds, of silver
　　and gold,
His coffers are full, He has riches
　　untold.
　　I'm the child of a King!...
　　I'm the child of a King!
　　With Jesus my Saviour, I'm the child,
　　I'm the child of a King!

2 My Father's own Son, the Saviour
　　　of men,
Once wandered o'er earth as the
　　poorest of them; 　　　[high,
But now He is reigning for ever on
And will give me a home in heaven
　　by and by.

3 I once was an outcast stranger on
　　earth, 　　　　　[birth!
A sinner by choice, and an alien by
But I've been adopted, my name's
　　written down—
An heir to a mansion, a robe, and a
　　crown!

4 A tent or a cottage, why should I
　　care? 　　　　　[there!
They're building a palace for me over
Tho' exiled from home, yet still I
　　may sing: 　　　　　[King!
All glory to God, I'm the child of a

699 MY Father will not let me fall,
　　　　　His strong and loving arms
　　　　　enfold me;
To Him I trust my life, my all,
　　And know that He will safely hold
　　me.
　　Just as He promised, promised to do,
　　　When first to Him I trembling came;
　　Now I have trusted, proven Him true,
　　Hallelujah to His Name.

2 My Saviour will not let me stray,
　　The path He trod is plain before
　　　me;
And He who said, "I am the Way,"
　　Is watching, ever watching o'er me.

3 I trust Him as a little child,
   Content beneath His wings to
      hide me;
Tho' all around is rough and wild,
   He walks the path of peace beside
      me.

4 His love will still remember me,
   In life, in death, in joy, and
      sorrow;
Whate'er betide, He still will be
   My Guide to-day, my Hope to-
      morrow.

700 WHO is this that's waiting,
            waiting,
   Just outside the door?
Who is He that's knocking, knocking,
   Has He knocked before?
Rise and bid Him enter in,
   Peace and hope He'll bring;
'Tis thy Saviour knocking, knocking,
   'Tis thy Lord and King.

   Let Him in! Let Him in!
   He waits outside the door;
   Let Him in ere He departs
   To return no more!

2 Don't you hear Him saying, saying,
   Come, O come to Me;
'Twas for you that, dying, dying,
   I hung on the tree.
Come and see My hands, My side;
   Look on Me and live;
Though your sins be many, many,
   Pardon I can give.

3 Still His voice is calling, calling,
   Sweet the tones and low;
Bid Him enter quickly, quickly,
   Ere He turns to go!
Must His pleading be in vain?
   Must He, then, depart,
All because His pleading, pleading,
   Reaches not your heart!

4 Sometime you'll be waiting, waiting,
   Just outside the gate;   [ing,
Sometime you'll be pleading, plead-
   Then 'twill be too late!
Now accept your Heavenly Guest!
   He'll forgive your sin!
While He still is waiting, waiting,
   Rise and let Him in!

701 JESUS is standing in Pilate's
            hall,
   Friendless, forsaken, betrayed by all;

Hearken, what meaneth the sudd
   call:
   What will you do with Jesus?
What will you do? what will you do?
   Neutral you cannot be,
   Some day your heart will be asking,
   What will He do with me?

2 Jesus is standing on trial still;
   You can be false to Him if you wil
   You can be faithful thro' good
      ill—
   What will you do with Jesus?

3 Will you evade Him as Pilate trie
   Or shall you choose Him whate
      betide?
   Vainly you struggle from Him
      hide—
   What will you do with Jesus?

4 Shall you, like Peter, your L
      deny?   [fi
   Or shall you scorn from His foes
   Daring for Jesus to live or die—
   What will you do with Jesus?

5 "Jesus, I give Thee my heart to-da
   Jesus, I'll follow Thee all the wa
   Gladly obeying Him, will you sa
   "This will I do with Jesus."

702 SO strange it seemed a
            wondrous,
   When it first came to me,
The story of my Saviour,
   I asked, "Can such things be
I felt my heart replying,
   "Oh, if I only knew!
The Cross, the thorns, the dying
   O is it, is it true?"

   I love to hear it spoken,
   I love to read it through;
   But O for word or token
   To tell me it is true!

2 And when I heard the story
   Told o'er and o'er again,
How Jesus, now in glory,
   Was walking still with men;
Was filling hearts with gladness,
   And scatt'ring sunshine thro';
My own heart longed in sadness
   To know if it were true!

3 Then softly was it spoken,
   "Come, lean upon My breast,
Ye weary ones, heart-broken,
   And I will give you rest."

My heart, so sad and lonely,
　A little closer drew ;
I cried, " O Lord, if only
　I felt and knew it true ! "

A voice came sweet and tender !
　It seemed to touch my woe ;
I felt my heart surrender—
　I cried, " O Lord, I know ! "
My Saviour, Thou hast spoken !
　The old, old story's new !
And Thou dost give the token !
　I know, I know it's true !
　　My Saviour, O my Saviour !
　　The old, old story's new !
　　My strength, my joy for ever,
　　I know, I know it's true.

03 WEARY and wand'ring and
　　　　sunken in sin,
　Vile as a sinner could be,
Jesus beheld, and to Bethlehem
　　　came,
　Left His bright throne for me.
　　All for me,...all for me ?
　　Lord, was it all for me ?...
　　From the throne to the manger, from there
　　　to the Cross,
　　Yes, it was all for me.

Footsore and weary He toil'd all
　the way,
　Even to Gethsemane ;
Oft I have met Him and heard His
　sweet voice
　Praying for me, for me.

Still I rejected your Saviour and
　mine,
　Till I beheld on the tree,
Suffering, dying, my Saviour and
　yours,
　Dying for you and for me.

04 WHO is this that cometh from
　　　　Edom,
　Crimson red His garments dyed,
In His hands are cruel nail-prints,
　And a spear-wound in His side ?
Say, who is this " Man of Sorrows?"
　Why is He thus pierced and
　　scarred ?
Why with face and form so kingly !
　Why His beauteous visage marred?
　　It is Christ,...the King of glo - - ry,
　　Who His life...a ransom gave,...
　　Bow before Him, and adore Him,
　　Jesus Christ the mighty...to save....

2 Who is this, despised and rejected,
　Who the wine-press trod alone ?
Who is this by all forsaken,
　Left to comfort there are none ?
Who is this, oppressed, afflicted,
　Yet no murmur ever heard ;
As a Lamb led to the slaughter,
　Yet He answers not a word !

3 Who is this with bearing so kingly,
　And a crown His brow adorns,
Not of gold and gems befitting,
　But of mocking, cruel thorns ?
Why with many stripes thus beaten ?
　Why thus scourged and spit upon ?
Why His anguish in the garden,
　Kneeling, praying all alone ?

4 Who is this on Calvary's mountain,
　Dying there such shameful death ?
Who for His tormentors praying,
　With His last expiring breath ?
Who is this that earth should tremble
　And the sun in darkness hide,
Rocks be rent and graves be opened,
　When He bowed His head and
　　died ?

705 SEEK ye first, not earthly
　　　　pleasure,
　Fading joy and failing treasure,
　But the love that knows no measure,
　Seek ye first, seek ye first.

2 Seek ye first, not earth's aspirings,
　Ceaseless longing, vain desirings,
　But your precious soul's requirings
　Seek ye first, seek ye first.

3 Seek ye first God's peace and blessing
　Ye have all if this possessing ;
　Come, your need and sin confessing,
　Seek Him first, seek Him first.

4 Seek Him first, then, when forgiven,
　Pardon'd, made an heir of heaven,
　Let your life to Him be given :
　Seek this first, seek this first.

5 Seek the coming of His kingdom ;
　Seek the souls around to win them,
　Seek to Jesus Christ to bring them :
　Seek this first, seek this first.

706 I WAS wandering and weary
　　　　When my Saviour came unto
　　　　me ;
　For the ways of sin grow dreary,
　　And the world has ceased to woo
　　　me :

And I thought I heard Him say,
As He came along His way :
   " O wand'ring souls, come near Me,
   My sheep should never fear Me—
   I am the Shepherd true ! "

2 At first I would not hearken,
   And put off till the morrow ;
But life began to darken,
   And I was sick with sorrow ;
And I thought I heard Him say,
As He came along His way :

3 At last I stopp'd to listen—
   His voice could not deceive me ;
I saw His kind eyes glisten,
   So anxious to relieve me ;
And I thought I heard Him say,
As He came along His way :

4 I thought His love would weaken,
   As more and more He knew me ;
But it burneth like a beacon, [me ;
   And its light and heat go thro'
And I ever hear Him say,
As He goes along His way :

707 THE door of God's mercy is open
   To all who are weary of sin,
And Jesus is patiently waiting,
   Still waiting to welcome you in.
Come, says the Saviour, come enter the gate,
I watch by the portals both early and late,
Lest some precious soul, not far from the goal,
Should wander away into darkness and hate,
And miss it for ever, the pearly gate.

2 The world is e'er wantonly wooing
   Your soul from the ways of the
     blest,
But Jesus is tenderly bidding
   You turn to His heavenly rest.

3 So many who hear the glad message
   Will never its mandates obey,
But turn from the precious, dear
     pleadings,
   And wilfully wander away.

4 Sad hearts there will surely be
     moaning
   Outside of the gateway of life,
And praying to Him they rejected
   When earth with gay pleasure
     was rife.

5 The door of God's mercy is open,
   Invitingly open to all,
Who list to the voice of the Master,
   And hearing, shall heed His sweet
     call.

708 JESUS was standing beside
     grave,
Weeping, but knowing His power
     save ;
" Take ye away now the stone fr
     the door,"
   And Christ will His power displa
They roll'd the stone away, for Christ was th
   that day,
And call'd upon a man to leave the darker
   grave.
We'll roll the stone away, for He is here to-d
   And waits to show His mighty power, I
   power to save.

2 Jesus is speaking to you in song,
   Asking why you have delayed
     long ? [of si
While men are lying in grave-cloth
   For whom Jesus died on the Cros

3 Jesus is standing by hearts of sin
   Knocking and saying, " Let N
     come in." [do
Rouse, then, ye sleeper, and open t
   For Jesus has power to save.

709 MY blessed Lord was cru
     fied—
The day was dark, and grief w
     wide ; [vai
For hope was crushed, and all seem
Until that Saviour rose again.
   Ring out the blessed news again !
   Oh ! bear aloft the strain ;
   The mighty Lord is ris'n in pow'r—
   He died, but not in vain !

2 He brings His great salvation nig
   And on His love bids us rely ;
He bought our peace thro' grief a
     pain,
   But oh ! He did not die in vain !

3 O, wondrous news of life and lov
That Jesus lives and reigns above
He made the path to glory plain ;
Ah, no ! He did not die in vain.

710 JESUS is calling, is calling,
     calling,
   Jesus is calling—
Open your heart's door wide and
   Him in.

711 ABOVE this earthly home
     ours,
Of chilling winds and fading flowe

There is a home all bright and fair,
And all our hopes are centred there.

Oh happy home,...Oh mansions blest,...
Where all God's wea - - ry ones may rest ;
For in that bright...unclouded day,...
Our God shall wipe all tears away.

There we shall meet the lov'd and lost
Who over death's dark river cross'd ;
There we shall see our Saviour's face,
And praise the wonders of His grace.

Here we may suffer grief and pain,
And tears may flow like falling rain ;
But there, where shines eternal day,
God's hand shall wipe all tears away.

12 I HAVE a Friend, an ever-
　　　　lasting Friend,
He is so kind, He is so good to me ;
He bore my sins, He suffered to the
　　　end, 　　　　[victory.
　That I might win a glorious

me to this Friend, He's waiting now for thee,
He'll be so kind, so loving, warm and true,
'll break your bands, from sin He'll set you
　　　free,
He'll be an everlasting Friend to you.

This Friend of mine, O how He longs
　　　to give
　　The help you need in this dark
　　　world of sin ;
He bids you come, no longer sinful
　　　live,
　And thro' His Name a crown of
　　　glory win.

Thro' ages past He's proved a
　　　glorious Friend,
　None ever asked and were by Him
　　　denied ;
His blood was shed that you and I
　　　might spend 　　　[side.
　Eternity at His, our Saviour's

13 WHEN in His beauty my
　　　　Saviour I see,
When I shall look on His face,
Tongue cannot tell of the joy it will
　　　be,
　　Saved by His wonderful grace.....

ved,..saved,..Saved by His wonderful grace!..
ved,..saved,..Granted in heaven a place ;..
ved,..saved,..Saved by His wonderful grace!..
　Glory to Jesus, I know I am saved,
　Saved by His wonderful grace !..

2 Long I had wander'd in pathways
　　　of sin,
　Often His grace I had spurned ;
Often resisted His strivings within,
　Ere to the Saviour I turn'd....

3 How I rejoice that salvation is free,
　That I was not turn'd away ;
How I rejoice that my Saviour I'll see
　Where I may praise Him for aye....

714 I TAKE my portion from Thy
　　　　hand,
And do not seek to understand ;
For I am blind, while Thou dost see,
Thy will is mine, whate'er it be.

　　Whate'er it be ! whate'er it be !
　　I do not fear, whate'er it be !
　　Thy love divine sustaineth me ;
　　Thy will is mine, whate'er it be.

2 When darkness doth Thy face
　　　obscure,
And many sorrows I endure,
I think of Christ's Gethsemane ;
Thy will is mine, whate'er it be.

3 When tender joys to me are known,
I render thanks to Thee alone ;
I know my cup is filled by Thee ;
Thy will is mine, whate'er it be.

4 Thus calmly do I face my lot,
Accept it, Lord, and doubt Thee not ;
Lo ! all things work for good to me ;
Thy will is mine, whate'er it be.

715 GONE from my heart the
　　　　world with all its charm,
Now thro' the blood I'm saved from
　　　sin's alarm ;
Down at the Cross my heart is
　　　bending low,
The precious blood of Jesus washes
　　　white as snow.

　　I love Him, I love Him,
　　Because He first loved me,
And purchased my salvation on Mount Calvary.

2 Once I was far away, deep down in
　　　sin,
　Once was a slave to passions fierce
　　　within ;
Once was afraid to meet an angry
　　　God,
　But now I'm cleansed from ev'ry
　　　stain thro' Jesus' blood.

3 Once I was bound, but now I am
   set free,
Once I was blind, but now the light
   I see ;   [live,
Once I was dead, but now in God I
And tell the world around the peace
   that He doth give.

716 THERE'S a dear and precious
      book,
Though it's worn and faded now,
Which recalls the happy days of long
   ago ;
When I stood at mother's knee,
With her hand upon my brow,
And I heard her voice in gentle tones
   and low.

Blessed book,...precious book,...
On thy dear old tear-stained leaves I love to
   look ;...   [narrow way
Thou art sweeter day by day, as I walk the
That leads at last to that bright home above.

2 There she read of Jesus' love,
As He blest the children dear,
How He suffered, bled and died
   upon the tree ;
Of His heavy load of care,
Then she dried my flowing tear
With her kisses as she said it was
   for me.

3 Well, those days are past and gone,
But their memory lingers still,
And the dear old Book each day has
   been my guide ;
And I seek to do His will,
As my mother taught me then,
And ever in my heart His words
   abide.

717 MY heart was oppressed with
      the load of my sin,
And it bent with the weight of
   its woe ;   [burden fell off,
At a touch of His hand all the
   Do you wonder my loving Him so?

My Saviour is precious to me,
My Saviour is precious to me,
And the more He is known by His loved
   and His own,
More precious He's certain to be.

2 Then He filled me with peace that
   the world knoweth not,
That is with me wherever I go ;
'Tis the very same calm that is
   filling His heart,
Do you wonder my loving Him so?

3 Then He shelters, and blesses, a
   watches o'er me,   [low
Be my pathway the high or t
I am safe, for His arm is protecti
   His child,
Do you wonder my loving Him s

4 Oh, will you not love Him who fi
   loved you?
Just respond and His sweetne
   you'll know,
And never again will you want oth
   love,
Nor will wonder my loving Him

718 OH, aching heart, with sorro
      torn,
Thy Lord is near and knows ;
He knows it all—the feet way-wor
The weary cares and woes,
The load of grief in anguish borne,
Thy Lord is near,....He knows.

He knows,...He knows,...
The Lord is near, He knows.

2 Oh, fainting soul, with doubts o
   pressed,
Thy Lord is near and knows ;
He knows it all—how thou a
   pressed
On every side with foes ;
He waits to be thy cherished Gues
Thy Lord is near,....He knows.

3 Oh, weary head, that fain would re
Thy Lord is near and knows ;
He knows it all, and on His breast
Thou mayest now repose ;
Drop every care at His behest ;
Thy Lord is near,....He knows.

4 Oh, lonely one, live thou thy be
Thy Lord is near and knows ;
He knows it all, sees ev'ry test,
Yes, every tear that flows ;
Rejoice, faint heart, His way is bes
Thy Lord is near,....He knows.

719 I HAVE a Friend so preciou
      So very dear to me,
He loves me with such tender lov
He loves so faithfully :
I could not live apart from Him,
I love to feel Him nigh,
And so we dwell together,
   My Lord and I.

He knows how much I love Him,
  He knows I love Him well ;
But with what love He loveth me
  My tongue can never tell ;
It is an everlasting love
  In every rich supply,
And so we love each other,
    My Lord and I.

He knows how I am longing
  Some weary soul to win,
And so He bids me go and speak
  The loving word for Him ;
He bids me tell His wondrous love,
  And why He came to die,
And so we work together,
    My Lord and I.

So up into the mountains
  Of heaven's cloudless light,
Or away into the valleys
  Of darkness or of night,
Though round us tempests gather,
  And storms are raging high,
We'll travel on together,
    My Lord and I.

And when the journey's ended
  In rest and peace at last,
When every thought of danger
  And weariness is past,
In the Kingdom of the future,
  In the Glory by and by,
We'll live and reign together,
    My Lord and I.

20   JUST one touch as He moves
      along,
Push'd and press'd by the jostling
    throng,
Just one touch and the weak was
    strong,
  Cured by the Healer divine.
Just one touch as He passes by,
He will list to the faintest cry,
Come and be saved while the Lord is nigh,
  Christ is the Healer divine....

Just one touch and He makes me
    whole,   [soul,
Speaks sweet peace to my sin-sick
At His feet all my burdens roll,
  Cured by the Healer divine.

Just one touch and the work is done,
I am saved by the blessed Son,
I will sing while the ages run,
  Cured by the Healer divine.

4 Just one touch and He turns to me,
  O the love in His eyes I see !
I am His, for He hears my plea,
  Cured by the Healer divine.

5 Just one touch, by His mighty power
  He can heal thee this very hour,
Thou canst hear tho' the tempests
    low'r,
  Cured by the Healer divine.

721   ON the ocean of life we are
      sailing,
  For the Canaan above we are
    bound ;
We are certain the port to be gaining,
  Since the heavenly Pilot we've
    found.
Pil - - ot me,...pil - - ot me ;...
  Take the helm in Thine own hand,
  Bring my sinking barque to land.
Pil - - ot me,...pil - - ot me,...pil - - ot me....

2 For He knows where the dangers are
    lurking,
  Where the rocks and the hidden
    reefs lie ;   [breaking,
We are safe tho' the billows are
  And the hungry waves dash moun-
    tain high.

3 Soon the haven our barques will be
    nearing,
  The Jerusalem golden and fair ;
Soon the lights of the city appearing,
  Soon the home of the ransomed
    we'll share.

722   OH, to be like Him,
      Tender and kind,
    Gentle in spirit,
      Lowly in mind ;
    More like to Jesus
      Day after day,
    Filled with His Spirit
      Now and alway.
Yes, to be like Him, we must abide
Near to our Saviour, close to His side.

2 Oh, to be like Him,
    Quick to obey,
  Childlike and truthful,
    Ready to say,
  " I and my Father
    Purpose have one,
  Thine, not my will,
    Ever be done."

3 Oh, to be like Him,
 Tempted in vain,
 Dwelling with sinners,
 Yet without stain ;
 Giving our life-work
 Sinners to save,
 Triumphing over
  Death and the grave.

723 WHERE shall I flee for refuge
 Hiding when storms are near ?
Where find a place of safety,
 Dwelling without a fear ?

 Jesus alone can save me,
  All of my joys increase ;
 From ev'ry storm He'll shield me,
  Giving my soul sweet peace.

2 Softly I hear Him calling,
 " Come unto Me and rest ;
Here in My arms find shelter,
 Close to My loving breast."

3 Burdens oft-times oppress me,
 Burdens so hard to bear ;
Oh, then, how sweet His whisper,
 " Cast upon Me thy care."

4 Thus would I ever journey,
 On toward my home above ;
Resting alone on Jesus,
 Whom, tho' unseen, I love.

724 I ENTERED once a home of
  care,
 Old age and penury were there,
 Yet peace and joy withal ;
I ask'd the lonely mother whence
Her helpless widowhood's defence,
 She told me, " Christ was all."

 Christ is all, all in all,
 Yes, Christ is all in all.

2 I stood beside a dying bed
Where lay a child with aching head,
 Waiting for Jesus' call ;
I mark'd his smile, 'twas sweet as
  May,
And as his spirit passed away,
 He whisper'd, " Christ is all."

3 I saw the martyr at the stake,
The flames could not his courage
  shake,
 Nor death his soul appal ;
I asked him whence his strength
  was giv'n,
He look'd triumphantly to heav'n,
 And answered, " Christ is all."

4 I saw the Gospel herald go
 To Afric's sand and Greenland
  snow,
 To save from Satan's thrall.
No home or life he counted dear,
'Midst wants and perils own'd
  fear,
 He felt that " Christ is all."

5 I dream'd that hoary time had fle
And earth and sea gave up their dea
 A fire dissolved this ball ;
I saw the Church's ransom'd thron
I heard the burden of their song,
 'Twas " Christ is all in all."

6 Then come to Christ, oh, come t
  day,
The Father, Son, and Spirit say,
 The Bride repeats the call,
For He will cleanse your guil
  stains,   [pain
His love will soothe your wea
 For " Christ is all in all."

725 THERE'S no love to me li
  the love of Jesus,
 Ever, always just the same ;
E'en tho' of this world you may
  most lowly,   [Nam
 Jesus still loves you, bless H

 There never was one like Jesus,
  Ever always true is He ;
 There never was one like Jesus,
  There's no love like His love to me.

2 When far, far away, and in conden
  nation,
 Feeling no one cared for me,
There came a sweet voice, I sha
 ne'er forget it—   [Thee
 " Jesus, thy Saviour, still lov

3 O wonderful love is the love of Jesu
 Who on Calvary's cruel tree
Was wounded and died to make fu
  atonement
 For a poor sinner, lost, like me.

726 A MESSAGE sweet is borne
  me
 On wings of joy divine,
A wondrous message, glad and fre
 That thrills this heart of mine.

 O glorious song,...that all day long...
  With tuneful note is ringing ;
 I'm saved by grace,...amazing grace,...
  And that is why I'm singing.

I'm saved by grace, by grace alone,
Thro' Christ whose love I claim,
No other could for sin atone,
Hosanna to His Name.

I hear the message that I love
When morning dawns anew,
I read it in the sun above,
That shines across the blue.

I hear it in the twilight still,
And at the sunset hour—
I'm sav'd by grace ! what words can thrill
With such a magic power.

Oh, wondrous grace for all mankind,
That spreads from sea to sea !
It heals the sick and leads the blind,
And sets the pris'ner free.

The soul that seeks it cannot fail
To see the Saviour's face,
And Satan's power cannot prevail
If we are saved by grace.

27 IT pleased the Lord to bruise
His only Son
On Calvary,....
That He might ransom sinners such
as you,
And set you free.....
He hid His face from Jesus, whom
He lov'd
So tenderly,....
With all His heart in yearnings deep
and true,
On Calvary.....

Although the piercing wail went up
on high
From Calvary,....
" My God, oh, why hast Thou for-
saken Me
On Calvary ? "....
The heav'ns return'd nor echo, groan
nor sigh
On that dark day,....
And all that He might freely pardon
me
On Calvary.....

And canst thou, sinner, stand be-
neath the Cross
Of Calvary,....
To see His life's blood dropping
surely down
Unheedingly ;....

And treat His cruel suffering as dross
On Calvary,....
While He is wearing sorrow's heavy
crown
In agony.....

4 The Cross unfolds the wondrous love
divine,
On Calvary,....
And shows in woe love's majesty
supreme
On Calvary.....
Then yield to Him that burden'd
heart of thine
At Calvary,....
And then the Cross will be thy theme
throughout
Eternity.....

728 MY stubborn will at last hath
yielded ;
I would be Thine, and Thine alone ;
And this the pray'r my lips are
bringing,
Lord, let in me Thy will be done.

Sweet will of God, still fold me closer,
Till I am wholly lost in Thee.

2 I'm tired of sin, footsore and weary,
The darksome path hath dreary
grown,
But now a light has ris'n to cheer me;
I find in Thee my Star, my Sun.

3 Thy precious will, O conqu'ring
Saviour,
Doth now embrace and compass
me ;
All discords hushed, my peace a
river,
My soul a prisoned bird set free.

4 Shut in with Thee, O Lord, for ever,
My wayward feet no more to roam ;
What pow'r from Thee my soul can
sever ?
The centre of God's will my home.

729 O GOLDEN day, when light
shall break
And dawn's bright glories shall
unfold,
When He who knows the path I take
Shall ope for me the gates of gold.
Earth's little while will soon be past,
My pilgrim song will soon be o'er,

The grace that saves shall time out-
last,
And be my theme on yonder shore.

Then I shall know, as I am known,
And stand complete before the throne ;
Then I shall see my Saviour's face,
And all my song be, " Saving grace."

2 Life's upward way, a narrow path,
Leads on to that fair dwelling
place,
Where safe from sin, and storm, and
wrath,   [grace.
They live who trust redeeming
Sing, sing, my heart, along the way,
The grace that saves will keep and
guide,
Till breaks the glorious crowning day
And I shall cross to yonder side.

3 I dimly see my journey's end,
But well I know who guideth me.
I follow Him, that wondrous Friend,
Whose matchless love is full and
free.
And when with Him I enter in,
And all the way look back to trace,
The conqueror's palm I then shall
win   [grace.
Thro' Christ and His redeeming

730 FAR away my steps have wan-
dered,
On the rugged mountain's brow ;
But to Thee my heart is crying,
Gentle Shepherd, save me now !

Save me now ! save me now !
Gentle Shepherd, save me now !
Unto Thee my heart is crying,
Gentle Shepherd save me now !

2 Thou hast borne my weight of sorrow
At Thy feet I humbly bow ;
And my heart with Thee is pleading,
Gentle Shepherd, save me now !

3 Though Thy love I long have
slighted,
Though ungrateful I have been,
To Thy fold my faith has brought
me ;
Let my weary soul come in.

4 Though Thy love I long have
slighted,
O'er my wasted years I weep ;
In Thy blessed arms of mercy,
Shield and save Thy wand'ring
sheep.

731 THO' the angry surges roll
On my tempest-driven soul,
I am peaceful, for I know,
Wildly tho' the winds may blow,
I've an anchor safe and sure,
That can evermore endure.

And it holds, my anchor holds ;
Blow your wildest, then, O Gale,..
On my barque so small and frail ;
I shall never, never fail,
For my an - - chor...holds,...my anchor hol‹

2 Mighty tides about me sweep,
Perils lurk within the deep ;
Angry clouds o'ershade the sky,
And the tempest rises high ;
Still I stand the tempest's shock,
For my anchor grips the rock.

3 Troubles almost whelm the soul ;
Griefs like billows o'er me roll ;
Tempters seek to lure astray ;
Storms obscure the light of day ;
I can face them and be bold,
I've an anchor that shall hold.

732 O CONDESCENSION wonde‹
ful !
O boundless love surpassi‹
thought !
That Christ the mighty Counsell‹
From heaven to earth salvati‹
brought !

O love divine ! O matchless grace !
O mercy flowing full and free !
With wondrous love and winning voice,
We hear Him whisper, " Come to Me.

2 O joy to know that He is mine !
This wondrous Friend, beyo‹
compare !
O joy above all human joy,
He will a place for-me prepare !

3 O peace that passeth human though‹
The peace of God so freely giv'‹
The world cannot this peace destro‹
This peace that fills the soul wi‹
heaven !

733 I KNOW that afar in Go‹
boundless realm,
Perhaps 'mid the starry spaces
Lies the promised home of the sai‹
redeemed,
Replete with celestial graces ;

In dreams I have walked on the
streets of gold,
As I sought for my own fair
dwelling,
And voices I knew and loved of old
I've heard in the music swelling.

That beautiful city is home to me,
Each day it is growing dearer ;
And voices that call from beyond the sea
Are drawing me nearer and nearer.

That beautiful city with jasper walls,
Ne'er closes its pearly portals,
And the healing pow'r of its holy
Light
Sweeps over the blest immortals ;
There sorrow and tears shall be
wiped away
In the dawn of an endless morning,
Our triumphs of faith like stars shall
shine,
Bright crowns for the soul's
adorning.

The longings of life shall be satisfied,
The fetters of earth be broken,
And the words imprisoned within
the soul
With rapture shall then be spoken ;
The music that sorrow hath hushed
awhile,
And the silence of life's sad story
Shall leap into songs of perfect joy,
Attuned to eternal glory.

734 THERE is a land mine eye
hath seen
In visions of enraptur'd thought,
So bright that all which spreads
between
Is with its radiant glories fraught.

Oh, land of love,...of joy and light,...
Thy glories gild...earth's darkest night ;...
Thy tranquil shore,...we, too, shall see,...
When dawn shall break...and shadows flee.

A land upon whose blissful shore
There rests no shadow, falls no
stain ;
There those who meet shall part no
more,
And those long parted meet again.

Its skies are not like earthly skies,
With varying hues of shade and
light !
It hath no need of suns to rise
To dissipate the gloom of night.

4 There sweeps no desolating wind
Across the calm, serene abode ;
The wand'rer there a home may find
Within the paradise of God.

735 LIKE a shepherd, tender, true,
Jesus leads,....Jesus leads,....
Daily finds us pasture new,
Jesus leads,....Jesus leads ;....
If thick mists....are o'er the way,....
Or the flock....'mid danger feeds,...
He will watch them lest they stray,
Jesus leads,....Jesus leads....:

2 All along life's rugged road,
Jesus leads,....Jesus leads,....
Till we reach yon blest abode,
Jesus leads,....Jesus leads,....
All the way...before, He's trod,....
And He now...the flock precedes,...
Safe into the folds of God
Jesus leads,....Jesus leads.....

3 Thro' the sunlit ways of life
Jesus leads,....Jesus leads,....
Thro' the warrings and the strife,
Jesus leads,....Jesus leads ;....
When we reach...the Jordan's tide,...
Where life's bound'ry....line re-
cedes,....
He will spread the waves aside,
Jesus leads,....Jesus leads.....

736 WHEN angry waves about me
roll,
And hide my path across life's sea,
No fear alarms my trusting soul,
For well I know who pilots me.

Yes, well I know...who pilots me...
Across life's ev - - er troubled sea ;...
The winds may rave...and waves may swell,...
While Jesus pi - - lots, all is well....

2 Day after day, tho' tossed about,
And often dang'rous rocks I see,
There comes to me no fear nor doubt,
For well I know who pilots me.

3 Tho' each new day brings trials sore,
Tho' rougher still the ocean be,
I know that I shall reach the shore,
For well I know who pilots me.

4 My Saviour's love still guides me on,
My only chart and compass He ;
I'll trust Him till the journey's done,
For well I know who pilots me.

737 THERE was One who was
willing to die in my stead
That a soul so unworthy might live
And the path of the Cross He was
willing to tread,
All the sins of my life to forgive.

They are nail'd to the Cross, they are nail'd
to the Cross,
O how much He was willing to bear !
With what anguish and loss, Jesus went to
the Cross !
And He carried my sins with Him there !

2 He is tender and loving and patient
with me,   [dross,
While He cleanses my heart of its
But " there's no condemnation "—I
know I am free,
For my sins are all nail'd to the
Cross.

3 I will cling to my Saviour and never
depart,
I will joyfully journey each day,
With a song on my lips and a song
in my heart,   [away.
That my sins have been taken

738 BEYOND the sea....that rolls
between....
This world of care....and things unseen....
There is a land....of endless day,....
Where all our tears....are wiped
away....

Beyond the sea,..the restless, rolling sea,..
I hear my loved..ones gently calling me...
I soon shall leave the troubled shores of time...
And dwell for aye..in that celestial clime....

2 Beyond the sea....lies heav'n's fair
shore,....   [o'er ;....
Where all of sin....and earth are
Where care and toil....have passed
away ;....   [stray.....
Where weary feet....no more shall

3 No more shall beat....the flood of
years....   [worn ;....
Across these forms....so frail and
No more shall roll...the sea of tears...
Across these hearts....by anguish
torn....

4 Beyond the sea....there's rest and
peace,....   [come ;....
There Jesus bids....His children
Beyond the sea....the tempests
cease,....   [home."....
There angels sing....a " welcome

739 I NEVER can forget the day
I heard my mother kindly say
" You're leaving now my tende
care ;
Remember, child, your mother
pray'r."

Whene'er I think of her so dear,
I feel as if she still were here ;
A voice comes floating on the air,
Reminding me of mother's pray'r.

2 I never can forget the voice
That always made my heart rejoice
Tho' I have wandered, God know
where,
Still I remember mother's prayer.

3 Tho' years have gone, I can't forge
Those words of love, I hear them yet
I see her by the old armchair,
My mother dear, in humble pray'r.

4 I never can forget the hour
I felt the Saviour's cleansing pow'r
My sin and guilt He cancell'd there
'Twas there He answer'd mother
pray'r.

O praise the Lord for saving grace !
We'll meet up yonder, face to face,
The home above together share,
In answer to my mother's pray'r.

740 WHEN I'm sad and heav
laden,
Burdened with the weight of sin,
Jesus is the very Friend I need ;
To the bloodstained Cross He poin
me,
And He gives me peace within,
Jesus is the very Friend I need.

O He is the best of friends,
And His goodness never ends,
And His love will ev'ry human though
exceed ;
Let me love Him more and more,
Till I stand on glory's shore ;
O Jesus is the very Friend I need.

2 When I'm struggling with tempt
tion,
When my strength shall almost fa
Jesus is the very Friend I need ;
For His arm will bring deliv'rance.
And His grace will still prevail,
Jesus is the very Friend I need.

3 When I drink the cup of sorrow,
When I tread the path of grief,
Jesus is the very Friend I need ;

In His Word is consolation,
In His presence sweet relief,
  Jesus is the very Friend I need.

When I reach the silent river,
When I wait beside the tide,
  Jesus is the very Friend I need;
He will bear me o'er the billows
To the radiant morning side,
  Jesus is the very Friend I need.

41 THOU my ransom price hast paid,
  Blessed Son of God,
Since on Thee my heart is stayed,
  Keep me under the blood.

> Keep me under the blood, dear Lord,
>   Calvary's crimson flood;
> Not mine own, but Thine alone,
>   Keep me under the blood.

At the Cross where first I knelt,
  Full of sinful pride,
Where I first salvation felt,
  Let me still abide.

Where to self and sin I died,
  Where, the nails were driven,
Let me still for cleansing hide
  In Thy dear side riven.

Shouting with my latest breath
  Praises to our God,
Who my soul has saved and kept
  By His precious blood.

42 WHEN I was but a little child,
  how well I recollect,
How I would grieve my mother with
  my folly and neglect;
And now that she has gone to heaven
  I miss her tender care;
O Saviour, tell my mother, I'll be
  there.

> Tell mother I'll be there, in answer to her
>   pray'r;
> This message, blessed Saviour, to her bear:
> Tell mother I'll be there, heav'n's joys with
>   her to share;
> Yes, tell my darling mother I'll be there.

Tho' I was often wayward, she was
  ever kind and good,
So patient, gentle, loving, when I
  acted rough and rude:
My childhood griefs and trials she
  would gladly with me share;
O Saviour, tell my mother, I'll be
  there.

3 When I became a prodigal, and left
    the old roof tree,
  She almost broke her loving heart
    in mourning after me.
  And day and night she prayed to
    God to keep me in His care;
  O Saviour, tell my mother I'll be
    there.

4 One day a message came to me, it
    bade me quickly come,
  If I would see my mother ere the
    Saviour took her home;
  I promised her, before she died, for
    heaven to prepare,   [there.
  O Saviour, tell my mother I'll be

743 I PRAISE the Lord that one
    like me
  For mercy may to Jesus flee;
  He says that whosoever will
  May seek and find salvation still.

> My Saviour's promise falleth never,
> He counts me in the Whosoever.

2 I was to sin a wretched slave,
  But Jesus died my soul to save;
  He says that whosoever will
  May seek and find salvation still.

3 I look by faith and see this word
  Stamp'd with the blood of Christ,
    my Lord;
  He says that whosoever will
  May seek and find salvation still.

4 I now believe He saves my soul,
  His precious blood hath made me
    whole;
  He says that whosoever will,
  May seek and find salvation still.

744 SOME day 'twill all be over—
    The toils and cares of life;
  Some day the world be vanquished
    With all this mortal strife;
  Some day, the journey ended,
    I'll lay my burden down;
  Some day, in realms supernal,
    Receive, at last, my crown.

> Some day,...some happy day,...
> The Lord will wipe all tears away,...
> And I shall go to dwell with Him,....
> To dwell with Him...some happy day..

2 Some day I'll see the mansions
    Of heaven's city fair;
  Some day I'll greet with pleasure
    The dear ones waiting there;

Some day I'll hear the voices
  Of God's angelic throng;
Some day I'll join the chorus
  In heaven's immortal song.

3 Some day I'll see the Saviour,
  And know Him face to face;
Some day receive, unmeasured,
  The blessings of His grace;
Some day He'll smile upon me
  From that white throne above;
Some day I'll know the fulness
  Of His undying love.

745 BROTHER, don't stay away,
  Brother, don't stay away,
Brother, don't stay away, don't stay
  away.
My Lord says there's room enough,
Room enough in the heavens for you,
My Lord says there's room enough,
  don't stay away.

746 HE who hath led will lead,
  All through the wilderness,
He who hath fed will surely feed;
  He who hath blessed will bless;
He who hath heard thy cry,
  Will never close His ear;
He who hath marked thy faintest
  sigh
  Will not forget thy tear.
He loveth always, faileth never,
So rest on Him to-day, for ever.

2 He who hath made thee whole
  Will heal thee day by day;
He who hath spoken to thy soul
  Hath many things to say.
He who hath gently taught,
  Yet more will make thee know;
He who so wondrously hath wrought
  Yet greater things will show.

3 He who hath made thee nigh,
  Will draw thee nearer still;
He who hath given the first supply
  Will satisfy and fill.
He who hath given thee grace,
  Yet more and more will send;
He who hath set thee in the race
  Will speed thee to the end.

4 He who hath won thy heart
  Will keep it true and free;
He who hath shown thee what thou
  art,
  Will show Himself to thee.

He who hath bid thee live,
  And made thy life His own,
Life more abundantly will give,
  And keep it His alone.

747 WHEN your spirit bows
    sorrow
  From the load it bears,
Go and tell your heart to Jesus,
  Don't you know He cares ?
Yes, there is One who bears your burden
  Ev'ry sorrow shares;
Go and tell it all to Jesus—
  Don't you know He cares ?

2 Have your feet become entangled
  In the tempter's snares ?
There is One who died to save you
  Don't you know He cares ?

3 Have you been by grief o'ertaken,
  Stricken unawares ?
Yet ye will not be forsaken,
  Don't you know He cares ?

4 Is your body filled with anguish,
  With the pain it bears ?
Think of how the Saviour suffered
  Don't you know He cares ?

5 Loss of friends and loss of fortune
  Life a dark look wears;
Yet the Saviour still is with you,
  Don't you know He cares ?

6 So amid life's cares and struggles,
  Blending songs with prayers—
Always put your trust in Jesus,
  Don't you know He cares ?

748 ONE thing I of the Lo
    desire,
  For all my path hath miry been
Be it by water or by fire,
  Oh make me clean, oh make r
    clean !
So wash me, Thou,..without, within,..
  Or purge with fire,..if that must be t..
No matter how,..if only sin..
  Die out in me,..Die out in me...

2 If clearer vision Thou impart,
  Grateful and glad my soul shall b
But yet to have a purer heart
  Is more to me, is more to me.

3 Yea, only as this heart is clean
  May larger vision yet be mine,
For mirror'd in its depths are see
  The things divine, the thir
  divine.

I watch to shun the miry way,
    And staunch the springs of guilty thought;
But, watch and struggle as I may,
    Pure I am not, pure I am not.

49 THE trusting heart to Jesus clings,
    Nor any ill forebodes,
But at the Cross of Calv'ry sings,
    Praise God for lifted loads!

> Singing I go along life's road,
> Praising the Lord, praising the Lord,
> Singing I go along life's road,
> For Jesus has lifted my load.

The passing days bring many cares,
  "Fear not," I hear Him say;
And when my fears are turned to prayers,
    The burdens slip away.

He tells me of my Father's love,
    And never-slumb'ring eye;
My everlasting King above
    Will all my need supply.

When to the throne of grace I flee,
    I find the promise true,
The mighty arms upholding me
    Will bear my burdens too.

50 ERE you left the homestead in the vanished long ago,
When your heart was happy and your soul was pure as snow,
You were bade to Jesus' feet, His shelt'ring love to know;
    Don't forget the promise made to mother.

> n't forget those tender hands that soothed your cares away;
> n't forget that gentle face, those tresses thin and grey;   [you to-day;
> d don't forget her Saviour, who is calling
> Don't forget the promise made to mother.

When you sought the world, she bade you take this faithful Friend,
Begged you to confess Him, and in Him your soul defend;
Oft you vowed to claim Him and to trust Him to the end,
    Don't forget the promise made to mother.

Far from grace you wander'd in the weary passing years,
Patiently she suffered and endured her grief and fears;

Many times you told her you would heed the pray'rs and tears;
    Don't forget the promise made to mother.

4 Once again you promised when her pilgrim work was done,
When she went in triumph to receive her golden crown;
When she said, " Thro' Christ alone were life and vict'ry won; "
    Don't forget the promise made to mother.

751 I READ that whosoever
    May from wrath flee;
God will reject me never,
    For that means me.

> For that means me,
> Yes, that means me;
> When I read " whosoever,"
> That means me.

2 His blood is efficacious,
    His love is free;
To sinners He is gracious,
    And that means me.

3 Christ died for ev'ry nation,
    On Calv'ry's tree;
He died for our salvation,
    And that means me.

4 I read the promise given
    That o'er death's sea,
We'll live with Him in heaven,
    And that means me.

752 THE sun will never set
    In Summer-land;
No eyes with tears are wet
    In Summer-land;
No shade of dark'ning night
Will shut the view from sight,
Nor e'er becloud the light,
    In Summer-land.

2 No one will lose the way
    In Summer-land;
Nor ever go astray
    In Summer-land;
No mountain hard to climb,
Yet all is grand, sublime,
With endless summer clime,
    In Summer-land.

3 No death is ever known
    In Summer-land;
For life is on the throne
    In Summer-land;

No mourning for the dead,
No heavy hearts, like lead,
But endless joy instead,
In Summer-land.

753 SOMEWHERE the sun is
shining,
Somewhere the song-birds dwell;
Hush, then, thy sad repining,
God lives, and all is well.

Some - - where,...some - - where,
Beautiful Isle of Somewhere !
Land of the true where we live anew,
Beautiful Isle of Somewhere !

2 Somewhere the day is longer,
Somewhere the task is done :
Somewhere the heart is stronger,
Somewhere the guerdon won.

3 Somewhere the load is lifted,
Close by an open gate ;
Somewhere the clouds are rifted,
Somewhere the angels wait !

754 WHEN the world and sin
oppose,
We will follow Jesus ;
He is greater than our foes,
We will follow Jesus.
On His promise we'll depend,
He'll be with us to the end,
He will guard us and defend :
We will follow Jesus.

755 BOTH weak and blind, dear
Lord, I am,
For now Thy face I cannot see,
But I can hear Thy gentle voice
Speak words of love to me.

O some day...I shall see,...
And some day...clasp Thy hand....
Yes, some day...see Thy face,...
When in Thy courts I stand.

2 But I can feel Thy gentle touch,
And I can read Thy blessed Word,
And with Thy mighty throbbing love
My lonely heart is stirred.

3 Till then, dear Lord, but lead me on,
And guide me in the better way,
Lest, groping in the darkness here,
My feet shall go astray.

4 And when at last my journey's o'er,
Earth's heavy burdens are laid
down ;   [joy,
When tears are changed to pearls of
My cross to jewelled crown.

756 OH, I can't tell it all, of t
wonderful love,
How, when lost in my sins, Jes
found me ;
With a heart full of love, how I
came from above,
Threw His strong arms of mer
around me.

Oh, I can't tell it all ; no, I can't tell it all ;
But my heart is so full of His glory,
That wherever I go in this wide world belo
I am telling the wonderful story.

2 Oh, I can't tell it all, how He free
forgave ;
How the blood flowed with wo
derful healing ;
O'er my lost, guilty soul, how
cleansed and made whole,
While low at the Cross I w
kneeling.

3 Oh, I can't tell it all, what a Frier
He has been,
Now He's borne all my sorrov
and sadness ;
How He saves me to-day, bids tl
clouds chase away,
How He turns all my mournin
to gladness.

4 Oh, I can't tell it all, but His lo
you may know,
You may have Him, this wonde
ful Saviour ;
You may taste of His bliss, you ma
say, I am His,
And He is my portion for ever.

5 Oh, I can't tell it all, but as long
I've breath
I will still tell the wonderful stor
When my life work is done and
crown I have won,
I will tell it for ever in glory.

757 AFTER the earthly shado
have lifted,
And o'er the hill-tops morning
see,
Sweetest of prospects, I shall beho
Him,
Jesus, the Saviour of sinners li
me.

When I behold Him, Christ, in His beauty
When with the ransom'd His face I shall
O how my heart in rapture will praise Hin
Praise Him for saving a sinner like me.

Helpless He found me, lifted me to
　　Him ;
　Whisper'd of pardon abundant
　　and free ;
Breath'd He His peace o'er my sin-
　　stricken spirit ;
　Pointed my vision to Calvary's
　　tree.

Now in His presence daily I'm living,
　Walking by faith where mine eyes
　　cannot see ;
For He is guiding home to that city,
　Built for His lov'd ones—saved
　　sinners like me.

58 HOLY Bible, book divine,
　　Precious treasure, thou art
　　　mine ;
Mine to tell me whence I come,
Mine to tell me what I am.

　Mine,....mine,...book divine,
　Precious treasure, thou art mine ;
　O thou holy book divine,
　Precious treasure, thou art mine !

Mine to chide me when I rove,
Mine to show a Saviour's love ;
Mine thou art to guide and guard,
Mine to punish or reward.

Mine to Comfort in distress,
Suff'ring in this wilderness ;
Mine to show by living faith,
Man can triumph over death.

Mine to tell of joys to come,
And the rebel sinner's doom ;
O thou holy book divine,
Precious treasure, thou art mine !

59 WHAT hinders your coming to
　　Jesus,
　What hinders your coming to-day?
He offers His grace and His pardon,
　Tell Jesus what stands in the way.

　What is it that hinders your coming ?
　　You may find this salvation to-day ;
　The Saviour is ready and waiting,
　　O why do you longer delay ?

If pleasures and earthly enjoyment
　Have hindered your coming before
O tarry no longer, but prove Him,
　Who offers you joy evermore.

The fearful, the troubled and doubt-
　　ing,
　May lovingly lean on His breast ;
O trust Him who offers salvation,
　Come now to His arms and be blest

4 What hinders your coming to Jesus?
　　The fear that you may not hold
　　　out ?
　His mercy endureth for ever,
　　O how can you linger in doubt ?

760 FAR from home and kindred,
　　　Wandering away,
Where is he I think of,
　Pray for day by day ?
Once home's brightest sunshine,
　Once its joy and light,
Still his mother's darling,
　Where is he to-night ?

　　For the Shepherd, Jesus,
　　　Leaves the rest behind,
　　Seeks the lost and wand'ring,
　　　Seeks until He find.

2 Far he may be straying,
　From the heavenly fold,
Yet the tender Shepherd,
　With a love untold,
And a great compassion
　Filling all His mind,
Will be following after,
　Seeking till He find.

3 Ah ! no heart can harden
　So He cannot teach ;
And no sheep can wander
　Where He cannot reach ;
So I keep on praying,
　Wheresoe'er he be,
Bring him home, Good Shepherd,
　Bring him back with Thee.

4 May the bells of heaven
　Ring for him with joy ;
May rejoicing angels
　Smile upon my boy ;
May the Father meet him
　Coming back alone,
Saying, " Loved and lost one,
　Welcome, welcome home ! "

761 I WAS far away from Jesus,
　　　dead in trespasses and sin,
　　And I thought for one so vile no
　　　hope could be ;
　But the blessed Lord of Glory
　　stooped and raised me to Him-
　　self,　　　　　　　　　[me.
And He put His loving arms around

　He put His loving arms around me,
　He put His loving arms around me,
　I look'd into His face, it beamed with tender
　　grace,
　As He put His loving arms around me.

2 Then He whispered to me pardon
thro' the all atoning blood
Which He shed for my transgressions on the tree ;
And the blessed peace of heaven
came into my weary soul,
As He put His loving arms around
me.

3 Day by day He guides and keeps me
and in the blessed narrow way,
From the ban of sin and death He
makes me free ;
There's no evil can befall me while
I'm resting in His grace, [me.
And He has His loving arms around

4 In the hour of deepest trial, when all
earthly comfort fails,
And no cheering ray of sunshine I
can see ;
Then to Him I bring my sorrow, and
He wipes away my tears, [me.
As He puts His loving arms around

5 Oh, this blessed life in Jesus ! sinner,
won't you hear His call ?
From the power of sin's dominion
He can free ;
Yield thy heart to Him this moment
and with joy thou'lt surely find,
That He'll put His loving arms
around thee.

He'll put His loving arms around thee,
He'll put His loving arms around thee,
Look up into His face, it beams with tender
grace,
And He'll put His loving arms around thee.

762 WITH ev'ry power, with heart
and soul,
I belong to Jesus !
He shall my ev'ry thought control,
I belong to Jesus !

I belong to Jesus !
I belong to Jesus !
I belong to Jesus,
He belongs to me.

2 What though temptations sore beset,
I belong to Jesus !
What though earth's cares annoy
and fret,
I belong to Jesus !

3 In vain the world my heart allures,
I belong to Jesus !
In weakness this my soul assures,
I belong to Jesus !

4 No threat'ning danger then I see,
I belong to Jesus !
Through time and through eterni
I belong to Jesus !

763 WHEN weary and faint
and ready to die,
To the Rock in the desert for safe
I fly ;
There 'neath its cool shelter fr
storms I would hide, [abi
My soul is refresh'd as in Him

O come, all ye weary, and blissfully prove,
That Christ is the Rock, and His shadow is lo

2 When thirsty and parched with
heat of the day,
To the Rock that was smitten
haste me and say,
" Give me a cool drink from T
bountiful store,"
And quickly and freely the
waters pour.

3 Though billows of sorrow around
may roll,
And dangers of midnight m
trouble my soul,
I'll haste to the Rock that is hig
than I,
And safely I'll rest till the ni
passeth by.

764 I BELONG to the King, I
a child of His love,
I shall dwell in His palace so fa
For He tells of its bliss in y
heaven above,
And His children its splend
shall share.

I belong to the King, I'm a child of His love
And He never forsaketh His own ;
He will call me some day to His palace abo
I shall dwell by His glorified throne.

2 I belong to the King, and He lo
me, I know,
For His mercy and kindness so f
Are unceasingly mine, wheresoe
I go,
And my refuge unfailing is He

3 I belong to the King, and His p
mise is sure, [l
That we all shall be gathered
In His kingdom above, by li
water so pure, [pa
When this life with its trials

65 LORD, Thou hast granted
    salvation to me,
  What wilt Thou have me to do ?
From Satan's bondage at last I am
    free,
  What wilt Thou have me to do ?

What wilt Thou have me to do ?
  Where wilt Thou have me to go ?
Jesus, my Master, Thy will shall be mine,
  What wilt Thou have me to do ?

Since I am saved by the Crucified
    One,
  What wilt Thou have me to do ?
I would point others to God's only
    Son,
  What wilt Thou have me to do ?

Pardon is granted thro' Him who
    hath died,
  What wilt Thou have me to do ?
I am so happy with Thee at my side,
  What wilt Thou have me to do ?

Ready and willing Thy voice to obey,
  What wilt Thou have me to do ?
Bid me to follow Thee day unto day,
  What wilt Thou have me to do ?

66 I SHALL lay the cross aside,
    Some day, some glad day ;
Safely pass to Canaan's side,
  Some day, some glad day ;
If I live a life of pray'r,
And the cross for Jesus bear,
I a glorious crown shall wear,
  Some day, some glad day.

I the sinner's Friend shall see,
  Some day, some glad day ;
See the wounds once made for me,
  Some day, some glad day ;
I shall press close to His side,
Who for me was crucified,
And shall then be satisfied,
  Some day, some glad day.

I shall meet the friends of yore,
  Some day, some glad day ;
And with them the Lamb adore,
  Some day, some glad day ;
There at Jesus' sacred feet
Saints of ev'ry clime I'll meet,
Hold with them communion sweet,
  Some day, some glad day.

I shall lean on Jesus' breast,
  Some day, some glad day ;
Find a sweet, a perfect rest,
  Some day, some glad day ;

On that bright eternal shore
All our sorrows will be o'er,
We shall meet to part no more,
  Some day, some glad day.

767 HAVE you accepted the friend-
    ship of Jesus ?
  Do you walk with Him day by day
Resting secure in His blessed assur-
    ance,
  " Lo, I am with you alway ? "

By and by,...by and by,...
  They who walk with Him here below,
In His glorified likeness awaking,
  As they are known, shall they know.

2 Dear as a mother, or sister, or
    brother,
  To His infinite heart of love
Is he that doeth the will of the
    Father,
  Seeking for strength from above.

3 Servants no longer, but friends He
    doth call us,
  If we do what His love commands,
Yesterday, now, and for ever His
    promise
  Fixed and unchangeable stands.

768 LEAD me gently home, Father,
    Lead me gently home,
When life's toils are ended,
  And parting days have come ;
Sin no more shall tempt me,
  Ne'er from Thee I'll roam,
If Thou'lt only lead me, Father,
  Lead me gently home.

    Lead me gently home, Father,
      Lead me gently,
    Lest I fall upon the wayside,
      Lead me gently home....

2 Lead me gently home, Father,
    Lead me gently home ;
In life's darkest hours, Father,
  When life's troubles come,
Keep my feet from wand'ring,
  Lest from Thee I roam,
Lest I fall upon the wayside,
  Lead me gently home.

769 JESUS of Nazareth, Healer of
    men,
  Curer of halt and of blind ;
Worker of wonders again and again,
  Seeking the sad ones to find.

    Jesus of Nazareth, tell it again,
    Died on the Cross for sinful men.

2 Jesus of Nazareth, Curer of sin,
  Seeker for lost and defiled ;
Striving so kindly the straying to
  win,
  Loving each penitent child.

3 Jesus of Nazareth, dying for all,
  Hanging in pain on the tree,
Suff'ring so meekly that we who may
  call,
  Pardon thro' Him may have free.

770 JUST as I am I come to Thee,
  Myself I cannot better make ;
The precious blood my only plea,
  Oh, save me for Thy mercy's sake.
  Just as...I am,...
  Just as I am I come to Thee,...
  Oh hear me, bless me, save me, Lord,
  Just as I am I come to Thee.

2 Just as I am, yet this I know,
  The blood will all-sufficient be ;
I shall be whiter than the snow,
  Made fully whole in trusting Thee.

3 Just as I am, I come to-day,
  My hungry soul cries out for Thee ;
I can no longer stay away,
  Thine, wholly Thine, I long to be.

4 Just as I am, my Life, my Love,
  My soul here finds a perfect rest ;
While, like the weary, wand'ring
  dove ;
  Safe folded in Thy love I rest.

771 OH, awful load for that bow'd
  Head,   [form,
Terrific weight for that marr'd
He bore *your* sins, *your* burden
  dread,
  And brav'd *your* judgment's fear-
    ful storm.
  Thy death, Lord Jesus, evermore,
  Shall be our song on yonder shore :
  We'll praise the blessed One who bore
  Our load of sin upon the tree.

2 Transferred to Him, the guiltless, see
  Your guilt, in blood your debt was
    paid ;
Behold, to set the captive free,
  Jesus the great sin-off'ring made.

3 Believe, believe, thou guilty one,
  That all thy sins' deserved doom
Was borne by Christ ; God's Holy
  Son   [tomb.
  For thee has bow'd Him to the

772 THERE is singing up in heav
  such as we have never know
Where the angels sing the praises
  the Lamb upon the throne ;
Their sweet harps are ever tune
  and their voices always clear,
Oh, that we might be more like the
  while we serve the Master here.
  Holy, holy, is what the angels sing.
  And I expect to help them make the cou
  of heaven ring ;
  But when I sing redemption's story they w
  fold their wings,   [vation brin
  For angels never felt the joys that our salv

2 But I hear another anthem blendi
  voices clear and strong,
  " Unto Him that hath redeemed
  and has bought us," is the song
We have come thro' tribulations
  this land so fair and bright,
In the fountain freely flowing I
  hath made our garments white.

3 Then the angels stand and listen, i
  they cannot join that song,
Let the sound of many waters, I
  that happy, blood-washed thron
For they sing about great tria
  battles fought and vict'ries won
And they praise their great R
  deemer, who hath said to the
  " Well done."

4 So, although I'm not an angel, ye
  know that over there
I will join a blessed chorus that t
  angels cannot share ;
I will sing about my Saviour, w
  upon dark Calvary,
Freely pardoned my transgressior
  died to set a sinner free.

773 YEARS I spent in vanity a
  pride,
Caring not my Lord was crucified
Knowing not it was for me He die
  On Calvary.
  Mercy there was great and grace was fre
  Pardon there was multiplied to me,
  There my burdened soul found liberty,
  At Calvary.

2 By God's Word at last my sin
  learned,   [spurne
Then I trembled at the law I
Till my guilty soul imploring, turn
  To Calvary.

Now I've given to Jesus ev'rything,
Now I gladly own Him as my King,
Now my raptured soul can only sing
    Of Calvary.

Oh ! the love that drew salvation's
    plan,
Oh ! the grace that brought it down
    to man,
Oh ! the mighty gulf that God did
    span
       At Calvary.

774 MY Father has many dear
        children ;
Will He ever forget to keep me ?
He gave His own Son to redeem them
And He cannot forget to keep me.

  He'll never forget to keep me,...
  He'll never forget to keep me,...
  He gave His own Son to redeem me,
  And He cannot forget to keep me.

Our Father remembers the sparrows,
Their value and fall He doth see ;
But dearer to Him are His children,
And He'll never forget to keep me.

  He'll never forget to keep me,...
  He'll never forget to keep me,...
  But dearer to Him are His children,
  And He'll never forget to keep me.

The words of the Lord are so price-
    less,
How patient and watchful is He ;
Tho' mother forget her own offspring,
Yet He'll never forget to keep me.

  He'll never forget to keep me,...
  He'll never forget to keep me,...
  Tho' mother forget her own offspring,
  Yet He'll never forget to keep me.

O brother, why don't you accept
    Him ?
He offers salvation so free ;
Repent and believe and obey Him,
    And He'll never forget to keep
    thee.

  He'll never forget to keep thee,...
  He'll never forget to keep thee,...
  Repent and believe and obey Him,
  And He'll never forget to keep Thee.

775 WHAT were we when mercy
        found us ?
Captives unto death and sin ; [us,
Clouds and darkness closed around
All was hopeless night within.

We were lost, but Jesus found us,
Burst the bonds of death that bound us,
Wrapt the robe of grace around us,
And the heirs of glory crowned us.

2 What are we since mercy found us ?
    Blameless, spotless in His sight ;
Sons and saints His Word has
    crowned us,
    Called to walk with Him in light.

3 What we shall be ? That's a story
    Never uttered or expressed !
We shall see Him in His glory,
    And be folded to His breast.

776 UNANSWERED yet ? The
        prayer your lips have pleaded
    In agony of heart these many
    years ?
Doth faith begin to fail ? Is hope
    departing ?
    And think you all in vain those
    falling tears ?
Say not the Father hath not heard
    your prayer,
You shall have your desire, some-
    time, somewhere.

2 Unanswered yet ? tho' when you
    first presented
    This one petition at the Father's
    throne,
It seemed you could not wait the
    time of asking,
    So urgent was your heart to make
    it known.
Tho' years have passed since then,
    do not despair,
The Lord will answer you some-
    time, somewhere.

3 Unanswered yet ? Nay, do not say
    " ungranted ; "
    Perhaps your part is not yet
    wholly done ;
The work began when first your
    prayer was uttered,
    And God will finish what He has
    begun ;
If you will keep the incense burning
    there,
His glory you shall see sometime,
    somewhere.

4 Unanswered yet ? Faith cannot be
    unanswered ;
His feet are firmly planted on the
    Rock ;

Amid the wildest storms she stands
undaunted,
   Nor quails before the loudest
   thunder shock.
She knows Omnipotence has heard
her prayer,
   And cries, " It shall be done,"
sometime, somewhere.

777 COME home ! come home !
    You are weary at heart,
For the way has been dark,
And so lonely and wild ;
   O prodigal child !
Come home ! O come home !

2   Come home ! come home !
For we watch and we wait,
And we stand at the gate,
While the shadows are piled ;
   O prodigal child !
Come home ! O come home !

3   Come home ! come home !
From the sorrow and blame,
From the sin and the shame,
And the tempter that smiled,
   O prodigal child !
Come home ! O come home !

4   Come home ! come home !
There is bread and to spare,
And a warm welcome there ;
Then, to friends reconciled,
   O prodigal child !
Come home ! O come home !

778 THERE is something strangely
tender
In His parting words so sweet,
" Do not let your heart be troubled,
For we by and by shall meet
In the home of many mansions
Which I go now to prepare,
And when I am ready, dear ones,
I will come and take you there."
  " Ah," He whisper'd when He left them,
    " I am coming back again,
  And will take you to your new home,
    Ever near Me to remain."

2 Ah, those words, so strangely tender,
Still keep echoing all round,
And tho' they have gone to glory,
And have reached the hallow'd
   ground,   [them,
The sweet promise has not failed
They are with their Lord to-night,
We shall find them ready waiting,
Just within the gates of light.

3 Don't you hear the words so tende
Don't they echo in your heart 1
Don't they woo you from this pe
   life,
That with which you soon m
   part ?
Those who wait His coming gloric
Then will form His royal train,
Oh, the rapturous hour of meetir
When the Lord comes back
   reign.

779 I LOVE to think my Fath
knows
Why I have missed the path I cho
And that I soon shall clearly see
The way He led was best for me.
  He knows it all,...He knows it all,...
  My Father knows,...He knows it all ;...
  Thy bitter tears,...how fast they fall !
  He knows, my Father knows it all.

2 I love to think my Father knows
The thorns I pluck with ev'ry ro
The daily griefs I seek to hide
From the dear souls I walk beside

3 I love to think my Father knows
The strength or weakness of my fc
And that I need but stand and see
Each conflict end in victory.

780 MY soul is so happy in Jesu
    For He is so precious to n
His voice it is music to hear it,
   His face it is heaven to see.
  I am happy in Him,...
  I am happy in Him ;...
  My soul with delight He fills day and ni
  For I am happy in Him.

2 He sought me so long ere I kn
   Him,   [fo
When wand'ring afar from
Safe home in His arms He h
   brought me,
To where there are pleasu
   untold.

3 His love and His mercy surround n
His grace like a river doth flow
His Spirit, to guide and to comfor
  Is with me wherever I go.

4 They say I shall some day be l
   Him,
My cross and my burden lay dow
Till then I will ever be faithful,
  In gathering gems for His crow

81 HOW I praise Thee, precious
　　　Saviour,
That Thy love laid hold of me ;
Thou hast saved and cleansed and
　　　filled me,
That I might Thy channel be ;

Channels only, blessed Master,
　But with all Thy wondrous power,
Flowing through us, Thou canst use us
　Ev'ry day and ev'ry hour.

Just a channel, full of blessing,
　To the thirsty hearts around ;
To tell out Thy full salvation,
　All Thy loving message sound.

Emptied that Thou shouldst fill me,
　A clean vessel in Thine hand ;
With no pow'r but as Thou givest
　Graciously with each command.

Witnessing Thy power to save me,
　Setting free from self and sin ;
Thou hast bought me to possess me,
　In Thy fulness, Lord, come in.

Jesus, fill now with Thy Spirit
　Hearts that full surrender know ;
That the streams of living water
　From our inner man may flow.

82 I AM on the Gospel highway,
　　　Pressing forward to the goal,
Where for me a rest remaineth,
　In the home-land of the soul ;
Ev'ry hour I'm moving onward,
　Not a moment to delay ;
I am going home to glory
　In the good old-fashioned way.

　In the good old-fashioned way,
　In the good old-fashioned way,
　　I am going home to glory
　In the good old-fashioned way.

From the snares of sinful pleasure,
　Here my feet are always free ;
Tho' the way may be called narrow,
　It is wide enough for me ;
It was wide enough for Daniel,
　And for David in his day ;
I am glad that I can follow
　In the good old-fashioned way.

Many friends have gone before me,
　They have laid their armour down ;
With the pilgrims and the martyrs,
　Have obtained a robe and crown ;
On this road they fought their
　　battles,
　Shouting vict'ry day by day ;

I shall overcome and join them
　In the good old-fashioned way.

4 Just a few more steps to follow,
　Just a few more days to roam ;
But the way grows more delightful
　As I'm drawing nearer home ;
When the storms of life are over,
　And the clouds have rolled away,
I shall find the gates of heaven
　In the good old-fashioned way.

　Then palms of victory, crowns of glory,
　Palms of victory I shall wear.

783 I'LL cling closer to Jesus ;
　　　I'll cling closer to Him ;
I'll cling closer to Jesus,
　The mighty to save.

784 DO you know the world is
　　　dying
For a little bit of love ?
Ev'rywhere we hear their sighing
For a little bit of love ?
For the love that rights a wrong,
Fills the heart with hope and song ;
They have waited, oh, so long !
For a little bit of love.

　For a little bit of love,
　For a little bit of love ;
　They have waited, oh, so long,
　For a little bit of love.

2 From the poor of ev'ry city,
　For a little bit of love,
Hands are reaching out in pity
　For a little bit of love ;
Some have burdens hard to bear,
Some have sorrows we should share ;
Shall they falter and despair
　For a little bit of love ?

　For a little bit of love,
　For a little bit of love ;
　Shall they falter and despair
　For a little bit of love ?

3 Down before their idols falling,
　For a little bit of love,
Many souls in vain are calling
　For a little bit of love ;
If they die in sin and shame,
Someone surely is to blame
For not going, in His Name,
　With a little bit of love.

　With a little bit of love,
　With a little bit of love ;
　For not going, in His Name,
　With a little bit of love.

4 While the souls of men are dying
   For a little bit of love,
While the children, too, are crying
   For a little bit of love ;
Stand no longer idly by,
You can help them if you try ;
Go then, saying, " Here am I,"
   With a little bit of love.

> With a little bit of love,
> With a little bit of love ;
> Go then, saying, " Here am I,"
> With a little bit of love.

785 ONLY one word for the Master,
   Lovingly, quietly said :
Only a word ! Yet the Master heard,
   And some fainting hearts were fed.

2 Only a cry from the sinner,
   Bitterly earnest and wild ;
" Help, Lord, I die ! " rose in agony,
   And the Saviour saved His child.

3 Only an hour with the children,
   Pleasantly, cheerfully given ;
Still seed was sown in that hour
      alone,   [heaven.
   Which would bring forth fruit for

786 THERE is a land mine eyes
      shall see   [down ;
   When I shall lay life's armour
But all its bliss is not for me,
   If I must wear a starless crown.

> A starless crown, when life is done,
> No glitt'ring gems which I have won !
> Forbid it, Lord, that there should be
> A starless crown in Heav'n for me.

2 The gains of earth are all but loss—
   Eternal joys are all for me,
When I by faith uplift the cross,
   And lead one soul, dear Lord, to
      Thee.

3 Forbid it, Lord, that I should be
   Content to live for self alone ;
Oh, may some soul I win for Thee
   Adorn my crown when life is done.

787 ONCE upon the tide I drifted,
   With no guide to yonder
      shore ;
But I've found a side once rifted,
   Where I'm safe for evermore.

> I am anchored, safely anchored,
> Anchored, never more to roam,
> Anchored by the side of Jesus,
> Anchored in the soul's bright home.

2 Let the storms sweep o'er life's oce
   They can do me no more harm ;
Anchored far from their commotio
   I am resting 'neath His arm.

3 Here my peace flows like a river,
   Here my soul o'erflows with son
Prayer and praises to the Giver
   Fill my glad heart all day long.

4 When this life below is ended,
   I shall anchor on that shore ;
When my praises will be blended
   With ten thousand thousand mo

788 FAR away in the depths of
      spirit to-night
   Rolls a melody sweeter than psal
In celestial-like strains it unceasin;
      falls
   O'er my soul like an infinite cal

> Peace ! peace ! wonderful peace,
> Coming down from the Father abov
> Sweep over my spirit for ever, I pray,
> In fathomless billows of love !

2 What a treasure I have in t
      wonderful peace,   [so
   Buried deep in the heart of n
So secure that no power can mine
      away,
   While the years of eternity roll

3 I am resting to-night in this wond
      ful peace,
   Resting sweetly in Jesus' contro
For I'm kept from all danger
      night and by day,
   And His glory is flooding my so

4 And methinks when I rise to th
      city of peace,   [se
   Where the Author of peace I sh
That one strain of the song whi
      the ransomed will sing
   In that heavenly kingdom will be

5 Ah, soul ! are you here witho
      comfort and rest,   [of tim
   Marching down the rough pathw
Make Jesus your Friend ere t
      shadows grow dark ;
   O accept of this peace so sublim

789 I CANNOT drift beyond T
      love,
   Beyond Thy tender care ;
Where'er I stray, still from above
   Thine eye beholds me there.

I cannot drift so far away
   But what Thy love divine
Upon my path, by night and day,
   In mercy sweet doth shine.

I cannot drift beyond Thy sight,
   Dear Lord, the thought is sweet ;
Thy loving hand will guide aright,
   My weary, wand'ring feet.
When rough and dark my lonely way
   I shall not be forgot,   [day
Thro' all life's changeful, shadow'd
   Thou wilt forsake me not.

I cannot drift away from Thee,
   No matter where I go ;
Still Thy dear love doth gladden me,
   Thou all my way dost know.
Where'er I journey Thou art there,
   In wind and wave I hear
Thy voice, in tones of music rare,
   And know that Thou art near.

90 MY soul in sad exile was out
      on life's sea,
   So burden'd with sin and distress'd
Till I heard a sweet voice saying,
    "Make Me your choice ; "
   And I entered the "Heaven of
     Rest."

e anchored my soul in the Haven of Rest,
'll sail the wide seas no more ;
e tempest may sweep o'er the wild, stormy
   deep,
n Jesus I'm safe evermore.

I yielded myself to His tender
   embrace,
   And faith taking hold of the Word,
My fetters fell off, and I anchor'd
   my soul ;
   The "Haven of Rest" is my Lord.

The song of my soul, since the Lord
   made me whole,
   Has been the old story so blest,
Of Jesus, who'll save whosoever will
   have
   A home in the " Haven of Rest."

How precious the thought that we
   all may recline,
   Like John, the beloved and blest,
On Jesus' strong arm, where no
   tempest can harm,
   Secure in the " Haven of Rest."

Oh, come to the Saviour, He
   patiently waits
To save by His power divine ;

Come, anchor your soul in the
   " Haven of Rest,"
   And say, " My beloved is mine."

791 LIKE a bird on the deep, far
     away from its nest,
   I have wander'd, my Saviour,
    from Thee ;
But Thy dear loving voice called me
   home to Thy breast,
   And I knew there was welcome
    for me.

Welcome for me, Saviour, from Thee ;
A smile and a welcome for me,
Now, like a dove, I rest in Thy love,
And find a sweet refuge in Thee....

2 I am safe in the ark ; I have folded
    my wings
   On the bosom of mercy divine ;
I am filled with the light of Thy
   presence so bright,
   And the joy that will ever be mine.

3 I am safe in the ark ; and I dread
    not the storm,
   Tho' around me the surges may
    roll ;
I will look to the skies, where the
   day never dies,
   I will sing of the joy in my soul.

792 I KNOW my heavenly Father
     knows
   The storms that would my way
    oppose,
But He can drive the clouds away,
   And turn my darkness into day.

He knows,....He knows,....
The storms that would my way op - - pose,
   He knows,....He knows,....
And tempers ev'ry wind....that....blows.

2 I know my heavenly Father knows
   The balm I need to soothe my woes ;
   And with His touch of love divine,
   He heals this wounded soul of mine.

3 I know my heavenly Father knows
   How frail I am to meet my foes ;
   But He my cause will e'er defend,
   Uphold and keep to me the end.

4 I know my heavenly Father knows
   The hour my journey here will close,
   And may that hour, O faithful Guide,
   Find me safe sheltered by Thy side.

793 I HAVE giv'n up all for Jesus,
This vain world is nought
to me,
All its pleasures are forgotten
In rememb'ring Calvary ;
Though my friends despise, forsake
me,
And on me the world looks cold,
I've a Friend that will stand by me
When the pearly gates unfold.

Life's morn will soon be waning,
And its evening bells be toll'd,
But my heart will know no sadness
When the pearly gates unfold.

2 When the voice of Jesus calls me,
And the angels whisper low,
I will lean upon my Saviour,
Through the valley as I go ;
I will claim His precious promise,
Worth to me the world of gold,
" Fear no evil, I'll be with thee
When the pearly gates unfold."

3 Just beyond the waves of Jordan,
Just beyond its chilling tide,
Blooms the tree of life immortal,
And the living waters glide ;
In that happy land of spirits
Are there stores of bliss untold,
And the angels are awaiting
Where the pearly gates unfold.

794 WHEN this passing world is
done,
When has sunk yon glowing sun,
When we stand with Christ in glory,
Looking o'er life's finished story,

Then, dear Lord, shall I fully know,
Not till then, how much I owe ;
Then, dear Lord, shall I fully know,
Not till then, how much I owe.

2 When I stand before the throne,
Dressed in beauty not my own ;
When I see Thee as Thou art,
Love Thee with unsinning heart,

3 When I hear the wicked call
On the rocks and hills to fall ;
When I see them start and shrink
On the fiery deluge brink,

4 When the praise of heav'n I hear,
Loud as thunders to the ear ;
Loud as many waters' noise,
Sweet as harp's melodious voice,

795 JUST when I am dishearten
Just when with cares c
press'd,
Just when my way is darkest,
Just when I am distress'd,
Then is my Saviour near me,
He knows my ev'ry care ;
Jesus will never leave me,
He helps my burdens bear.

His grace is enough for me, for me,
His grace is enough for me ;
Thro' sorrow and pain, thro' loss or gain
His grace is enough for me.

2 Just when my hopes have vanish
Just when my friends forsake,
Just when the fight is thickest,
Just when with fear I shake ;
Then comes a still small whisper,
" Fear not, my child, I'm near,'
Jesus brings peace and comfort,
I love His voice to hear.

3 Just when my tears are flowing,
Just when with anguish bent,
Just when temptation's hardest,
Just when with sadness rent ;
Then comes a thought of comfort
" I know my Father knows,"
Jesus has grace sufficient
To conquer all my foes.

796 BOW'D beneath your burd
is there none to share ?
Weary...with the journey, is th
none to care ?
Courage, way-worn trav'ler, he
your Lord's commands,
There's a thought to cheer yc
Jesus understands.

Yes,...He understands,
All His ways are best,
Hear,...He calls to you,
" Come to Me and rest."
Leave the unknown future in the Maste
hands,
Whether sad or joyful, Jesus understands.

2 Ev'ry heavy burden He will glac
share ;
Are you sad and weary ? Jesus k
a care :
Well He knows the pathway o
life's burning sands,
Courage, fainting pilgrim, Jes
understands.

Tho' temptation meet you, Jesus
can sustain,
Life has vexing problems which He
can explain ;
Serve Him where He sends you, tho'
in distant lands ;
Do not doubt or question, Jesus
understands.

Weary heart, He calls you, "Come
to Me and rest,"
Does the path grow rugged ? yet
His way is best ;
Leave the unknown future in the
Master's hands,
Whether sad or joyful, Jesus under-
stands.

97 I'M pressing on the upward
way,
New heights I'm gaining ev'ry day ;
Still praying, as I onward bound,
"Lord, plant my feet on higher
ground."

Lord, lift me up and let me stand,
By faith, on heaven's table-land ;
A higher plane than I have found,
Lord, plant my feet on higher ground.

My heart has no desire to stay
Where doubts arise and fears dismay ;
Tho' some may dwell where these
abound,
My pray'r, my aim is higher ground.

I want to live above the world,
Tho' Satan's darts at me are hurled ;
For faith has caught the joyful soun l
The song of saints on higher ground.

I want to scale the utmost height,
And catch a gleam of glory bright ;
But still I 'll pray till heav'n I 've
found,
"Lord, lead me on to higher ground."

98 O HOUSE of many mansions,
Thy doors are open wide,
And dear are all the faces
Upon the other side ;
Thy portals, they are golden,
And those who enter in
Shall know no more of sorrow,
Of weariness and sin.

O house of many mansions,
Thy doors are open wide,
And dear are all the faces
Upon the other side.

2 O house of many mansions,
My weary spirit waits,
And longs to join the ransom'd
Within thy pearly gates,
Who enter thro' thy portals,
The mansions of the blest ;
Who come to thee aweary,
And find in thee their rest.

3 O house of many mansions,
O house not made with hands,
I sigh for thee while waiting
Within these border lands ;
I know that but in dying
Thy threshold is cross'd o'er ;
There shall be no more sorrow
In thy for-ever-more.

799 HOW dear to my heart is the
story of old,
The story that ever is new,
The message that saints of all ages
have told,
The message so tender and true.

The story that never grows old,....
Though over and over 'tis told,....
The story so dear, bringing heaven so near,
Sweet story that never grows old.

2 It came to my heart when, all fet-
tered by sin,
I sat in the prison of doubt ;
Like angel of old, the glad story
came in
And led me triumphantly out.

3 It comes to my soul when the tempter is nigh
With snares for my way-weary
feet ;
It tells of the rock that is higher
than I,
And leads to its blissful retreat.

4 When sorrow is mine, and on pillows
of stone
My aching head seeks for repose,
This story brings comfort and peace
from the throne,
My desert blooms forth like the
rose.

5 When down in the "valley and
shadow of death,"
I enter the gloom of the grave,
I'll tell the old story with life's latest
breath,
Of Christ and His power to save.

800 THE Lord hath declared, and
    the Lord will perform ;
" Behold ! I am near to deliver,
A refuge and fortress, a covert in
    storm ; "
He keepeth His promise for ever.

  For ever ! for ever ! O not for a day !
  He keepeth His promise for ever !
  To all who believe, to all who obey,
  He keepeth His promise for ever !

2 Who seek Him shall find Him, shall
    find Him to-day,
The word is to all, " whosoever ! "
No soul that entreateth He turneth
    away ;
He keepeth His promise for ever.

3 Tho' often my toil seems but labour
    in vain,
I leave with the Lord my en-
    deavour !
I patiently wait for the sunshine and
    rain,
He keepeth His promise for ever.

4 My heart may sink low in the depths
    of its woe,
But never, He tells me, O never !
The frail, bruised reed will He break
    and I know
He keepeth His promise for ever.

5 The bonds that unite us in earth's
    dearest ties,
The rude hand of Time will dis-
    sever ;   [skies ;
But we shall renew them again in the
He keepeth His promise for ever.

801 THEY shall be comforted ;
    sorrowing heart,
Soon every cloud will for ever depart;
Joy, wondrous joy, in that beautiful
    day,
When God shall wipe ev'ry tear-drop
    away.

  Never a sorrow, never a fear,
  Never a shadow, never a tear,
  They shall be comforted in that sweet day,
  When God shall wipe ev'ry tear-drop away.

2 They shall be comforted, Jesus says
    so,   [know ;
  True and eternal His promise we
Gentle His smile, and how tender
    His voice,
Bidding His children in Him to
    rejoice.

3 They shall be comforted ; yea ev
    here,
Blessed the mourner whom Jes
    shall cheer ;
Sunbeams of glory thro' tim
    fleeting show'rs,   [our
Heaven around us—this Saviour

4 They shall be comforted ; rise th
    and shine,
Shine in the beauty of love so divin
Let others find there the " s
    waters " flow,   [s
They may be comforted, Jesus sa

802 BEHOLD the precious Lamb
    God,
Who died upon the tree,
That guilty sinners, such as I,
Might thro' His grace be free.

  Thy bound - - - less love I'll sing,
  Thy grace....so full and free,
  'Tis under Thy protecting wing
  My soul delights to be !

2 Behold the healing streams of gra
  That from His side did flow,
I plunged beneath the crimson flo
  That washes white as snow.

3 Behold the Cross He bore for me,
  Whereby He saved my soul ;
His matchless grace shall be n
    theme
While countless ages roll.

803 I HAVE perfect peace to-da
    All my sins are washed away
Hiding 'neath the crimson blood,
I am reconciled to God.

  Under the blood, under the blood,   [blo
  Pardoning and cleansing I found under t
  Under the blood, under the blood,
  There I for ever will hide, under the blood.

2 What a work the Lord has done !
What a work of grace begun !
All my sins are cover'd o'er ;
He remembers them no more.

3 Wondrous is God's grace to me,
Making me for ever free,
Sanctifying me to God,
Thro' the all-prevailing blood.

4 So in gladness I go on,
Till the Master's work is done,
Trusting in atoning blood,
Walking in the love of God.

04 PEACE like a river is flooding
    my soul,
Since Christ, my Saviour, maketh
    me whole ;   [be—
Sweet peace abiding my portion shall
Jesus, my Saviour, is precious to me.

> Pre - - cious to me,.....
> Pre - - cious is He ;.....
> Jesus shall ever..be   pre - - cious to me...

Joy is abounding—my heart gaily
    sings,
Cleave I the heavens, mount up on
    wings ;   [free—
Christ hath exalted, my soul He set
Jesus, my Saviour, is precious to me.

Oh, precious Jesus, how lovely Thou
    art !
Come, and abiding, rule in my heart ;
Break ev'ry fetter, Thy face let me
    see,   [me.
Then Thou shalt ever be precious to

05 I KNOW not the hour of His
    coming,
Nor how He will speak to my
    heart ;
Or whether at morning or mid-day
    My spirit to Him will depart.

> But I know..I shall wake in the likeness
> Of Him..I am longing to see ;
> I know..that mine eyes shall behold Him,
> Who died..for a sinner like me.

I know not the bliss that awaits me,
    At rest with my Saviour above ;
I know not how soon I shall enter
    And bathe in the ocean of love.

Perhaps in the midst of my labour
    A voice from my Lord I shall hear ;
Perhaps in the slumber of mid-night,
    Its message may fall on my ear.

I know not, but oh I am watching,
    My lamp ever burning and bright !
I know not if Jesus will call me
    At morning, at noon, or at night.

06 I CANNOT tell thee whence it
    came,
This peace within my breast ;
But this I know, there fills my soul
    A strange and tranquil rest.

> There's a deep, settled peace in my soul,...
> There's a deep, settled peace in my soul,...
> Though the billows of sin near me roll,
> He abides, Christ abides.

2 Beneath the toil and care of life
    This hidden stream flows on ;
My weary soul no longer thirsts,
    Nor am I sad and lone.

3 I cannot tell the half of love,
    Unfeigned, supreme, divine,
That caused my darkest, inmost self,
    With beams of hope to shine.

4 I cannot tell thee why He chose
    To suffer and to die ;
But if I suffer here with Him,
    I'll reign with Him for aye.

807 IN land or store I may be poor ;
    My place unknown, my name
    obscure ;
Of this I have the witness sure ;
    O bless the Lord, I've Jesus.

> What tho' the world its gifts deny,
> I've riches more than gold can buy—
> The key to treasures in the sky !
> O bless the Lord, I've Jesus !

2 On life's rough sea how frail my
    barque !
But in the storm and densest dark
I have a safe and trusted ark :
    O bless the Lord, 'tis Jesus !

3 When shadows deep around me fall,
And gloom and fear my soul enthrall,
There is an arm beneath them all :
    O bless the Lord, 'tis Jesus !

4 Soon will this fleeting life be o'er ;
O then, upon the other shore
I'll be with Him for evermore,
    For evermore with Jesus !

808 LIFE wears a different face to
    me
Since I found my Saviour ;
Rich mercy at the Cross I see,
    My dying, living Saviour.

> Golden sunbeams round me play,
> Jesus turns my night to day,
> Heaven seems not far away,
> Since I found my Saviour.

2 He sought me in His wondrous love,
    So I found my Saviour ;
He brought salvation from above,
    My dear, almighty Saviour.

3 The passing clouds may intervene
    Since I found my Saviour ;
But He is with me though unseen,
    My ever-present Saviour.

4 A strong hand kindly holds my own
Since I found my Saviour ;
It leads me onward to the throne,
Oh, there I'll see my Saviour !

809 IF I could only tell Him as I
know Him,
My Redeemer who has brightened
all my way ;
If I could tell how precious is His
presence,
I am sure that you would make
Him yours to-day.

Could I tell..it, could I tell..it,
How the sunshine of His presence lights my
way;
I would tell..it, I would tell..it,
And I'm sure that you would make Him yours
to-day.

2 If I could only tell you how He loves
you,
And if we could thro' the lonely
garden go,   [pardon,
If I could tell His dying pain and
You   would   worship   at   His
wounded feet, I know.

3 If I could tell how sweet will be His
welcome
In that home whose matchless
beauty ne'er was told ;
The Father's mansions stand by
living waters,
And the trees of healing shades
the streets of gold.

4 But I can never tell Him as I know
Him :
Human tongue can never tell all
love divine ;   [Him ;
I only can entreat you to accept
You can know Him only when you
make Him thine.

810 OH, bless the Lord, He cleansed
my soul,
And filled my lips with singing ;
He came in my poor, sinful heart,
And set the joybells ringing.

Oh, praise the Lord, He first loved me,
I feel new life upspringing ;
He came in my poor, sinful heart,
And set the joybells ringing.

2 He placed my feet upon the Rock,
The only sure foundation ;
He shows me wonders of His grace,
The blessings of salvation.

3 His promise is " for all the days."
His love for me is caring ;
While in the " Father's House
above,
A mansion He's preparing.

4 His love is calling, seeking still,
Come, ev'ry burden bringing ;
The touch of Christ within yo
heart
Will set the joybells ringing.

811 FOR God so lov'd this sin'
world,
His Son He freely gave,
That whosoever would believe,
Eternal life should have.

'Tis true, O yes, 'tis true,....
God's wonderful promise is true ;....
For I've trusted, and tested, and tried
And I know God's promise is true.....

2 I was a wayward, wand'ring chil
A slave to sin and fear,
Until this blessed promise fell
Like music on my ear.

3 The " whosoever " of the Lord,
I trusted was for me ;
I took Him at His gracious word,
From sin to set me free.

4 Eternal life begun below
Now fills my heart and soul :
I'll sing His praise for evermore,
Who has redeemed my soul.

812 *Special Solo, for words see N
573.*

813 JUST to trust in the Lord, ju
to lean on His Word,
Just to feel I am His ev'ry day
Just to walk by His side with H
Spirit to guide,
Just to follow where He leads t
way.

Just to say what He wants me to say,....
And be still when He whispers to me
Just to go where He wants me to go,..
Just to be what He wants me to be.

2 When my way darkest seems, wh
are blighted my dreams,
Just to feel that the Lord knowe
best ;
Just to yield to His will, just to tru
and be still,
Just to lean on His bosom a
rest.

Then my heart will be light, then my
    path will be bright,
  If I've Jesus for my dearest friend ;
Counting all loss but gain, such a
    friend to obtain,   [end.
  True and faithful He'll be to the

14 ON the Cross my Saviour
        bought me,
In the wilderness He sought me,
To His blessed fold He brought me,
    For He loves even me,
    He loves even me ;
To His blessed fold He brought me,
    Jesus loves even me.

Soft as ev'ning dewdrops falling,
Is His voice so sweetly calling,
More and more my soul enthralling,
    For He loves even me,
    He loves even me ;
More and more my soul enthralling,
    Jesus loves even me.

Since that happy day He found me,
Everlasting arms surround me ;
With His mercies He hath crowned
    me,
    For He loves even me,
    He loves even me ;   [me,
With His mercies He hath crowned
    Jesus loves even me.

All my needs to Him I'm bringing,
To His keeping hand I'm clinging,
And my heart for joy is singing,
    For He loves even me,
    He loves even me ;
And my heart with joy is singing,
    Jesus loves even me.

Tho' the ills of life may grieve me,
Yet I know He'll never leave me,
To His glory He'll receive me,
    For He loves even me,
    He loves even me ;
To His glory He'll receive me,
    Jesus loves even me.

15 THERE'S One **above** all
        earthly friends,
Whose love all earthly love tran-
    scends,
It is my Lord and Christ divine,
My Lord, because I know He's mine.
I know He's mine,.. this Friend so dear,..
He lives with me,.. He's ever near ;..
Ten thousand charms..around Him shine,..
And, best of all, I know He's mine.

2 He's mine because He died for me,
  He saved my soul, He set me free ;
  With joy I worship at His shrine,
  And cry, " Praise God, I know He's
      mine."

3 He's mine because He's in my heart,
  And never, never will we part ;
  Just as the branch is to the vine,
  I'm joined to Christ ; I know He's
      mine.

4 Some day upon the streets of gold
  Mine eyes His glory shall behold,
  Then, while His arms around me
      twine,
  I'll cry for joy, " I know He's mine."

816 I WAS poor as the poorest out-
        cast from the fold,
  I sank by the wayside with hunger
      and cold ;
  But He bade me look up, all His
      riches behold ;
  O the wealth of the world is Jesus.
I was poor as the poorest outcast from the fold,
But He gave me great treasures of silver and
    gold,
And a mansion above that will never grow old,
For the wealth of the world is Jesus.

2 I was poor as the poorest, I shrank
      from the throng,   [me long ;
  I hid in the darkness that dwelt with
  But He came like the morning, with
      sunlight and song,
  Now the light of my life is Jesus.

3 I was poor as the poorest, I wandered
      alone.   [stone ;
  No dwelling had I, and my pillow a
  But I heard someone whisper, " I'll
      make thee My own " ;
  Now the peace of my heart is Jesus.

4 I was poor as the poorest, no riches
      had I,
  But Jesus, my Saviour, came down
      from the sky,
  And He went to the Cross, there to
      suffer and die,   [Jesus.
  And my soul was redeemed by

5 I was poor as the poorest till Jesus
      stooped low,
  And washed me and cleansed me as
      white as the snow ;
  I have bathed in the blood, I am
      under the flow,
  O the power to save is Jesus.

817 IN looking through my tears one day
   I saw Mount Calvary ;
Beneath the Cross there flowed a stream
   Of grace enough for me.....

   Grace is flowing from Calvary,....
      Grace as fathomless as the sea,....
   Grace for time and eternity,....
      Grace enough for me !

2 While standing there my trembling heart,
   Once full of agony,
Could scarce believe the sight I saw
   Of grace enough for me....

3 While I beheld my ev'ry sin
   Nailed to the cruel tree,
I felt a flood go thro' my soul
   Of grace enough for me....

4 When I am safe within the veil,
   My portion there will be
To sing thro' all the years to come
   Of grace enough for me....

818 WHERE shall I go, Lord, where shall I go ?
Wisdom to guide me Thou wilt bestow ;
Help me to go, Lord, where Thou dost lead,
Trusting Thy promise, " Grace for all need."

What shall it be,..Lord, what shall it be ?..
   How can I serve..Thee, serve Thee best ?..
Speak unto me, Lord, speak unto me,
   Help me to shrink from no test.

2 What shall I say, Lord, what shall I say ?   [day ;
Thou art my Teacher, *teach* me to-
Only and ever help me to be
Speaking for Thee, Lord, speaking for Thee.

3 What shall I read, Lord, what shall I read ?
Here Thy protection ever I need ;
Led by Thy Spirit sent from above,
E'en through temptation safely I'll move.

4 Purchased by Thee, Lord, now I am Thine,
Time, thought, and effort never-more mine ;   [be
Thou hast redeem'd me, help me to
Shining for Thee, Lord, *only* for Thee.

819 THE way of the cross mea[ns] sacrifice,
   As to God you yield your all.
To be laid on the altar, the place [of] death,
   Where fire will surely fall.

'Tis the way of the Cross, are you willing this ?
   What does bearing the Cross mean to you
You who've given yourself, your all to God
   To God are you wholly true ?

2 As the voice of song and prayer raise,
   How easy to say, " We give all !
Till some rougher cross lies ju[st] before,
   And sterner is duty's call.

3 Do not falter then, or, true to dea[th]
   Just die on the cross in the way,
Till the fulness of life from t[he] Living One
   Is filling you day by day ?

4 'Tis the plan of life, for you die [to] live—
   One with Jesus crucified ;   [yo]
With the life alone to be liv'd thr[u]
   Of the risen, the glorified.

820 TO me, dear Saviour, yes, [to] me,
   Speak out Thy utmost will,
What Thy great love doth bid me [do]
   I surely can fulfil.

There is not in my heart left one treasu[re] dear Lord,
   That I would not yield gladly to Thee,
Only let in Thy mercy, Thy pleadings heard,
   They shall gladly be answered by me.

2 To me, dear Saviour, yes, to me,
   Thy gracious pardon show,
That not one sin I've ever sinned
   May unforgiven go.

3 To me, dear Saviour, yes, to me,
   The floodgates open wide,
That even I may stoop and wash
   Within the crimson tide.

4 To me, dear Saviour, yes, to me,
   To me, the least of all,
With all my consciousness of gui[lt]
   Thou hast for me a call.

5 To me, dear Saviour, yes, to me,
   Thy saving power be given,
Then shall I know why I have live[d]
   And what on earth is heaven.

821 NO, no, no, He never will forsake me,
No, no, no, no evil can o'ertake me ;
　His love will ever last,
　Till all of earth is past,
Oh, no, He never will forsake me.

No, no, no, He never will deceive me,
No, no, no, His words shall never grieve me ;
　I know His love is true,
　And what He says He'll do,
Oh, no, He never will deceive me.

No, no, no, He never will desert me,
No, no, no, no grief can ever hurt me ;
　For on His throbbing breast
　I can most sweetly rest,
Oh, no, He never will desert me.

No, no, no, He never will reject me,
No, no, no, His blood will e'er protect me ;
　And when before His throne
　I shall not stand alone,
No, no, He never will reject me.

822 TELL me about the Master !
　　I am weary and worn tonight,
The day lies behind me in shadow,
　And only the ev'ning is light !
Light with a radiant glory
　That lingers about the West,
My poor heart is a-weary, a-weary,
　And longs like a child for rest.

Tell me about the Master !
　Of the wrongs He for us forgave ;
Of love and of tender compassion,
　Of love that was mighty to save ;
Sad is my heart and a-weary
　Of woes and the trials of life,
Of the wrongs that are stalking in noonday,
　Of falsehood, and sin, and strife.

Yet what I know of sorrow
　And temptations that oft befall,
The infinite Master had suffered,
　And knoweth and pitieth all.
Tell me the sweetest old story
　That falls on each wound like balm
And my heart that was bruised and broken,
　Shall grow well, and strong, and calm.

823 IF waves of affliction should over thee roll,
　Tho' tempests around thee may sweep,
No storms on life's ocean can injure thy soul,
　The Saviour has promised to keep.
Hold thy faith steady, be not afraid,
Jesus will keep ev'ry promise He's made.

2 Whene'er thou art weary, and long seems the road,
　If laden with care thou art press'd,
Thy Saviour has promised to carry thy load,
　Has promised to give thee His rest.

3 If thou hast been praying for more of His grace,
　Hast pray'd to know more of His will,
Hast pray'd to be held in His loving embrace,
　He's promised such pray'rs to fulfil.

4 Thy dear, loving Saviour has gone to prepare
　A mansion in glory for thee,
He's promised to take thee to live with Him there,
　If thou only faithful wilt be.

824 IN tender compassion and wonderful love,　　　[high ;
　The Father looks down from on
He knoweth the raven hath need of its food,
　And heareth in mercy its cry.
The raven He feedeth, then why should I fear ?
To the heart of the Father His children are dear ;
So, if the way darkens or storms gather o'er,
I'll simply look upward and trust Him the more.

2 His arm is abundantly able to save,
　His eye is a guide to my feet ;
Since love sought and found me, I constantly dwell
　With Him in companionship sweet

3 No need have I ever to trouble my breast,
　Or fear what the morrow may bring ;
The heart of the Father is planning my way,
　And I am a child of a King.

825 THO' your sins may be red
and like scarlet,
Outnumb'ring the sands on the
shore,
Yet thro' Christ and His infinite
mercy
They're cleans'd and remember'd
no more.

Remember'd no more,
Remember'd no more,
Yet thro' Christ and His infinite mercy,
Your sins are remember'd no more.

3 Hear the voice that in love now
entreats you
To enter the wide-open door
That will lead to the kingdom of
heaven,
Where sins are remember'd no
more.

3 At the door of your heart Christ is
knocking,
He often has knock'd there before,
Let Him in, He'll forgive your transgressions,
And they'll be remember'd no
more.

826 WHEN my heart is sad with
life's cares and toils,
I will hush my troubled spirit's
anxious cry,
For the day is coming fast when my
cares shall all be past,
I shall see Him, I shall see Him
by and by.

I shall see Him ! My Redeemer !
O my heart, be brave, be strong !..
I shall see Him, and I'll praise Him,
With an everlasting song.

2 When the path is rough and the way
is hard,
And no resting for my weary feet
is nigh ;
I will bravely press along, singing
still my hopeful song,
I shall see Him, I shall see Him
by and by.

3 When the day grows dark, and the
clouds o'erhang,
And they close out all the sunshine from the sky ;
Tho' in darkness I abide, He is still
my faithful Guide,
I shall see Him, I shall see Him
by and by.

4 Then, my heart be brave, and m
soul rejoice,
For His promise standeth sure
on it rely ;
And for all the care and pain the
shall be eternal gain,
When I see Him, when I see Hi
by and by.

827 BLEST revelation, wondro
salvation,
God in love doth for the lost
earth provide ;
Sins like a mountain, lost in t
fountain,
Calv'ry's stream for ever flows,
cleansing tide.

Safe in the hollow of His hand,....
Safe in the hollow of His hand,....
To His promise clinging, evermore I'm singin
I am safe within the hollow of God's ha

2 Nothing can harm me, naught c
alarm me,
Fiercely tho' the tempest rage o'
sea and land ;
Waking or sleeping, safe in H
keeping,
Kept within the hollow of H
mighty hand.

3 Come, all ye burdened and hea
laden,
Without doubting all your ca
upon Him roll ;
Gracious for ever, strong to deliv
Ye shall surely find sweet rest un
your soul.

828 AFTER the sowing of sin is
done,
After the glory of earth has been wo
After the sands of thy life have
run,
Oh, what shall thy reaping be ?

Sowing, sowing, sowing in Satan's migl
Reaping, reaping, reaping eternal night

2 After the pleasures of sin are all pa
After the wealth of the world
amassed,
When the death-angel you face
the last,
Oh, what shall thy reaping be ?

Sowing, sowing, sowing in Satan's migl
Reaping, reaping, reaping eternal night

Come to the Saviour of sinners, come
    home !
Why will you longer so aimlessly
    roam ?   [come,
While He is pleading, O wanderer,
    The Master is waiting for thee.
Come home, come home, like as a weary dove,
Come home, come home, unto thy Father's
   love.

Cease from thy waywardness, Jesus
    invites ;
List to the Bride who with pleading
    unites,   [incites,
While the blest Spirit to prayer now
    The Master is waiting for thee.
Come home, come home, like as a weary dove,
Come home, come home, unto thy Father's
   love.

29 O TELL me more of Christ,
    my Saviour ;
  On this glad theme dwell o'er and
    o'er ;   [favour,
His boundless grace, His saving
    His precious name, O tell me more !
   O tell me more ! so much I need
   His power to keep, His hand to lead ;
   O tell me more of Him I love,
   Until I see His face above,...

O tell me more of love's sweet story,
   If you would cheer and comfort me
How Jesus wept, the King of glory,
   Those tender tears of sympathy.

O tell me more ! How waves of
    sorrow
Shall hear His voice say, " Peace,
    be still ; "
How after night, bright dawns the
    morrow,   [will.
   To those who trust His blessed

O tell me more ! And I repeating
   The happy news, shall spread the
    joy ;   [pleting,
Come, blessed Lord, Thy work com-
   Till songs of praise our lips employ.

30 IS there a heart that is willing
    to lay
  Burdens on Jesus' breast ?
He is so loving, and gentle, and
    true—
    Come unto Him and rest.
   Lord, it is I who need Thy love,
   Need Thy strength and power ;
   Oh, keep me, use me, and hold me fast,
   Each moment, each day, each hour.

2 Is there a heart that is lonely to-day,
    Needing a faithful Friend? [side,
  Jesus will always keep close by your
    Loving you to the end.

3 Is there a heart that has failed to
    o'ercome
  Sin with its mighty power ?
  Jesus is stronger than Satan and sin,
    Trust Him this very hour.

4 Is there a heart that is longing to
    bring
  Blessing to some lost soul ?
  Jesus is willing the weakest to use,
    Let Him thy life control.

831 I CANNOT breathe enough of
    Thee,
  O gentle breeze of love ;
More fragrant than the myrtle tree
The Rose of Sharon is to me,
  The Balm of Heaven above.

2 I cannot gaze enough on Thee,
  Thou Fairest of the Fair ;
My heart is filled with ecstasy,
As in Thy face of radiancy
  I see such beauty there.

3 I cannot work enough for Thee,
  My Saviour, Master, Friend ;
I do not wish to go out free,
But ever, always willingly,
  To serve Thee to the end.

4 I cannot sing enough of Thee,
  The sweetest name on earth,
A note so full of melody
Comes from my heart so joyously,
  And fills my soul with mirth.

5 I cannot speak enough of Thee,
  I have so much to tell ;
Thy heart it beats so tenderly
As Thou dost draw me close to Thee,
  And whisper, " All is well."

832 FILLED with my sin to the
    Saviour I came,
This power has changed me, all praise
    to His Name ;
Grace all sufficient He gives me each
    day,   [way.
Trusting I follow where He leads the
   Oh,..what a change,..since He came into my
   heart,
   Oh,..what a change,..since He bade sin depart,
   Oh,..what a change,..Jesus wrought in my
   soul,   [whole..
   Oh,..what a change, since His blood makes me

2 Changed all my grief to a heart full
        of song,
And now I'm confiding in Him all
        day long ;   [shown,
Tender compassion and love He has
Cleansed me and healed me, and
        called me His own.

3 When thro' the portals of glory I've
        passed,
I then shall be changed to His image
        at last ;   [shine,
I shall be like Him in beauty to
Ever to live in His presence divine.

833 ALL for Jesus ! all for Jesus !
        All my being's ransom'd
                pow'rs ;
All my thoughts and words and
        doings,
All my days and all my hours.
All for Jesus ! all for Jesus !
All my days and all my hours.

2 Let my hands perform His bidding,
Let my feet run in His ways ;
Let my eyes see Jesus only ;
        Let my lips speak forth His praise.
All for Jesus ! all for Jesus !
        Let my lips speak forth His praise.

3 Worldlings prize their gems of beauty,
Cling to gilded toys of dust,
Boast of wealth, and fame, and
        pleasure ;
        Only Jesus will I trust.
Only Jesus ! only Jesus !
        Only Jesus will I trust.

4 O what wonder ! how amazing !
Jesus, glorious King of kings,
Deigns to call me His beloved,
        Lets me rest beneath His wings.
All for Jesus ! all for Jesus !
        Resting now beneath His wings.

834 IF you are sad and weary, and
        burdened down with care,
And feel that you have wandered
        from the right ;
Tho' all your life seems dreary, your
        load seems hard to bear,
        Just tell Him you are coming
        home to-night.

Just tell Him you are coming home to-night,
Just tell Him you are coming home to-night;
If, weary and distressed, you long for peace and
        rest,
Just tell Him you are coming home to-night.

2 The Saviour loves you dearly, an
        longs your soul to win,
His precious love would mak
        your burden light ;
Heed now His tender pleading, an
        turn away from sin,
        Just tell Him you are comin
        home to-night.

3 He offers you forgiveness, and peac
        and joy, and rest,
He wants to make your pathwa
        fair and bright ;
His loving arms are open to fold yo
        to His breast,
        Oh, tell Him you are coming hon
        to-night.

835 MASTER, speak ! Thy servan
        heareth,
Waiting for Thy gracious Word
Longing for Thy voice that cheeret
Master, let it now be heard.
I am list'ning, Lord, for Thee :
What hast Thou to say to me ?

2 Speak to me by name, O Master,
        Let me know it is to me ;
Speak, that I may follow faster,
        With a step more firm and free,
Where the Shepherd leads the floc
        In the shadow of the Rock.

3 Master, speak ! tho' least and lowes
        Let me not unheard depart ;
Master, speak ! for oh, Thou knowe
        All the yearning of my heart.
Knowest all its truest need ;
        Speak ! and make me blest indeed

4 Master, speak ! and make me read
        When Thy voice is truly heard,
With obedience glad and steady,
        Still to follow ev'ry word.
I am list'ning, Lord, for Thee ;
Master, speak, oh, speak to me !

836 SHOULD the new daw
        breaking, a burden bring,
That your soul deems hard to bea
Seek a boon of grace for a little spac
        There is always time for pray'r
There is always time in the morning's prim
        And the golden noon-tide fair ;
There is always time 'neath the even-chim
        There is always time for pray'r.

2 With a lift of heart let the day begi
        And a moment respite spare,

Ere you press along with the toiling
throng ;
   There is always time for pray'r.

When your weary feet falter on the
path,
Tho' to pause you do not dare,
Would you find the stress of the
noon grow less ?
   There is always time for pray'r.

When the late light dies with the
setting sun,
Would you taste a balm for care ?
With a lift of heart let the day
depart ;
   There is always time for pray'r.

837 MY soul crieth out for the
Spirit,   [know
I'm hung'ring and thirsting to
The fulness of blessing He giveth ;
   Now fill me while humbly I bow.

Come in, come in ! Holy Spirit,
   Thy work of great blessing begin ;
By faith I lay hold of Thy promise,
   And claim complete vict'ry o'er sin.

O Spirit of God and of Jesus,
Blest Trinity, come and possess
My body, my soul, and my spirit,
   And fill me with Thy holiness.

My body make meet for Thy temple ;
My heart make Thou whiter than
snow ;
My spirit make loving and gentle—
   Oh, fill me, while humbly I bow.

Oh, ye that are thirsting for fulness,
Make room by forsaking all sin ;
Surrender to Him your whole nature,
   By faith let the Spirit come in.

838 WHEN the waves are rolling
fast,
And I face the threat'ning blast,
And a dark, forbidding cloud my
barque enfolds ;
Tho' the billows round me roll,
There's a calm within my soul,
Hallelujah ! praise the Lord, my
anchor holds.

I an face the tempest's shock, for I'm anchored
to the Rock,
And His mighty arm my feeble strength
upholds ;
o' the billows round me roll, there's a calm
within my soul,
Hallelujah ! praise the Lord, my anchor holds.

2   Satan tries by ev'ry art,
   And with many a fiery dart,
To affright me from the Christ my
faith beholds ;
But I trust Him more and more,
And I've proved Him o'er and o'er,
Hallelujah ! praise the Lord, my
anchor holds.

3   I am waiting for a day   [away,
   When the storms have passed
And the haven of sweet rest my eye
beholds ;
When my voyage is complete,
And I bow at Jesus' feet,
Praise the Lord for evermore, my
anchor holds.

839 SOMEBODY did a golden
deed,
Proving himself a friend in need ;
Somebody sang a cheerful song,
Bright'ning the skies the whole
day long—
   Was that somebody you ?

2 Somebody thought 'tis sweet to live,
Willingly said, " I'm glad to give ; "
Somebody fought a valiant fight,
Bravely he lived to shield the right—
   Was that somebody you ?

3 Somebody idled all the hours,
Carelessly crushed life's fairest
flowers ;
Somebody made life loss, not gain,
Thoughtlessly seemed to live in
vain—
   Was that somebody you ?

4 Somebody filled the day with light,
Constantly chased away the night ;
Somebody's work bore joy and peace,
Surely his life shall never cease—
   Was that somebody you ?

840 O SOFTLY the Spirit is
whisp'ring to me,
With tender compassion, with pitying plea ;
I hear His beseeching, and earnestly
pray,
That Jesus will make me a blessing
to-day.

Lord, make..me a blessing to-day,
A blessing to some one, I pray ;..
In all that I do, in all that I say,
O make me a blessing to-day.

2 Some heart may be longing for only
    a word,
Whose love by the Spirit is quickened
    and stirred ;
Now grant, blessed Saviour, this
    service to me,
Of speaking a comforting message
    for Thee.

3 Some soul may be plung'd in the
    darkest despair,
Whose shadows would melt in the
    sunlight of pray'r ;
O give me, dear Saviour, I humbly
    implore,
The sweet consolation that soul to
    restore.

841   IN the warfare that is raging
        For the truth and for the
        right,
When the conflict fierce is raging
    With the powers of the night ;
God needs workers, brave and true:...
May He, then, depend on you ?

    May the Lord..depend on you ?....
    Loyalty..is but His due,..
    Say, O spirit, brave and true,....
    That He may depend on you.

2 See, they come on sable pinions,
Come in strong Satanic might—
Powers come and dark dominions
    From the regions of the night.
God requires the brave and true :....
May He, then, depend on you ?

3 From His throne the Father sees us ;
    Angels help us to prevail ;
And our leader true is Jesus,
    And we shall not, cannot fail ;
Triumph crowns the brave and true,..
May the Lord depend on you ?

842   SAVED by grace, oh, wonder-
        ful story,
Jesus, the Saviour, has come from
    on high ;
Saved by grace, an heir to His glory,
    I shall inherit it by and by.

    Saved by grace, Oh, wonderful story !
      Sing it o'er and o'er again ;
    Saved by grace, oh, tell of His glory !
    Jesus is coming, coming again.

2 Saved by grace, and justified freely,
Jesus, the Crucified, rose from the
    grave ;

Saved by grace, oh, marvello
    dealing ;
Life everlasting to me He gave.

3 Saved by grace, and sanctifi
    through Him,
Christ, the Ascended, now plea
    for His own ;
Saved by grace, I sing hallelujah !
    I shall behold Him upon H
    throne.

843   JESUS the Saviour, dying o
        Calv'ry,
Purchased my pardon, setting n
    free ;   [Hir
Love so abundant, should I not ser
    When He so gladly suffer'd for m

    Lord,..I am Thine,..Saviour Divine !..
    Oh,..what a joy..just to know..Thou s
    mine !..

2 Oh, what a Saviour, tender an
    loving,
Guarding my footsteps lest
    should stray ;
Love so abundant, leading me eve
    Out of the darkness into the day

3 Constant Companion, leaving n
    never,
Bidding me follow close by H
    side ;
He is my Refuge, safely I shelter,
    Knowing He loves me whate'
    betide.

844   I HAVE a mighty Saviour,
        His love is all my song,
And since His grace redeemed me
    I praise Him all day long.

    He brought me out of darkness,
    He turned my night to day,
    For when I knew His pard'ning love
    The sin clouds rolled away.

2 No friend so kind and tender,
    And none so true as He ;
Unworthy of His goodness,
    His grace my song shall be.

3 I would that you might know Hir
    As Friend and Saviour too ;
For what He is to others
    He'll surely be to you.

4 Some day in realms of glory
    I'll see Him face to face,
And sing through endless ages
    Of His redeeming grace.

45 MY times are in my heav'nly
     Father's hands,
  Their changeful scenes I should
     not fear ;
The reason why, He fully under-
     stands,
  He will not cause a needless tear.

My times are in His hands...
What's best for me He understands,..
I'll ever trust in His unchanging love,
'Twill lead me to my home above.

My times are in my heav'nly Father's
     hands,
  The joy He sends a blessing brings ;
His light will sparkle on life's golden
     sands ;   [wings.
  I'll hide beneath His shelt'ring

My times are in my heav'nly Father's
     hands,
  Used for His glory may they be ;
Until in that most beautiful of lands,
  I'll sing of Him who died for me.

46 I HAD heard the Gospel call,
     Off'ring pardon free for all,
And I hearkened to the blessed in-
     vitation ;
  Laid my sins at Jesus' feet,
  Tasted there redemption sweet,
And He saved me with an utter-
     most salvation.

Jesus saves,...Jesus saves,..
'esus saves me with an uttermost salvation ;
  Tho' I cannot tell you how,
  Jesus fully saves me now,
With a full, and free, an uttermost salvation.

  Now the load of sin is gone,
  And by faith I travel on,
And I rest no longer under con-
     demnation ;
  For the blood has been applied,
  And my soul is satisfied
With this full and free, this utter-
     most salvation.

  From the mire and from the clay
  Jesus took my feet away,
And He placed them on the Rock,
     the sure Foundation ;
  Whether now I live or die,
  This shall be my constant cry,
Jesus saves me with an uttermost
     salvation.

847 LORD, fill us with Thy Spirit's
     might,
  That we may live as in Thy sight,
  And teach us how to pray aright ;
     We ask in Jesu's Name.

2 Lord, cleanse our hearts from ev'ry
     sin,
  And let Thy love so dwell within
  That Thou canst use our lips to win
     Some souls for Jesu's Name.

3 As we for others intercede,
  Lord, let Thy power be felt indeed,
  And some from Satan's grasp be
     freed ;
     We ask in Jesu's Name.

4 On all children lay Thy hand,
  That each may live as Thou hast
     planned,
  To serve in home or foreign land ;
     We ask in Jesu's Name.

To be sung at the close of the meeting.

5 The prayers that we have offered,
     Lord,
  " In faith," according to Thy Word,
  We thank Thee, Father, Thou hast
     heard,
     And praise in Jesu's Name. AMEN.

848 BE careful what you sow,
     For seed will surely grow ;
  The dew will fall,
     The floods will come,
     The clouds grow dark,
     And then the sun,
  And he who sows good seed to-day
     Shall reap good seed to-morrow ;
  And he who sows good seed to-day
     Shall reap with joy to-morrow.

     Be careful what you sow,...
     For seed will surely grow,...
     And he who sows good seed*to-day
     Shall reap with joy to-morrow.

2 Be careful what you sow,
     For seed will surely grow ;
  Where it may fall
     You cannot know,
     In sun or shade,
     'Twill surely grow,
  And he who sows good seed to-day
     Shall reap good seed to-morrow ;
  And he who sows good seed to-day
     Shall reap with joy to-morrow.

3 Be careful what you sow,
  The weeds you plant will grow ;
    The scattered seed
      From thoughtless hand
    Must gathered be,
      By God's command ;
  And he who sows wild oats to-day
    Must reap the crop to-morrow ;
  And he who sows wild oats to-day
    Shall reap with tears to-morrow.

4 Then let us sow good deeds,
  And not the briars and weeds ;
    Then harvest time
      Its joys shall bring,
    And when we reap
      Our hearts shall sing ;
  And he who sows good seed to-day
    Shall reap good seed to-morrow ;
  And he who sows good seed to-day
    Shall reap with joy to-morrow.

849 JESUS, Thy strength we need,
  Sowing Thy precious seed ;
  In thought, or word, or deed,
    Oh, lead us by Thy hand.

2 May we this hour be led
  In righteous paths to tread ;
  And, by Thy manna fed,
    Oh, lead us by Thy hand.

3 As this brief fleeting day
  Passes so swift away,
  May we from Thee not stray—
    Oh, lead us by Thy hand.

4 And when the hour draws nigh
  When death shall dim our eye,
  Take us to Thee on high—
    Oh, lead us by Thy hand.

850 WHEN the storm is raging and
    the heart is sad,
  Listen for the whispers of Jesus ;
  Surely you will hear them, and
    they'll make you glad,
    Listen for the whispers of Jesus.
  Listen....listen !....
  Listen for the whispers of Jesus !   [glad,
  Surely you will hear them and they'll make you
    Listen for the whispers of Jesus !

2 When beneath a burden you are
    bending low,
  Listen for the whispers of Jesus ;
  When your friends forsake you and
    the sad tears flow,
    Listen for the whispers of Jesus.

3 When the night seems endless, wh
    for courage pressed,
  Listen for the whispers of Jesus
  When the soul is weary and you si
    for rest,
  Listen for the whispers of Jesu

851 O'ER death's sea in yon bl
    city,
  There's a home for ev'ry one ;
  Purchased with a price most costl
  'Twas the blood of God's dear S
    In that city, bright city,
      Soon with loved ones I shall be :
    And with Jesus live for ever,
      In that city beyond death's sea.

2 Here we've no abiding city,
    Mansions here will soon decay
  But that city God's built firmly
    It can never pass away.

3 I have lov'd ones in that city,
    Those who left me years ago ;
  They with joy are waiting for me.
    Where no farewell tears e'er flo

4 T'ward that pure and holy city,
    Oft my longing eyes I cast ;
  Jesus whispers sweetly to me,
    Heav'n is yours when earth is pa

852 "IT is finished !" Jesus cri
    I will trust ! I will trust !
  As He bows His head and dies !
    I will trust ! I will trust !
  All my load on Him was laid ;
  And my debt He freely paid ;
  He my peace with God has made ;
    I will trust ! I will trust !
    I will trust !..I will trust !....
      And I will not be afraid !....
    I will trust !....I will trust !....
      And I will not be afraid !

2 Jesus, hear my cry to Thee,
    I will trust ! I will trust !
  Thou alone art all my plea ;
    I will trust ! I will trust !
  In Thy hands I leave my case,
  Trusting fully in Thy grace ;
  All my hope in Thee I place ;
    I will trust ! I will trust !

3 Wherefore should I doubt or fear
    I will trust ! I will trust !
  Thou, my Lord, art ever near ;
    I will trust ! I will trust !

May I close to Thee abide,
Ever keeping near Thy side,
There from ev'ry storm to hide ;
　　I will trust ! I will trust !

53　　I'VE been redeemed, all glory
　　　　　　to the Lamb,
Jesus has loved me, I'm saved, I
　　know I am ;
O wondrous love that caused my
　　Lord to die,
Now I will serve Him, then reign
　　with Him on high.

　　e been redeemed, yes, I have been redeemed,
　　Glory to Jesus ! 'tis sweet for me to know ;
　　e been redeemed, yes, I have been redeemed,
　　O hallelujah ! my soul is white as snow.

O sinner, listen, I once was lost like
　　you,
But Jesus found me, and saved me
　　thro' and thro' ;
Now He is waiting for you to make a
　　start,
Come to Him quickly and choose
　　the better part.

I'm so glad I've found the way of life,
Free from all sorrow, from sin, and
　　from strife ;
I am so glad I'm in this holy way,
O hallelujah ! I'm happy night and
　　day.

I'm going home, all glory to the
　　Lamb,
Jesus will take me now just as I am ;
Soon I'll be there with friends who've
　　gone before ;
O happy meeting ! we'll meet to
　　part no more.

4　　NEVER alone in this earthly
　　　　　　way,
　　Somebody cares, Somebody cares ;
I have a Helper each busy day ;
　　Somebody cares, 'tis Jesus.
Somebody cares when the clouds
　　hang low,
Cares when my heart is o'erwhelmed
　　with woe,
Cares, and is marking my path below ;
　　Somebody cares, 'tis Jesus.

　　Some - - body cares for me,
　　Some - --body cares for me,
　　In all my life His kind hand I see,
　　Somebody cares, 'tis Jesus.

2　When I am singing a happy song,
　　Somebody cares, Somebody cares ;
　When I am fighting against the
　　　wrong,
　　Somebody cares, 'tis Jesus.
Somebody cares when I stand alone,
Cares when the pleasures of earth are
　　gone,
Cares when my false hopes with
　　wings have flown ;
　　Somebody cares, 'tis Jesus.

3　When I am weary and long for rest,
　　Somebody cares, Somebody cares ;
　When by the tempter I'm sorely
　　　pressed,
　　Somebody cares, 'tis Jesus.
Somebody cares, and, whate'er
　　betide,　　　　　　　　[side,
Walks ev'ry hour by the Christian's
Love so amazing will e'er abide,
　　Somebody cares, 'tis Jesus.

855　　DAY is dying in the west,
　　　　　　Heav'n is touching earth with
　　　　　　　rest,
Wait and worship while the night
Sets her evening lamps alight
　　Through all the sky.

　　Holy, Holy, Holy, Lord God of Hosts !
　　Heav'n and earth are full of Thee ;
　　Heav'n and earth are praising Thee,
　　　O Lord, most high !

2　While the deep'ning shadows fall,
Heart of love enfolding all,
Thro' the glory and the grace
Of the stars that veil Thy face,
　　Our hearts ascend.

3　When for ever from our sight
Pass the stars, the day, the night,
Lord of angels, on our eyes
Let eternal morning rise,
　　And shadows end.

856　　CAME He to Bethlehem's
　　　　　　manger,
　　Infant, yet glorious Lord ;
Stood He in Temple and uttered
　　Wondrous and mystical word ;
Toiled He in workshop, and lowly,
　　Bore He the burden of life ;
Calmly, and sweetly, and purely,
　　Mixed He in anger or strife.

　　Love brought Him down from the glory,
　　Love made Him come from the sky,
　　Love is His heart for the sinner,
　　Led Him to suffer and die.

2 Passed He the fiery temptation,
　　Was He the homeless and lone,
Was He despised and rejected,
　　Claimed He dark sorrow His own ;
Came He to Olivet's garden,
　　Drank He the dregs of the cup,
Say, was that holy cheek sullied,
　　Gave He His precious life up.

3 Went He to Pilate and Herod,
　　Bore He the lash and the nail,
Prayed He His Father to pardon,
　　Died He with agony's wail ;
Lay He in grave of the stranger,
　　Rose He in majesty grand,
Went He to claim as a victor
　　Trophies as countless as sand.

857 GOD will take care of me ;
　　　　Here will I rest,
　　Trusting His promise true,
　　　　Safe on His breast.
　　Changeful may be my lot,
　　His mercy changeth not ;
　　No child of His forgot,
　　　　In Jesus blest.

2 God will take care of me ;
　　　Hushing my fear ;
　When dangers round I see,
　　　His voice I hear ;
　Then let my soul be brave,
　High though the wind and wave,
　Greater His power to save,
　　　Tenderly near.

3 God will take care of me ;
　　　Holding the helm ;
　Storms that may sweep the sea
　　　Will not o'erwhelm.
　Soon, ev'ry billow pass'd,
　I shall my anchor cast,
　Safe, safe at home at last,
　　　In joy's bright realm.

858 THERE'S joy in the home-land,
　　　there's plenty and peace,
A welcome for souls gone astray ;
Glad songs over sinners returning to
　　　God !—
　Tell someone the story to-day.

Tell someone the story to-day,....
　Tell someone,..tell someone ;..
Tell someone the story, 'twill add to His
　glory :
　Tell someone the story to-day.

2 The sinful and weary find pard
　　　and rest,
　The lame may be healed in
　　　way ;
Believing in Jesus, each soul may
　　　blest—
　Tell someone the story to-day.

3 For love like the Master's, for w
　　　dom to win,
　For patience and tenderness, pra
And, weeping, go forth to the hi
　　　ways of sin—
　Tell someone the story to-day

4 The parting commandment of Jes
　　　your King,
　Be earnest and swift to obey ;
To help the Good Shepherd
　　　" other sheep " bring,
　Tell someone the story to-day.

859 I HAVE a dear Saviour w
　　　loves me, I know,
　And whose will I delight to do.
He's present to cheer me where
　　　I go—
　Was there ever a Friend so tru

Was there ever a Friend so true ?
Was there ever a Friend so, true ?..
I often have proved Him, I ever will love H
Was there ever a Friend so true ?

2 This wonderful Friend is a hel
　　　indeed ;
　He has promised to lead me th
And closer He comes than a brot
　　　in need—
　Was there ever a Friend so tru

3 He soothes me in sorrow with so
　　　in the night,
　And inspires me with hopes ane
He fills me with courage my batt
　　　to fight—
　Was there ever a Friend so tru

4 His love is a fountain of blessing
　　　pure,
　Ever flowing for me, for you ;
His pow'r is unfailing, His prom
　　　is sure—
　Was there ever a Friend so tru

860 BECAUSE of His love
　　　　Saviour died,
　For sin of the world was crucifi

With His own blood our ransom paid,
And for our souls deliv'rance made.

Because of His love, His sacrifice !
Because of His love, oh, what a price !
He suffered and died, was crucified,
Because of His love, because of His love.

Because of His love, oh, blessed
thought,
Were wonderful deeds of mercy
wrought ;
The wind and wave obey'd His will,
Hush'd by His wondrous " Peace,
be still."

Because of His love, His blest command,
We'll send the glad word to ev'ry
land ;
His Name above all names we'll sing,
And crown Him Saviour, Priest,
and King.

861 SHOW me the way, dear
Saviour !
The shadows are falling fast.
And through the clouds above me
No ray of light is cast ;
The storm is wildly raging,
The thunders loudly roar,
The restless waves are dashing
Against the wreck-strewn shore.

Show me the way, dear Saviour,
That Thou wouldst have me go,
Show me the way, dear Saviour,
For Thou alone dost know.

Show me the way, dear Saviour !
The night is so wild and dark ;
I cannot stem the current
Unless Thou guide my barque ;
Oh, fiercer grows the tempest,
And wilder rolls the sea ;
Help ! help me, O my Saviour,
I trust alone in Thee.

Show me the way, dear Saviour !
My courage is failing fast ;
My storm-toss'd barque is sinking
But I'll be saved at last.
Come nearer, nearer to me,
And speak the word of peace
That stills the angry waters,
And bids the tempest cease.

862 IS it nothing to you that
heaven's King
Came down to this world of woe,

That He suffered and bled, and rose
from the dead,
That eternal life you might know?

Is it nothing to you that grace is free,
And that God in His love doth call ?
Is it nothing to you ? Is it nothing to you ?
Is it nothing, nothing to you ?

2 Is it nothing to you that by and by
You must travel death's dark vale,
Where Jordan's waves the pathway
laves,
And all but Christ doth fail ?

3 Is it nothing to you that some sweet
day,
In the heavenly land so fair,
You may join the song that the ran-
somed throng
Are for ever singing there ?

863 ARE you with some sorrow
burdened,
On your way no ray of light ?
Strain your ear, all heaven's watch-
ing ;
God can give you songs by night.

Weary soul,..cease your repin - - ing,
Burdened one.. God's ways are right,
Ev'ry cloud..has silver lin - - ing ;
God can give..you songs by night..

2 Paul and Silas, prison-fastened,
Shook the jail with earthquake
might ;
Bands were rent and doors were
opened ;
God had given songs by night.

3 It is oft in saddest moments
That our souls take highest flight ;
And to strains of sweetest music
God doth set the songs by night.

864 O SO long was my barque
toss'd about on life's sea,
But I've anchored in Jesus at last ;
And I heard a sweet voice gently
calling to me,
And I've anchored in Jesus at last.

All my doubtings are over, my struggling is past
And the load of my sin at His feet I have cast,
I have anchor'd in Jesus at last....

2 Safely moor'd to the Rock which no
tempest can shake,
I have anchored in Jesus at last ;

Tho' the billows in fury around me
  may break,
  I have anchored in Jesus at last.

3 In the harbour of faith there is
    safety and rest,
  I have anchored in Jesus at last ;
And a deep settled peace now is
    filling my breast,
  I have anchored in Jesus at last.

4 Deeper groweth my peace as I'm
    nearing the shore,
  I have anchored in Jesus at last ;
And by simply believing I'm safe
    evermore,
  I have anchored in Jesus at last.

865 GIVE me a sight, O Saviour,
    Of Thy wondrous love to me,
Of the love that brought Thee down
    to earth,
  To die on Calvary.
    Oh, make me understand it,
      Help me to take it in,..
    What it meant to Thee, the Holy One,
      To bear away my sin.

2 Was it the nails, O Saviour,
    That bound Thee to the tree ?
Nay, 'twas Thine everlasting love,
    Thy love for me, for me.

3 Oh, wonder of all wonders,
    That through Thy death for me,
My open sins, my secret sins,
    Can all forgiven be.

4 Then melt my heart, O Saviour,
    Bend me, yea, break me down,
Until I own Thee Conqueror,
    And Lord and Sov'reign crown.

866 JUST beyond the river Jordan,
    Just across its chilling tide,
There's a land of life eternal,
    Thro' its vales sweet waters glide.
By the crystal river flowing
    Grows the tree of life so fair ;
Many loved ones wait our coming
    In the Upper Garden there.
We..shall meet them some bright morning,..
  Rest - - ing by the waters fair ;..
They..are waiting for our coming,..
  In..the Upper Garden there...

2 Growing in the Upper Garden,
    " Flowers the earth too rudely
      pressed,"
In that land shall reach perfection
    By the heav'nly Gard'ner dressed ;

Where the flowers bloom for ever,
    Death can find no entrance ther
All is life and light eternal.
    All is joy beyond compare.

3 There the buds from earth tran
    planted
    For our coming watch and wait
In the Upper Garden growing,
    Just within the golden gate ;
Though our hearts may break wi
    sorrow,
    By the grief so hard to bear,
We shall meet them some gl
    morning
    In the Upper Garden there.

867 SHE came to Jesus, one of c
    Who sent her He has n
      revealed ;
This only are we plainly told,
    How she by simple faith w
      healed.
    Oh ! touch Him too, oh ! touch Him to
    There's virtue still in Christ for thee ;
    His blood can cleanse, His power can sav
      Though crimson-dyed your sins may b

2 She heard, she came, she touch'd t
    hem
    Of His loose garment in the way
Immediately through her weak fra
    She felt the thrill of health th
      day.

3 I came with all my guilt and sin ;
    Knelt in contrition at His feet ;
The Holy Spirit entered in,
    And wrought in me a chan
      complete.

4 Oh come to Him, and rest assure
    Whate'er thy sin He'll welco
      thee ;
Who ever came to Him was cured
    And from all doubts and fear s
      free.

868 A HOMELESS Strang
    amongst us came,
    To this land of sin and mournin
He walked in a path of sorrow a
    shame,   [scornin
    Thro' insult, and hate, a
A Man of Sorrows, of toils, of tea
    An outcast man and lonely ;
But He looked on me, and th
    endless years,
    Him must I serve, Him only.

And then from this sad and sorrowful
  land,
  This land of tears, He departed;
But the light of His eyes, and the
  touch of His hand,
  Had left me broken-hearted;
And I clave to Him as He turn'd
  His face
  From the land that was mine no
  longer,
The land I'd loved in the golden days
  Ere I knew the love that was
  stronger.

And I must abide where He abode,
  And follow His steps for ever;
His people, my people; His God,
  my God,
  In the land beyond the river;
His face in glory I'll soon behold,
  And dear ones who've gone before
  me.
With the blood-bought throng in
  that heavenly fold
  I'll sing redemption's story!

39 O SHIPWRECKED soul, far
        out on sin's dark wave,
With no help near, no life-line
  thrown to save;
No boat to launch, no crew with
  courage brave;
  Thy only help is Jesus.

Jesus has conquer'd the storm-toss'd sea,
Walk'd the wild billows of Galilee;
He is the Saviour for you, and me;
Jesus, only Jesus.

O shipwrecked soul, no wave can
  drown the voice
Of Him who speaks to make thy
  soul rejoice;
'Midst tempest swirl, make Jesus
  now thy choice;
  Thy only help is Jesus.

O shipwrecked soul, He waits with
  pitying eye,
Behold thee; He'll hear thy helpless
  cry;
O venture now, trust fully, He is
  nigh;
  Thy only help is Jesus.

70 A LAMP in the night, a song
        in time of sorrow;
A great glad hope, which faith can
  ever borrow,

To gild the passing day with the
  glory of the morrow,
  Is the hope of the coming of the
  Lord.

Blessed hope,..blessed hope,..
  Blessed hope of the coming of the Lord;
How the aching heart it cheers;
How it glistens through our tears;
  Blessed hope of the coming of the Lord.

2 A star in the sky, a beacon bright to
     guide us;
   An anchor sure to hold when storms
     betide us;
   A refuge for the soul, where in quiet
     we may hide us,
     Is the hope of the coming of the
     Lord.

3 A call of command, like trumpet
     clearly sounding,
   To make us bold when evil is sur-
     rounding;
   To stir the sluggish heart, and to
     keep in good abounding,
     Is the hope of the coming of the
     Lord.

4 A word from the One to all our
     hearts the dearest,
   A parting word to make Him aye
     the nearest;
   Of all His precious words, the
     sweetest, brightest, clearest,
     Is the hope of the coming of the
     Lord.

871 WHERE He may lead me I
         will go,
For I have learned to trust Him so
And I remember 'twas for me,
That He was slain on Calvary.

Jesus shall lead me night and day,
Jesus shall lead me all the way:
He is the truest Friend to me,
For I remember Calvary.

2 O I delight in His command,
   Love to be led by His dear hand,
   His divine will is sweet to me,
   Hallowed by blood-stained Calvary.

3 Onward I go, nor doubt nor fear,
   Happy with Christ, my Saviour,
     near;
   Trusting some day that I shall see
   Jesus, my Friend of Calvary.

872 EV'RY *step* with Jesus
　　Thus we love to go,
Down life's shady pathway
　　Into ev'ning's glow.

Ev'ry power for Jesus,
　Brain and heart and will,
Used at highest pressure
　Till the pulse be still ;
Crown of Glory waiting,
　On the further shore,
Sing with glad rejoicing,
　Praises evermore.

2 Ev'ry *day* with Jesus
　　When the morning breaks,
Whispering life's secrets
　　Ere the road we take.

3 Ev'ry *nerve* for Jesus
　　Strained in mighty toil,
Just to bring the Master
　　Heaps of golden spoil.

4 Ev'ry *man* for Jesus,
　　What a mighty throng,
Then would swell the chorus
　　Of the victor's song !

CHOIR PIECES

873 WILL you come and help us
　　　in our work,
　　For Jesus' sake ?
Will you fight with enemies that lurk,
　　For Jesus' sake ?
The pow'rs of evil stronger grow,
Within, without, we meet the foe ;
Will you lend a hand to strike a blow,
　　For Jesus' sake ?

For Jesus' sake, for Jesus' sake,
What will you do for Jesus' sake ?
Let each one bring some worthy thing
　　For Jesus' sake.

2 Will you make the homes of darkness
　　bright
　　　For Jesus' sake ?
Will you be an ever-shining light
　　For Jesus' sake ?
Against all forms of deadly sin,
Against all evil thoughts within,
Will you strike as one who means to
　win
　　For Jesus' sake ?

3 Will you curb the quick and angry
　　word
　　　For Jesus' sake ?
Will you bear the yoke of our dear
　　Lord
　　　For Jesus' sake ?
When work is hard and duty dry,
And easy seems the tempting lie,
Will you speak the truth, although
　you die,
　　For Jesus' sake ?

4 Will you turn from every evil way
　　For Jesus' sake ?
Will you climb up higher day by day
　　For Jesus' sake ?

Amid the stress of earthly strife,
Amid a world with evil rife,
Will you try to live the higher life
　　For Jesus' sake ?

874 HAVE you toiled all night ne
　　　the shore in vain ?
　　Push away from the shore, laun
　　　out ;
　Where the flood is deep cast yo
　　　nets again,
　　Push away from the shore, laun
　　　out ;
　There a blessing waits for your sou
　　　to take,　　　　　　　[stra
　　Haste away from the barr
　Toil no more in vain where t
　　　surges break,
　　Launch out is your Lord's co
　　　mand.

Launch out,..launch out,..
Push away from the shore, launch out,.
God's grace flows free, like a mighty se
And the Master calls, " Launch out ! "

2 Have your souls grown faint wi
　　　the vigil long ?
　　Push away from the shore, laun
　　　out ;
　Put your trust in Christ, He v
　　　make you strong,
　　Push away from the shore, laun
　　　out ;
　Be no more content with a mea
　　　share
　　From your Father's abunda
　　　store ;
　Ask Him largely now, He will h
　　　your pray'r,
　　And give till you want no more

Jesus bids to-day ev'ry weary soul
   Push away from the shore, launch
     out ;
Hear His loving voice, He will make
   you whole,
   Push away from the shore, launch
     out ;
Leave the shore of sin with its
   shallowness,
   It has nothing of life to give ;
Look to Jesus now, who alone can
   bless,
   Launch out on His grace and live.

75   ARE you sowing the seed of
     the kingdom, brother,
   In the morning bright and fair ?
Are you sowing the seed of the
   kingdom, brother,
   In the heat of the noonday's glare?

r the harvest time is coming on,..
And the reapers' work will soon be done,..
ll your sheaves be many, will you garner any
'or the gath'ring at the harvest home ?

Are you sowing the seed of the
   kingdom, brother,
   In the still and solemn night ?
Are you sowing the seed of the
   kingdom, brother,
   For a harvest pure and white ?

Are you sowing the seed of the
   kingdom, brother,
   All along the fertile way ?
Would you glean golden sheaves in
   the harvest, brother,
   Come and join the ranks to-day.

76   PRAISE the Lord with heart
     and voice,
   Joyfully serving your King,
Come and worship at His throne,
   Lovingly, gratefully sing ;
Happy ev'ry hour, trusting in His
wer,
   Unto the Giver of our salvation
    praises bring.

   Praise Him ! sing with melody,
    Heart and voice.
   Praise Him everlastingly,
    Come, rejoice ;
   Hail Him, Lord, most glorious,
   Mighty One victorious,
    Praise His Holy Name.
   Praise Him, heav'nly company,
    Angels bright.

Crown Him now and evermore,
   Lord of light :
Praise Him, all creation,
God of our salvation,
Boundless in majesty,
King eternal ;
   Praise His Name.

2 Praise the dear Redeemer's Name,
   Crown Him with beauty and light,
Just and true are all His ways,
   Wonderful, boundless His might ;
Glad hosannas swelling, loud His
   goodness telling,
   Fountain of blessing our joy
    eternal, day and night.

3 Praise the Lord with heart and voice,
   Ever adoringly raise
Hallelujahs sweet and strong,
   Unto the " Ancient of Days ; "
Shout with acclamation, hail Him
   all creation,
   Worship Jehovah, O come rejoic-
    ing, sound His praise.

877   CHRIST, our mighty Captain,
     leads against the foe ;
We will never falter when He bids
   us go ;
Tho' His righteous purpose we may
   never know,
   Yet we'll follow all the way.

Forward ! forward ! 'tis the Lord's command,
Forward ! forward ! to the promised land ;
Forward ! forward ! let the chorus ring :
We are sure to win with Christ, our King !

2 Satan's fearful onslaught cannot
   make us yield,
While we trust in Christ, our Buckler
   and our Shield ;
Pressing ever on—the Spirit's sword
   we wield,
   And we follow all the way.

3 Let our glorious banner ever be un-
   furled—
From its mighty stronghold evil
   shall be hurled ;
Christ, our mighty Captain, over-
   comes the world,
   And we follow all the way.

4 Fierce the battle rages, but 'twill not
   be long,
Then triumphant shall we join the
   blessed throng,   [song—
Joyfully uniting in the victor's
   If we follow all the way.

878 LIFE-TIME is working time,
  Spend no idle days ;
Jesus is calling thee
  On the harvest ways.
Working with a willing hand,
  Sing a song of praise ;
    Work, ever work for Jesus !

..Swiftly the hours of labour fly,..
Freighted with love let each pass by !..
There is joy in labour for the struggling
    neighbour,
  Work, ever work for Jesus !

2 Life-time is working time,
    Learn where duty lies ;
  Grasp ev'ry passing day
    As a precious prize,
  Glad to help the sorrowing,
    Glad to sympathise ;
      Work, ever work for Jesus !

3 Life-time is working time,
    Do thy honest part ;
  Though in discouragements
    Bear a cheerful heart.
  Trusting Jesus as Thy Friend,
    Ne'er from Him depart,
      Work, ever work for Jesus !

879 STANDING in the market
    places all the season through,
  Idly saying, " Lord, is there no work
    that I can do ? "
  O how many loiter, while the Master
    calls anew—
      " Reapers ! reapers ! Who will
        work to-day ? "

Lift..thine..eyes and look upon the fields
    that stand..
Ripe..and..ready for the willing gleaner's
    hand..
    Rouse ye, O sleepers !
    Ye are needed as reapers !
Who will be the first to answer, " Master,
    here am I ?"..
Far..and..wide the ripened grain is bending
    low,..
In..the..breezes gently waving to and fro,..
    Rouse ye, O sleepers !
    Ye are needed as reapers,
And the golden harvest days are swiftly
    passing by.

2 Ev'ry sheaf you gather will become
    a jewel bright
  In the crown you hope to wear in
    yonder world of light.

Seek the gems immortal that a
    precious in His sight !
  " Reapers ! reapers ! Who w
    work to-day ? "

3 Morning hours are passing, and t
    ev'ning follows fast ;
  Soon the time for reaping will f
    evermore be past ;
  Empty-handed to the Master w
    you go at last ?
    " Reapers ! reapers ! Who w
      work to-day ? "

880 COME to the ark of refuge,
    Come to the place of rest ;
  Safe in this quiet harbour,
    Naught can thy peace molest ;
  Come with thy guilt to Jesus,
    Weary and sore distrest ;
      List to His plea,
      " Come unto Me,
    And I will give you rest."....

    O message of mercy !
      Unbounded, unknown !
    He died to redeem thee ;
      O make Him now thine own !
    By faith in His mercy,
      By trust in His grace ;
    With saints in His kingdom,
      He'll give thy soul a place.

2 Come to the heart that loves thee
    Come to the soul's true home,
  Come while the Lord invites thee,
    Come while there yet is room ;
  Tell Him thy ev'ry sorrow,
    Nought from this Friend wit
      hold ;
      He'll hear thy prayer,
      Thy burden bear :
    Trust in His love untold.....

3 Christ is the soul's sure refuge ;
    When breaks the world's fier
      blast,
  He will protect His children
    Till all is overpast ;
  When storms without are raging,
    Rest and be not afraid ;
      Look to the Lord,
      Hope in His Word,
    Trust and be undismayed.....

881 O LISTEN to our wondro
    story,
  Once we dwelt among the lost ;

Yet Jesus came from heav'n's glory,
　Saving us at awful cost.

Who saved us from eternal loss ?
Who but God's Son upon the Cross !
What did He do ?　He died for you !
Where is He now ?　Believe it, thou !
In Heaven interceding !

No angel could our place have taken,
　Highest of the high though He ;
Nail'd to the Cross, despis'd forsaken,
　Was one of the Godhead three !

Will you surrender to this Saviour ?
Now before Him humbly bow ?
You, too, shall come to know His favour,
　He will save, and save you now !

882　I MUST needs go home by the way of the Cross,
　There's no other way but this ;
I shall ne'er get sight of the Gates of Light,
　If the way of the Cross I miss.

The way of the Cross leads home,..
The way of the Cross leads home ;..
It is sweet to know, as I onward go,
The way of the Cross leads home.

I must needs go on in the blood-sprinkled way,
　The path that the Saviour trod,
If I ever climb to the heights sublime,
　Where the soul is at home with God.

Then I bid farewell to the way of the world,
　To walk in it never more ;
For my Lord says, " Come ! " and I seek my home,
　Where He waits at the open door.

883　I LOVE the Gospel story,
　'Tis God's redeeming love,
It comes with light and glory
　From Him who reigns above.
I love the blessed story,
Its theme the Lamb of God,
Who left His home in glory,
　For me to shed His blood.

I love the Gospel story,
　It never can grow old ;
It helps me on to glory,
　The more I hear it told.

2 I love the Gospel story,
　It keeps me ev'ry hour ;
For Christ, the Prince of Glory,
　Imparts His saving pow'r.
I love the blessed story,
　'Tis manna to my soul ;
The balm of life and glory,
　It makes my spirit whole.

3 I love the Gospel story,
　It cheers me day by day ;
My hope, my joy, my glory,
　I own its gentle sway.
I love the blessed story,
　My portion evermore ;
'Twill be my theme in glory,
　When earthly cares are o'er.

884　DEAR Lord, I need Thy saving care about....me ;
　Into Thine arms of refuge would I flee ;....
I could not live, I dare not die without....Thee,
　In mercy then abide, abide with me.

Abide with me—I need Thee ev'ry hour ;..
Abide with me, I fear the tempter's pow'r,..
Abide with me, in sunshine and in show'r,
In life,..in..death,..O Lord, abide with me.

2 When foes without, and foes within assail....me,
　And I am tossed upon a troubled sea ;....
When, in my weakness, hope and courage fail....me,
　In mercy then abide, abide with me.....

3 When o'er my way the sun is brightly shin - - ing,
　My Counsellor, my Guide and Keeper be,....
And in the hour of sorrow and re-pin - - ing,
　In mercy then abide, abide with me.....

4 When I am near the dark and unknown riv - - er,
　Lord, who in earth or heav'n can save but Thee ?....
'Tis Thou alone hath power to de-li - - ver,
　In mercy then abide, abide with me....

885 BY the way of the Cross we're
going,
Home to the land above ;
We will fear not the hosts of evil,
Kept by a Father's love.

Home,....home, home,....
Home to the Land above,..
By the way of the Cross we're going,
Home to the land of love.

2 By the way of the Cross we're going ;
Jesus has gone before ; [steps,
We will follow our Master's foot-
Home to the golden shore !

3 By the way of the Cross we're going ;
Rough though the path may be ;
There's a hand that will guide us
safely
Home, blessed Lord, to Thee !

886 WHO are the soldiers of Jesus
Christ ?
Who who are they ?
What is the fight that they wage on
earth ?
Why do they watch and pray ?
Ah ! they are God's own children ;
He is near them,
He will cheer them ;
Truth is the cause for which they
strive
In battle fray.

They are stepping bravely onward,
They are eager with the hope of youth,
They never fear the foe,
But strike a gallant blow
For God and the cause of truth ;
They are ever climbing homeward,
They are looking unto higher things,
Free as the flag that waves o'erhead,
Soldiers of the King of kings.

2 Who are the soldiers of Jesus Christ ?
Who, who are they ?
Are they the heroes of earthly war,
Eager to smite and slay ?
No, they are something nobler ;
And the story
Of their glory
Rings with the power of faith and
love,
That lights their way.

3 Who are the soldiers of Jesus Christ ?
Who, who are they ?
Are they the lovers of empty joys,
Things that will pass away ?

No, they would lead for ever
Lives of beauty,
Lives of duty,
Lives that are hid with Christ in Go
No more to stray.

4 Who are the soldiers of Jesus Chris
Who, who are they ?
Are they the rich and the great
earth,
Holding a mighty sway ?
No, in a grander kingdom,
Ever fairer,
Ever rarer,
Bright with the crown of endless li
They'll shine like day.

887 "LOYALTY unto Christ " t
trumpet now is sounding,
And the echoes answer from t
fields of sin ;
Nations are awakening,
Idol thrones are shaking,
For the great Millennium is comi
in.
Like a mighty army,
The heralds of the Cross are marc
ing over land and sea ;
Bearing through the darkness
The light that leadeth to salvati
full and free.

Long and loud, " Loyalty unto Christ "
sing ;
Till ev'ry human tongue,
Shall hear His praises sung !
Let the hills, valleys and desert places rin
With " Loyalty unto Christ our Lord a
King.".

2 "Loyalty, faith and works," in ho
consecration,
Shall the scattered nations unto H
restore ;
Then the world shall own Him,
And with joy enthrone Him,
King of kings and Lord of lords
evermore.
See the darkness rifting !
The Gospel light of truth is spreadi
to the perfect day !
Clouds are backward drifting !
Renew endeavour ! for the Ki
prepare the way !

3 "Loyalty unto Christ ! " O wha
mighty power,
Where the hosts of God united
His Name !

Then would angels greet us,
Christ Himself would meet us,
And baptise us with the Pentecostal
flame.
Then would come the triumph,
And Christ be known and lov'd, His
praise be sung from shore to
shore;
Earth would then, in glory,
Become the kingdom of the Lord
for evermore.

88 WHAT are you seeking day by
day,
Working with heart and hand?
Is it for honour in the fray?
Is it for wealth or land?
Turn from the eager longing thirst,
Turn from the world's great strife,
Seek ye the Kingdom of Heaven first,
Seek ye eternal life.

For the kingdom of Heav'n is better
Than pearls of a priceless worth,..
Than treasures great, or pomp of state,
Than the kingdom of all the earth.
It ever abideth within you,
This home of the life divine,
Let the dark clouds roll from your heart
and soul,
Let the Light of the Kingdom shine.

What are you seeking day by day?
Is it for something new?
Is it for pleasures bright and gay,
Brief as the morning dew?
Seek ye the kingdom evermore,
Joys shall be added then,
Greater than all that you felt before,
Ever renew'd again.

What are you seeking day by day,
Comrade so brave and true?
Is it for some great thing to say?
Some noble deed to do?
Give to the Master heart and hand,
Follow in truth and love,
So shall you share in His work and
stand
Crown'd in the life above.

Enter the kingdom, child of truth,
Seeking the Saviour's face;
Enter the kingdom, maid and youth,
Come in your strength and grace;
Enter the kingdom one and all,
Cease from the path to stray,
Hear ye the voice of the Master, call
"I am the Living Way."

889 HARK! 'tis the clarion sound-
ing the fight,
Turn from each siren charmer.
Banners are waving, swords gleam-
ing bright,
Gird on the heavenly armour.
Stern is the conflict, fierce the foe;
Cowards and traitors will backward
go!
Brave men are wanted, hearts all
aglow,
Wanted to battle for Jesus.

Soldiers of God, we join you to-day,
Join in our grand endeavour, .
Soldiers of God, advance to the fray,
For the truth is triumphant for ever.

2 Haste to the rescue, souls in their
need
Loud for relief are calling;
Must they for ever hopeless plead?
None hear the cry appalling?
Broken in spirit, wounded by sin,
Foemen around them, and fear
within;   [win;
Speed ye to help them freedom to
Speed with the Gospel of Jesus.

3 Soon 'twill be over, danger all past;
Ended the marches dreary.
After the warfare, rest comes at last,
Sweet rest for soldiers weary.
Crown after conflict; ease after
pain;
Parting shall never be known again;
Joy everlasting all shall obtain;
All who are faithful to Jesus.

890 OH, Christian, rise and shine,
and give God the glory;
Christian, rise and shine, and give
God the glory (*Repeat*);
Christian, rise, rise and shine.
Do you want to be a really happy
Christian (*Repeat*),
Do you want to be a really happy
Christian, full of joy, joy divine?
Yes, I want to be a really happy
Christian (*Repeat*),
Yes, I want to be a really happy
Christian, full of joy, joy divine!
Then you must rise and shine, and
give God the glory (*Repeat*);
You must rise and shine, and give
God the glory;
You must rise, rise and shine.

891 ON to the front, for the fight
is on !
This is not the time for dreaming !
See ! on the breeze of the early dawn,
Banners of the foe are streaming !
Into position for battle drawn,
And with weapons brightly gleam-
ing,
Now from the hill-top of vantage
ground,
Loud their battle cries resound.

> Onward to the conflict ! . . . .
> Fearless, like a soldier true ; . .
> Press into the bat - - tle, . .
> Your Commander calls for you.

2 On to the front, nor the danger fear,
Satan's forces cannot harm you ;
Let not the hordes that are pressing
near
In their proud array alarm you ;
Be not dismayed by the foeman's
cheer,
Let no evil power disarm you ;
Trust in the Lord for your strength
to win
Over all the ranks of sin.

3 On to the front ! He who smote the
sea,
And its angry waves divided,
Is thy Commander, and surely He
For the vict'ry hath provided.
Trust in His power, and ever be
By His love and wisdom guided ;
Keep up the fight till the whole
world sings
Praise unto the King of kings.

892 LORD, bring some wand'rers
home to-night—
Some who have gone astray ;
Oh, give them grace to come to-night
Let them no more delay !

> To-night, Lord ! to-night, Lord !
> Bring wand'rers home to-night !
> To-night, Lord ! to-night, Lord !
> Bring wand'rers home to-night !

2 May none Thy mercy spurn to-night,
Thy Holy Spirit grieve ;
May prodigals return to-night ;
May sinners now believe.

3 Let none unblest depart to-night,
Unsaved and unforgiven ;
Over some yielding heart to-night
Let there be joy in heaven.

893 CONQUERORS and ove
comers now are we,
Thro' the precious blood of Chri
we've victory ;
If the Lord be for us, we can nev
fail,
Nothing 'gainst His mighty pow
can e'er prevail.

> Con - - querors are we, . . thro' the blood.
> thro' the blood ; . .
> God will give...us victory,...thro' the blood,
> thro' the blood ; ...
> Thro' the Lamb for sinners slain,
> Yet who lives and reigns again,
> More than conquerors are we.

2 In the Name of Israel's God we'
onward press,
Overcoming sin and all unrighteou
ness ;
Not to us, but unto Him the prai
shall be,
For salvation and for blood-boug
victory.

3 Unto him that overcometh shall k
giv'n
Here to eat of " hidden manna
sent from heav'n ;
Over yonder he the victor's pal
shall bear,
And a robe of white and golde
crown shall wear.

894 WHEN out in sin and darkne
lost,
Love found me ;
My fainting soul was tempest tosse
Love found me ;
I heard the Saviour's words so bles
Love found me ;
Come, weary, heavy-laden rest,
Love found me.

> Oh, 'twas love, . . love, . .
> Love that moved the mighty God,
> Love, love, 'twas love found me.

2 The Spirit roused me from my slee
Love found me ;
Conviction seized me strong a
deep,
Love found me ;
Although I long withstood His grac
Love found me ;
He wooed me to His kind embrac
Love found me.

I'll praise Him while He gives me
    breath,
        Love found me ;
For saving from an endless death,
        Love found me ;
Christ is my Advocate above,
        Love found me ;
I'm yoked to Him in perfect love,
        Love found me.

And when I reach the gold-paved
    street,
        Love found me ;
I'll sit adoring at His feet,
        Love found me ;
And sing hosanna round the throne,
        Love found me ;
Where I shall know as I am known,
        Love found me.

95 WHERE the flag is flying,
        where the fight is keen,
    Where the trumpet call is ringing,
There you find the soldiers, steady
        and serene,   [singing.
    There you find the sound of
Servants of the Master, scorning fear
        or flight,
Fighting for the Truth, the Life, the
        Light !

    Soldiers of the Master, onward tread,
    Telling out the grand old story !
    Ready day by day Jesus to obey,
    Soldiers of the King of Glory.

Where the darkness reigneth, where
    the pow'r of sin,
    Binds the heart of man in sadness,
There you find the soldiers, waiting
        souls to win,
    Bringing them to light and glad-
        ness,
Servants of the Master, strong in
        love and might,
Fighting for the Truth, the Life, the
        Light !

Where the doubts are thickest,
    where the strength of youth
    Falls beneath the chains of error,
There you find the soldiers, with the
        lamp of truth,
    Freeing men from thoughts of
        terror.
Servants of the Master, strong in
        faith and sight,
Fighting for the Truth, the Life, the
        Light !

4 Where the pallid suff'rer, weary,
        worn, and weak,
    On his bed of pain is lying,
There you find the soldiers, words of
        hope to speak,
    Comforting the sick and dying.
Servants of the Master, watching in
        the night,   [Light !
Fighting for the Truth, the Life, the

5 Where from angel chorus thro' the
        heavenly dome,
    Rings a song of triumph splendid,
There you find the soldiers entering
        their home,
    By the heavenly hosts attended.
Servants of the Master, clad in spot-
        less white,   [Light !
One with Him in Truth, in Life, in

896 OUR heavenly home is bright
        and fair,
    And we'll sing the new song ;
No pain or sorrow enter there,
    We will sing the new song.

    Wait a little while,
    Then we'll sing the new song ;
    Wait a little while,
    Then we'll sing the new song.

2 Our Saviour and Lord to heav'n is
        gone,
    We will sing the new song ;
He whom we fix our hopes upon ;
    And we'll sing the new song.

3 And when we behold His blessed face,
    We will sing the new song ;
We'll praise Him for His wondrous
        grace,
    And we'll sing the new song.

897 SADLY from the field of con-
        flict,
    Where the wounded and the slain...
Lay with pale and upturn'd faces,
    Some in peace and some in pain,
Slow we bore a dying soldier,
    Who had fallen in the fight,
And to us he faintly whisper'd,
    " Comrades, let me sleep to-night"

    Let him sleep,..calmly sleep,..
        While the days and the years go by,
    Let him sleep,..sweetly sleep,..
        Till the call of the roll on high,
    Let him sleep,..calmly sleep,..
        While the years go by.

2 On the ground we softly laid him,
    Thinking he no more will wake,.....
When, with eyelids widely open,
    Pointing upward, thus he spake :
" Comrades, listen ! don't you hear
    it,
    Hear the roll-call there on high ?
Hark ! my name the Saviour's
    calling,
    Jesus, Captain, here am I ! "

3 Oh ! from many a field of battle
    Earnest pray'r has gone to God,.....
From the lips of dying soldiers,
    As their life-blood drench'd the
    sod ;
And to many came the message :
    Son, thy sins are all forgiv'n ;
And their lips with joy responded,
    When the roll was called in heav'n.

Now they sleep,..calmly sleep,..
    While the days and the years go by,
Now they sleep,..sweetly sleep,..
    Till the call of the roll on high,
Now they sleep..calmly sleep,..
    While the years go by.

898 JESUS ! blessed Name,.....
    Jesus ! still the same,.....
I will sing it more and more,
Till we meet on heaven's shore.

899 HOMEWARD I go rejoicing !
    O lovely promised land,
Far in the distance gleaming,
    I see thy shining strand.

Homeward,..to join the ransomed,..
    Beyond the borders of the crystal sea ;..
Homeward,..to joys eternal,..
    And oh, how sweet the rest will be !

2 Homeward to meet my Saviour
    On that eternal shore,
Wonderful land of Canaan,
    Where sorrows come no more.

3 Homeward I go believing
    That there shall be no night
In that eternal city,
    Where God Himself is light !

900 THERE is One who under-
    stands our hearts,
    Jesus, the best Friend of all ;
And for ev'ry need His grace imparts,
    Jesus, the best Friend of all.

Jesus, the best Friend of all ;..
Jesus, the best Friend of all,..
    He knows our ev'ry care,
    And will ev'ry burden bear,
Jesus, the best Friend of all.

2 He will soothe and comfort in di
    tress,
    Jesus, the best Friend of all ;
He will sympathise, and help, an
    bless,
    Jesus, the best Friend of all.

3 In temptation He will help th
    stand,
    Jesus, the best Friend of all ;
Will support thee with His stron
    right hand,
    Jesus, the best Friend of all.

4 There is One who died for you an
    me,
    Jesus, the best Friend of all ;
He will give us pardon full and fre
    Jesus, the best Friend of all.

901 WE sing of a story the Mast
    told
    Of God's great love ;
A love that can never grow fai
    or cold,
    Where'er we rove ;
A love that waits to welcome us
    When from our sins we turn,
Whose depth and height are infin
    Whose fulness none can learn.

Then arise and come to the Father !
    He will meet you on the way ;
All the lost to His arms He will gather,
    In His home of eternal day ;
For the bells of the city of God shall ri
    And the choirs of heav'n shall sing,
" Let joy abound, let songs resound,
    For the loved and lost is found ! "

2 O all who have wander'd away a
    fed
    On husks of sin ;
O ye who are faint for the Livi
    Bread,
    And sad within ;
Whose thoughts are turning lon
    ingly
    Towards the Father's home,
No longer stay, make no delay,
    For Jesus bids you come.

3 That house of the Father is full
    light,
    Our home above :

There waits you a robe of immortal
　　white,
　　　　A ring of love.
O Father, grant us all Thy grace
　To leave our sin behind,
To enter straight the narrow gate,
　And seek Thee till we find.

02 A BAND of faithful reapers we,
　　Who gather for eternity,
The golden sheaves of ripened grain
From ev'ry valley, hill, and plain ;
Our song is one the reapers sing,
In honour of their Lord and King—
The Master of the harvest wide,
Who for a world of sinners died.

　　To the harvest field away,
　　　For the Master calleth ;
　　There is work for all to-day,
　　　Ere the darkness falleth.
　　Swiftly do the moments fly,
　　Harvest days are going by,
　　Going, going, going, going by.

We are a faithful gleaning band,
And labour at our Lord's command,
Unyielding, loyal, tried and true,
For lo ! the reapers are but few ;
Behold the waving harvest field
Abundant with a golden yield ;
And hear the Lord of the harvest say
To all : " Go reap for Me to-day."

The golden hours like moments fly,
And harvest days are passing by ;
Then take thy rusty sickle down,
And labour for a fadeless crown ;
Why will you idly stand and wait ?
Behold, the hour is growing late !
Can you to judgment bring but
　　leaves, 　　　　　　[sheaves ?
While here are waiting golden

03 THE fight is on, the trumpet
　　sound is ringing out,
　The cry " To arms ! " is heard
　　afar and near ;
The Lord of hosts is marching on to
　victory, 　　　　　　[appear.
　The triumph of the Christ will soon

ᵗe fight is on, O Christian soldier,
And face to face in stern array,
ᵗth armour gleaming, and colours streaming,
The right and wrong engage to-day !
ᵗe fight is on, but be not weary ;
Be strong, and in His might hold fast ;
God be for us, His banner o'er is,
We'll sing the victor's song at last !

2 The fight is on, arouse, ye soldiers
　　brave and true !
　Jehovah leads and vict'ry will
　　assure ;
　Go, buckle on the armour God has
　　given you,
　And in His strength unto the end
　　endure.

3 The Lord is leading on to certain
　　victory ;
　The bow of promise spans the
　　eastern sky ;
　His glorious name in ev'ry land shall
　　honoured be ;
　The morn will break, the dawn of
　　peace is nigh.

904 WHEN dark'ning clouds ob-
　　scure our sky, 　　[nigh,
　And friends are few, and troubles
　On One alone we may rely,
　　Jesus ! precious Saviour !

2 Friends, basking in the summer ray
　Of brighter hours, have pass'd away ;
　But One is left in sorrow's day,
　　Jesus ! precious Saviour !

3 When hopes, like autumn leaves, are
　　dead,
　And ev'ry joy of earth is fled,
　Sweet pillow—rest for heart and
　　head,
　　Jesus ! precious Saviour !

4 Jesus hath died thine heart to win,
　His precious blood atones for sin,
　His loving arms would take thee in ;
　　Jesus ! precious Saviour !

5 Oh, let Him fold thee to His breast,
　There find a true, a perfect rest,
　And thou shalt be for ever blest,
　　By Jesus ! precious Saviour !

905 CHRIST has need of soldiers,
　　brave and staunch and true ;
　In the front of battle there's a place
　　for you ;
　Ever marching onward through a
　　world of sin,
　For the heav'nly country is the prize
　　we win.

　　On - - ward !..soldiers of the Cross,
　　　Doubting never..trusting ever ;..
　　On - - ward !..soldiers of the Cross,
　　　Trusting the Lord, heeding His Word,
　　　Onward to victory !

2 Satan would oppose us, tempt our
souls to stray,
But through Him who loves us we
shall win the day ;
Other valiant soldiers in the ages
past,
O'er this upward pathway reach'd
their home at last.

3 Let us then with courage press our
upward way,
With our gaze on Jesus, ever watch
and pray ;
Blazon'd on our banner, " Christ, the
Lord of all,"
While we shout, Hosanna, Satan's
hosts must fall.

906 LET us never mind the scoffs
or the jeers of the world,
For we all have a cross to bear ;
It will only make the crown the
brighter to shine,
When we have the crown to wear.

907 AWAY to the harvest field,
toilers, away ;
Go, gather the golden grain whilst it
is day ;
Strength meet for thy labour thy
Lord will bestow,
Away to the harvest field, labourers,
go ;
For now is the time to be doing thy
best,
Soon, soon will be coming the season
for rest.
Away,..away,..away,..away,..
For soon..will be ended
The bright, the bright harvest day.

2 Behold how the ripen'd grain bends
to the earth !
The harvest is ready, oh, why such a
dearth   [toil ?
Of labourers ready and willing to
Will they listlessly suffer the rich
grain to spoil ?
No, it must not be so ; to the field
hie away,
With heart and with hand to work
whilst it is day.

3 O say not, " No work of that sort
can I do ; "
For some kind of toil is there even
for you ;

For if the keen sickle thy hand ma
not wield,
Bind together the sheaves, or e
glean in the field.
If you follow the reapers over t
ground,
Full many a rich golden ear shall
found.

4 And when the last sheaf to the garn
has come,
And saints join with angels to sho
" Harvest home,"
When labour is over, then rest a
reward,
And the welcome " Well done !
from the lips of the Lord.
Away to the harvest field, toil whi
you may,
Soon, soon will be ended the brig
harvest day.

908 MAKE the Lord a full co
fession,
When on Him you call ;
Do not carry half the burden,
Tell the Saviour all.
Tell the Saviour all,....
Tell the Saviour all,....
Make to Him a full confession,
Tell the Saviour all.

2 Not alone the great temptations
That the heart appal,
But the little cares and burdens,
Tell the Saviour all.

3 For the eye that guards creation,
Sees a sparrow fall ;
All your troubles will not tire Him
Tell the Saviour all.

909 HARK to the sounds of voice
Hark to the tramp of feet !
Is it a mighty army
Treading the busy street ?
Nearer it comes and nearer,
Singing a glad refrain ;   [awa
List what they say as they has
To the sound of a martial strain
" Marching beneath the banner,
Fighting beneath the Cross,
Trusting in Him who saves us,
Ne'er shall we suffer loss !
Singing the songs of homeland,
Loudly the chorus rings,
We march to the fight in our armour brig
At the call of the King of kings."

Out of the mist of error,
  Out of the realms of night,
Out of the pride of learning,
  Seeking the home of light ;
Out of the strife for power,
  Out of the greed of gold,
Onward they roam to their heavenly
    home,
  And the treasure that grows not
    old.

Out of the bonds of evil,
  Out of the chains of sin,
Ever they're pressing onward,
  Fighting the fight within ;
Holding the passions under,
  Ruling the sense with soul ;
Wielding the sword in the Name of
    the Lord,
  As they march to their heavenly
    goal.

On then, ye gallant soldiers,
  On to your home above !
Yours is the truth and glory,
  Yours is the power and love.
Here are ye trained for heroes,
  Yonder to serve the King ;
Marching to the light, 'neath the
    banner white,
  With a song that ye love to sing.

0 BEAUTIFUL words of Jesus,
      Spoken so long ago,
Yet, as we sing them over,
  Dearer to us they grow ;
Calling the heavy laden,
  Calling to hearts oppressed,
" Come unto Me, ye weary,
  Come, I will give you rest."

  Hear the call of His voice so sweet ;
  Bring your load to the Saviour's feet ;
  Lean your heart on His loving breast,
  Come, O come and He will give you rest.

Beautiful words of Jesus,
  Cheering us day by day ;
Throwing a gleam of sunshine
  Over a cloudy way ;
Casting on Him the burden
  We are too weak to bear,
He will give grace sufficient,
  He will regard our pray'r.

Beautiful words of Jesus,
  Tokens of endless rest,
When, by and by, we enter
  Into His presence blest ;

There we shall see His beauty,
  Meet with Him face to face ;
There shall we sing His glory,
  Praising His matchless grace.

911 SAY, brother,* will you meet us,
        Say, brother, will you meet us,
Say, brother, will you meet us
  On Canaan's happy shore ?

  By the grace of God we'll meet you,
  By the grace of God we'll meet you,
  By the grace of God we'll meet you,
    On Canaan's happy shore !

May be sung " sister," " children."

912 WHAT are you building, brother?
        So busily day by day ?
Is it a mighty castle of stone ?
  Is it a house of clay ?
Whose is the plan you build on ?
  What are the stones and lime ?
Is it based on the Rock of eternity,
  Or the sands of the shores of time?

  Then build on the Rock, the Rock that ever
    stands,
  O build on the Rock, and not upon the sands ;
  You need not fear the storm or the earthquake
    shock,
  You're safe for evermore if you build on the
    Rock.

2 What are you building, brother ?
    You work at it every day ;
Something is added, something is
    changed,
  Something is cast away.
Is it a house of pleasure ?
  Is it a house of sin ?
Or a temple divine for the Light of
    lights
  To descend and abide within ?

3 Brother, a time is coming,
    When all shall be tried by fire ;
Storms of the world shall beat on
    your house,
  Winds of a fierce desire.
Then, if you based it wrongly,
  Great will the ruin be ;
But if built on the firm and un-
    changing Rock,
  It will stand for eternity.

4 Build on the Rock, then, brother,
    How grandly it towers above !
Piercing the clouds and the starry
    skies,
  Lost in the heights of love !

Heaven and earth shall perish,
  Grow like a garment old ;
But the Rock is the same, and it
    shall not fail,
  Through the ages of time untold.

913 AS of old, when the hosts of
  Israel,
Were compelled in the wilderness
    to dwell,
Trusted they in their God to lead
    the way
To the light of perfect day.

So the sign of the fire by night,
  And the sign of the cloud by day,
Hov'ring o'er, just before,
  As they journey on their way,
Shall a guide and a leader be,
  Till the wilderness be past,
For the Lord our God in His own good time
  Shall lead to the light at last.

2 To and fro, as a ship without a sail,
Not a compass to guide them through
    the vale ;
But the sign of their God was ever
    near,
Thus their fainting hearts to cheer.

3 All the days of their wand'rings
    they were fed,
To the land of the promise they
    were led ;
By the hand of the Lord, in guid-
    ance sure,
They were brought to Caanan's shore

914 EV'RY morning the red sun
  Rises warm and bright ;
But the evening cometh on,
  And the dark cold night ;
There's a bright land far away,
Where 'tis never-ending day.

2 Ev'ry spring the sweet young flow'rs
  Open fresh and gay ;
Till the chilly autumn hours
  Wither them away.
There's a land we have not seen,
Where the trees are always green.

3 Little birds sing songs of praise
  All the summer long ;
But in colder, shorter days,
  They forget their song :
There's a place where angels sing
Ceaseless praises to their King.

4 Christ our Lord is ever near
    Those who follow Him ;
But we cannot see Him here,
    For our eyes are dim :
There's a happy, glorious place,
Where His people see His face.

5 Who shall go to that fair land ?
    All who love the right ;
Holy children there shall stand
    In their robes of white :
For that heaven so bright and bles
Is our everlasting rest.

915 WHAT will you do with t
    King called Jesus ?
  Many are waiting to hear you sa
Some have despised Him, rejecti
    His mercy ;
  What will you do with your Kii
    to-day ?
What can you witness concerni
    His goodness,
  Who died to save you from sin
    bitter thrall ?
Who will declare Him the fairest
    thousands ?
  Who now will crown Him the Lo
    of all ?

What will you do with the King called Jesu
What, oh, what will you do with Jesus ?
He waits to bless all who humbly confess
Faith in His blood and righteousness.

2 What will you do for the King call
    Jesus ?
  He who for you left His thro
    above,
Here 'mid the lowly and sinful
    labour,
  Daily unfolding His Father's lov
Look on the fields white already
    harvest,
  Who now is willing to toil wi
    the few ?
What will you do for the de
    Saviour, Jesus ?   [yo
  Lo, He is waiting—He calls

3 What will you do with the Ki
    called Jesus ?
  Who will submit to His gen
    sway ?
Where are the hearts ready now
    enthrone Him ?
  Who will His kind comman
    obey ?

Come with your ointments most
    costly and precious,
    Pour out your gifts at the dear
      Saviour's feet ;
Render to Him all your loyal devo-
    tion ;
    Seek to exalt Him by praises meet.

16 BY AND BY we'll see the
    King,
    And crown Him Lord of all.

17 WHY are you marching along
    to war ?
      Soldiers true,
      Who are you ?   [for ?
What is the cause you are fighting
    Why are you never sad ?
O we are only rank and file,
Treading the path for many a mile ;
Still ev'ry face must bear a smile,
    For Jesus has made us glad.

We've enlisted in the cause victorious,
Of the everlasting Lord,
We are marching in the ranks all glorious,
Resplendent with the shield and sword.
Christ is our Captain, Christ our might,
    So we fight,
    Seeking right ;
Christ is leading us to light
    In the all victorious army.

Who are the foes that you fight
    withal,
      Ye who stand,
      Sword in hand ?
Do you not fear in the strife to fall,
    Struck by a deadly blow ?
Strong are the foes that bar our way,
Many the sins we have to slay,
Still we shall rise and win the day,
    Tho' oft in the dust laid low.

What is the secret of your great
    pow'r,
      Soldier bright,
      Full of might ?
Why are you fearless in danger's
    hour—
    Strong with the foe to cope ?
Jesus it is that makes us strong,
Trusting in Him we march along,
He ever fills our hearts with song,
    Our eyes with the light of hope.

4 Where is the home you are marching
    to,
      Hearts of youth,
      Hearts of truth ?
Is there a kingdom beyond the blue,
    Where you may rest from strife ?
Jesus has said that we shall stand,
Victors of faith at His right hand,
Crown'd in the light of God's own
    land
    With joy and eternal life.

918 THEY come and go, the seasons
    fair,
    And bring their spoil to vale and
      hills ;
But oh, there is waiting in the air,
    And a passionate hope the spirit
      fills.
Why doth He tarry, the absent
    Lord ?
When shall the kingdom be restor'd,
And earth and heav'n with one
    accord,
    Ring out the cry that the King
      comes ?

What will it be when the King comes ?
What will it be when the King comes ?
What will it be when He comes ? . . . .
What will it be when the King comes ?

2 The floods have lifted up their voice ;
    The King hath come to His own,
      His own !
The little hills and vales rejoice,
    His right it is to take the crown.
Sleepers, awake, and meet Him first !
Now let the marriage hymn out-
    burst !
And powers of darkness flee, dis-
    perst :
    What will it be when the King
      comes ?

3 A ransomed earth breaks forth in
    song,
    Her sin-stain'd ages overpast ;
Her yearning, "Lord, how long,
    how long ? "
    Exchanged for joy at last, at last !
Angels carry the royal commands ;
Peace beams forth throughout all
    the lands ;
The trees of the field shall clap their
    hands ;
    What will it be when the King
      comes ?

4 Oh, brother, stand as men that
  wait,
  The dawn is purpling in the East,
And banners wave from heaven's
  high gate;
  The conflict now, but soon the
  feast!
Mercy and truth shall meet again;
Worthy the Lamb that once was
  slain!
We can suffer now—He will know
  us then;
  What will it be when the King
  comes?

919 I KNOW that my Redeemer
  liveth,
  And on the earth....again shall
  stand!....
I know eternal life He giveth,
  That grace and power are in His
  hand.

I know, I know..that Jesus liveth,
  And on the earth..again shall stand;
I know, I know..that life He giveth,
  That grace and power..are in His hand.

2 I know His promise never faileth,
  The word He speaks....it cannot
  die;....
Tho' cruel death my flesh assaileth,
  Yet I shall see Him by and by.

3 I know my mansion He prepareth,
  That where He is....there I may
  be;....
O wondrous thought, for me He
  careth,
  And He at last will come for me.

920 INTO the valleys of blessing
  My Shepherd leads;
Peace is my spirit possessing,
  My soul He feeds.
Pastures so green are around me,
  Waters of life shall flow;
Fairest of flowers surround me,
  Ever I onward go.

My Shepherd leads along the way,
Kept by His care I cannot stray;
  In tender love,
  To realms above,
My Shepherd leads me home!

2 Into the ways that are weary
  My Shepherd leads;
Dark tho' the skies be, and dreary,
  He knows my needs,

Heavy the load I am bearing,
  Love hath my pathway planned;
Trusting, I'm still.forward faring,
  Led by my Shepherd's hand.

3 Into the land all immortal
  My Shepherd leads;
Unto the glorious portal
  My way He heeds.
Mansions of heavenly splendour
  Wait me when I shall come.
Led by my Shepherd so tender,
  Unto my Father's home.

921 THERE is a place of rest,
  The sweetest and the best,
The saints have found it down t
  ages hoary.!
  Life that is hid in Him
  Is full right to the brim
Of love, and peace, and ecstasy, an
  glory.

922 WHEN we have reached t
  heav'nly plains,
  And joined the hosts above,
One song shall swell the rapturo
  strains,
  The song of Jesus' love.
When we have reached the pear
  gate,
  And passed its portals through,
The saints, with holy joy elate,
  Shall tune their harps anew.

..Rejoice,..rejoice, for Christ Himself is nea
His wondrous love I feel,..His tender voice
  hear,..
And when..at last we meet with Him above
One song shall swell the rapturous strains, t
  song of Jesus' love.

2 While years eternal roll along
  Their ever ceaseless round,
Like ocean's waves shall swell t
  song,
  The glad, triumphant sound.
There life's fair river, broad a
  deep,
  Reflects its golden ray;
Where eyes have never learned
  weep,
  Where joys shall ne'er decay.

3 Then we shall see as we are seen,
  And know as we are known,
And walk the fields of fadeless gree
  While gazing on the throne.

And when are tuned the harps of
　　gold
To ev'ry blissful sound,
And ages long have onward rolled,
　Jesus shall King be crowned.

23 I BELIEVE God answers
　　prayer ;
I am sure God answers prayer ;
I have proved God answers prayer :
　Glory to His Name.

24 IN a world so full of weeping,
　　While the years are rolling
　　　on,
Christian souls the watch are keeping
　While the years are rolling on !
While our journey we pursue,
With the haven still in view,
There is work for us to do,
　While the years are rolling on !

　　Are rolling on !....
　　Are rolling on !....
　Oh, the good we may be doing,
　While the years are rolling on !

There's no time to waste in sighing,
　While the years are rolling on !
Time is flying, souls are dying,
　While the years are rolling on !
Loving words a soul may win
From the wretched paths of sin ;
We may bring the wand'rers in,
　While the years are rolling on !

Let us strengthen one another,
　While the years are rolling on !
Seek to raise a fallen brother,
　While the years are rolling on !
This is work for ev'ry hand,
Till throughout creation's land,
Armies for the Lord shall stand,
　While the years are rolling on !

Friends we love are quickly flying,
　While the years are rolling on !
No more parting, no more dying,
　While the years are rolling on !
In the world beyond the tomb
Sorrow never more may come,
When we meet in that blest home,
　While the years are rolling on !

25 FROM Jesus' lips we hear the
　　call,
In tones of tenderness to all,

" Ye burdened sinners, come to Me,
Though heavy-laden you may be."

　　He'll wash your sins away,
　　He'll wash your sins away,
　The blood of Christ, the bleeding Lamb,
　　Will wash your sins away.

2 He would not have one sinner lost,
For well He knows what pardon cost,
O seek His mercy while you may,
And Christ will wash your sins away.

3 Too long you have remained in sin,
Forsake it, hate it—now begin ;
Tho' Satan long has held the sway,
Yet Christ can wash your sins away.

4 And some have erred and turned
　　aside,
And, Peter-like, their Lord denied,
To such He calls in love to-day,
And seeks to wash your sins away.

926 GO forth, go forth for Jesus
　　now !
　Be working ! Be watching !
The Lord Himself will teach you how
　To watch and pray ;
'Tis not for thee thy field to choose,
No work He gives must thou refuse,
　Be working ! Be watching ! Be
　　praying !

　Go forth to work, to watch and pray !
　'Tis Jesus who calls thee ;
　The harvest waits for thee to-day,
　Go bring some sheaves for God !

2 Go forth, go forth to all the world !
　O stay not ! Delay not !
But let love's banner be unfurl'd,
　And grace be told ;
O let redeeming love be sung,
A song of joy on ev'ry tongue !
　Be working ! Be watching ! Be
　　praying !

3 Go forth, let hearts and hands be
　　strong !
　Be working ! Be watching !
O stay the mighty power of wrong
　Where'er ye may !
Equipped with love and strength
　　divine,
The victory is surely thine ;
　Be working ! Be watching ! Be
　　praying !

927 I HAVE a Friend, a precious
     Friend,
   A Helper in the time of need ;....
He will my soul keep to the end,
   A Helper in the time of need.....

O Jesus is a Friend, and He cares for me,
He cares for me, He cares for me ;
O Jesus is a Friend, and He cares for me,
   A Helper in the time of need....

2 He turns to light the darkest hour,
   A Helper in the time of need ;....
In pain He soothes with wondrous
     pow'r,
   A Helper in the time of need.....

3 Thro' dangers hid or dangers known,
   A Helper in the time of need ;....
His wings of love are o'er me thrown,
   A Helper in the time of need.....

4 Where'er I go, where'er I stray,
   A Helper in the time of need ;....
A Guardian all along my way,
   A Helper in the time of need.....

928 WHEN my steps are slow and
     weary,
   Shadows o'er me cast,
And the way seems long and dreary,
Jesus holds me fast.

He will hold me fast,
Till my journey's past :
Ransomed by His precious blood,
Jesus holds me fast.

2 Oft when storms and clouds sur-
     round me,
   He has held me fast ;
With His strong right arm around
     me,
Jesus holds me fast.

3 When my faint heart dreads the
     morrow,
   He will hold me fast ;
When my spirit bows in sorrow,
Jesus holds me fast.

4 When the summons, " Come up
     higher,"
   Reaches me at last,
Face to face I'll see my Saviour :
He has held me fast.

929 IF you have heard that our
     God is love,
   Go tell it, go tell it !

That He is reigning in heaven abov
   Go tell of His love to-day.

Tell of a Saviour so kind and true,
Tell of His love and His mercy too,
Tell of the good He would have us do,
   Go tell of His love to-day.

2 If you can sing the dear Saviou
     praise,
   Go sing it, go sing it !
Unto Him gladly your voices no
     raise,
   Go sing of His love to-day.

3 If you can turn other hearts to Go
   Go do it, go do it !
Bid them to follow where Jesus b
     trod,
   Go do what you can to-day.

930   *Choir Piece, for words see
       No.* 460.

931   *Choir Piece, for words see
       No.* 21.

932 THERE'S a city of such beau
     Mortal eye hath never seen
Filled with radiance brighter th
     the noon-day sun,....
Streets of gold and streams of cryst
   Trees of ever living green,
Jesus reigns, exalted One, in glo
     land.

Then crowns of glory, palms of victory,
   Harps of gold triumphant anthems ble
Hosannahs ringing, praises singing,
   We shall come, our trophies bringing,
     that glory land.

2 There the ransomed dwell eterna
   Out of tribulation come,
Undreamed music fills the soul th
     endless days,....
Hope so dear and aspirations
   Down on earth there freely bloo
Life's real treasures ne'er decay
     glory land.

3 Would you see this heavenly city
   Would you drink its rapture in
There's a place prepared for all w
     will believe,....
Jesus earnestly invites you,
   He will guide you, cleanse your s
And a mansion freely give in glo
     land.

"Unto Him that overcometh,"
  Is the promise full of love;
Fiery trials in the furnace proves the
  gold,....
After conquest in life's conflict,
  Faith sustained by grace above,
Comes the victor's joy untold in
  glory land.

33   OUR service for God has been
    barren and dry,
  And barren it shall remain,
Until we are blest with the fire from
  on high,
  And sound of abundance of rain.

There's sound of abundance of rain,
There's sound of abundance of rain;
O God we draw near, and by faith we can hear,
The sound of abundance of rain.

The prophets of Pride and the priests
  of Desire
  Are "calling" and "cutting" in
    vain;
The "halting" are waiting for wit-
  ness of fire,
  And sound of abundance of rain.

The altars of God that our sins have
  destroyed
  We must build with "the things
    that remain;"
And prove to the world that no pro-
  mise is void
  By sound of abundance of rain.

To each may the faith of Elijah be
  given,
  To pray till the answer we gain,
And the sinners acknowledge the
  witness of heav'n
  And sound of abundance of rain.

34   GO tell to souls benighted, of
    the Lord who came,
Speak His Name—love proclaim;
Go tell the Gospel story, that the lost
  may know,
  Bring salvation near.
O bid them come repenting, bid
  them come to-day,
Help them say, "I obey."
Bear the blessed message, hasten
  now to go,
  Go with love sincere.

Press on - - ward..ere the night is falling,
On - - ward..hear the Saviour calling,
  Hear Him gently, sweetly say,
  "I will be with thee alway,"
    Peace and joy to bring.
Press on - - ward..never danger fearing,
On - - ward..brightest hope is nearing,
  Darkness shall no more enthrall,
  Christ our light shall shine for all,
  He shall reign our King.

2 In lands beyond the rolling of the
    ocean foam,
  Wand'rers roam—bring them home;
O lead them to the Saviour and His
  pard'ning love—
  He will give them rest,
And they who long have wandered
  soon will learn to see
How to be truly free,
Living for the kingdom of the land
  above,
  Safe and glad and blest.

3 Go bear the joyful message ev'ry-
    where you may,
  Work and pray—day by day;
Lift burdens from the weary, cheer
  the grieving heart—
  Walk where Jesus trod.
O be a beam of sunshine that reflects
  His light,
Pure and bright, in the night,
Helping many sinners choose the
  "better part"
  In the love of God.

935   SING me the song that tells
    of Jesus,
  That is the song which has music's
    sweetest tone,
Coming from heaven like perfume
  on breezes,
  Fills all my soul with the joy that
    is His own.
Bears me in spirit to bright realms
  of glory,
  Holds me enraptured with visions
    of delight;
Gives me to hear what the saint
  dar'd not utter,
  When He returned to the shadow
    and the night.

Sing me the song that tells of Jesus,
  Sing to this heart and bid its throbbing cease,
Sing me that song for it chastens my spirit,
  Calming my soul with its magic spell of peace.

2 This song has wings like eagle's pinions,
Oft has it borne me to God's own paradise ;
There I have sung with angels in chorus,
Knows not my soul of a trance of joy like this.
But when returning to life's din and battle,
Spells still are o'er me and sounds are in mine ear,
Taking the glare from the earthly and fleeting,
Filling my life with what the angels hear.

3 " Worthy the Lamb " who died to save us ;
" Worthy the Lamb "—let it sound thro' earth and sky ;
" Worthy the Lamb " sing the angels in chorus,
" Worthy the Lamb " our redemption draweth nigh.
Worthy of honour from highest archangels,
Worthy of glory of the universe around ;
Worthy of majesty, pow'r, adoration,
" Worthy the Lamb," the lov'd and lost are found.

936 *Choir Piece, for words see No. 57.*

937 WHEN God sees the flowers Need His tender care,
He sends little raindrops With a blessing there.

Busy little raindrops,
Let us be to-day,
As we strive to scatter blessings,
All along the way,

Helpful little raindrops
Will we be to-day,
Doing work for Jesus
In a raindrop's way.

2 We are little raindrops,
God has sent us here,
From His fount of blessing,
Bringing hope and cheer.

3 Ev'ry drop reflecting
God's most tender love,
Helps to light the pathway
To the home above.

4 Tho' we are but raindrops,
We are glad to know
That we have a mission
In this world below.

938 I LOVE to think of Chris my King,
Who did salvation freely bring ;
So while I live I mean to sing,
Hallelujah ! grace is free.

O Hallelujah ! grace is free,
This my song shall ever be ;
Jesus died to set me free,
Hallelujah ! grace is free.

2 O wondrous is the crimson flood !
O precious is the cleansing blood !
My Jesus as my surety stood,
Hallelujah ! grace is free.

3 What greater love can ever be,
To die upon a cruel tree,
And ransom such a wretch as me
Hallelujah ! grace is free.

4 And when I reach that silver stran
And join that holy, happy band,
This song I'll sing in that brig land,
Hallelujah ! grace is free.

CLOSING

939 THRO' the love of God our Saviour,
All will be well.
Free and changeless is His favour,
All, all is well.
Precious is the blood that heal'd us,
Perfect is the grace that seal'd us,
Strong the hand stretched forth to shield us,
All must be well.

2 Tho' we pass thro' tribulation,
All will be well.
Ours is such a full salvation,
All, all is well.
Happy still in God confiding,
Fruitful if in Christ abiding,
Holy thro' the Spirit's guiding.
All must be well.

3 We expect a bright to-morrow ;
All will be well.

Faith can sing thro' days of sorrow,
　　All, all is well.
On our Father's love relying,
Jesus ev'ry neéd supplying,
Or in living or in dying,
　　All must be well.

40 THE night draws near, our
　　　　day of praise is o'er,
Our songs, our hearts uplifted rise
　　once more,
As at Thy feet, O Lord, our off'rings
　　pour,
　　And then, " Good night, good
　　　night ! "

The day of life has oft-times dark-
　　ened been,
Fierce storms have raged, with
　　fitful lights between ;
But still at even, o'er the changing
　　scene,
　　Has come—sweet word—" Good
　　　night ! "

The task will soon be o'er, however
　　hard,
The lonely struggle, watched still
　　by the Lord,
With Him is thine exceeding great
　　reward,
　　Till then, " Good night, good
　　　night ! "

Go forth in earnest, steadfast lives
　　to prove
Thy teaching true ; deep rooted in
　　His love,
Fruits budding here, to ripen soon
　　above,
　　Where none shall say, " Good
　　　night ! "

" Good night ! "   The longest day
　　must have an end,
The happiest hours will to their
　　closing tend,
Beyond, afar, th' eternal day we'll
　　spend,
　　" Good night, good night, good
　　　night ! "

41 OUR friends on earth we meet
　　　　with pleasure,
While swift the moments fly,
Yet ever comes the thought of sad-
　　ness
That we must say good-bye.

We'll never say good-bye in heav'n,
　　We'll never say, good-bye,..
For in that land of joy and song
　　We'll never say, good-bye.

2 How joyful is the thought that
　　　lingers,
　　When lov'd ones cross death's sea,
That when our labours here are
　　ended,
　　With them we'll ever be.

3 No parting words shall e'er be spoken
　　In that bright land of flow'rs ;
But songs of joy and peace and glad-
　　ness
　　Shall evermore be ours.

942 GOD be with you till we meet
　　　　again,
　　By His counsels guide, uphold you,
　　With His sheep securely fold you ;
God be with you till we meet again.

Till we meet,.. till we meet,..
Till we meet at Jesus' feet ;..
Till we meet,.. till we meet,..
　　God be with you till we meet again.

2 God be with you till we meet again,
　　'Neath His wings protecting hide
　　　you,
　　Daily manna still provide you ;
God be with you till we meet again.

3 God be with you till we meet again,
　　When life's perils thick confound
　　　you,
　　Put His arms unfailing round you ;
God be with you till we meet again.

4 God be with you till we meet again,
　　Keep love's banner floating o'er
　　　you,
　　Smite death's threat'ning wave
　　　before you ;
God be with you till we meet again.

943 GLORY be to the Father, and
　　　　to the Son, and to the Holy
　　　　Ghost.
　　As it was in the beginning, is now,
　　and ever shall be, world without
　　end.　　　　　　　　　AMEN.

944 FATHER, in high heaven
　　　　dwelling,
　　May our ev'ning song be telling
　　Of Thy mercy large and free ;

Through the day Thy love hath fed
us, [us,
Through the day Thy care hath led
With divinest charity.

2 This day's sins O pardon, Saviour,
Evil thoughts, perverse behaviour,
Envy, pride, and vanity ;
From the world, the flesh, deliver,
Save us how, and save us ever,
O Thou Lamb of Calvary.

3 From enticements of the devil,
From the might of spirits evil,
Be our shield and panoply ;
Let Thy power this night defend us,
And a heav'nly peace attend us,
And angelic company.

4 Whilst the night dews are distilling,
Holy Ghost, each heart be filling
With Thine own serenity ;
Softly let our eyes be closing,
Loving souls on Thee reposing,
Ever blessed Trinity.

945 LORD, dismiss us with Thy
blessing,
Fill our hearts with joy and peace;
Let us each, Thy love possessing,
Triumph in redeeming grace ;
Oh, refresh us, oh, refresh us,
Travelling through this wilder-
ness !

2 Thanks we give, and adoration,
For Thy Gospel's joyful sound ;
May the fruits of Thy salvation
In our hearts and lives abound ;
May Thy presence, may Thy presence
With us evermore be found.

3 So whene'er the signal's given,
Us from earth to call away,
Borne on angels' wings to heaven,
Glad the summons to obey,
We shall surely, we shall surely
Reign with Christ in endless day.

946 BLEST be the tie that binds
Our hearts in Christian love ;
The fellowship of kindred minds
Is like to that above.

2 Before our Father's throne
We pour our ardent pray'rs ;
Our fears, our hopes, our aims are
one,
Our comforts and our cares.

3 We share our mutual woes ;
Our mutual burdens bear ;
And often for each other flows
The sympathising tear.

4 When we asunder part,
It gives us inward pain ;
But we shall still be joined in heart
And hope to meet again.

947 SUN of my soul, Thou Saviour
dear,
It is not night if Thou be near ;
Oh, may no earth-born cloud arise,
To hide Thee from Thy servant's
eyes !

2 When the soft dews of kindly sleep
My wearied eyelids gently steep,
Be my last thought, how sweet to
rest
For ever on my Saviour's breast.

3 Abide with me from morn till eve,
For without Thee I cannot live ;
Abide with me when night is nigh,
For without Thee I dare not die.

4 If some poor wand'ring child of
Thine
Have spurn'd to-day the voice divine,
Now, Lord, the gracious work begin,
Let him no more lie down in sin.

5 Watch by the sick, enrich the poor
With blessings from Thy boundless
store ;
Be ev'ry mourner's sleep to-night
Like infant's slumbers, pure and
light.

6 Come near and bless us when we
wake,
Ere thro' the world our way we take,
Till, in the ocean of Thy love,
We lose ourselves in heav'n above.

948 ABIDE with me ; fast falls the
eventide ;
The darkness deepens ; Lord, with
me abide ;
When other helpers fail, and comforts flee,
Help of the helpless, oh, abide with
me !

2 I need Thy presence ev'ry passing
hour ;
What but Thy grace can foil the
tempter's pow'r ?

Who like Thyself my guide and stay
  can be ?
Thro' cloud and sunshine, oh, abide
  with me !
Swift to its close ebbs out life's little
  day ;
Earth's joys grow dim, its glories
  pass away ;
Change and decay in all around I see ;
O Thou, who changest not, abide
  with me !
I fear no foe with Thee at hand to
  bless,   [bitterness ;
Ills have no weight, and tears no
Where is death's sting ? where,
  grave, thy victory ?   [me.
I triumph still if Thou abide with

949 THE day Thou gavest, Lord,
  is ended ;
  The darkness falls at Thy behest ;
To Thee our morning hymns as-
  cended,
  Thy praise shall sanctify our rest.
We thank Thee that Thy Church
  unsleeping,   [light,
  While earth rolls onward into
Thro' all the world her watch is
  keeping,
  And rest not now by day or night.
As o'er each continent and island
  The dawn leads on another day,
The voice of pray'r is never silent,
  Nor dies the strain of praise away.
The sun that bids us rest is waking
  Our brethren 'neath the western
  sky ;
And hour by hour fresh lips are
  making   [high.
  Thy wondrous doings heard on
So be it, Lord ! Thy throne shall
  never,   [away ;
  Like earth's proud empires, pass
Thy kingdom stands and grows for
  ever,   [sway.
  Till all Thy creatures own Thy

950 SAVIOUR, again to Thy dear
  Name we raise
With one accord our parting hymn
  of praise ;
We stand to bless Thee ere our wor-
  ship cease,   [of peace.
Then, lowly kneeling, wait Thy word

2 Grant us Thy peace upon our home-
  ward way ;
  With Thee began, with Thee shall
  end the day ;
Guard Thou the lips from sin, the
  hearts from shame,
That in this house have called upon
  Thy Name.

3 Grant us Thy peace, Lord, thro' the
  coming night,   [light ;
Turn Thou for us its darkness into
From harm and danger keep Thy
  children free,   [Thee.
For dark and light are both alike to

4 Grant us Thy peace throughout our
  earthly life ;
Our balm in sorrow and our stay in
  strife ;
Then, when Thy voice shall bid our
  conflict cease,   [peace.
Call us, O Lord, to Thine eternal

951 PRAISE God, from whom all
  blessings flow ;
Praise Him, all creatures here below ;
Praise Him above, ye heav'nly host,
Praise Father, Son, and Holy Ghost.

952 I HOPE to meet you all in
  glory,
  When the storms of life are o'er ;
I hope to tell the dear old story,
  On the blessed shining shore.

    On the shining shore,
      On the golden strand,
    In our Father's home,
      In the happy land :
    I hope to meet you there,
    I hope to meet you there—
    A crown of vict'ry wear—
      In glory.

2 I hope to meet you all in glory,
  By the tree of life so fair ;
I hope to praise our dear Redeemer,
  For the grace that brought me
  there.

3 I hope to meet you all in glory,
  Round the Saviour's throne above ;
I hope to join the ransomed army,
  Singing now redeeming love.

4 I hope to meet you all in glory,
  When my work on earth is o'er ;
I hope to clasp your hands rejoicing
  On the bright eternal shore.

CHORUSES

None of the following Choruses are to be found in any other part of the book.

GOSPEL

1 I AM the Door, I am the Door,
By Me if any man enter in
He shall be saved, he shall be saved,
He shall be saved.

For Gospel Temperance Meetings.

2 A CERTAIN man of whom we read,
Who lived in days of old,
Though he was rich he felt his need
Of something more than gold.
Oh, yes, my friend, there's something more,
something more than gold :
To know your sins are all forgiv'n is something
more than gold.

2 It happened on a certain day
This little man was told
That Jesus soon would pass that way
With something more than gold.

3 He climbed a tree above the crowd,
So that he might behold
The Blessed One with power to give
Something more than gold.

4 The Saviour came along the way,
And saw him on the tree,
Then calling to him Jesus said,
" I must abide with thee."

5 So he obeyed, and soon he found,
The half had not been told,
The blessing Jesus brought to him
Was better far than gold.

3 LOOK to Him now, look to Him
now,
Jesus is waiting to save ;
Look to Him now, look to Him now
Jesus is waiting to save.

4 WHO'LL be the next ?
Who'll be the next ?
Who'll be the next to follow Jesus
Who'll be the next to follow Jesus
now,
Follow Jesus now ?

5 TELL the Saviour all,....
Tell the Saviour all ;....
Make to Him a full confession,
Tell the Saviour all.

6 COME away, come away,
Come away to Jesus ;
Come away, come away home !
For Jesus waits to save you.

7 STEAL away, steal away,
Steal away to Jesus,
Steal away, steal away home,
For Jesus waits to save you.

8 ETERNITY, eternity,
Where will you spend eternity ?
Eternity, eternity,
Where will....you spend eternity

TESTIMONY

9 O GLORY ! O glory, what rap-
ture is mine !
The King in His beauty I see ;
I'm singing His praises since Jesus
divine
Extended His mercy to me.

10 I KNOW,....I know,....
I have another building ;
I know,....I know,....
'Tis not made with hands.

11 I WANT ev'rybody to know
Of Jesus who loveth me so !
My time I will give as long as I
live
To help ev'rybody to know.

12 O....WHAT He's done for me !
O....what He's done for me !
If I tried to eternity, I never could
tell
All He's done for me !

3 OH, wondrous bliss! oh, joy
     sublime!
   I've Jesus with me all the time!
Oh, wondrous bliss! oh, joy sub-
     lime!
   I've Jesus with me all the time!

4 'TIS Jesus in the morning hour,
   'Tis Jesus thro' the day;
'Tis Jesus in the eventide,
   'Tis Jesus all the way.

I'll praise Him in the morning hour,
   I'll praise Him thro' the day;
I'll praise Him in the eventide,
   I'll praise Him all the way.

5 GET right with God,....
   Get right with God,....
Oh, do not let the Spirit now de-
     part;....
   Get right with God,....
   Get right with God,:....
And grant Him glad admission to
   thy heart.

6 SAVED, saved, oh glory to God!
   I have the assurance divine;
Saved, saved, oh glory to God!
   His Spirit bears witness with
   mine.

17 SINCE I....have learned the
     sto - - ry,
   This song I love to sing,....
Oh, Jesus has the world redeemed
   From darkness unto glory.

18 I'M satisfied with Jesus here,
   He's ev'rything to me;
His dying love has won my heart,
   And now He sets me free.

19 HALLELUJAH to His Name!
   Hallelujah to His Name!
He is guiding, cheering, loving all
   the way!
     O glory to His Name!

20 THE Lamb, the Lamb, the bleed-
     ing Lamb,
   I love the sound of Jesus' Name,
It sets my spirit in a flame—
   Glory to the bleeding Lamb!

21 AND when I reach the pearly
     gates,
   Then I'll put in this plea;
I was a guilty sinner,
   But Jesus died for me.

22 OH! the blood, the precious
     blood,
   Jesus shed on Calvary;
Oh! the blood, the precious blood;
   Praise the Lord, it cleanseth me....

CONSECRATION AND HOLINESS

3 EV'RY step of the way, my Lord,
   Yes, ev'ry step of the way;
Thy all is mine, and I am Thine,
   For ev'ry step of the way.

4 I'M going thro', Jesus, I'm going
     thro';
   I'll pay the price whatever others do;
I'll take the way with the world-
     despised few;
I've started out, Jesus, I'm going
     thro'.

5 I'LL be true, Lord, to Thee,
I'll be true, Lord, to Thee;
     And whate'er befall,
     I shall conquer all,
If I'm only true to Thee.

6 JESUS, Master, search me, prove
   me,
   With Thy fire try my heart;
All I am and have I yield Thee;
   All I want Thou art.

27 MORE, more like Jesus
     I would ever grow;
More of His love constantly prove—
   More of His likeness show.

28 HE will break ev'ry fetter,
   He will break ev'ry fetter,
   He will break ev'ry fetter,
   And will set you free.

2 He has broken ev'ry fetter,
   He has broken ev'ry fetter,
   He has broken ev'ry fetter,
   And has set me free.

29 JESUS, keep me in Thy ful-
     ness;
   Keep me yielded, keep me
     pure;
Keep me telling of Thy glory;
   Keep me steady, keep me sure.

30 STEP by step, step by step,
    I will follow Jesus,
    Ev'ry day, all the way,
    Keeping step with Jesus.

31 POW'R to cleanse the leper,
    pow'r to raise the dead, [oil,
    Pow'r filled the empty cruse with
    Ready waiting for the workers, who
        in Jesu's step will tread, [toil.
    And leave a life of ease for one of

32 NEARER, yes, nearer, my Saviour,
    Oh draw me yet nearer to Thee!
    Nearer, yes, nearer, my Saviour,
    And perfect Thy likeness in me!

33 THY love,..Thy boundless love,
    Thy love,..all-conq'ring love,..
    Shed in..my heart abroad;
    Give me this perfect love.

34 THERE'S nothing too hard fo
    Thee,.....
    There's nothing too hard for Thee
    Nothing, nothing,
    There's nothing too hard for Thee.

2 I'm trusting alone in Thee,....
    I'm trusting alone in Thee;
    Trusting, trusting,
    I'm trusting alone in Thee.

GENERAL

35 MARCH on! we shall win the
    day;
    March on! hear the Saviour say:
    " March on till the vict'ry's won,"
    And you shall hear the glad " Well
    done."

36 MY burden's great, my faith is
    small;
    Ah, that's the trouble with us all!
    A little more faith! a little more
    faith!
    A little more faith in Jesus.

37 COMING by and by, 'tis coming
    by and by;
    A better day is dawning in yonder
    sky;
    So never give up trusting, nor ques-
    tion Him or why,
    For victory is coming by and by.

38 SATISFIED,....satisfied,....
    I know I'll be fully satisfied;....
    When mine eyes shall behold
    All the wonders untold,
    I know I'll be satisfied...

39 I SHALL be like Him, I shall be
    like Him,
    And in His beauty shall shine;
    I shall be like Him, wondrously like
    Him,
    Jesus, my Saviour divine.

40 I FEEL like going on, brother,
    I feel like going on;
    I'm on my way to Zion,
    And I feel like going on.

41 'TIS well, 'tis well,
    'Tis well with the righteous, well
      In sorrow's night,
      In pleasures bright,
    'Tis well with the righteous, we

42 CONFIDE it to Jesus, He
    comfort and cheer you,
    Each burden and sorrow He
    share;
    Confide it to Jesus, He's waiting
    hear you,
    Go, tell Him the story in prayer

43 SOME thro' the waters,
    Some thro' the flood,
    Some thro' the fire,
    But all thro' the blood;
    Some thro' deep sorrow, trial ar
    pains,
    God leads His dear children alon

44 SOMETHING whispers, can
    be,....
    There is hope for one like me?...
    I will seek His mercy full and free,
    Jesus bled and died for me.

45 IN tune with Thee,....in tune wi
    Thee,...
    Lord, keep my heart in tune....wi
    Thee.

46 SINCE I have been forgiven,
    His dear face I see;....
    While we walk together,
    This world's a heaven to me.....

A LITTLE talk with Jesus makes
   things right, all right,
A little talk with Jesus makes things
right, all right;
   Thank God, I always find,
   In trouble of ev'ry kind,
That a little talk with Jesus makes
things right, all right.

48 I AM determined to hold out to
   the end,
Jesus is with me, on Him I can
   depend;
And I know I have salvation, for I
   feel it in my soul,
I am determined to hold out to the
   end.

INDEX TO FIRST LINES

INDEX OF CHORUSES

The following appear throughout the Hymn Book

The following Refrains are suitable as Choruses